Contemporary Feminist Theories

Contemporary Feminist Theories

Edited by Stevi Jackson and Jackie Jones

NEW YORK UNIVERSITY PRESS
Washington Square, New York

Introduction, selection, and arrangement of material
© Stevi Jackson and Jackie Jones 1998
Individual chapters © The contributors 1998

First published in the U.S.A. in 1998 by
NEW YORK UNIVERSITY PRESS
Washington Square
New York, N.Y. 10003

Published in the United Kingdom by
Edinburgh University Press,
22 George Square, Edinburgh

CIP data available from the Library of Congress
ISBN 0-8147-4248-3 (clothbound)
ISBN 0-8147-4249-1 (paperback)

Typeset in Baskerville and Futura by
Norman Tilley Graphics, Northampton,
and printed and bound in Finland by WSOY

Contents

Chapter 1

Thinking for Ourselves: An Introduction to Feminist Theorising

Stevi Jackson and Jackie Jones

Feminist theory seeks to analyse the conditions which shape women's lives and to explore cultural understandings of what it means to be a woman. It was initially guided by the political aims of the Women's Movement – the need to understand women's subordination and our exclusion from, or marginalisation within, a variety of cultural and social arenas. Feminists refuse to accept that inequalities between women and men are natural and inevitable and insist that they should be questioned. Theory, for us, is not an abstract intellectual activity divorced from women's lives, but seeks to explain the conditions under which those lives are lived. Developing this understanding has entailed looking at the material actualities of women's everyday experience and examining the ways in which we are represented and represent ourselves within a range of cultural practices, such as the arts and the media.

Thinking as a feminist involves challenging much of what has counted as 'knowledge'. Because we have historically lived in male-dominated societies, women have more often been the objects of knowledge than the producers of it. As a result, much of what has passed as objective knowledge of the world has been produced by men, framed by their particular location in society as men – and usually white, middle-class and heterosexual men. Feminist modes of theorising contest androcentric (or male-centred) ways of knowing, calling into question the gendered hierarchy of society and culture. Feminist theory is about thinking for ourselves – women generating knowledge *about* women and gender *for* women. Yet this immediately raises questions. Who are the 'we' doing the thinking and who are the 'ourselves' for whom we claim to be thinking: women in general or only some women? Are certain women being left out of the picture? Are we not in danger of perpetuating the same faults we have criticised in male thinkers – marginalising women not like 'ourselves', casting them as 'other'?

Women are not a homogenous group. This is not merely to restate a truism – that we are not all alike – but to underline the social significance of differences among us. We are differently located within global and local social contexts and differently represented in art, literature and other media. Distinctions of

1

nationality, ethnicity, education, language, family, class, employment, ability/ disability and sexuality are important. These are not merely differences, which can be acknowledged and passed over; these differences are often hierarchical, producing inequalities among women which intersect with gender inequality. Hence, while we need to pay attention to commonalities among women, we cannot afford to ignore these crucial differences.

Nor do we all think alike. 'Woman' is not coterminous with 'feminist'; to be a feminist implies a particular politicised understanding of being a woman. Moreover, while feminists may share some common assumptions, these do not necessarily lead us to think in the same ways about these shared concerns. There are many strands of feminist thinking and numerous areas of contention and debate within feminism. Feminist theory has been produced both from the grass roots and from within the academy, although in recent years it has increasingly housed itself in – or removed itself to – the academy. This has given rise to concerns that theory is being done by 'hegemonic' feminists from 'hegemonic' countries – those of affluent northern Europe and North America. However, even those of us who are similarly located as, for example, white, middle-class professionals and academics, do not necessarily share the same perspectives. Academic feminism is itself diverse, reflecting the differing political affiliations, theoretical traditions and disciplinary backgrounds which feminists bring to their theorising.

Feminist theory is not, and has never been, a static phenomenon. This is one reason why it has proved so difficult to capture within classifications such as 'liberal', 'marxist' or 'radical' (Maynard 1995). Diversity and change are interlinked. As feminism has evolved, theorising has taken many different directions and forms. Individual feminists have also changed their views over time and this is evident in the reflexive, self-critical tenor of much feminist work. Feminists are constantly reflecting on their own ideas, changing their stances in response to debates and challenges from other feminists. Hence individual theorists cannot always be pinned down to a single statement of their position, since this is continually being developed and modified.

Feminist theory has now grown into a vast field. In the 1970s it was still possible for each one of us to keep track of feminist thought as a whole, to have an overview of it, if not detailed knowledge. This is now impossible. While some feminists, especially in the 1970s, attempted a grand synthesis in order to account for the totality of women's subordination, much theorising since has focused on specific aspects of social life or cultural production, or on specific applications of particular theories. Given that it is now so difficult for a single person to have an in-depth knowledge of the whole of feminist theory, overviews of it are often partial and incomplete. One reason for embarking upon this collection was the dissatisfaction with existing introductions to feminist theory which often failed fully to track change and capture diversity. Hence this volume draws on the expertise of a range of feminists in order to reflect the breadth of feminist theory and shifts within it. Each of the chapters maps the development of feminist thought in a particular area over time and suggests future directions. Each author has provided an overview while adopting her own perspective on the field she surveys.

This collection has been written by feminists based in Britain, but each chapter draws on and engages with theory produced elsewhere, especially in North America and Western Europe. While each country has its own tradition of feminist thought, feminist ideas have always crossed national boundaries. In the past, theory has been dominated by white anglophone feminists from Britain, Australia and especially the US. More recently, with the questioning of the dominance of white Western feminism, new voices have joined and challenged the terms of feminist debates, making us more sensitive to differences, international issues and the intersections between the global and the local.

The Historical Context

The chapters in this volume cover developments in feminist theory since 1970. While there were certainly important feminist thinkers writing earlier in the twentieth century, such as Virginia Woolf, Charlotte Perkins Gilman, Simone de Beauvoir and Betty Friedan, the rise of Second Wave feminism provided the impetus for a rapid growth in feminist thought. The feminist theory we know today has derived from that period but has developed and diversified through a constant process of debate, critique and reflection. As a result, different strands of theory and new objects of theoretical inquiry have emerged at different times in this process. Hence, some of the chapters in this book take as their point of departure feminist writings of the early 1970s (see Chapter 2); others deal with forms of theorising which have emerged in more recent social and political contexts (see Chapter 8). It is safe to say, though, that none of the theory produced today could have developed without the ground-breaking work done by feminists in the 1970s.

The late 1960s and early 1970s witnessed an upsurge of youthful left activism throughout the western world. This was the context in which the Women's Liberation Movement emerged, along with others such as Gay Liberation and Black Power. It was a period of incredible energy and excitement generated by an optimistic belief in the possibility of radical social change. Feminist work of this period was inspired by grass roots activism, although it was written largely by young, white, university-educated women. This early theory was premised on the need to understand the causes of women's oppression in order to overturn the male dominated social order. This is why work produced in this era often seems with hindsight to be offering totalising explanations. Even at this time, however, there were political differences among women.

In the US two founding works of what came to be known as radical feminism were published in 1970: Kate Millett's *Sexual Politics* and Shulamith Firestone's *The Dialectic of Sex*. These books were radical as distinct from the strong liberal reformist feminist current in the US, but they also came to be defined as radical feminist in opposition to Marxist feminism. In the British context, where Marxism was a much stronger influence, Juliet Mitchell's *Women's Estate* was published a year later and written within a Marxist framework. Marxist and radical feminism quickly became defined as two major and opposing tendencies within the women's movement, the former seeking alliance with the class politics of the left, the latter arguing for a more autonomous movement and forms of theorising which broke with Marxism. Even at this stage, however, it is important to note that these were not homogenous and mutually exclusive groups: there were differences within them and common interests between them (see Chapter 2). Moreover, many feminists did not identify wholeheartedly with either camp.

While the works mentioned above constituted major statements on the underpinnings of male domination, feminists were not concerned only with generating 'grand theory'. There was a strong emphasis from the beginning on the need to theorise from our experience as women, in keeping with the slogan 'the personal is political'. Feminism changed the agenda of politics and theory, making areas of life previously seen as personal into areas of political struggle and objects of theoretical analysis. For example, an early anthology of US writings, *Sisterhood is Powerful* (Morgan 1970), included chapters entitled 'The Politics of Orgasm' and 'The Politics of Housework'. Sexuality and housework were to become central theoretical concerns in the 1970s (see Chapters 2 and 9). There was also much work done at this time which aimed to make women visible and to recover, for example, women's history and literature (see Sheila Rowbotham's *Hidden from History* 1973; Ellen Moers's *Literary Women* 1976; Elaine Showalter's *A Literature of Their Own* 1977).

At this time, feminism was also having an impact within academic institutions. Many activists in the movement were also students, lecturers and researchers and began to bring their feminist concerns into their academic work. Hence the construction of theory moved easily between activist and academic circles. The academic world was itself an arena of struggle for feminists. Women were still a tiny minority of those with secure academic posts and feminists were a marginal, powerless and youthful group – but they did have political skills deriving from their activism. They began to organise to challenge the existing male-dominated curriculum, campaigning on two fronts. Within established disciplines, women were caucusing and sharing ideas, with the aim of putting feminist knowledge and ways of thinking on the agenda.[1] At the same time they began to agitate for the formation of women's studies as a distinct academic field, and one informed by feminist politics (see Chapter 17). The groundwork done in the 1970s led to the formal establishment of women's studies in Britain at the end of the decade.

The first Masters degree course in Britain at the University of Kent was followed by others at the Universities of York and Bradford, and subsequently elsewhere, with undergraduate degrees following somewhat later.

The growth in feminist intellectual work also led to the establishment of feminist academic journals. In the US, *Signs* was launched in 1976; in France, *Questions Féministes* was founded in 1977, and was succeeded, after a split among its collective in 1980, by *Nouvelles Questions Féministes*; in Britain *m/f* appeared in 1978 followed by *Feminist Review* in 1979. In 1978 the first truly international women's studies journal was established, *Women's Studies International Quarterly*, which later became *Women's Studies International Forum*. These journals were absolutely central to the development of feminist thought, providing a forum for debating and circulating ideas at a time when mainstream journals were often reluctant to publish feminist work. Many classics of feminist theory first appeared in these journals including writings by Heidi Hartmann, Adrienne Rich, Catharine MacKinnon, Nancy Chodorow, Christine Delphy, Monique Wittig and Michèle Barrett. The importance of these journals can also be gauged by their continued success: those we have cited, with the exception of *m/f*, are still thriving and have been joined by many others.

The need to find outlets for feminist writing, as well as a desire for feminist control of the publishing process also led, in the 1970s, to the founding of independent feminist (including lesbian and black feminist) presses. In Britain these included Virago, set up in 1973; Onlywomen, who printed as well as published, founded in 1974; The Women's Press, established in 1977; Sheba, formed in 1980 as a collective; and Pandora, started in 1981 as an imprint of Routledge and Kegan Paul. These publishers started with very radical intent, with political and feminist convictions determining their lists. Some of them have survived, although mostly now incorporated into larger mainstream commercial organisations. While the early success of identifiably feminist presses established feminist publishing, it was only with the advent of women's studies in the academy that feminist lists within mainstream publishing houses appeared (Jones 1992). Ironically, as women's studies became commercially viable, feminist publishing arguably became deradicalised (Scanlon and Swindells 1994), especially with gender studies coming to the fore in mainstream publishers' lists in the 1990s (Robinson and Richardson 1994).

By the 1990s women's studies had become a highly professionalised established field of study, with national and international women's studies associations now part of the academic landscape. It should be noted, however, that the place of women's studies in the academy is far from secure. It is still often marginalised and underfunded within academic institutions and its autonomy is constantly under threat. However, feminist influence remains strong in many disciplines and courses on women and gender appear to be thriving. It is now largely within the academy that feminist theory (or what counts as feminist theory) is generated and for many young women, their first contact with explicitly feminist ideas is through academic courses.

As feminism has become more entrenched in the academy, changes have occurred at the level of grass roots feminism. There is no longer a visible, unified Women's Liberation Movement. In Britain, as in many Western countries, the movement has become more fragmented since the last Women's Liberation Movement conference in 1978. These conferences became unmanageable partly because they had grown too big and unwieldy. They had also become more diverse. It became increasingly difficult to contain differences among women within a single movement and to sustain the idea of a universal sisterhood. These differences, especially around issues of sexuality and 'race', as well as the older problem of class, led to fractures within the movement which proved nigh on impossible to heal.

Feminism as grass roots political activity did not disappear. Women have continued to be active up to the present day in single issue campaigns around, for example, pornography, reproductive rights, violence against women and women's legal rights. Even here, however, there are often major differences and divisions – the heated debates around pornography being a case in point (see Jackson and Scott 1996). Feminists also became involved, and made specific contributions to, broader social movements such as the peace movement (Roseneil 1995) and campaigns for lesbian and gay rights (Green 1997). Feminist ideas have also had some influence within mainstream politics and wider public debates.

Academic feminism has, in turn, been influenced by these changes in feminist politics, with feminist theory itself becoming more diverse and more inclined to focus on the particular, rather than attempting to capture the generality of women's situation. The recognition of differences among women has become a central theoretical issue in its own right. For some, this has brought the category 'women' itself into question. As we indicated at the beginning of the chapter, women can no longer be thought of as a homogenous group sharing a common oppression and a common identity. This is not to say that there are not commonalities among us as well as differences. 'Women' may no longer be thought of as a *unitary* category but it might still potentially be a *unifying* one (see Brah 1991).

Along with the changes generated by feminist politics, feminist theory has also been affected by academic developments, by new forms of theory and shifting disciplinary hierarchies. With the rise of poststructuralist and postmodernist perspectives, which have emphasised the instability of language and meaning (see Chapter 13), the influence of social scientific perspectives within feminist theory has waned. There has been a 'cultural turn' within feminism with literary and cultural theory in the ascendant (Barrett 1992). For example, where once feminist academic production was preoccupied with such issues as the economic and sexual exploitation of women, attention has shifted to the pleasures of popular cultural consumption and the fashioning of cultural identities (see Chapter 15).

Feminists have become aware of the sources of pleasure in women's lives as well as the sources of pain and deprivation; they are less inclined to dismiss pleasure as 'false consciousness' and are more likely to take seriously as meaningful activities the pleasure of watching soap operas or reading romance. This need not mean, however, being uncritical of cultural practices. Moreover, the focus on meaning and discourse is not limited to explorations of pleasure, play and leisure; the cultural turn has not always entailed the side-lining of issues of social exclusion, but has recast them in new ways. Feminist analyses of the deployment of discourse have addressed such issues as the legal regulation of women's lives (see Chapter 5) and the maintenance of heterosexual hegemony (see Chapters 9 and 10). The consequences of these theoretical developments are debated in many of the chapters of this book.

More recent issues have not entirely eclipsed older ones; it remains vitally important that we consider, in Barrett's terms, both 'things' – the material facticity of women's subordination – and 'words' – the language and discourse we use to think about and make sense of the world. We continue to live in a world where large-scale inequalities still have a profound impact on women's lives, and the ways in which social structures are both constraining and enabling cannot be ignored. It is necessary for feminists to remain engaged with socio-economic issues and the persistence of material inequalities associated with the new world economic order (see Chapter 3). Feminist theory of the future will need to take account of the ways in which the social worlds of women are shaped both materially and discursively, and be alert to the structural constraints on our lives as well as the scope for agency and creativity.

Common Themes and Key Debates

While challenging conventional academic orthodoxies within existing disciplines, feminist scholarship has also tested the boundaries between disciplines. Women's studies has, since its inception, been interdisciplinary, and feminist theory has increasingly become so. Feminists continue to generate theory from within existing disciplines, as is evident in many of the chapters in this book. However, even here, they frequently range beyond the boundaries of those disciplines, drawing on feminist insights from elsewhere. It is not unusual to find feminist philosophers, sociologists, literary critics and legal theorists, for example, drawing on common bodies of work, citing similar sources and intervening in the same debates from very different academic locations.

This is, arguably, part of a wider trend, but it is a trend which feminists have led. There are good reasons why feminist theory has been in the forefront of the move towards interdisciplinarity. In the first place, our critique of androcentric knowledge led us to be less reverential towards the founding principles of our disciplines, even where we built on those foundations. We also had a political interest in critique and in sharing analytical tools with other feminists intent on questioning received 'truths'. Our political interests as feminists also led us to focus on common objects of theorising, even where we disagree about the appropriate theoretical stance to take. To take some examples from this volume, feminist theorists from diverse theoretical and disciplinary backgrounds have engaged with issues of gender, sexuality and the body, identity, ethnicity and 'race'. This is evident not only in those chapters addressed to these specific issues, but also in those which cover particular forms of theory. Feminists also have a shared interest in understanding the location of women within a changing world order, hence the increasing interest in exploring the complexities of the post-colonial era and the often heated debates around postmodernism.

Feminists also share a highly reflexive orientation to the process of theorising and have consistently questioned its purpose and its political implications. They have been keen to question the dichotomies between theory on the one hand and activism, experience and research on the other and have sought, in a variety of ways, to establish connections between theory and our understanding of every-day life. Feminist theory, as we have pointed out, began from the politicisation of personal experience. Today, we find ourselves confronting a paradox. If feminist theory is to retain its political relevance, it must continue to make sense to women in terms of everyday knowledges and practices. Yet the concept of experience has increasingly been problematised and the idea of women as a unified collectivity is no longer tenable.

Experience never comes to us in a raw form. In everyday life, we constantly work over, interpret, make sense of our experiences – we are all practical theorists (Smith 1987). Conversely, concepts and theories are 'in actuality' and activated in 'organised social relations' (Smith 1997: 393). Hence the dichotomy between theory and experience is a false one: theory is never abstracted from experience. The problem becomes not the relationship between theory and experience but that between everyday lay theorising and more formalised theorising which attempts to transcend the localised contexts of our everyday lives. This move is necessary if feminism is to retain its critical edge and its explanatory power.

The complex social conditions which shape women's lives cannot be grasped merely from the perspective of everyday 'lived experience' – the task of theory is to make those conditions intelligible in terms of that lived experience. But women's lived experience is diverse; women are differently located within complex social relations and the forms of lay theorising they employ depend on their cultural milieux. Feminist theory, cannot, therefore, be totalising; it cannot explain the world for all women, at all times, in all places. It has moved away from universalising statements towards the local and particular. It might now be better characterised as a *process* of theorising rather than as a privileged body of knowledge. The term 'theorising' implies that the thinking is fluid and provisional, and continually being modified, whereas 'theory' implies something static – a fixed point of reference. All this is in keeping with Mary Maynard's call for 'middle-order theorising', emphasising grounded generalisations (Maynard 1995; see also Chapter 17).

Paying attention to the local and particular, and grounding our generalisations, raises the issue of the relation between theory and research; the empirical investigation of women's lives. While this book focuses on theory, the relationship between the two emerges in a number of contributions (for example, Chapters 2, 11 and 15). Theory is of little use if it has no relationship to the actualities of life as it is lived. Theory informs the way in which feminists frame their research, and their findings are interpreted through a further process of theorising. Some theory, however, appears to be completely abstracted from empirical modes of knowing. Indeed, there are those who would deny the possibility of reliable knowledge, or of a 'reality' which has an existence independent of the discourses through which we construct it. This position is associated with 'strong' forms of postmodernism (see Chapter 13).

Postmodernism has been identified as one of the major theoretical and political challenges facing feminism at the end of the millennium (de Groot and Maynard 1993). Postmodernism shares with feminism a scepticism about universal truth claims, an awareness of knowledge as something constructed from specific locations. Like feminism it questions the idea of a stable, pre-social self and casts doubt on the pretensions of disembodied rationality. Despite these points of convergence, however, postmodernism could be seen to threaten the intellectual project of feminism since it undermines the attempt to understand structural inequalities: instead, the world is seen as fluid and constantly shifting so that persistent inequalities of gender, class or 'race' are erased. It follows that postmodernism also threatens feminism's political, emancipatory project and 'breaches the link between politics and scholarship which has formed the important bases for the generation of feminist knowledge' (ibid.: 157).

Since postmodernism has considerable currency on the contemporary intellectual scene, most of the chapters in this volume engage with it to some degree, although the contributors have differing perspectives on it. The problems we have identified are less evident in 'weaker' forms of postmodernism (see Chapter 13). Moreover, there are signs that some theorists at least are retreating from strong postmodern positions (see Chapter 2). Whether postmodernism itself proves to be a product of a particular historical moment remains to be seen. Nonetheless postmodernism has been a provocative and, for some, productive influence. It is important that feminists engage with all forms of theorising as they happen, extracting what might be useful to us rather than turning our backs on major arenas of intellectual debate.

The key challenges facing feminist theory today remain those we outlined at the beginning of this Introduction: understanding diversity among women and understanding the complex changing world within which women are variously located. We live in uncertain times, an era characterised by an increasingly globalised division of labour and transnational capitalist enterprise on the one hand, and fierce parochial nationalisms, civil wars and dramatically shifting national boundaries on the other hand. The hype about a global community linked by the information super highway and ease of travel across continents should be balanced against the realities of the majority of women's (and men's) lives still bounded by local contexts. The gulf between rich and poor is widening and, generally, where men are poor, women are poorer and bear the brunt of coping with the consequences of poverty. In some contexts, especially in affluent nations, women's opportunities appear to be expanding with increased participation in paid work and education; but even here this trend applies only to some women (Walby 1997). Elsewhere in the world women are still struggling for very basic rights.

Feminist theory for the future must continue to acknowledge the specific local-ised actualities and global contexts which shape women's lives in a changing world. What we have said entails a recognition of the many, and often vast, differences among women, but acknowledges that women are still a recognisable social category in all these local contexts. While women constitute an extremely diverse collectivity, feminism cannot afford to abandon the category women, to ignore the persistent, patterned inequalities between women and men which are evident all over the world. We have only just begun to find ways of theorising diversity and working across our differences, to learn that we speak from specific locations and can never speak for all women. Yet, collectively, and individually, as differently located women, we are thinking for ourselves.

Note

1. Sociology is a good example since it was one of the first disciplines on which feminism made a real impact. A landmark was the British Sociological Association conference in 1974 which was held on the theme of 'Sexual Divisions in Society'. Subsequently a Women's Caucus and a Sexual Divisions Study Group were set up ensuring that women became better represented within the BSA and feminist ideas began to gain a wider hearing within the discipline as a whole (see Allen and Leonard 1996). Women in sociology were involved in campaigning for courses on women within the discipline and were also instrumental in establishing Women's Studies as a distinct academic field.

References

Allen, Sheila and Diana Leonard (1996) 'From sexual divisions to sexualities: changing sociological agendas', in J. Weeks and J. Holland (eds) *Sexual Cultures*, Basingstoke: Macmillan.

Barrett, Michèle (1992) 'Words and things: materialism and method in contemporary feminist analysis', in Michèle Barrett and Ann Phillips (eds) *Destabilizing Theory: Contemporary Feminist Debates*, Oxford: Polity Press.

Brah, Avtar (1991) 'Questions of difference and international feminism', in Jane Aaron and Sylvia Walby (eds) *Out of the Margins: Women's Studies in the Nineties*, London: Falmer.

de Groot, Joanna and Mary Maynard (1993) 'Facing the 1990s: problems and possibilities for women's studies', in Joanna de Groot and Mary Maynard (eds) *Women's Studies in the 1990s: Doing Things Differently?*, Basingstoke: The Macmillan Press Ltd.

Firestone, Shulamith (1970) *The Dialectic of Sex: The Case for Feminist Revolution*, New York: William Morrow.

Green, Sarah (1997) *Urban Amazons*, Basingstoke: The Macmillan Press Ltd.

Jackson, Stevi and Sue Scott (1996) *Feminism and Sexuality: A Reader*, Edinburgh: Edinburgh University Press.

Jones, Jackie (1992) 'Publishing feminist criticism: academic book publishing and the construction and circulation of feminist knowledges', *Critical Survey*, 4, 2: 174–82.

Maynard, Mary (1995) 'Beyond the big three', *Women's History Review*, 4, 3: 259–81.

Millett, Kate (1977) *Sexual Politics*, London: Virago.

Mitchell, Juliet (1971) *Women's Estate*, Harmondsworth: Penguin.

Moers, Ellen (1976) *Literary Women: The Great Writers*, London: The Women's Press.

Morgan, Robin (ed.) (1970) *Sisterhood is Powerful: An Anthology of Writings from the Women's Liberation Movement*, New York: Vintage.

Robinson, Victoria and Diane Richardson (1994) 'Publishing feminist criticism: redefining the women's studies discourse', *Journal of Gender Studies*, 3, 1: 87–94.

Roseneil, Sasha (1995) *Disarming Patriarchy*, Buckingham: Open University Press.

Rowbotham, Sheila (1973) *Hidden from History: 300 Years of Women's Oppression and the Fight Against It*, London: Pluto Press.

Scanlon, Joan and Julia Swindells (1994) 'Bad apple', *Trouble & Strife*, 28: 41–6.

Smith, Dorothy (1987) *The Everyday World as Problematic*, Buckingham: Open University Press.

Smith, Dorothy (1997) 'Comment on Hekman's "Truth and Method: Feminist Standpoint Theory Revisited"', *Signs*, 22, 2: 392–98.

Showalter, Elaine (1977) *A Literature of Their Own: British Women Novelists from Brontë to Lessing*, London: Virago.

Walby, Sylvia (1997) *Gender Transformations*, London: Routledge.

Chapter 2

Feminist Social Theory

Stevi Jackson

Feminist social theory has been concerned with understanding fundamental inequalities between women and men and with analyses of male power over women. Its basic premise is that male dominance derives from the social, economic and political arrangements specific to particular societies. This mode of theorising derives its concepts and methods from the social sciences and focuses on the material conditions of women's lives and the ideological processes which legitimate and help to perpetuate women's subordination. Like all forms of feminist theory, social theory takes diverse forms and has, over the last three decades, given rise to considerable debate. In this chapter I will map out the key points of contention while tracing the development of feminist social theory, beginning with its founding statements in the 1970s. I will also discuss the place of social theory within feminist theory as a whole.

During the 1970s social science perspectives were at the forefront of feminist analysis, but have since been displaced from their central position by literary and cultural theory. Michèle Barrett (1992) has characterised this shift as a 'cultural turn' in feminist theory, a change of emphasis from 'things' to 'words'. Where once feminist theory was preoccupied by 'things' such as housework, inequalities in the labour market or male violence, now it has come to be more concerned with 'words', with issues of representation and subjectivity. However, while social scientific perspectives are less influential than they once were, they have maintained a significant presence within feminist theory into the 1990s and still, I will argue, have much to offer feminism at the turn of the millennium.

Feminism and Marxism

In the 1970s and early 1980s most feminist theory was addressed to a single, basic question: how can we account for women's subordination? Many feminists looked to Marxism as a means of answering this question – not only those who identified as Marxist or socialist feminists, but also some who identified themselves as radical feminists. Since the women's movement emerged in a period of widespread radical Left activism, feminists were generally familiar with, and

12

often sympathetic to, Marxist ideas. Marxism offered an analysis of oppression as systematic, built into the structure of society. Hence women's subordination could be seen as social in origin, as neither given by nature nor an accidental feature of relations between men and women. Marxism was also a theory of social change, one which held out the promise of a more egalitarian future society. Yet, for all its appeal, Marxist theory could not easily accommodate feminism. Marxism was developed to explain capitalist class relations – the exploitation of the proletariat – and required considerable modification to accommodate gender relations.

Throughout the 1970s and early 1980s, feminists sought in a variety of ways to extend, modify or reformulate Marxist ideas, giving rise to a series of debates on the relationship between capitalism and male domination, often referred to as the patriarchy debates (see, for example, Stacey 1993). The differing positions taken on this issue were related to political differences among feminists, particularly on the relationship between women's liberation and class struggle. Many textbooks on feminist theory give the impression that feminists were split into two opposing camps: Marxist or socialist feminists versus radical feminists. In fact the theoretical divisions which emerged in the course of the 1970s were far more complex. Rather than there being a split between two distinct variants of feminism, there was a continuum between those who saw women's subordination as a consequence of capitalism and those who saw it as a consequence of patriarchy, of a system of male domination. Theorists at both ends of the spectrum drew upon Marxism, but in rather different ways: while the more orthodox sought to fit feminist analysis into existing Marxist conceptual frameworks, others experimented with more radical reworkings of Marxism, taking from it only what seemed productive for feminism.

Within these debates patriarchy was a highly contentious concept. Hardened Marxists insisted that women's oppression was rooted in capitalist social relations; for them the analysis of patriarchy was a product of 'bourgeois feminism' and antithetical to class struggle (see, for example, Petty et al. 1987). Marxist feminists, on the other hand, recognised male domination as a systematic feature of modern society and did not generally reduce women's subordination to a side effect of capitalism – although some were reluctant to conceptualise patriarchy as a separate social system co-existing with capitalism. Many worried that the concept of patriarchy was ahistorical; some felt that it aptly described past societies based literally on the rule of fathers, but was not applicable to our own (Rubin 1975; Barrett 1980). Some shared Sheila Rowbothom's (1981) concern that positing the existence of patriarchy as a system which long predated capitalism might lead feminists into a fruitless search for its pre-historic origins. However, not all feminists who used the concept of patriarchy were interested in unearthing its origins; some resisted its use as a transhistorical concept (e.g. Delphy 1984) while others sought to historicise it (e.g. Walby 1986).

Another source of concern was the difficulty of establishing the central dynamics of patriarchy. Among those who have used the term patriarchy, whether from a Marxist perspective or not, there is no consensus on how to define or theorise it (see Beechey 1979; Barrett 1980; Walby 1986). These disagreements entailed another set of differences, cutting across the capitalism–patriarchy continuum, about where the causes of women's subordination should be located. Many Marxist feminists argued that rather than being rooted, like class, in relations of production, women's subordination was either a consequence of specific relations of reproduction or was primarily ideological. Some theorists at the radical feminist end of the spectrum also developed analyses of reproduction and sexuality, sometimes influenced by Marxist ideas or concepts. The range of feminisms which this produced is represented diagrammatically in Figure 2.1.

In outlining these perspectives I will deal first with those who concentrated on economic analysis, on productive relations, then with those who focused on reproduction and, finally, with theories focusing primarily on ideology. Ideology figures to some degree in all feminist theories, hence its location in the centre of the vertical axis in Figure 2.1. Certain perspectives on ideology, however, proved particularly significant for the development of feminist perspectives in the 1980s, ultimately producing a shift away from materialist analysis on the part of many Marxist feminists.

Relations of Production: Capitalist or Patriarchal?

Just as Marxist analysis takes the productive relations of a given society as its point of departure, so too did many feminists. A wide range of theorists sought explanations for male domination in terms of the exploitation of labour, from orthodox Marxists seeking to attribute women's subordination to capitalism to radical feminists arguing that the productive processes of modern society entail both capitalist and patriarchal relations. This form of analysis was founded on two aspects of women's economic situation. First, women's position in the labour market differs from that of men in that they tend to be lower paid, concentrated into fewer occupations, to be employed less continuously than men and frequently on a part-time basis; second, in addition to any paid employment women undertake, they are typically also engaged in unpaid domestic work in the home.

For those with orthodox Marxist preoccupations, the most obvious line of enquiry was to relate these facts to the capitalist economy. The conditions of women's employment led to women being dubbed a 'reserve army of labour': a pool of cheap, flexible and disposable labour, which could be called on when needed by capital and laid off at other times. While this model works in some situations, such as when women take over men's work in times of war, it is less applicable to others (see Breugel 1979; Walby 1986). If women are employed because their labour is cheaper than that of men, why are they not always given

Figure 2.1: The 'Patriarchy Debates' – Explanations for Women's Subordination

Explanations emphasising	Capitalist relations	Patriarchy + Capitalism	Male dominance or patriarchal relations
Production	Traditional Marxism **Barrett** (UK) – Marxist feminist (women's subordination not reducible to capitalism, but concept of patriarchy inappropriate)	Some Marxist feminists e.g. **Hartmann** (USA) Materialist dual systems theory **Walby** (UK)	Materialist radical feminists **Delphy** (France)
Culture/ideology		Psychoanalytic Marxist feminism e.g. **Mitchell** (UK)	
Sexuality			Heterosexuality as a class relation, e.g. **Wittig** (France) Subordination through sexuality **MacKinnon** (USA), **Jeffreys** (UK)
Reproduction		Relations of production vs relations of reproduction. Some Marxist feminists e.g. **McDonough and Harrison** (UK)	Male control over reproduction as basis of sex-class: **Firestone** (USA) Differing male and female relationships to reproduction: **O'Brien** (Canada)

jobs in preference to men? Women may be a flexible labour force, but that flexibility is not utilised in such a way that they are potential replacements for male workers. Indeed women rarely do the same jobs as men and are employed instead in a different range of occupations. Moreover, this approach does not explain why it should be *women* who constitute the reserve army – it is simply taken for granted that women's primary role is a domestic one and that this renders them marginal to the wage economy.

Women's domestic work was itself the subject of much debate. Marxists theorised housework in terms of the contribution it made to capitalism, within what became known as 'the domestic labour debate' which dominated theoretical discussions on housework in many Western countries, particularly in Britain and Canada, throughout the 1970s. The debate was premised on Capital's need for a constantly replenished labour force. It is largely women who do the work this entails – they cook the meals and wash the shirts necessary to make existing workers ready for each new day and care for the next generation of workers. Marxist feminists initially sought to establish that this work was socially necessary, essential to the functioning of capitalism (see, for example, Benston 1969). However, what began from feminists' attempts to challenge the orthodox Marxist view that housework was marginal to capitalism subsequently became a highly technical discussion. The debate became concerned with such issues as whether housework produced 'surplus value', in what sense housework or its products had a value and whether that value was embodied in the labour power of the housewife's husband and realised through his wage (for summaries see Rushton 1979; Kaluzynska 1980; Walby 1986).[1]

In focusing exclusively on fitting housework into Marx's labour theory of value the debate lost its feminist impetus and by the end of the 1970s it had run its course. The problems proved insoluble because domestic labour is not performed under the same conditions as wage labour and cannot be explained in terms of a theory designed to analyse wage labour. Moreover, participants in the domestic labour debate took divisions of labour between men and women for granted: they never paused to consider why it was women who performed domestic labour or why men apparently 'needed' to have it done for them. The competing claims made about the value of domestic labour were entirely contingent upon the position of the housewife's *husband* within the capitalist economy. It was in terms of *his* labour that *her* work was conceptualised. Yet relations between husbands and wives, particularly inequalities between them, were largely ignored. For most Marxists it was unthinkable that working-class men might be oppressors in their own homes or that 'bourgeois' women might also be oppressed (Delphy and Leonard 1992).

From the early 1970s a rather different approach to domestic labour was being developed by French materialist feminists, particularly Christine Delphy. According to Delphy, the peculiarities of housework arise from the social relations within which it is performed. She argues that these relations are patriarchal and that within families men systematically exploit and benefit from women's labour within a domestic mode of production (Delphy 1976, 1977, 1984). Women's domestic work is undertaken as a personal service to a male head of household. He effectively appropriates her whole person and the labour she embodies, so that the work she does is potentially limitless and depends on his requirements. Hence housework has no fixed job description; it does not directly involve the exchange of a set number of hours or an agreed amount of work for a given return. The maintenance a wife receives is not related to the work she does, but is determined by her husband's income and his generosity. The direct appropriation and non-exchange of women's labour is particularly clear when a wife is also in employment, earning enough to meet her own maintenance costs, but is still expected to do the housework. In this situation she is clearly working for nothing. Delphy argues that within the domestic mode of production men constitute a class of exploiters while women are an exploited class.

Delphy's analysis provoked hostile responses from Marxist feminists (see Jackson 1996). The grounds for such criticism were generally technical, such as the question of whether two modes of production can co-exist within one society (Kaluzynska 1980; Molyneux 1979). However, at the root of Marxist feminists' objections was an unwillingness to entertain the possibility that men might benefit directly from the work their wives do (see, for example, Barrett 1980: 216–17). Delphy was also taken to task for not considering the relationship between the domestic and capitalist modes of production. Others, however, have done so, notably Sylvia Walby (1986). Walby concentrates less on the direct benefits men gain from their wives' work, and more on the ways in which these benefits are mediated through the exchange of labour power. She argues that a man realises the value of the domestic labour he has appropriated when he exchanges his labour power – which his wife's work has produced – for a wage which he controls. This, for Walby, is the main mechanism of exploitation within the patriarchal mode of production.[2]

Neither Delphy nor Walby see women's exploitation within the domestic mode of production as the sole basis of their subordination. Another, obviously material aspect of women's situation is their disadvantaged position in the labour market. As we have seen, this is not directly explicable in terms of ready-made Marxist concepts. Marxism cannot explain why women and men should not be exploited equally in the capitalist economy. By extending materialist analysis, however, it may be possible to explore the interconnections between capitalism and patriarchy in the structuring of labour markets. This is a theme explored by the American Marxist feminist, Heidi Hartmann (1976; 1981), and subsequently developed by Walby (1986).

Hartmann's perspective, though recognised as Marxist feminist, is not dissimilar to Delphy's. Both argue that patriarchy exists as a distinct system of inequality alongside capitalism, and that patriarchy is founded upon male control of women's labour. Harmann differs from Delphy in that she devotes more attention to women's paid work outside the home and seeks to establish the interconnections between patriarchy and capitalism. Using historical analysis she argues that the development of capitalism within societies which were already patriarchal had consequences for gender divisions in both the home and the workplace. During the nineteenth century, organised working-class men used their social advantage to exclude women from well paid, skilled occupations and to marginalise them in the labour market. A vicious circle was established, such that women's disadvantage in the labour market constrained them into dependence on marriage for survival. Within marriage they exchanged domestic services for maintenance, and housework and childcare became their primary responsibilities. Because of the burden of domestic work they could not compete in the labour market on equal terms with men, thereby compounding their original disadvantage.

This suggests some interesting possibilities for grounding theory in history, but history is itself contested terrain. Some Marxist feminists argued for the primacy of class relations in history (see, for example, Humphreys 1977), while others, such as Michèle Barrett (1980), were less inclined to reduce women's subordination to class relations. Barrett argued that women's subordination was not a product of the logic of capitalist development, but had become thoroughly enmeshed with the material structures of contemporary capitalist societies. The research which accumulated during the 1980s swung the balance towards a recognition of the importance of patriarchal relations and the resilience of male domination under changing historical conditions (see Walby 1986; Mark-Lawson and Witz 1990; Seccombe 1986; Jackson 1992a).

Relations of Reproduction and the Control of Women's Sexuality

An alternative to relating women's subordination in productive relations was to suggest that it was located in social relations of reproduction. After the domestic labour debate most Marxist feminists defined housework as unproductive but it continued to be regarded as reproducing labour power.[3] More specifically, it was argued, turning our attention to motherhood 'would lead to an analysis of the role of women in reproducing labour power and the forces and relations of production more generally' (Barrett and McIntosh 1979: 102). The obvious danger here is biological reductionism: all the complex ways in which capitalist social relations are reproduced, as well as women's subordination itself, are reduced to women's reproductive capacities (Edholm, Harris and Young 1977; Delphy 1984; Delphy and Leonard 1992). Despite this problem, reproduction was, for a time, a central concept in Marxist feminist analysis.

The idea that women's subordination is rooted in reproduction has a respectable history within Marxism, deriving from Engels's thesis that the 'world historic defeat of the female sex' occurred with the rise of private property and the establishment of men's right to pass on property to their heirs and hence monopolise individual women's reproductive capacities. Engels's work is now known to be badly flawed. It is based on the assumption of a 'natural' sexual division of labour and the presupposition that men possess an innate desire to transmit property to their biological offspring. These problems, however, did not deter Marxist feminists from using Engels to authorise a search for the roots of women's subordination in relations of reproduction. For example, Rosin McDonough and Rachel Harrison locate patriarchy in men's control of women's sexuality and procreative functions. They suggest that the emergence of social classes divided women into two groups: 'those who procreated heirs (future owners of the means of production) and those who procreated future ... labourers'. Thus women perform 'two economic functions necessary to perpetuate the social relations of capitalist production' (McDonough and Harrison 1978: 34). Once again the reproduction of class relations is reduced to biology, an error compounded by the classic functionalist teleology: projecting current functions into the past and treating them as causal origins.

The attraction of the idea of relations of reproduction is that it keeps Marxist analysis of productive, class relations intact while simultaneously providing a means for arguing that patriarchy currently exists to service capitalism. Other Marxist feminists, however, are wary of leaving the Marxist perspectives on productive labour relations untouched by feminism, and are therefore sceptical of arguments based only on reproduction (see, for example, Beechey 1979). It is not only those who wish to avoid troubling Marxist conceptualisations of capitalism who concentrate their efforts on reproduction. This has also been a strategy adopted by some who seek to displace class relations from the privileged place they occupy in Marxism, and concentrate on the significance of gender relations in the progress of human history.

One of the best-known examples of this tendency is Shulamith Firestone (1972). Often taken as an exemplar of radical feminism, Firestone's analysis is in fact highly individual and idiosyncratic. She attributes women's subordination directly to their reproductive functions. 'Unlike economic class, sex-class sprang directly from biological reality: men and women were created different, and not equal' (Firestone 1972: 16). Although Firestone claims to employ Marx's dialectical method, in her hands this amounts to little more than overturning the Marxist view of history as class struggle in favour of an alternative view of history as founded upon 'the division of society into two distinct biological classes for procreative reproduction, and the struggles of these classes with one another' (1972: 20). She claims that the organisation of the biological family is the crucible of all forms of domination and inequality, and that this is the motor of history, but there is nothing in her model to explain how such historical changes come about.

A far more sophisticated account of the historical development of relations of reproduction is offered by Mary O'Brien (1981). O'Brien's conceptualisation of reproduction includes the biological processes of conception, gestation and birth and the social relations involved in nurturing a child. She argues that paying attention to reproduction is no more biologistic than Marxist accounts of production. Both production and reproduction start from basic human needs: to eat and breed, to survive as individuals and as a species. However, in satisfying these basic human needs we enter into *social* relationships, and it is these which shape the conditions under which we produce and reproduce and which have, historically, produced structural inequalities of class and gender. O'Brien also suggests mechanisms for social change in the sphere of reproduction, and posits two major historical transformations: the discovery of biological paternity and the recent development of technologies of fertility control. The outcome of the latter is still uncertain and is a site of feminist struggle. The discovery of paternity, however, presaged the beginnings of patriarchy. This knowledge simultaneously included men in reproduction and excluded them from it. Men became aware of their alienation from their own seed and of their lack of an experiential sense of generational continuity. To establish their place in the succession of generations they needed to appropriate the fruits of women's reproductive labour as their own, co-operating with other men to maintain their individual rights. O'Brien thus supplies what is missing in analyses deriving from Engels, an explanation of why men should seek to pass on property to their biological offspring; but whether she does, in fact, avoid biological reductionism is a moot point.

Whereas O'Brien treats sexual acts primarily as moments in the reproductive cycle, other feminists have focused on sexuality itself. Another influential variant of the argument that women's oppression is founded on sexuality is that offered by Catharine MacKinnon. She begins by establishing parallels between the object of Marxist analysis, labour, and the object of feminist analysis – in this case sexuality. 'Sexuality is to feminism what work is to Marxism: that which is most one's own, yet most taken away' (MacKinnon 1982: 515). Gender divisions and women's subordination are founded on heterosexuality, which 'institutionalises male sexual dominance and female sexual submission' (1982: 533). In making sexuality so central to the analysis of women's subordination, MacKinnon over-privileges sexuality and gives insufficient weight to other forms of male domination.

An alternative analysis is offered by Monique Wittig who began developing her analysis of heterosexuality in the late 1970s. Drawing on Delphy's work on the exploitation of women's labour within marriage and Guillaumin's conceptualisation of the public and private appropriation of women's bodies and labour, she analyses heterosexuality as a class relationship which is founded upon both sexual and labour relations (Wittig 1992; Delphy 1984; Guillaumin 1981). She likens lesbians to runaway slaves; as fugitives from their class they are no longer 'women'. Wittig's analysis is a contentious one, and rejected by some other French materialists, particularly Delphy, for implying that it is possible to escape patriarchy by opting out of heterosexuality.

Wittig was not alone in arguing for lesbianism as an act of political resistance. This idea had been in circulation in the USA since the early 1970s (see Radical-esbians 1970). In Britain, Leeds Revolutionary Feminists argued that hetero-sexual feminism was a contradiction in terms (Onlywoman Press 1980). As in Wittig's analysis, revolutionary feminists saw women as a class, but they, unlike Wittig, did not define this in Marxist terms and, like MacKinnon, focused exclusively on men's sexual appropriation of women. Prominent among this group was Sheila Jeffreys, who has continued to argue that sexual exploitation and violence are central to the maintenance of patriarchal domination (see, for example, Jeffreys 1990).

Theorists such as O'Brien, MacKinnon, Jeffreys and Wittig, while highly controversial, have had a lasting impact on diverse strands of feminist theory and politics. O'Brien's analysis is still drawn on by those interested in women's em-bodied specificity (e.g. Brodribb 1992); Wittig has influenced some feminist Queer theorists, notably Judith Butler (1990); the work of MacKinnon and Jeffreys informs some radical feminist theories of sexuality, especially critiques of pornography. More orthodox Marxist feminist analyses of reproduction, on the other hand, have proved to be less durable. Among Marxist feminists, the most significant developments have taken place in the sphere of ideology and culture.

Ideology, Discourse and the Turn to Culture

Since the early 1980s many of those who once saw themselves as Marxist fem-inists have turned their backs on materialist analyses of such things as housework and labour markets in favour of a focus on language, discourse and represen-tation. The associated decline in the influence of social scientific analysis has meant that macro-level models of social structure, of patriarchy and capitalism, have disappeared from much Marxist-feminist analysis.[4] This 'cultural turn' (Barrett 1992) became increasingly evident in the 1980s, but its origins can be discerned in the late 1970s, presaged by Marxist feminist interest in ideology and psychoanalysis.

Juliet Mitchell's *Psychoanalysis and Feminism* (1974) reflects the 1970s preoccu-pation with structural analysis, but places particular emphasis on ideology and the psyche. She draws heavily on the work of French structuralists, on Althusser's Marxism, Lacan's psychoanalysis and on Lévi-Strauss's anthropological work on kinship. Althusser's reformulation of Marxism, particularly the idea that ideology was relatively autonomous from economic relations, was potentially attractive to feminists. If ideology no longer had to be seen as a superstructural reflection of the economic base of society, this created a space to theorise women's subordination without having to relate it to the capitalist mode of production. Mitchell argues that women's subordination once had a material base rooted in the social ordering of kinship but that under capitalism kin ties are no longer a fundamental form of social and economic organisation. Women's subordination, she suggests, is now primarily ideological; this ideology is reproduced in our psyches, guaranteed only by the continual replaying of the oedipal drama between generations. For Mitchell, the struggle against patriarchy must take the form of a 'cultural revolution' (Mitchell 1974: 414). However, she gives us no clues on how we are to break out of the cycle by which, according to her psychoanalytic reasoning, a universal oedipal drama determines our psychic functioning.

Mitchell's work was important insofar as it rehabilitated psychoanalysis, which many feminists had rejected, introduced English-speaking feminists to the work of Jacques Lacan, and was indicative of a growing interest in the structuralist tradition of French theory, soon to be superseded by post-structuralism. Other Marxists and Marxist feminists were also experimenting with combinations of Althusserian theory, psychoanalysis, structural linguistics and semiology, particularly the idea that ideology is effective through the capacity of language to shape our thoughts and desires (see, for example, Coward and Ellis 1977). These bodies of theory were also central to the project of the Marxist feminist journal *m/f*, which was launched in 1978. Once the ideas of Michel Foucault (1980) were added to this mixture, the emphasis shifted from linguistic and semiotic structures to a more fluid notion of discourse. Foucault, another French theorist, reconceptualised power as diffuse and dispersed rather than concentrated into the hands of ruling classes. Moreover, for Foucault, the concept of ideology is untenable since 'truth' is an effect of discourse. Hence ideology could no longer be seen as 'false', with effects discoverable by 'scientific' Marxism. The one, fragile, link which had moored these new analyses of the symbolic realm to the material world was severed. Gradually these new forms of feminist theory evolved into poststructuralist and postmodern feminisms.

The influence of these ideas were felt first among Marxist feminists. In part this was a response to the perceived failure of Marxism to deal with issues which were important to feminist analysis, such as subjectivity and sexuality. Moreover, those who had sought to explain women's subordination within Marxism, whether in terms of productive relations, reproduction or ideology faced the difficulty of explaining why women should occupy particular niches within the social hierarchy. They often found themselves sliding into universalistic and biologistic accounts at odds with both materialism's emphasis on the primacy of the social and their desire as feminists to avoid identifying women's subordination with 'nature'. Poststructuralism and postmodernism offered perspectives which were radically anti-essentialist – which challenged the idea that 'men' and 'women' were given, natural, essential categories. Increasingly the category 'women' was called into question. The editors of *m/f*, for example, argued that there is no unity to 'women', or to 'women's oppression', that differing discourses construct varying definitions of 'women' (Adams, Brown and Cowie 1978). This deconstruction of 'women' was to become a central theme in some of the most celebrated works of postmodern feminism (for example, Riley 1988; Butler 1990; see also Chapter 10).

In this context the immediate concern was to counter the idea of 'women' as a fixed, natural category, to emphasise its historical, cultural and contextual specificity. There was, however, another, and compelling, reason for questioning the category 'women', in that it often served to conceal differences among women. The analyses of women's oppression which shaped feminist debate were framed almost entirely from a white Western perspective. By the end of the 1970s white feminists found themselves confronted by black women, Third World women and women of colour, angrily denouncing those who had excluded them or unthinkingly subsumed them under the banner of 'sisterhood', without allowing them to speak for themselves. Hazel Carby summed this up when she asked of white feminists 'what exactly do you mean when you say WE?' (Carby 1982: 233). As the clamour of critique grew in the 1980s it became abundantly clear that 'women' was not, and could not be, a unitary category, and that any theory attempting to distil women's subordination into a single explanation was doomed to exclude the experiences of the majority of the world's female population (Flax 1990). Moreover, attention was increasingly being drawn to the complexities of women's lives in a post-colonial era with its global economy, its history of colonial diasporas and its current labour migrations and displacements of refugees.

All of this was taken by some feminists as a further mandate for post-modern theorising, seen as a means of avoiding the exclusions of an assumed universal womanhood and the simplifications of causal models of oppression (see, for example, Riley 1988). Some critics have suggested that postmodernists are simply taking refuge in an impenetrable elitist theory which does not require them to confront the realities of racism (Modleski 1991). However, there are feminist post-colonial theorists who speak from the position of the previously marginalised 'other', and hence from a rather different location from that occupied by white theorists. Theorists such as Gayatri Spivak (1988), while engaging with postmodernist theory and concerned primarily with culture, rarely lose sight of material inequalities. Whether postmodernism is the only means of coping with the complexities of gender in a postcolonial world, or whether materialist, structural analyses still have something to offer is a matter of debate.

Theorising Diversity and Complexity

There is no doubt that the ways in which gender intersects with other forms of inequality, especially those founded on racism and colonialism, has been under-theorised. Some materialist feminists have paid attention to the construction of 'race' as a category (Guillaumin 1995) and to women's location within the global division of labour (Mies 1986), but this has not been sufficient to answer the post-modernists' accusation that materialist analysis cannot capture the multiplicity of differences among women, that the term 'patriarchy' conceals such differences, that the concept 'women' itself denies diversity of experience. Moreover, it is becoming clear that issues of 'race' and racism can no longer be understood in terms of a binary relationship between Black and White, since ethnic, religious, national and cultural differences are themselves so complex and context specific (Brah 1992; Ang-Lygate 1995). There is no reason why a social structural analysis, provided it is not crudely reductionist, should be unable to deal with the diverse locations occupied by women within local and global contexts. Moreover, there are dangers in abandoning this form of analysis. Taken to its logical con-clusion, the cultural turn implied the abandonment of analyses of the material conditions of women's lives, the denial of any over-arching systems of power, and a move towards a focus on culture and the discursive construction of difference.

The claims of postmodernists to have a monopoly on theorising diversity and complexity have been contested, notably by Sylvia Walby (1992). While accept-ing that postmodernists have much to offer in sensitising us to varying cultural constructions of gender, she argues that they go too far in fragmenting the categories of 'women', 'race' and 'class'. In neglecting the social context of power relations, and in viewing power as diffuse and dispersed, postmodernism fails to recognise that systematic oppressions of gender, class and race persist. Seeing these in terms of 'difference' serves to deny inequality. Moreover, while Walby accepts that gender relations are culturally and historically variable, this is not in her view sufficient to justify the abandonment of attempts to explain them. There are also cross-cultural regularities and historical continuities in gender relations. The signifiers 'woman' and 'man', she maintains, 'have sufficient historical and cross-cultural continuity … to warrant using such terms' (Walby 1992: 36). She recognises that many feminist theories have not dealt adequately with historical change and cultural variations, but this she attributes to uni-causal analyses rather than the concept of patriarchy *per se*. Similarly, she is critical of traditional Marxist models which reduced all relations of inequality to class. She argues that rather than abandoning attempts to explain inequality, we should be developing theories of gender, class, and ethnicity which recognise the intersections between them and which place them in the context of the international division of labour. To do so we need to retain the structural concepts of patriarchy, capitalism and racism. She concludes:

> We do not need to abandon the notion of causality in the face of the complexity of the social world. We do not have to move from analysis of structure to that of discourse to catch that

complexity; neither do we have to resort to capitalism as the sole determinant in order to have a macro-social theory.

(Walby 1992: 48–9)

Feminist Social Theory in the 1990s

In the 1990s materialist feminist analyses are not particularly fashionable in academic circles. Somewhat prematurely, and I would say groundlessly, a theoretical tradition little more than twenty-five years old has been declared by some to be outmoded. There is a tendency in some recent feminist writing to assume that theories which emerged in the first decade of second-wave feminism have now been superseded, and that feminists who continue to work within these theoretical frameworks are no longer producing relevant work. In particular, feminist postmodernists constantly warn us against these older theoretical traditions, implying that they claim to have discovered the ultimate cause of women's oppression or that they assume universal applicability for theories generated from a particular historical and social location (see, for example, Flax 1990). Such accusations are not always just. Some feminists were always critical of attempts to construct totalising theories of women's oppression and sceptical of trans-historical, universalistic explanations (Delphy 1984; Walby 1990).

While warning of totalising tendencies in feminist theory, Jane Flax (1990) also indicates some points of convergence between feminism and postmodernism. She is substantially correct to say that feminists have always been sceptical about claims to 'objectivity' and 'truth', since these so often turned out to be very particular truths constructed from an androcentric perspective. We have also long been aware that language and discourse are not transparent media of communication, that they construct rather than reflect meaning. We have also recognised that the idea of a unitary, fixed, rational self is not tenable, that it does not match the complexities and contradictions of our lived experience as women and as feminists. Since postmodern theories speak to these concerns, it is perhaps not surprising that feminists have been attracted to them. Materialist feminists, too, have sometimes drawn on aspects of postmodern theorising but have remained wary of its tendency to discount the world of 'things' in favour of 'words' (Jackson 1992b). Since materialist social scientific perspectives presuppose a 'real' world outside and prior to discourse, it will always be irreconcilable with much postmodernist thinking.

There are signs, though, that some feminists are retreating from the extreme anti-materialist implications of postmodernism, and are edging back towards accepting the existence of structural inequalities. In this context the term 'materialist feminism' has been reinvented by American theorists such as Rosemary Hennessy (1993) and Donna Landry and Gerald Maclean (1993). Both texts claim some Marxist antecedents and both are motivated by the wish to avoid the politically disabling consequences of postmodernism consequent upon the denial of any material reality outside language and discourse. Hence Hennessy argues that materialist feminism needs to retain a 'critique of social totalities like patriarchy and capitalism' (1993: xii). Neither of these texts has a very clear idea of what materialist feminism has been and is in the European context, and both see it as a form of Marxism infused with postmodernism. Hennessy comes close to defining it in this way, saying that materialist feminism 'is distinguished from socialist feminism in part because it embraces postmodern conceptions of language and subjectivity' (1993: 5). Whatever its failings, if this work represents a trend towards a more materially grounded discourse analysis, it is to be welcomed.

There has also been a recent, renewed interest in political economy, in particular with analyses of women's household production (Folbre 1994; Fraad et al. 1994; Gibson-Graham 1996). These new analyses, while Marxist in orientation, are less concerned with macro-level analysis of economic and social structures than with contextualised and localised processes and practices. As a result of this shift it has become possible to think what was previously unthinkable in Marxist circles: that women's work in the home is productive, that household production entails exploitation and hence a class relationship between women as producers and men as appropriators of their wives' surplus labour. In this respect the analyses of Harriet Fraad et al. (1994) and J. K. Gibson-Graham (1996) converge with the older materialist feminist perspective developed by Delphy (1984). Interestingly in Delphy's more recent collaborative work with Diana Leonard (Delphy and Leonard 1992), more emphasis is placed on the processes of family production and exploitation and less on the structure within which these processes take place – the domestic mode of production. Nonetheless Delphy and Leonard retain a commitment to structural analysis which is less evident in newer approaches.

What has made these newer approaches possible is a re-visioning of Marxism through the lens of postmodernism, a questioning of the ways in which it has represented capitalism. Where earlier Marxist feminists took Marxism's account of capitalism as given, now it is seen as a discursive construction, a particular representation of the world rather than a sacrosanct, unquestionable 'truth'. The clearest account of this is in the work of J. K. Gibson-Graham (two feminist writers who have adopted a joint, singular authorial identity), who seek to deconstruct Marxist and other representations of capitalism (Gibson-Graham 1996). Gibson-Graham does not embrace the form of postmodernism which denies the existence of material, extra-discursive phenomena. Rather, she suggests that by dismantling the hegemonic representation of capitalism as a monolithic global system or structure we can reveal what this representation conceals: the persistence of non-capitalist processes and practices. In this way she is able to analyse the appropriation of women's surplus labour within households (following Fraad et al. 1994) as a non-capitalist class process.

Once class relations are thought of as contextualised processes rather than relationships between social groups pre-defined by their location within the economy, objections to treating relations between husbands and wives in class terms evaporate. Once capitalism is no longer seen as a total system into which everything must fit, it is no longer necessary to analyse women's domestic work in terms of its functionality for capitalism or to locate it outside 'the economy'. And, once attention shifts from systems to processes the difficult and contentious problem of accounting for the co-existence of two (or more) modes of production no longer exists. While some of us may have reservations about the abandonment of the concept of social structure in favour of an emphasis on process,[5] analyses such as these do allow us to focus on the material conditions of women's lives in varied and different contexts.

In the meantime, older forms of materialist analysis have not disappeared, despite imputations of their irrelevance in these supposedly postmodern times. The concept of patriarchy continues to be debated (see Pollert 1996) and feminist social scientists continue to demonstrate that material factors shape women's lives in determinate ways. There has, however, been a move away from 'grand theory' which seeks to explain all aspects of women's subordination and a move towards forms of theory which are more sensitive to local contexts and to differences among women. Often this has emerged from a productive engagement with the work of postmodern feminists. Mary Maynard (1995) has recently suggested that the way forward lies in developing what some sociologists have called 'middle range theories'. Such theories emphasise the specifics of given social contexts, institutions and relationships, offering grounded generalisations rather than universalistic, totalising models of entire societies and are more easily integrated with empirical research. Middle-range theories would enable us to use materialist and structural methods of analysis without constructing huge, theoretical edifices which are remote from everyday life and insufficiently flexible to account for the varying life patterns of differing groups of women.

A trend in this direction is already discernible and has been facilitated by growing bodies of feminist research, giving rise to new theoretical developments which are empirically grounded. Feminists continue to develop theory around such issues as gender segregated labour markets (Witz 1992; Siltanen 1994) and issues of power and exploitation within families (Delphy and Leonard 1992; Folbre 1994; Fraad et al. 1994; Van Every 1995). The emphasis on understanding the local, situated contexts of women's lives has also enabled feminists to make connections between aspects of gendered social relations which were previously seen as discrete and separate, such as sexuality and work. Hence, for example, Lisa Adkins (1995) has drawn our attention to the sexualisation of women's labour in the service sector and Gillian Dunne (1996) has explored the ways in which lesbians have a specific relation to the labour market which differs from that of heterosexual women. There has also been a recent resurgence of debate around heterosexuality, which is increasingly conceptualised as encompassing both sexual and non-sexual aspects of life and analysed both as an institution and in terms of its specific and situated practices (see especially Richardson 1996).

Paying attention to the specific contexts of women's lives also entails accounting for the effects of social change, some of which derive from feminist struggle – for example women's increased participation in paid work and their lesser dependence on male breadwinners (see Walby 1990, 1997). It also means being sensitive to differences among women and to the materiality of these differences. There is now a strong strand of theory, again empirically grounded, exploring the intersections between gender and racial inequalities (Afshar and Maynard 1994; Mirza 1997). Here, too, there is innovative work being done, drawing on ideas from post-colonial theory, originally developed around cultural analysis, but grounding them sociologically, relating them to the specific contexts of migrant women's accounts of post-colonial diaspora (Ang-Lygate 1996, 1997).

The challenge for feminist social theory today is to analyse the localised contexts of women's everyday existence and the meanings women give to their lives without losing sight of structural patterns of dominance and subordination. I would argue that a materialist analysis which pays attention to systematic inequalities is as relevant now as it ever was and remains necessary to grapple with the complexities of a post-colonial world, with the intersections of gender, ethnicity and nationality. The material foundations and consequences of institutionalised racism, the heritage of centuries of slavery, colonialism and imperialism and the continued international division of labour, are at least as important as culturally constituted difference. We live our lives now within a global context characterised by extremely stark material inequalities. Even within the wealthy Western nations the material oppression suffered by women has not gone away, and for many women the situation is worsening as a result of unemployment and cuts in welfare provision. Intersections between class, gender and racism are clearly important issues here, too, and need to be pursued in terms of structural patterning of inequality as well as multi-layered identities. The continued vitality of approaches which deal with such inequalities is crucial for feminist politics and theory.

Notes

1. It should be noted that the Wages for Housework campaign, which argued that housework was productive labour and a hidden source of profit for capitalism (Dalla Costa and James 1972), represented a minority view. Most other Marxists and Marxist feminists disagreed. It was generally held that productive work is that which directly produces 'surplus value' – the wealth created by workers over and above the costs of employing them (the source of profit). Since housework only made an indirect

contribution, by servicing existing and future workers, it could not be seen as productive. Whether or not housework could be thought of as having value or creating value via the husband's labour power was a more contentious and widely debated issue.

2. Walby prefers the term 'patriarchal' as opposed to 'domestic' mode of production since, she argues, it more accurately denotes the form of exploitation occurring in marriage.

3. This distinction between production and reproduction is not only spurious and nonsensical it is also counter to Marx's claim that the two processes are inextricably linked since, for Marx, every process of production is simultaneously a process of reproduction (Beechey 1979; Walby 1986).

4. This trend can be traced, for example, in the pages of the Marxist feminist journal, *Feminist Review*, which was established in 1979. Issues such as welfare provision, education and women's work accounted for a large proportion of its content in the early 1980s but have now all but vanished from sight.

5. Gibson-Graham does not regard structural analyses as invalid – what she suggests is that different forms of analysis are suited to different forms of political critique.

References

Adams, Parveen, Beverley Brown and Elizabeth Cowie (1978) 'Editorial', *m/f*, 2: 3–5.

Adkins, Lisa (1995) *Gendered Work: Sexuality, Family and the Labour Market*, Milton Keynes: Open University Press.

Afshar, Haleh and Mary Maynard (eds) (1994) *The Dynamics of 'Race' and Gender*, London: Taylor & Francis.

Ang-Lygate, Magdalene (1995) 'Shades of meaning', *Trouble and Strife*, 31: 15–20.

Ang-Lygate, Magdalene (1996) 'Everywhere to go but home: on (re)(dis)(un)location', *Journal of Gender Studies*, 5 (3): 375–88.

Ang-Lygate, Magdalene (1997) 'Charting the spaces of (un)location: on theorizing diaspora', in H. Mirza (ed.) *Black British Feminism*, London: Routledge.

Barrett, Michèle [1980] (1990) *Women's Oppression Today*, London: Verso.

Barrett, Michèle (1992) 'Words and things: materialism and method in contemporary feminist analysis', in M. Barrett and A. Phillips (eds) *Destabilizing Theory: Contemporary Feminist Debates*, Oxford: Polity: 201–19.

Barrett, Michèle and Mary McIntosh (1979) 'Christine Delphy: towards a materialist feminism', *Feminist Review*, 1: 95–106.

Beechey, Veronica (1979) 'On patriarchy', *Feminist Review*, 3: 66–82.

Benston, Margaret (1969) 'The political economy of women's liberation', *Monthly Review* 4.

Brah, Avtar (1992) 'Questions of difference and international feminism', in J. Aaron and S. Walby (eds) *Out of the Margins: Women's Studies in the Nineties*, London: Falmer.

Brodribb, Somer (1992) *Nothing Mat(t)ers*, Melbourne: Spinifex.

Bruegel, Irene (1979) 'Women as a reserve army of labour: a note on recent British experience', *Feminist Review*, 3: 12–23.

Butler, Judith (1990) *Gender Trouble: Feminism and the Subversion of Identity*, New York: Routledge.

Carby, Hazel (1982) 'White women listen! Black feminism and the boundaries of sister-hood', in Centre for Contemporary Culture Studies (eds) *The Empire Strikes Back: Race and Racism in 70s Britain*, London: Hutchinson.

Coward, Rosalind and John Ellis (1977) *Language and Materialism*, London: Routledge and Kegan Paul.

Dalla Costa, Mariarosa and Selma James (1972) *The Power of Women and the Subversion of the Community*, Bristol: Falling Wall Press.

Delphy, Christine (1976) 'Continuities and discontinuities in marriage and divorce', in D. Leonard Barker and S. Allen (eds) *Sexual Divisions and Society*, London: Tavistock.

Delphy, Christine (1977) *The Main Enemy*, London: Women's Research and Resources Centre.

Delphy, Christine (1984) *Close to Home: A Materialist Analysis of Women's Oppression*, translated and edited by Diana Leonard, London: Hutchinson.

Delphy, Christine and Diana Leonard (1992) *Familiar Exploitation: A New Analysis of Marriage in Contemporary Western Societies*, Oxford: Polity.

Dunne, Gillian (1996) *Lesbian Lifestyles*, Basingstoke: Macmillan.

Edholm, Felicity, Olivia Harris and Kate Young (1977) 'Conceptualizing women', *Critique of Anthropology*, 3: 101–30.

Firestone, Shulamith (1972) *The Dialectic of Sex*, London: Paladin.

Flax, Jane (1990) 'Postmodernism and gender in feminist theory', in L. Nicholson (ed.) *Feminism/Postmodernism*, New York: Routledge.

Folbre, Nancy (1994) *Who Pays for the Kids? Gender and the Structures of Constraint*, London: Routledge.

Foucault, Michel (1980) *Power/Knowledge: Selected Interviews and Other Writings, 1972–1977*, Brighton: Harvester Press.

Fraad, Harriet, Stephen Resnick and Richard Wolff (1994) *Bringing it All Back Home: Class, Gender and Power in the Modern Household*, London: Pluto Press.

Gibson-Graham, J. K. (1996) *The End of Capitalism (as we knew it): A Feminist Critique of Political Economy*, Oxford: Blackwell.

Guillaumin, Colette (1981) 'The practice of power and belief in nature. Part 1: The appropriation of women', translated by Linda Murgatroyd, *Feminist Issues*, 1 (2): 3–28.

Guillaumin, Colette (1995) *Racism, Sexism, Power and Ideology*, London: Routledge.

Hartmann, Heidi (1976) 'Capitalism, patriarchy and job segregation by sex', *Signs*, 1: 137–68.

Hartmann, Heidi (1981) 'The unhappy marriage of marxism and feminism: towards a more progressive union', in L. Sargent (ed.) *Women and Revolution: the Unhappy Marriage of Marxism and Feminism*, London: Pluto Press.

Hennessy, Rosemary (1993) *Materialist Feminism and the Politics of Discourse*, New York and London: Routledge.

Humphries, Jane (1977) 'Class struggle and the persistence of the working class family', *Cambridge Journal of Economics*, 1: 241–58.

Jackson, Stevi (1992a) 'Towards a historical sociology of housework', *Women's Studies International Forum*, 15 (2): 153–72.

Jackson, Stevi (1992b) 'The amazing deconstructing woman', *Trouble and Strife*, 25: 25–31.

Jackson, Stevi (1996) *Christine Delphy*, London: Sage.

Jeffreys, Sheila (1990) *Anticlimax: A Feminist Perspective on the Sexual Revolution*, London: The Women's Press.

Kaluzynska, Eva (1980), 'Wiping the floor with theory: a survey of writings on housework', *Feminist Review*, 6: 27–54.

Landry, Donna and Gerald MacLean (1993) *Materialist Feminisms*, Oxford: Blackwell.

McDonough, Roisin and Rachel Harrison (1978) 'Patriarchy and relations of production', in A. Kuhn and A. M. Wolpe (eds) *Feminism and Materialism: Women and Modes of Production*, London: Routledge & Kegan Paul.

MacKinnon, Catharine A. (1982) 'Feminism, Marxism, Method and the State: An Agenda for Theory', *Signs*, 7 (3): 515–44.

Maynard, Mary (1995) 'Beyond the "big three": the development of feminist theory in the 1990s', *Women's History Review*, 4 (3): 259–81.

Mies, Maria (1986) *Patriarchy and Accumulation on a World Scale: Women in the International Division of Labour*, London: Zed Books.

Mirza, Heidi (1997) *Black British Feminism*, London: Routledge.

Mitchell, Juliet (1974) *Psychoanalysis and Feminism*, Harmondsworth: Penguin.

Modleski, Tania (1991) *Feminism Without Women*, New York: Routledge.

Molyneux, Maxine (1979) 'Beyond the domestic labour debate', *New Left Review*, 116: 3–27.

O'Brien, Mary (1981) *The Politics of Reproduction*, London: Routledge & Kegan Paul.

Onlywomen Press (ed.) (1980) *Love Your Enemy*, London: Onlywomen Press.

Petty, Celia, Deborah Roberts and Sharon Smith (1987) *Women's Liberation and Socialism*, London and Chicago: Bookmarks.

Pollert, Anna (1996), 'Gender and class revisited: or, the poverty of "patriarchy"', *Sociology*, 30 (4): 639–60.

Radicalesbians (1970) *Woman-Identified Woman*, New York: Gay Flames.

Richardson, Diane (ed.) (1996) *Theorising Heterosexuality: Telling it Straight*, Buckingham: Open University Press.

Riley, Denise (1988) *'Am I that Name?' Feminism and the Category of 'Women' in History*, London: Macmillan.

Rowbotham, Sheila (1981) 'The trouble with "patriarchy"', in R. Samuel (ed.) *People's History and Socialist Theory*, London: Routledge & Kegan Paul.

Rubin, Gayle (1975) 'The traffic in women: notes on the "political economy" of sex', in R. Reiter (ed.) *Toward an Anthropology of Women*, New York: Monthly Review Press.

Rushton, Peter (1979) 'Marxism, domestic labour and the capitalist economy: a note on recent discussions', in C. C. Harris (ed.) *The Sociology of the Family: New Directions for Britain*, Keele: Sociological Review Monographs.

Seccombe, Wally (1986) 'Patriarchy stabilized: the construction of the male breadwinner wage norm in nineteenth-century Britain', *Social History*, 11 (1): 53–76.

Siltanen, Janet (1994) *Locating Gender: Occupational Segregation, Wages and Domestic Responsibilities*, London: UCL Press.

Spivak, Gayatri Chakravorty (1988) *In Other Worlds*, London: Routledge.

Stacey, Jackie (1993) 'Untangling feminist theory', in D. Richardson and V. Robinson (eds) *Introducing Women's Studies*, Basingstoke: Macmillan.

Van Every, Jo (1995) *Heterosexual Women Changing the Family: Refusing to be a 'Wife'*, London:

Taylor and Francis.

Walby, Sylvia (1986) *Patriarchy at Work*, Oxford: Polity.

Walby, Sylvia (1990) *Theorizing Patriarchy*, Oxford: Blackwell.

Walby, Sylvia (1992) 'Post-post-modernism? Theorizing social complexity', in M. Barrett and A. Phillips (eds) *Destabilizing Theory: Contemporary Feminist Debates*, Oxford: Polity.

Walby, Sylvia (1997) *Gender Transformation*, London: Routledge.

Wittig, Monique (1992) *The Straight Mind and Other Essays*, Hemel Hempstead: Harvester Wheatsheaf.

Witz, Anne (1992) *Patriarchy and the Professions*, London: Routledge.

Witz, Anne and Jane Mark-Lawson (1990) 'Familial control or patriarchal domination? The case of the family system of labour in nineteenth century coal mining', in H. Corr and L. Jamieson (eds) *Politics of Everyday Life*, Basingstoke: Macmillan.

Further Reading

Introductions

Jackson, S. et al. (1992) *Women's Studies: A Reader*, Section 1, Hemel Hempstead: Harvester Wheatsheaf.

Stacey, J. (1997) 'Feminist Theory, capital "F" capital "T"', in D. Richardson and V. Robinson *Introducing Women's Studies*, 2nd edition, Basingstoke: Macmillan.

Key texts and collections

Adams, Parveen and Elizabeth Cowie (1990) *The Woman in Question*, London: Verso.

Afshar, Haleh and Mary Maynard (eds) (1994) *The Dynamics of 'Race' and Gender*, London: Taylor & Francis.

Barrett, Michèle [1980] (1990) *Women's Oppression Today*, London: Verso.

Barrett, Michèle and Anne Phillips (1992) *Destabilizing Theory*, Cambridge: Polity.

Bell, Diane and Renate Klein (1996) *Radically Speaking: Feminism Reclaimed*, Melbourne: Spinifex; London: Zed Books.

Collins, Patricia Hill (1990) *Black Feminist Thought*, Boston and London: Unwin Hyman.

Delphy, Christine (1984) *Close to Home*, London: Hutchinson.

Delphy, Christine and Diana Leonard (1992) *Familiar Exploitation*, Cambridge: Polity.

Firestone, Shulamith (1972) *The Dialectic of Sex*, London: Paladin.

Gibson-Graham, J. K. (1996) *The End of Capitalism (as we knew it): A Feminist Critique of Political Economy*, Oxford: Blackwell.

Hennessy, Rosemary (1993) *Materialist Feminism and the Politics of Discourse*, New York and London: Routledge.

hooks, bell (1982) *Ain't I a Woman? Black Women and Feminism*, Boston: South End Press; London: Pluto Press.

Jeffreys, Sheila (1990) *Anticlimax: A Feminist Critique of the Sexual Revolution*, London: The Women's Press.

Kuhn, Annette and Anne-Marie Wolpe (eds) (1978) *Feminism and Materialism*, London: Routledge & Kegan Paul.

Mirza, Heidi (1997) *Black British Feminism*, London: Routledge.

Mohanty, Chandra, Ann Russo and Lourdes Torres (eds) (1991) *Third World Women and the Politics of Feminism*, Bloomington: Indiana University Press.

Nicholson, Linda J. (ed.) (1990) *Feminism/Postmodernism*, New York: Routledge.

O'Brien, Mary (1981) *The Politics of Reproduction*, London: Routledge & Kegan Paul.

Sargent, Lydia (ed.) (1981) *The Unhappy Marriage of Marxism and Feminism*, London: Pluto Press.

Vogel, Lisa (1995) *Woman Questions: Essays for a Materialist Feminism*, London: Pluto Press.

Walby, Sylvia (1986) *Patriarchy at Work*, Cambridge: Polity.

Walby, Sylvia (1990) *Theorizing Patriarchy*, Oxford: Blackwell.

Weedon, Chris (1987) *Feminist Practice and Poststructuralist Theory*, Oxford: Blackwell.

Chapter 3

Feminist Theory and Economic Change

Lisa Adkins

Introduction

The focus on economic life in this chapter may appear somewhat out of place in a book concerned with current feminist theory since an interest in economic relations has long lost its centrality in feminist inquiry. This is linked to the broad shift in the disciplinary location of feminist thinking from the social sciences to the humanities and the arts: a movement which has been characterised as involving a shift in focus from things to words (Barrett 1990), from the social to the cultural (Adkins and Lury 1996) and as a turn to culture (Barrett 1992). This connects to a much broader shift within contemporary social thought in which the social sciences have been found wanting by a range of writers on a number of levels. Thus Michèle Barrett discusses the influence of poststructuralism in terms of this movement, and especially its devastating critiques of many of the key assumptions of the social sciences: 'In social science generally, such unexceptional concepts as "social structure", "role", "individual" or "labour market" have become contentious in terms of what they assume about a social totality or infrastructure, or the presumed characteristics of social actors' (Barrett 1992: 202).

Within feminist theorising this critique has meant, for example, that sociostructural analyses of gender – concerning, for instance, the organisation of economic relations or state relations – have generally lost their purchase and in some quarters their legitimacy. This shift also means that there is now relatively little feminist engagement with analyses emanating from the social sciences (see Chapter 2). At one time a substantial part of the feminist project appeared to centre around the excavation of key analyses at the heart of the social science disciplines, especially on analyses concerned with the nature of 'modern' societies (or with modernity as it is often termed). Feminist attention was directed both towards classic analyses of modern societies, for instance those by Karl Marx and Max Weber and to more contemporary understandings, for example the work of Jürgen Habermas. (See Sydie 1987 and Marshall 1994 for two excellent examples of this feminist tradition.) While this work was critical of these analyses (especially regarding the general absence of attention to gender) nevertheless, many feminists sought to develop these ideas to include a consideration of gender, especially to develop explanations of the specificity of gender relations within modernity and to consider the centrality of gender to modernity itself. However, recent critiques of enlightenment thinking[1] – on which analyses of modernity and the social sciences are seen to rest – especially critiques of rationality, universalism, and materialism appear almost to have lead to a wholesale rejection by feminist theorists of the disciplines associated with the social sciences. But a number of authors are now questioning this apparent rejection. For example, while Barrett (1992) notes the shift from things to words she also argues that moving in one direction or another is not adequate. Indeed she suggests the whole question of what value to give to the various subject matters will eventually have to be re-thought.

It is not my intention in this chapter to attempt to evaluate the relative merits of analyses of words or things, the social or the cultural, nor does it represent an attempt to simply re-state the significance of the social sciences in relation to feminism. Rather I take as my point of departure Barrett's observation that there 'are losses attached to a wholesale abandonment of the areas of study traditionally denoted by the academic disciplines of sociology, political economy, economics and politics' (Barrett 1992: 216).

In particular I aim to consider such potential losses in relation to recent sociological analyses which stress the ways in which there has been a shift in the production of the social, from one of social structures – be that of nation-state, the labour market, or the family – to the individual. In such analyses the social appears to be far more 'agentic' (where weight is given to the significance of agents and agency for the construction and organisation of the social) than has traditionally been the case with many sociological analyses. The latter are often critiqued for the over-emphasising the significance of 'external' structures, and therefore for negating the importance of agency in explanations of the production and organisation of the social. In stressing the passing away of the significance of the sociostructural and foregrounding the significance of agency these new analyses therefore seem quite far removed from those associated with the late 1970s and 1980s which a range of critics found wanting and which prompted the general move away from the social sciences. Moreover, they have been located as marking a turning point in sociological analyses and as reinvigorating the discipline. Key writers in this field include Ulrich Beck, Elisabeth Beck-Gersheim and Anthony Giddens (see Beck 1992; Beck and Beck-Gersheim 1995; and Giddens 1991, 1992). Discussing the impact of the recent writings of Giddens and Beck, Scott Lash (1994) argues that these analyses not only have immediate analytic and empirical purchase, but have had, and are continuing to have, a wide ranging impact. Thus he notes that Beck's *Risk Society* (1992) and Beck and Beck-Gersheim's *The Normal Chaos of Love* (1995) are bestsellers, read not simply by academics but by educated lay people. Similarly, Lash argues that Giddens's *Modernity and Self-Identity* (1991) and *The Transformation of Intimacy* (1992) have introduced a whole new audience to his work, including the British Labour Party and the wider left. On such developments Lash comments:

> After more than a decade in which literary critics, art and architecture and philosophers have dominated the 'theory scene' … it is gratifying that sociology can address the same major problems of the contemporary era with such political purchase and analytic power.
>
> (Lash 1994: 118)

But how much analytic and empirical purchase do these new analyses have in relation to gender? Can feminism too find a new political purchase through these analyses? What is this new sociology offering? Does it offer new ways of understanding gender which are more appropriate to the world than the old? Does it, for example, open up new ways of understanding gender which break free of the old problems associated with socio-structural analyses? If feminists do not engage with this new sociology what (following Barrett) is being lost? A revitalised empirical purchase? A new political salience?

Individualisation, Traditionalisation and the Economy

To address these issues this chapter concentrates on the economic sphere. This focus stems from a recognition that it is here that many of the changes associated with the freeing of agency from structure are often thought to be most marked. Lash (1994), for example, suggests this process 'is perhaps most powerfully instantiated in economic life' (Lash: 119). The idea of the progressive freeing of agency from structure – or what is often referred to as individualisation – has central place in the work of Beck and Beck-Gersheim. For Beck (1994) individualisation means 'the disintegration of the certainties of industrial society as well as the compulsion to find and invent new certainties for oneself and others without them' (Beck: 14). Individualisation therefore represents the idea that we are now constantly called upon to 'constitute ourselves as individuals: as individualised individuals' (Beck: 16). But, as Beck stresses, this does not represent simple freedom. On the contrary, he views individualisation as a compulsion: 'People are condemned to individualization. Individualization is a compulsion, but a compulsion for the manufacture, self-design and self-staging of not just one's own biography but also its commitments and networks as preferences' (Beck: 14).

All of this means that for Beck the cutting edge of social change is the process of individualisation, which he sees as dissolving traditional ways of life and modes of interaction.

This idea that individualisation is undoing previous forms of organisation may be paralleled by the more general – and classical – view that the onward march of modernity is destructive or incites the collapse of tradition: 'the capitalistic market, with its "imperatives" of continuous expansion destroys tradition' (Giddens 1992: 197). This notion – that the social is progressively de-tradition-alising – has recently revived itself in contemporary social and cultural theory (see, e.g., some of the opening chapters in Heelas, Lash and Morris 1996). But it is the process of individualisation which is being accorded central place in the current round of this process: 'individual subjects are themselves called upon to exercise authority in the face of ... disorder and contingency' (Heelas 1996: 2). In a range of current social theory individualisation and de-traditionalisation are therefore seen as going hand in hand.

De-traditionalisation is also, of course, a classical theme of feminist analyses. Put perhaps rather too simply many feminists have often seen an escape from tradition in relation to the gender order as key to any feminist project. In short there has been an emphasis in much feminist writing on the de-traditionalisation of gender. Many of the feminist critiques of analyses of modernity mentioned above, for example, focus on the ways in which men are often represented as modern, rational, cultured subjects within the context of modernity and women as traditional, irrational, 'natural' objects. As a counter to such views feminist critics have pointed to the patriarchal nature of such thinking and have em-phasised the modern rather than traditional experiences of women (for instance of alienation or anomie), and some have argued that the modern itself (for example becoming a wage-labourer) promises women emancipation. Such feminist critics have, in other words, taken issue with a representation of women which is closely tied to the tradition in relation to modernity and have sought to modernise women through the production of new discourses regarding women's relationship to modernity.

These themes also find expression in feminist writings on the economy. In her analysis of gender and the Japanese workplace Mary Saso (1990), for example, takes immense offence at the Japanese Ministry of Education's statement that 'If women are to continue to work on equal terms with men, women's self awakening is required in such fields as work morale and ethics'. She describes this statement as a loaded piece of prose 'in which it is presumed that a woman already ... work[s] on equal terms with a man and that, if she does not, the failure is due to her own lack of work consciousness'. (Saso 1990: xviii). But more than this she describes it as a 'quaint view' of working women. Indeed, throughout her text *Women in the Japanese Workplace* Saso attempts to undo what she sees as 'traditional' views of Japanese working women (or the 'quaintness trap' as she terms it) such as, 'the long apprenticeship of geisha and ... tea-pouring careers of "office ladies"' (Saso: xv). Thus, throughout, she emphasises the resist-ances, struggles and (what she sees as) the 'non-traditional' work (for example, manufacturing and entrepreneurial work) of Japanese working women. In short Saso's complaint regarding the Japanese Ministry of Education's statement is precisely about protesting against a 'non-modern' view of women – that women have not developed an adequate orientation to the modern world – that they are too traditional. Saso's agenda is therefore to demonstrate that Japanese women are decisively modern in terms of the economic sphere. For her the problem of gender in terms of the economy will therefore be solved by processes of de-traditionalisation. If, as Beck and others suggest, such processes currently go hand-in-hand with individualisation, then presumably the latter will be welcomed by Saso in that it may transform the gendered structuring of the economic.

But is there something else going on here? Is it enough just to say that the Japanese Ministry of Education statement simply constitutes an out-moded, 'non-modern' view of working women? Or that it is sufficient to assert and/or demonstrate that women are not traditional as a foil to such views? One of the central themes of this chapter is not that the Japanese Ministry of Education has an 'old-fashioned' view of women but rather that their statement is indicative of some broad shifts in the organisation of the economic sphere. Such shifts require precisely an interrogation of tradition if we are to understand recent developments in the gendering of the economic and of the current constitution of gender. In short this chapter points to the significance of a re-ordering of aspects of the economic sphere in which 'non-market' 'traditional' forms of organisation – such as workplace communities – are taking on increasing significance, and which may be constitutive of new forms of gendered hierarchies and new kinds of gendered workers. I suggest that, rather than a static hang-over of the past which must be or is being destroyed, tradition must be understood in terms of a process – traditionalisation – which is currently ongoing and, moreover, is a process which is highly significant for understanding some current shifts in the gendering of the economic sphere.

The Traditionalisation of the Economic?

I take the view that the traditional is not simply antithetical to the modern, but rather is simultaneously produced or co-constructed with the modern.[2] In his analysis of the restructuring of the economic sphere Lash (1994) gives us an example of this view (and in so doing he therefore questions the radical individualisation thesis as proposed by Beck and Giddens). In this analysis of the emergence and increasing significance of knowledge-intensive production – what Lash terms reflexive accumulation (see also Lash and Urry 1994) – he points to the formation and significance of non-market, or what at times he terms pre-modern relations: 'pre-modern and communal-traditional forms … can be conducive to information flow and acquisition which are the structural conditions of reflexive production ... communal regulation is optimal for the scope and power of information and communication structures' (Lash 1994: 127).

Here, then, 'tradition' is seen not as outmoded for workers or for economies, or as being destroyed by the processes of late modernity but rather as conducive to and incited by new forms of production. Moreover, Lash suggests these new 'pre-modern' forms are being constituted as agency is freed from structure. Indeed, for Lash, reflexive economies are characterised by structure forcing agency to be free because accumulation in such economies can only take place on the condition that agency can free itself from rule-bound 'Fordist' structures (the structures embodying the techniques and social relations of mass production and mass consumption). He points to the significance of fast innovation in this process, and that such innovation entails a lot more work going into the design of products. Production processes therefore increasingly involve knowledge-intensive design processes with the consequence that the material labour process is de-centred and succeeded by a de-materialised labour process (Lash and Urry 1994: 160). But knowledge intensity necessarily involves reflexivity:

> It entails self-reflexivity in that heteronomous monitoring of workers by rules is deplaced by self-monitoring. It involves ... structural reflexivity in that the rules and resources ... become the object of reflection for agency. That is, agents can reformulate and use such rules and resources in a variety of combinations in order chronically to innovate.
>
> (Lash 1994: 119)

In short, Lash is pointing to a major re-ordering of the labour market – in terms of the constitution of rules, resources, hierarchies and the nature of work and workers – invoked by the new structural conditions of accumulation: the liberation of agency from structure.

Lash looks to Germany and Japan for examples of reflexive production and in particular to demonstrate the significance of 'pre-modern', traditional forms in these regimes. He shows that promotion incentives in large firms in Japan are often tightly linked to the acquisition of knowledge or information, and that flows of information are optimised through personalised trust relations. Employment contracting is therefore often 'relational' where exchange relationships involve not only straightforwardly cash-nexus exchanges (where employers and employees are bound together only by the payment of wages for work done) but also symbolic exchanges of, for example, shared identities. All such forms are key to reflexive accumulation in that they optimise information flow. This emphasis on the significance of non-market exchanges for reflexive production is also stressed in relation to the German case. Here, inclusive information structures and highly reflexive production are achieved through the corporate governance of production systems, for instance through the technical college and apprenticeship systems. In both cases Lash stresses that what is at issue is an ethics of commitment and obligation not to the self but to a community, 'this community being the firm in the Japanese case and the Beruf [occupation] in the German case' (Lash 1994: 126). Practices in such communities are not simply a matter of the acquisition of money, power or status but are motivated towards 'workmanship (sic) or the good of the firm' (Lash 1994: 126). The freeing of agency from structure for Lash is therefore not a simple matter of the destruction of tradition but rather is constitutive of new traditional forms, and he terms this process reflexive traditionalisation. It is in the largest and most modern firms in Germany and Japan where it is suggested that such non-market, traditional structures are to be found, structures which many Anglo-Saxon firms are now attempting to develop.

Lash is also interested in what he terms the structural conditions of reflexivity, especially reflexivity winners and reflexivity losers. Amongst the latter he places women because of their exclusion from the new labour market spaces in reflexive economies:

> In countries like Germany this exclusion of women (and minorities) is exacerbated by the corporatist institutions of the apprenticeship, the welfare state and the education system, in which women perform welfare services, not in firms operating through the market, not by working in jobs in the welfare state, but (as excluded from labour markets) in the home. Hence the very low labour-force participation rate of women in Germany.
>
> (Lash 1994: 133)

In the Japanese case such exclusion takes on a different character. Saso's study shows, for example, that although women's employment rates in Japan are relatively high, 'a substantial portion of women's economic activity has been outside the large companies – especially in small companies or in family enterprises including farms' (Saso 1990: 7). In addition she shows that a high proportion of women work in manufacturing as production workers and that 'long serving women are usually found in small companies where wages are considerably lower than in larger companies' (Saso 1990: 69). That is to say, Saso's evidence suggests that women are excluded from precisely those spaces which Lash argues are those of reflexive production: large companies with emphases on information and knowledge where work is de-materialised.

The Gendering of Reflexive Production

This tendency towards the exclusion of women from reflexive production and therefore from the new traditional modes of economic organisation is striking on at least two counts. First, it seems more than a little ironic that women are apparently being excluded from such traditional forms and that such forms are viewed as innovative given that women's economic activity has often been found to be both non-cash nexus and/or non-market (in terms of employment and beyond). Such forms of labour have constituted a major focus of feminist inquiry especially since they have often been seen to be centrally linked to women's oppression and exploitation. Accounts abound of such work, including house-work, unpaid occupational work, emotional work and childcare (see e.g. Game and Pringle 1984; Delphy and Leonard 1992; Finch 1983; Hochschild 1983; Adkins 1995; Adkins and Lury 1996). Second, this exclusion is striking in that in Fordist and other 'non-reflexive' modes of accumulation it is the segregation of women within rather than their exclusion from employment which is widely viewed as constitutive of gender in terms of the labour market. Indeed there is extensive documentation of a historical shift from exclusion to segregation. Sylvia Walby, for example, has documented this change for patterns of women's employment in Britain from 1800–1945 (Walby 1986). And it is still women's segregation within particular occupations and at particular grades, rather than their exclusion from employment, which is generally seen to typify women's labour market situation and be the biggest problem for women in western labour markets today (see e.g. Walby 1990; Crompton and Sanderson 1990).

On this exclusion from the new reflexive classes Lash suggests that women may be part of a new lower class or underclass. But although this is for Lash a new class category, he suggests: 'the personnel filling these class positions are typically determined by more particularistic, "ascribed" characteristics – by race, country of origin and gender' (Lash 1994: 134). However, Lash does not attend to the processes of ascription – he simply assumes that in terms of reflexive economies these characteristics are already formed. Therefore he does not consider if there is a relationship between the new economies themselves and the construction of gender, nor does he interrogate the nature of women's exclusion from reflexive economies. He does go on to suggest, however, that 'civil society could be said to be built on the back of the labour of the new lower class today' (Lash 1994: 134). This idea – the formation of civil society (the sphere 'outside of' the economy and the state)[3] through the appropriation of the labour of others – is of course a familiar one in feminist analyses (see e.g. Pateman 1988 on the significance of the gender division of labour for the emergence of the civil sphere). Civil society is usually understood to represent a distinct sphere from the economy. But could Lash's suggestion – that civil society is constituted on the back of the new lower classes – be extended to include not just civil society but also the economy? Does this suggestion give us a way in to understanding the gendering of this new economic space?

Gendered Traditionalisation?

Let us take the case of the formation of workplace communities to think this issue through. Clearly for Lash the preconditions for the formation of new traditional, non market, work-place communities is the freeing of agency from structure –

the individualisation of workers. It is this individualisation and the associated agentic abilities to create new forms of occupational knowledges and resources, to become self-regulating workers, to perform relational non cash-nexus exchanges and to develop a sense of a shared workplace identity which, for Lash, marks reflexive economies off from Fordist regimes. In short it is individualisation which allows for the formation of traditional communities. Indeed, as many authors currently recognise, communities are becoming key across a range of domains in terms of the construction of a sense of identity and belonging in the context of the breakdown of social structures (see e.g. Bauman 1992; Weeks 1995). But a dimension which is often missing from these debates regarding the new significance of community is the earlier observation – from, for instance, critiques of the British community studies – that the formation of communities of interest often rests on a hidden gendered division of labour (see e.g. Davidoff 1976; Frankenberg 1976).

In her study of kin and quasi-kin relations of American-Italians in California, Michaela di Leonardo (1987), for example, describes the ways in which the very existence of a sense of community, identity and belonging depends on the work of women. She uncovers the ways in which the organisation of ritual celebrations and the continuous construction and maintenance of social networks are both dependent on the work of women and simultaneously create resources through which a sense of belonging and identity may be constructed. But more than this (and drawing on materialist feminist analyses) she shows how this work is performed in family relations of appropriation – how although women perform this labour they do not own it, and how men and children both benefit from and may mobilise the sense of community, belonging and identity constructed through this work as resources for exchange. Leonardo's work therefore reveals that whilst women may be key in the construction of community, the products of this work – a sense of identity and belonging – may not be accessible to women because this work is performed in relations of appropriation. Put another way, women cannot claim ownership and mobilise the products of their work as resources because they themselves do not own their labour through which it is constituted in the first instance. (See Chapter 2 for a full explication of the materialist feminist tradition.)

Leonardo's work clearly has important implications regarding current debates on traditionalisation. Most significantly it suggests that the process of traditionalisation, including the formation of communities, may itself rest on a hidden gendered productivity – a productivity which means that, while women are key in the construction of community (for instance, the resources to construct shared identities) they may not be able to claim membership or belonging in terms of that community in the same ways as men. Moreover, it also has important implications regarding understandings of the process of individualisation, upon which current traditionalisation (according to Lash's analysis) is seen to rest.

Specifically, in revealing the ways in which women's work releases resources which men may mobilise, Leonardo's research suggests that the appropriation of family labour may be key in the freeing of agency from structure.

Leonardo's research, taken together with Lash's observation regarding the exclusion of women from reflexive occupations and the intensity of women's welfare servicing in the family in relation to reflexive economies, therefore has profound implications for the current restructuring of the labour market. Specifically it suggests not only that processes of individualisation in the labour market may rest on market-place economic structures forcing agency to be free, but that individualisation, and the consequent agentic abilities of workers to build traditional economic forms in the workplace, may also significantly involve the appropriation of women's labour in the family. Individualisation in terms of labour market – becoming an individualised worker – appears therefore to be a gendered process which relies on, or is founded upon, the appropriation of women's labour in the private sphere (see Adkins and Lury 1996). Thus, the process of traditionalisation taking place in new economic spaces may also be said to be significantly dependent on the work of women. Indeed, many studies of small businesses have shown a similar process at work, namely that business networks and communities are often formed through the mobilisation of re-sources for exchange which may be non-market and non-cash nexus – for example, business honour, trust and respect – constituted through family relations of appropriation (see e.g. chapters in Westwood and Bhachu 1988 and Phizacklea and Ram 1996). In this sense one cannot help but wonder if the processes Lash describes in terms of reflexive economies represent a thoroughgoing institution-alisation of individualisation which is dependent on a traditional family division of labour.

Carol Pateman (1988) and Joan Acker (1990) have previously argued that a worker can only exist in the context of the gender division of labour, that a worker presupposes that he is a man who has a woman (a housewife) to take care of his daily needs. In this sense both Acker and Pateman (along with other feminists concerned with the specificity of women's labour, see e.g. Cockburn 1991; Delphy and Leonard 1992 and Mies 1986) suggest that women can never be workers in the same way as men because they are not free to exchange their labour on the same terms as men. For Pateman this explains why 'most women can find paid employment only in a narrow range of low-status low-paid occupations, where they work alongside other women and are managed by men' (Pateman 1988: 132). But in the context of reflexive economies, as mentioned above, it appears that women do not even have the opportunity to be labour market 'workers' at all. As Lash and Saso's evidence reveals, it is men rather than women who are achieving individualised worker status and are able to create new labour market resources as a consequence of this process. In terms of gender, individualisation and the attendant processes of traditionalisation in the labour market could, therefore, be said to represent a process of _re-traditionalisation_ both in terms of the labour market and the family: the exclusion of women from reflexive occupations and an intensification of the appropriation of family labour. Such a re-traditionalisation of gender suggests that, rather than individualisation acting upon already ascribed gender (as Lash suggests), gender may (in part) be being re-constituted or re-ordered by this new economic organisation. Put another way, men and women and the relations between them are being re-constituted through this process.

Social Women, Non-Social Men?

But if the freeing of agency from structure is (in part) dependent upon the appropriation of women's labour, how are we to understand the current organisation of the social? Can it be maintained that the 'social' is retreating (with agency being set free from social structure) when individualisation may depend on an ongoing – and perhaps intensifying – social organisation of gender? Clearly the analysis of traditionalisation suggested here – as dependent on a re-traditionalisation of gender – questions this assumption. But it also suggests that a new gendered bifurcation of the social may be emerging: namely, while the social may continue to be key in terms of the constitution of women, for men, although they may depend on the social, their definition as men is not limited to this. For example, they may act as individualised workers creating new resources and knowledges in the labour market which in turn is constitutive of the transformation of the workplace itself. In other words the social for men does not determine them but rather may afford them creative possibilities, not least the ability to be set free of social structures and act as self-regulating labour market agents rather than members of the social group 'men'.

Let us pursue this issue a little further. I mentioned above that it is more than a little ironic that 'traditional' forms of economic organisation are now viewed as innovative given women's relationship to non-market and non-cash nexus forms of labour. Research on these forms of labour have stressed the ways in which it is typically performed in relations of production in which it is difficult for women to exchange this labour in return for anything else, and that anything given in return is more gift-like than constituting the reciprocity of an exchange relationship. Indeed this research has typically stressed that these are appropriated forms of work. One example of what might be regarded as women's non-market and non-cash nexus labour market work is the sexual labour that many women tourist workers are required to perform (that is work which involves a sexual element, for example wearing 'sexy' uniforms or responding to and dealing with sexual innuendoes, which is performed as 'part of the job' alongside more 'regular' elements of jobs, such as serving customers; see Adkins 1995). In such cases sexual labour is not formally incorporated into an exchange relationship, nor is it cash nexus or simply market-orientated. But while this work may be regarded as 'traditional' (in that it does not bring with it monetary reward, power or status) it also does not bring with it the potential for labour market creativity, for instance, the ability to create labour market resources, but rather leads to specific forms of appropriation – in this instance the appropriation of sexuality. More than this in cases where sexual labour is required as 'part of the job' such forms of work often define a group of workers 'women'. In contrast, men tourist workers are not required to perform such sexual labour and are often afforded creative labour market possibilities, for instance, the opportunity to define themselves as possessing particular occupational competencies and knowledges in a way which women can not (because they can not escape a definition of themselves as a group of workers – women – who perform sexual labour). Here again individualisation and the social appear as gendered. Individualisation requires the social, but in this local context the social defines 'women' and yet at the same time affords men resources to be individualised – 'non-social' – workers. Men workers are therefore not defined as a group of workers 'men' but rather as individuals with abilities to claim specific capabilities and competencies.

The De-materialisation of Labour and New Productivities

In accounts of women's non-market, non-cash nexus work it is also typically stressed that such work is material in content. But more than this it is often stressed that the 'non-material' (e.g. the aesthetic, the symbolic) and the 'material' (e.g. tangibly productive labour) cannot be separated out. For example, Game and Pringle (1984) discuss the aesthetics of housework, Acker (1990) the embodied nature of women's labour market work, and in my own work I have stressed the sexualisation of labour. Thus, as I remarked earlier, some have argued that to fully understand the structuring of gender the distinction between the material and the non-material must be dissolved (see e.g. Barrett 1992; Adkins and Lury 1996). This last point is of some significance for current debates regarding the restructuring of the labour market. As we have seen in accounts of the emergent economies it is precisely the emptying out of labour in terms of material content (or its de-materialisation) which is seen to characterise reflexive production as opposed to non-reflexive production. But if women cannot escape the ongoing material construction of their labour even when this work may be formally 'non-material', through, for example, the embodied nature of their work (see e.g. Guillaumin 1981, 1995; Witz, Halford and Savage 1996) can they achieve a de-materialised worker status or become fully de-materialised workers? In the context of a mode of accumulation which is centred on information and knowledge – reflexive accumulation – one has to ask if de-materialised knowledge and information work is difficult for women to achieve because of their ongoing construction as embodied and material workers. In fact one has to ask if the very criteria of non-material knowledge and information for workers exclude women, that is, that these are gendered criteria. The de-materialisation of work and of workers may, in other words, be an important but neglected dimension of the gendered nature of both individualisation and the current round of traditionalisation.

In all this what is perhaps most striking is that 'non-market', 'non-cash-nexus' forms of work, which women have a long history of performing but which has not been remunerated, are now emerging as occupational resources for men workers which may be exchanged in reflexive economies. Moreover, the ability to exchange these forms of work are constitutive of new forms of workers and new workplace hierarchies. Put another way, it appears that a range of productivities have become exchangeable and are being mobilised in terms of the labour market But these are clearly gendered productivities in terms of exchange in that first, women are excluded from the new reflexive occupations in which such exchanges take place, and second, as existing research demonstrates, even when women perform such forms of production they are not exchangeable. It seems, therefore, that if feminists are to address the ways in which the labour market is currently being restructured, the issue of how and in what ways the exchange of such gendered productivities has been achieved must be tackled. In this chapter I have indicated that a number of processes may be key in this restructuring. These include the de-materialisation of labour (and especially criteria of work involving knowledge and information), individualisation, tra-ditionalisation and de-traditionalisation. But I have also stressed that what appears to be at issue in terms of these processes is a new bifurcation of the social in terms of gender. This bifurcation takes expression in, for example, the apparent intensification of women's servicing in the domestic sphere in relation to reflexive economies, the continued construction of women in the labour market as a group of workers, 'women', and men's ability to be self-regulating agents, capable of exchanging non-market, non-cash-nexus goods and participating in workplace communities.

Conclusions

One of the main arguments of this chapter has been that the current round of traditionalisation in terms of the labour market may be dependent on a re-traditionalisation or an intensification of tradition in relation to gender. It was suggested at the start that one of the themes of feminist analyses of the economy has been one of de-traditionalisation, and in particular that processes of de-traditionalisation are often held to be key to undoing the gendering of the labour market. The analysis of this chapter, however, suggests that, in terms of gender, rather than tradition standing in opposition to the modern, tradition may be co-constructed or created with the modern. As we have seen in the apparently most modern and innovative economies, those regarded as key to economic growth –

reflexive economies – accumulation may depend on a traditionalisation of gender, and in particular an intensified traditional gender division of labour.

It was also suggested earlier that some current analyses imply that individualisation may be transformative of the gendered structuring of the labour market. Indeed it was shown that in much current social and cultural theory individualisation and de-traditionalisation are viewed as going hand in hand. However, the analysis of individualisation offered here questions this assumption. In particular, individualisation may not de-stabilise the gendered structuring of the economic (as for example inferred by Saso's analysis), nor may individualisation go hand in hand with de-traditionalisation as implied more generally in recent social theory. Rather than being transformative of gender the organisation of individualisation may be central to the current organisation of gender oppression.

I want to end this discussion by returning to the issues raised at the start regarding the renaissance of sociology via analyses of the freeing of agency from structure and the empirical and analytical purchase such analyses may have for feminism. This chapter certainly supports the view that processes currently associated with individualisation may be key to the current organisation of gender, and in this sense supports Beck's (1994) view that many sociological categories (especially those associated with industrial society) are now inadequate. However, it also suggests that individualisation itself has a gendered productivity – that far from being transgressive of the social categories of gender, individualisation may re-embed 'women' in the social. Individualisation is therefore not emptying out gender but may be creating new lines of social domination, for instance, those of community, of networks and of new knowledges and forms of communication. In this sense these new sociological analyses may indeed have some important purchase for feminism, but only if the gendering of the new social/non-social and the relationship between them is made explicit. In this sense the argument of this chapter is clearly supportive of Barrett's suggestion that simply shifting either to things or words is inadequate, rather it appears that the things/words dichotomy may currently be key in terms of the organisation of gender. If feminism is to gain a new empirical, analytical and political purchase as currently being enjoyed by sociology, then perhaps critical attention should be directed at the emerging gendered social/non-social nexus.

Notes

1. That is, the European tradition of thought characteristic from the late eighteenth century onwards which broke from a religious worldview to one based on human reason, rationality and a belief in human progress. See also Chapter 13.
2. See also the contributions to Part II of Heelas, Lash and Morris 1996 for further examples of this view.
3. See Marshall (1994) for a very clear account of the development of (and disagreements over) the concept of civil society in social theory.

References

Acker, J. (1960) 'Hierarchies, Jobs and Bodies: A Theory of Gendered Organizations', in *Gender and Society*, vol. 4, no. 2, pp. 39–58.

Adkins, L. (1955) *Gendered Work: Sexuality, Family and the Labour Market*, Buckingham: Open University Press.

Adkins, L. and C. Lury (1996) 'The Cultural, the Sexual, and the Gendering of the Labour Market', in L. Adkins and V. Merchant (eds) *Sexualizing the Social: Power and the Organization of Sexuality*, Basingstoke: Macmillan.

Barrett, M. (1960) 'Feminism's "Turn to Culture"', in *Women: A Cultural Review*, vol. 1, no. 1, pp. 22–4.

Barrett, M. (1992) 'Words and Things: Materialism and Method in Contemporary Feminist Analysis', in M. Barrett and A. Phillips (eds) *Destabilizing Theory: Contemporary Feminist Debates*, Cambridge: Polity.

Bauman, Z. (1992) *Intimations of Postmodernity*, London: Routledge.

Beck, U. (1992) *Risk Society: Towards a New Modernity*, London: Sage.

Beck, U. (1994) 'The Reinvention of Politics: Towards a Theory of Reflexive Modernization', in U. Beck, A. Giddens and S. Lash (eds) *Reflexive Modernization: Politics, Tradition and Aesthetics in the Modern Social Order*, Cambridge: Polity.

Beck, U. and E. Beck-Gersheim (1995) *The Normal Chaos of Love*, Cambridge: Polity.

Beck, U. and E. Beck-Gersheim (1995) 'Individualization and "Precarious Freedoms": Perspectives and Controversies of a Subject-orientated Sociology', in P. Heelas, S. Lash and P. Morris (eds) *Detraditionalization: Critical Reflections on Authority and Identity*, Oxford: Blackwell.

Cockburn, C. (1991) *In the Way of Women: Men's Resistance to Sex Equality in Organizations*, Basingstoke: Macmillan.

Crompton, R. and K. Sanderson (1990) *Gendered Jobs and Social Change*, London: Unwin Hyman.

Davidoff, L. (1976) 'The Rationalization of Housework', in D. Leonard Barker and S. Allen (eds) *Dependence and Exploitation in Work and Marriage*, London: Longmans.

Delphy, C. and D. Leonard (1992) *Familiar Exploitation: A New Analysis of Marriage in Contemporary Western Societies*, Cambridge: Polity.

Finch, J. (1983) *Married to the Job: Wives' Incorporation in Men's Work*, London: George Allen and Unwin.

Frankenberg, R. (1976) '"In the Production of Their Lives, Men (?) ..."': Sex and Gender in British Community Studies', in D. Leonard Barker and S. Allen (eds) *Sexual Divisions and Society: Process and Change*, London: Tavistock.

Game, A. and R. Pringle (1984) *Gender at Work*, London: Pluto.

Giddens, A. (1991) *Modernity and Self-Identity: Self and Society in the Late Modern Age*, Cambridge: Polity.

Giddens, A. (1992) *The Transformation of Intimacy: Sexuality, Love and Eroticism in Modern Societies*, Cambridge: Polity.

Guillaumin, C. (1981) 'The Practice of Power and Belief in Nature, Part I: the Appropriation of Women', in *Feminist Issues*, vol. 1, no. 2, pp. 3–28.

Guillaumin, C. (1995) *Racism, Sexism, Power and Ideology*, London: Routledge.

Heelas, P. (1996) 'Detraditionalization and its Rivals', in P. Heelas, S. Lash and P. Morris (eds) *Detraditionalization: Critical Reflections on Authority and Identity*, Oxford: Blackwells.

Heelas, P., S. Lash and P. Morris (eds) (1996) *Detraditionalization: Critical Reflections on Authority and Identity*, Oxford: Blackwell.

Hochschild, A. (1983) *The Managed Heart: The Commercialization of Human Feeling*, Berkeley, University of California Press.

Lash, S. (1994) 'Reflexivity and its Doubles: Structure, Aesthetics, Community', in U. Beck, A. Giddens and S. Lash (eds) *Reflexive Modernization: Politics, Tradition and Aesthetics in the Modern Social Order*, Cambridge: Polity.

Lash, S. and J. Urry (1994) *Economies of Signs and Space*, London: Sage.

Leonardo, M. di (1987) 'The Female World of Cards and Holidays: Women, Families and the World of Kinship', in *Signs*, vol. 12, no. 3, pp. 440–53.

Marshall, B. (1994) *Engendering Modernity: Feminism, Social Theory and Social Change*, Cambridge: Polity.

Mies, M. (1986) *Patriarchy and Accumulation on a World Scale*, London: Zed.

Pateman, C. (1988) *The Sexual Contract*, Cambridge: Polity.

Phizacklea A. and M. Ram (1996) 'Being Your Own Boss: Ethnic Minority Entrepreneurs in Comparative Perspective', in *Work, Employment and Society*, vol. 10, no. 2, pp. 319–39.

Saso, M. (1990) *Women in the Japanese Workplace*, London: Shipman.

Sydie, R. A. (1987) *Natural Women, Cultured Men: A Feminist Perspective on Sociological Theory*, Milton Keynes: Open University Press.

Walby, S. (1986) *Patriarchy at Work: Patriarchal and Capitalist Relations in Employment*, Cambridge: Polity.

Walby, S. (1990) *Theorizing Patriarchy*, Oxford: Blackwell.

Weeks, J. (1995) *Invented Moralities: Sexual Values in An Age of Uncertainty*, Cambridge: Polity.

Westwood, S. and P. Bhachu (eds) (1988) *Enterprising Women*, London: Routledge.

Witz, A., S. Halford and M. Savage (1996) 'Organized Bodies: Gender, Sexuality and Embodiment in Contemporary Organizations', in L. Adkins and V. Merchant (eds) *Sexualizing the Social: Power and the Organization of Sexuality*, Basingstoke: Macmillan.

Further Reading

Due to the processes outlined in this chapter there are relatively few explicitly feminist engagements with recent shifts in the gendered constitution of the economic. But some important recent works include:

Cockburn, C. (1991) [see References].

Halford, S., M. Savage and A. Witz (1997) *Gender, Careers and Organisations*, Basingstoke: Macmillan.

Massey, D. (1994) *Space, Place and Gender*, Cambridge: Polity (see especially her chapter on 'Flexible Sexism').

McDowell, L. (1995) 'Body Work: Heterosexual Gender Performances in City Workplaces', in D. Bell and G. Valentine (eds) *Mapping Desire: Geographies of Sexualities*, London: Routledge.

Pringle, R. (1988) *Secretaries Talk: Sexuality, Power and Work*, London: Verso.

Witz, Halford and Savage (1996) [see References].

Chapter 4

Feminist Political Theory

Elizabeth Frazer

Politics and Gender

'Politics' is the practice of, and the study of, the power to govern. 'Practice of' should be taken to include: exercise of, organisation of, the influence of or pressure on government, and, of course, the resistance to governance and governmental power. This formulation differs in significant respects from other characterisations of 'politics' and 'the political' (e.g. Heller 1991; Crick 1992; Miller 1987). In particular, its *broadness* owes a good deal to feminist thought and activism. It is notable, though, that a perusal of both feminist and orthodox analyses of 'politics' reveals that it is an extraordinarily difficult term to define – although it is used so commonly, it is not easy to say exactly what is meant when an action, or an event, or a relationship is described as political (Heller [1991] discusses a number of different conceptions).

In what follows I describe conventional understandings of politics, and the challenges to these, practical and theoretical, that have been made by feminists. One of the most familiar slogans from western women's movements of the last thirty years has been 'the personal is political'. This slogan has been satisfyingly bewildering to male political theorists, who sneer that it makes no sense, that it lacks consistency, that it has totalitarian implications, and so on. Although their bewilderment should not convince us that there are any flaws at all in the slogan, it is nonetheless worthwhile to analyse precisely its exact meanings and implications.

Before doing this, though, I need to set the scene with a more general discussion of the project and methods of political theory, which will give some insight into debates and disputes within feminism.

According to some theorists the definition of politics I have started with is wrong because, they declare, 'politics' is the *practice of governing in a particular manner* – to govern 'politically' is to govern by mechanisms other than violence, through institutions and arrangements that are public, and by reference to the people who are governed (Crick 1992: 16–33; Philp 1994: 4–8). 'By reference to' does not explicitly entail any particular way of referring. It does not, for instance, entail

50

democracy in any form – political rule could be autocratic or monarchical. But it does mean that rulers engage in the conciliation of the various interests among the ruled. The point is, rulers consider the effect their rule will have, and, of course, consider how to behave so that their rule can continue.

Political theory comes in two, analytically distinct but connected, forms. First there is prescriptive political theory – theory of how governance ought to be done. This theory sets limits to governance, by analysing relevant concepts such as equality, rights, freedom, obligation and justice – ideals that should be realised, or at least must not be undermined, by government, if that government is to be legitimate. Second, descriptive political theory looks at how legitimate government can be done, by way of analysis of concepts and phenomena such as authority, power, law, decision-making, judgement.

The orthodox emphasis on politics as a particular form of governance, conciliatory and carried on through public institutions, has led political theorists and scientists to focus on a particular set of institutions: the state institutions of legislature, executive, judiciary, and their subsidiary agencies such as welfare bureaucracies, police, courts and so on. One absorbing aspect of politics is the competition for the power to govern: so political scientists have looked at parties, factions, interest groups, and such centres of power as are potential bases for claims to the power to govern, or bases for entry into the competition for this power – for instance, economic interests, or the military.

Predictably, the orthodox academic study of politics has tended to be a study of men and masculinity. This is so because classical and modern theorists and commentators have defined politics as a masculine business, and they have done this by reference to a commonsensical and received conception of femininity, elaborated and defined in such a way as to make it clear why feminine creatures, or women, cannot participate in, cannot constitute, politics. Aristotle defined the *polis* as separate from and contrasted with the household. Hegel and Rousseau elaborated whole theories of gender in order to demonstrate the difference between the public political world and the private domestic world. Liberal theorists like Locke and Mill, as individualists were sympathetic to women's rights, but nevertheless by deploying the same domestic versus public, political versus private distinctions managed to take for granted and to reinforce women's exclusion, *qua* women, from politics.

One of the first tasks of recent feminist political theory has been to expose the theories of gender that are for the most part implicit but often quite explicit in the classical and modern political theoretical texts. This project has produced a substantial body of critical literature (including Coole 1993; Elshtain 1981; Kennedy and Mendus 1987; Lloyd 1984; Okin 1979; Shanley and Pateman 1991). It has been conventional that those who teach and write about the history of political thought ignore this aspect of it. It has been presumed or pretended that the theories of gender and ponderings on the relation between the sexes that so often preoccupied the great philosophers was just an idiosyncratic oddity, attributable to the times they lived in. Feminists, in the first place, argue that we are entitled to ask why brilliant minds which did not hesitate to run against the grain of their times in many respects (for instance, in thinking about the sources of political power, or the standing of monarchs) nevertheless remained in thrall to this particular bit of 'common sense'. In the second place, they have revealed the way the very idea of political relations, political institutions and political rule is analysed by reference to a theory of gender and proper relations between the sexes.

Feminism: Political Movement and Political Theory

An important aspect of the contribution of feminism to political theory has been via feminist political practice. Feminism has been a constant feature of modern societies. As a political movement it has engaged with politics in the conventional sense, and has also widened the scope of political action in practically and theoretically significant ways.

First, there are organised campaigns for particular legislative measures – to secure women the vote, or to give them property rights, or to make abortion legal, or for equal opportunities legislation as regards employment or welfare. These campaigns have often been ignored by conventional political scientists and historians. Where they are attended to, they clearly must count as 'political' in the conventional sense – they are public interventions in the competition for the power to govern. Second, there are organised campaigns for other, non-legislative, but important social changes – more women into Parliament and thereby into government, more women into other powerful social positions such as in the professions and education (the campaigns for educational institutions, professions and other occupations to be open to women are relevant here, as are such campaigns as those for equal opportunities codes and the like inside organisations such as firms and clubs, women's sections within political parties, and so on). Again, such campaigns count as 'political' in the orthodox sense.

Third, there are the many organisations, connected to the pressure for formal social change, but mostly focused on informal change – self-help organisations like the telephone help lines and refuges for women sufferers of violence, or networks of women in particular occupations. Fourth, these organisations and campaigns are supplemented by and merge into cultural organisations and sites for women's organisation and action: publishing collectives, film-makers and theatre groups, shops, cafes and bars (see Griffin 1995; Lovenduski and Randall 1993; Kaplan 1992 for coverage of recent feminist political organisation and aims).

In feminism in the last thirty years changes in lifestyle, changes in values, changes in the way we relate to friends, colleagues, intimates, sexual partners, spouses and children have been emphasised as supremely important. (We must, however, remember that their importance did not escape feminists of previous generations [Spender 1983].) Cultural activity, inter-personal discussion and self-help have been identified as more important modes of social transformation than the conventional political strategies of organised, public campaigns, at the level of the national or local state, for administrative and legislative change.

The crucial theoretical point which connects with these forms of feminist activism is that *changes within the conventional political realm* and measures taken from within political institutions – legislation and governmental administration – *will not bring about the kind of social change that really makes a difference to people's lives*. In this, feminism is not so different from a number of other perspectives. Marxists, for instance, have always argued that social change can only be brought about by changes in the economy – changes, furthermore, not at the superficial level of the distribution of goods, but at the deeper, more fundamental and causal level of production. Conservatives have thought that social change can only occur organically, or incrementally, and must be deep-seated in ways of life, traditions, and traditional forms of social relations. But these shared ideas are less important than what distances feminism from these rival social and political theories and traditions. Another body of literature is dedicated to criticism of systems of social and political thought – capitalism, liberalism, socialism, marxism, conservatism etc. (rather than individual authors), and to the construction of a specifically feminist social and political theory (e.g. Bryson 1992; Jaggar 1983; Sargent [ed.] 1981).

Critically, the point feminists make is that the conceptions of gender that are implicit and explicit in these systems are not accidental, but necessary, and they are not insignificant. Given that all such analyses are at least partly *prescriptive* (they set out systematic ideas of how society ought to be organised), and as they have made their way, albeit imperfectly, into constitutions, systems of law, other social and political institutions, and into the popular culture of societies, they are also *constitutive*. Therefore, the ideal of gender incorporated in conservatism or liberalism, is likely to be felt within actually existing societies. If we are to transform gender relations one thing that we must understand is these ideological underpinnings.

In constructing feminist political theory a range of social phenomena beyond the workings of state and conventionally political institutions is taken into account. 'Ways of life' and 'traditions' are very important – because existing ones are frequently detrimental to women's interests. The values at the heart of traditional sexual relations are particularly significant; and not only values and ideas, but also practices – taken for granted, mundane, common-sense ways of doing things, underpinned by unspoken assumptions about sex roles, about how it is proper for whom to behave. This focus on meanings must be accompanied by a focus on material relations. Feminists have concentrated on women's positions in the labour and property markets, but have looked at these in relation to their positions in the 'domestic realm'. Reproduction – the bearing and rearing of children, the reproduction of the body in domestic labour and the provision of food – is as important and indeed is systematically connected to the division of burdens and rewards in the market for waged and salaried labour.

Positively, then, feminist political theory involves modelling and empirically scrutinising the connections between events and changes in state government and government policy, changes in laws, social relations in institutions like firms and households, and in locations like streets and homes, and finally meanings and values constructed and expressed in popular culture, and other cultural practices like the conduct of sexual and romantic relations, or pastimes like going to the pub.

The Basis of Legitimate Government

One of the most fundamental challenges launched from feminism to political theory is the argument that conventional models of the 'ideal political society' are anti-woman and anti-feminist. This challenge has generated disagreements and disputes between feminists which, it is fair to say, are as yet unresolved. These disputes are often characterised as being between 'maternalists' on the one hand, and a variety of their critics on the other. The argument proceeds as follows.

Political theorists have often approached the task of understanding the nature of political relations, their possibilities and their limits, by way of a narrative of *how society might be established*, how men might in idealised circumstances set up a system of government. Now, the obvious historical narrative about the founding of governments that would immediately spring to mind following a perusal of world history is a story of war, conquest, the dispossession of people who were in some sense in possession of lands and other goods, and the imposition of rule. Such a picture, clearly, does not meet modern standards of political legitimacy. The question that political theorists ask is: beginning from where we are now, and forgetting the actual bloodshed and violence that was undergone on the way to the current settlement, would reasonable men, without the use of violence and force, have arrived at some mode of government or some system of justice anything like the one we have? That is, an ideal story is used against which to measure the actual state of affairs. It has seemed to many theorists that the canons of reason and thereby the requirements of legitimacy are only met when a settlement is based on an agreement, a compact, a contract or the like. Genuine agreements, contracts and compacts can only be struck between parties who are in some sense equal in status and power (see Lessnoff [ed.] 1990) for a collection of the key social contract readings).

Feminists have criticised this scheme on a number of grounds. First, some argue that according to the contractarians, women, *qua* feminine individuals, could not be party to such a contract. Contract theorists characterise the kind of individual who can be party – a public reasoner (by contrast with an intimate feeler and expresser of emotion), an independent person (man) by contrast with the dependent person (woman), a public (male) actor by contrast with a private and domestic (female) behaver. Of course, liberal and other contract theorists state that the model for the party to the contract is really gender-neutral. Feminist scrutiny of the texts, however, reveals that this so-called neutral creature is much more like a man than he (*sic*) is like a woman (in the framework, of course, of a conventional model of gender) (Pateman 1988, 1989).

The question, then, is: where are the women in this model? One answer is that they are already disposed of – a close reading of a number of contract narratives shows that the classical writers assumed or described a process whereby marriage and fatherhood is already an institution, and the social contract is struck between heads of families (Pateman 1988, 1989). Another answer is that they are simply ignored. Very few theorists, especially of a liberal sort, could seriously argue these days that women are not fully autonomous individuals with adult and citizenship status, but they nevertheless construct ideal models of society which ignore the situation of real women, ignore crucial social relationships like motherhood, ignore social relations that are not voluntary but which nevertheless generate obligations and ties which are morally binding (Okin 1989: ch. 5).

This leads to a second group of feminist arguments: that as a model of a reasonable basis for society this is most bizarre. The most fundamental kind of reasonable relationship, it is argued, is not the compact or contract, the bargain struck, between equal individuals; rather it is the bond between parent and child – a relationship that is not chosen, as such, that is not voluntaristic in any strong sense, but one which generates obligations, emotional and passionate ties, commitments, the need to find a way to live together (Held 1990; Noddings 1984; Ruddick 1984).

Needless to say, there has been controversy about this suggestion that the basic social relationship of mother and child is a preferable alternative to contract, and could be deployed as a model for all social relationships. Critics argue that it amounts to the suggestion that women should stay locked into a set of social roles that have been imposed on them in societies where men have disproportionate power (Bubeck 1995; Dietz 1985). Rather than revalorising traditional femininity and domestic life, we should think about political, social, economic, cultural and personal life in such a way that women and men share equally its privileges and burdens.

The structure of this dispute is repeated in feminist considerations of the range of concepts closely relevant to questions of governance. The basic issue is the tension between the project of reclaiming and revaluing aspects of femininity that have been denigrated in contexts of masculine dominance, and rejecting masculine ideals, values and practices, on the one hand; or reconstructing these various ideas in such a way that they are applicable indifferently to men and women (that is, no longer gendered). The perceived problem with this latter course is that it entails giving up the pervasive social structure of sexual and gender difference (and to some feminist theorists, this would be a loss indeed).

Does justice mean something different when looked at from a woman's point of view? Does a just society acknowledge sexual difference? Some theorists have emphasised the masculinity of dominant theories of justice and inferred that justice itself is a masculine virtue which is antithetical to feminine virtues like 'care'; others argue that we must reconstruct justice to incorporate or at least be consistent with care, without letting justice go (Gilligan 1982; Okin 1989; Young 1990; Baier 1994). Does equality always imply sameness, or can we reconceptualise equality in order to encompass sexual (and other social) differences? Should we? This dilemma is particularly important, of course, in light of the difficulties that feminists have encountered in the workings of equal opportunities legislation (Phillips [ed.] 1987; Frazer and Lacey 1993: ch. 3). A central value in modern societies is 'freedom' and the governmental protection of freedom an important political preoccupation. What would it mean for women to be genuinely free? In particular, is the basic idea of 'freedom' as unconstrainedness and untrammelledness consistent with women's lives, and should it be consistent with a truly human life (Benhabib 1992)? How would democratic government have to be altered if women are to take their place as equal participants (Phillips 1991, 1993)?

In these discussions analysis proceeds at a number of levels – and the method feminists use is relevant to feminist theory of politics, as we shall see. First, theorists engage in conceptual analysis: they consider the meaning of, say, 'freedom' with a view to unpicking its various components, to considering its relations to and implications for other concepts (say, 'equality'). Feminist theorists, in particular, are on the look out for tensions or inconsistencies within existing analyses of concepts. For instance, if it turns out that according to a particular meaning of 'freedom' men, but not women, could realise freedom in existing societies, then that must be made clear. That is, second, conceptual analysis cannot proceed without an eye on social analysis: the analysis of how things are in actually existing societies. Third, we find analysis of how things might be – feminist theory always has a utopian moment (Benhabib 1986). And this utopian moment weds feminist theory firmly to feminist politics: utopianism in current feminism must engage with the politics of the possible. The point is that feminists are not cowed by traditional views of what is possible.

Politics Revisited

However, this reference to 'feminist politics' begs the question what is meant by politics. As we saw, politics has conventionally been defined as processes surrounding conciliatory governance via public institutions. We have also seen that in the western political tradition the contrast between public and private, between political and non-political, has been analysed in terms of the contrast between men and women, and their respective modes of life, that is, between masculinity and femininity. Needless to say, in this schema, the relationship between public and private is not one of equivalence with difference; rather, like the relationship between masculine and feminine on which it is predicated, it is a relationship of superiority and inferiority, or value and disvalue. The marginalisation and denigration of feminism, both as a theory and as a social and political movement, in academic political science and theory underlines the superior value attached to men's politics.

There are a number of complications in the responses to this. First, feminists are inclined to reject politics as such as a man's game. The emphasis rather is on social change and transformation by other than political means. Second, though, there is a move to reconstruct the concept and practice of politics – to insist that activity in personal and social life is political. There is obviously, on the face of it, potential for tension or even inconsistency here. However, it is important to note that feminists are not the only ones susceptible to this tension. There are strands within a number of political traditions in which politics as such is not unambiguously valorised.

Liberals, for instance, have tended to see the economy, especially the market economy – where voluntaristic contractual relations are entered into by free and autonomous adults – as the realm of freedom. By contrast, the polity is the realm of state power and authority, a realm in which individuals have to obey laws, and cooperate with others – a realm of non-freedom. (Similarly, in traditional liberal thought the domestic realm has been a realm of non-freedom, the realm of the body, of emotional and intimate ties and so on [Frazer 1996].)

For conservative thinkers, there is also something unattractive about politics: they see politics as an activity of struggle and conflict, rather than a realm of settled authority. Conservatives think of traditional relations, the relations between lord and serf, heads of household and servants, children and wives, as truly human relations where people know who they are, know their place. For traditional conservatism both the market with its naked self interest, its competitive relations, and the political sphere, the state, with its competition for the power to govern, are unattractive places.

Socialists have also disliked politics but for rather different reasons. Socialist thinkers, both of the Marxist sort who emphasise production relations and particularly the ownership of the means of production as the key set of social relations, and of the social democratic sort who think much more about just distributions of goods, have faith in the prospect of a reasonably ordered society, in which individuals and groups will be self-governing, and governance will be along universally agreed and just lines. Therefore, the antagonistic, the manipulative, the political nature of rule is both disliked, and, it is hoped, will be overcome.

Feminists are torn here. Whenever men have been inclined to say to women, as they often have, that women should not mind if they are excluded from the professions, or from waged work, or from public power, because these things are burdens rather than privileges, then women rightly retort that if this were indeed the case men should not have to deploy so much violence and aggression, formal and informal, in order to keep women out. That is, a good which is so jealously guarded by men must be a good indeed, and their protests that it is a bad can only be made in bad faith.

On the other hand, feminists have tended to join in the antipathy to politics in its traditional sense. Like socialists, many feminists have hoped and aimed for genuinely autonomous collective self-governance, governance by reason. In their case, though, there is an extra reason for repudiating politics in its traditional sense – that is, its historic association with masculinity. Hence, as a social and political movement, feminism has rejected traditional forms of organisation, especially the party form, traditionally run meetings and so on. There is ambivalence, to say the least, about the target of more women into parliaments; there is widespread conviction that legislative and administrative change cannot be the main goal.

The slogan 'the personal is political' has the potential to resolve this tension. But, as I have said, it deserves more careful analysis than it has sometimes received either within or without feminist thought – for its meaning is not only rhetorical (important though this may be) but is also analytic.

Let us start with the orthodox definition of politics, as conciliatory rule through state and public institutions. Even using this definition it is possible to give a clear analytic meaning to the slogan: there is a clear connection between, say, the domestic division of labour, and women's participation in the public, conventionally political realm. Disadvantage in the 'private' or 'domestic' or 'personal' realms is exported, spills over into, the public and political worlds. Further, it is obviously true to say that state government, and the legislation and administration which is its product, is directly relevant to our so-called 'private' lives. Who may legally have sexual relationships with whom, some aspects of the distribution of power and goods within families, the domestic division of labour itself, are all impinged upon if not straightforwardly determined by legislation and administration. Equally, legislation and administration are impinged upon, constrained by, conceptions and practices in society. Policies are designed and administered according to social definitions of proper social relations, of normality and so on. Thus, meanings of, say masculinity and femininity, which are constructed and maintained in society, in popular culture, in counter-cultures, in our mundane practices are directly relevant to policy, and for the political processes within which policy is designed.

Let us now focus on my preferred definition of politics as the processes surrounding the securing and deployment of the power to govern. This definition does not rule the governance of social institutions – firms, schools, voluntary organisations, and households – out of politics. Neither does it foreclose on any particular way of governing. The power to govern may be bolstered by economic, cultural, sexual or traditional power (or inhibited by the lack of these). Governance is nonetheless political. Wherever individuals are governed, there are questions about the legitimacy of that governance. There are also processes of securing and deploying and, of course, resisting, the power to govern: the processes and activities that constitute politics.

These remarks clarify why criticism of 'public versus private' distinctions is so central in feminist theory. All of these arguments point us towards challenging and indeed deconstructing these clear distinctions (Pateman 1989: ch. 6). However, it is important that 'public' and 'private' are then reconstructed, and it is fair to say that there is some way to go in this project (Squires 1994). Feminists argue that common-sense views about the private nature of domestic or sexual relations, must be challenged. This is not to argue that we are happy to see government inspectors in every bedroom and bathroom regulating sexual conduct (as some of feminism's liberal critics seem to think feminists mean) (Frazer and Lacey 1993: 74). Privacy is, in some contexts, undoubtedly a value. In rejecting traditional public versus private distinctions we must not reject this good as well.

And, equally, publicity and public life is a value. Recently some critics have begun to voice disquiet at feminism's concentration on interpersonal transactions, arguing that feminists must not forget the importance of publicity – of speaking and acting in those public arenas where the intention is that voice is audible and actions are visible to the public (Dietz 1991, 1992).

This point has been taken up in recent contributions to feminist democratic theory and feminist theories of justice, which concentrate on the particular constraints governing public speech, debate and action (for example, Benhabib 1994; Mouffe 1992, 1993). Questions about the limits of publicity and privacy, about the kinds of institutions in which women's and other hitherto marginalised voices can properly be heard and in which standards of public deliberation and dispute might be improved, and about the proper bases of political power, are now central to the agenda of feminist political theory.

References

Baier, Annette (1994) 'The Need for More than Justice', in *Moral Prejudices*, Cambridge MA: Harvard University Press.

Benhabib, Seyla (1992) *Situating the Self: Gender Community and Postmodernism in Contemporary Ethics*, Oxford: Polity Press.

Benhabib, Seyla (1994) Democracy and Difference: Reflections on the Metapolitics of Lyotard and Derrida', *Journal of Political Philosophy*, 2, 1–23.

Benhabib, Seyla (1996) *Critique, Norm and Utopia*, New York: Columbia University Press.

Bryon, Valerie (1992) *Feminist Political Theory: An Introduction*, Basingstoke: Macmillan.

Bubeck, Diemut (1995) *Care, Gender, and Justice*, Oxford: Clarendon Press.

Butler, Judith and Joan W. Scott (eds) (1992) *Feminists Theorize the Political*, New York: Routledge.

Coole, Diana (1993) *Women in Political Theory: From Ancient Misogyny to Contemporary Feminism*, 2nd edn, Hemel Hempstead: Harvester Wheatsheaf.

Crick, Bernard (1992) *In Defence of Politics*, 2nd edn (fp 1962), Harmondsworth: Penguin.

Dietz, Mary G. (1985) 'Citizenship with a Feminist Face: the Problem with Maternal Thinking', *Political Theory*, 13, 19–35.

Dietz, Mary G. (1991) 'Hannah Arendt and Feminist Politics' in Mary Lyndon Shanley and Carole Pateman (eds) *Feminist Interpretations and Political Theory*, Cambridge: Polity Press.

Dietz, Mary G. (1992) 'Feminism and Theories of Citizenship', in Chantal Mouffe (ed.) *Dimensions of Radical Democracy*, London: Verso.

Elshtain, Jean Bethke (1981) *Public Man, Private Woman: women in social and political thought*, Princeton NJ: Princeton University Press.

Frazer, Elizabeth (1996) 'Feminism and Liberalism', in James Meadowcroft (ed.) *The Liberal Political Tradition: Contemporary Reappraisals*, London: Edward Arnold.

Frazer, Elizabeth and Nicola Lacey (1993) *The Politics of Community: a Feminist Critique of the Liberal Communitarian Debate*, Hemel Hempstead: Harvester Wheatsheaf.

Gilligan, Carol (1982) *In a Different Voice: Psychological Theory and Women's Development*, Cambridge MA: Harvard University Press.

Griffin, Gabriele (1995) *Feminist Activism in the 1990s*, London: Taylor and Francis.

Held, Virginia (1990) 'Mothering versus Contract', in Jane Mansbridge (ed.) *Beyond Self Interest*, Chicago: Chicago University Press.

Heller, Agnes (1991) 'The Concept of the Political Revisited', in David Held (ed.) *Political Theory Today*, Oxford: Polity.

Jaggar, Alison M. (1983) *Feminist Politics and Human Nature*, Brighton: Harvester.

Kaplan, Gisela (1992) *Contemporary Western European Feminism*, London: UCL Press.

Kennedy, Ellen and Susan Mendus (eds) (1987) *Women in Western Political Philosophy*, Brighton: Harvester.

Lessnoff, Michael (ed.) (1990) *Social Contract Theory*, Oxford: Basil Blackwell.

Lloyd, Genevieve (1984) *The Man of Reason: Male and Female in Western Philosophy*, London: Metheun.

Lovenduski, Joni and Vicky Randall (1993) *Contemporary Feminist Politics: Women and Power in Britain*, Oxford: Oxford University Press.

Miller, David (1987) 'Politics', in David Miller et al. (eds) *The Blackwell Encyclopaedia of Political Thought*, Oxford: Blackwell.

Mouffe, Chantal (ed.) (1992) *Dimensions of Radical Democracy*, London: Verso.

Mouffe, Chantal (1993) *The Return of the Political*, London: Verso.

Noddings, Nell (1984) *Caring: a Feminine Approach to Ethics and Moral Education*, Berkeley: University of California Press.

Okin, Susan Moller (1979) *Women in Western Political Thought*, London: Virago.

Okin, Susan Moller (1989) *Justice, Gender and the Family*, New York: Basic Books.

Pateman, Carole (1988) *The Sexual Contract*, Oxford: Polity Press.

Pateman, Carole (1989) *The Disorder of Women*, Oxford: Polity.

Phillips, Anne (ed.) (1987) *Feminism and Equality*, Oxford: Blackwell.

Phillips, Anne (ed.) (1991) *Engendering Democracy*, Oxford: Polity.

Phillips, Anne (1993) *Democracy and Difference*, Cambridge: Polity Press.

Philp, Mark (1994) 'On Politics and its Corruption', *Political Theory Newsletter*, 6, 1–18.

Ruddick, Sara (1984) *Maternal Thinking: Towards a Politics of Peace*, London: Women's Press.

Sargent, Lydia (ed.) (1981) *The Unhappy Marriage of Marxism and Feminism: a Debate on Class and Patriarchy by Heidi Hartmann and Others*, London: Pluto Press.

Shanley, Mary Lyndon and Carole Pateman (eds) (1991) *Feminist Interpretations and Political Theory*, Oxford: Polity.

Spender, Dale (ed.) (1983) *Feminist Theorists: Three Centuries of Women's Intellectual Traditions*, London: Women's Press.

Squires, Judith (1994) 'Private Lives, Secluded Places: privacy as political possibility', *Environment and Planning D: Society and Space*, 12, 387–401.

Young, Iris Marion (1990) *Justice and the Politics of Difference*, Princeton NJ: Princeton University Press.

Further Reading

Bryson, Valerie (1992) *Feminist Political Theory: An Introduction*, Basingstoke: Macmillan.

Coole, Diana (1993) *Women in Political Theory: From Ancient Misogyny to Contemporary Feminism*, 2nd edn, Hemel Hempstead: Harvester Wheatsheaf.

Cooper, Davina (1995) *Power in Struggle: Feminism, Sexuality and the State*, Buckingham: Open University Press.

Chapter 5

Feminist Jurisprudence

Jane Scoular

Introduction

In 1994 the Criminal Justice and Public Order Act made it illegal for a man to rape his wife. This transformation was achieved simply by removing the word 'unlawful' from the statutory definition of rape as it appeared in the Sexual Offences (Amendment) Act 1976. Thus prior to the law's change of heart there were acts of rape which could be lawful, due to the law's conflation of a woman's agreement to the contract of marriage with her irrevocable consent to intercourse. The centuries of protection afforded to a husband is perhaps one of the most recent examples of what feminists have termed a patriarchal legal system. The law's failure to regulate what it considered a 'private sphere' has many consequences. As Lacey comments, 'It positively inscribes a certain view of marriage' (Lacey 1993: 96). This view is one which sees male sexual ownership of the wife as paramount. It is an absolute property right which is outside the courts' jurisdiction; its exercise will not be interfered with. Any idea that her free will or capacity for consent could survive this union, which subsumes her, is nonsensical.

This fetishised privileging of heterosexual penetrative intercourse acts as a clear demonstration of the law's wilful blindness not only to the harms of women but also to male experiences of intrusion, as the criminalising of marital rape was accompanied by the first legal recognition of male rape. Although no longer protected by the formal letter of the law these assumptions still pervade many areas of our legal system. Attempts made by feminists to challenge them have revealed that the very nature of law makes it an often perilous ally. This has in turn necessitated the creation of a feminist jurisprudence whose focus has moved in recent times to considering the complexities of our engagement with law.

The Nature of Law – Engaging with Liberal Law

It is arguably the case that in the Western world contemporary social and political institutions more nearly enshrine liberal values and principles than, say, socialist, anarchist, feminist or even conservative ones. This is especially the case with political institutions and the law. It is no surprise, then, that both the genesis (and arguably still the present dominant form) of feminist legal strategies follow the liberal legacy. This may be only in the loose sense that demands have been and are made for freedom, equality and independence from male domination without necessarily consciously embracing all of the tenets of liberal theory. A failure to recognise this has often resulted in the construction of the easy target of the 'straw liberal woman' who is easily knocked down simply for rhetorical effect (Bryson 1992: 60).

In 1960s America, notable achievements of the 'Second Wave' feminists included the landmark Equal Pay Act 1963 and the inclusion of sex discrimination in the 1964 Civil Rights Act. These gains were mirrored in Britain a decade on and, most appropriately, fall under the rubric of liberal feminist. Having at their basis the ideal that men and women are equal individuals and that this should be guaranteed, recognised, and protected by law, the previous absence of women is considered to be an omission, an oversight, which is remedied by 'adding women and stirring'. The limitations of such an approach (similar to the inadequacies of liberal political theory) are clear when differences do exist; whether biologically or because of women's socially constructed roles. Thus when 'women' are introduced into law they have a problem being heard, and are often forced to use a vocabulary which is particularly unsuited to our needs. The law's inability to accommodate difference has led to, for example, claims being made for 'pregnant persons' or the equation of pregnancy and male hernias. This experience of 'incorporatism' is defined by Smart: 'Basically these approaches leave law as it is, but seek to find the most successful way of squeezing the interests of women past the legislature and judiciary' (Smart 1989: 82).

The realisation that the law has assimilated women's claims only when they sit comfortably within its pre-existing paradigm has motivated feminist inquiry into the nature of law; attention has moved from women's explicit exclusion to implicit barriers in 'the design of law' and its operation (Reaume 1996: 278).

The Feminist Critique of Reason

The feminist critique of reason is often association with what has been called 'cultural feminism'. It reveals the apparent coherency of reason to be dependant upon the exclusion and subordination of those characteristics associated with the feminine. This especially applies to legal reasoning which gains legitimacy from being abstract and universal. The work in the 1970s of the feminist psychologist Carol Gilligan has influenced much of the writing and theorising in this area (Gilligan 1982). Gilligan attempted to explain why women's moral voice was devalued in contemporary moral psychology and moral theory (including law). Under the standard ethical schema Gilligan found that rights were assumed to be the norm and that any deviation was ascribed lesser value. This coincided with the discovery that women were more inclined to have an ethical outlook which valued care as opposed to rights. Thus in systems of moral reasoning women's voice was systematically devalued. Gilligan concluded that our ethical systems of justice must develop to take in the excluded feminine ethics of care.

Following from this and taking an even more explicitly biologically determinist position is the work of Robin West. Drawing on works by Dinnerstein (1987) and Chodorow (1978), West asserts that women's reproductive role or 'pregnability' leads to an apprehension of the world which goes beyond the limits of male reason: 'The potential for material connection with the other defines women's subjective, phenomenological and existential state, just as surely as the inevitability of material separation from the other defines men's existential state' (West 1988: 14).

This experience of connection shapes women's ethics around the values of sympathy, relatedness, love and care. Women's 'pregnability' and their role as primary care-takers means that their 'lives are not autonomous, they are profoundly relational', that they are 'giving selves' as opposed to 'liberal selves' (West 1988: 2–14). Women's suffering and harm go unnoticed by the legal system because women are not legal subjects. However, rather than demanding that women be recognised as such, she argues that women don't want to be equal in this way. This is not in the misogynistic sense that all women are masochists but that if the goal of liberalism or even radical engagement with the legal system is freedom and equality to benefit the subjective well-being of autonomous individuals, then, West posits, such goals do not coincide with what women desire.

While these works form part of the important (and ongoing) work which interrogates and deconstructs the political tool of abstract reason, there are dangers with both writers' conclusions, especially in relation to the discourse of law. Scales, for example, warns it could be the *Uncle Tom's Cabin* of our century (Scales 1986: 1,381). The danger of 'incorporatism' is that it could only be achieved by repressing contradictions and that this would be done at the expense of usurping women's language in order to further define the world in the male image (1986: 1,381–2). She is sceptical of the idea that 'the different voices of women can be grafted onto our right and rule based system' (1986: 1,383) as the law cannot accept multiplicity; '[it] creates the other and then devours it' (1986: 1,383). Thus if the ruling ideology is that of 'rights' then values of care are necessarily precluded. Any incorporation is superficial, and is, according to Scales, 'the one surest sign of fatal misunderstanding, and is the kiss of Judas' (1986: 1,384). The re-instatement of prescribed biological stereotypes of women as caring mothers, Carol Smart notes, would operate only to put women 'back in their place' (Smart 1989: 75). Radical critiques focus on this concern; MacKinnon, for example, argues: 'Women value care because men have valued us according to the care we give them. Women think in relational terms because our existence is defined in relation to them' (MacKinnon 1987: 39).

This applies even more strongly to West, where the problem is not the advocation of difference but its naturalisation in the maternal body. Pregnancy is not a 'hedonic experience' felt by all women; for example, childless women, some lesbian women and sterile women do not share in this experience. Also, having a child does not necessarily make women caring. Cornell sees the problem as being that of 'dereliction', that is, the reduction to masculine fantasy – where maternity ascribes women to their 'proper role within gender hierarchy' (Cornell 1991: 22). West's rooting of feminist theory in female 'nature' is essentialist in that it has the effect of collapsing or mapping the feminine on (into) femaleness. Her insistence on female reality (so consciousness-raising would be a matter of revealing a known female essence) is disputed by post-modern, and indeed most feminist, theory; women's biological structure affects not our psychic identity but our place in a gender hierachy.[1] It is the legal system's reinforcement of these sexualised (dominant and subordinate) positions that is the central focus of radical perspectives in law.

Radical Feminist Jurisprudence

In her groundbreaking work 'Feminism, Marxism, Method and the State' Catharine MacKinnon states: 'Sexuality is to feminism, what work is to marxism; that which is most one's own and yet that which is most taken away' (1982: 515). Providing what she considers to be the first feminist 'account of male power as an ordered yet deranged whole' (MacKinnon 1989: xi), she reworks marxist notions of power so that women get 'fucked' (metaphysically and literally) by the system. The state is categorically male; it legitimises male dominance by enforcing its epistemology through law. Women are defined in law (and in society) by the expropriation of their sexuality; 'man fucks woman, subject verb object' (MacKinnon 1989: 124). Women's gender identity is given to her or forced upon her as a result of the (often violent) expropriation of her sexuality. Women's objectified status is the 'truth' of female reality. Thus 'our' sexuality is as it is seen, objectified and fantasised by men. Law reinforces, legitimises this objectification: 'Law is not neutral (as it claims to be) vis-à-vis the gender divide; law is male' (Cornell 1991: 121).

Radical perspectives on the law are antithetical to liberal notions in that inequality rather than equality between individuals is assumed. The fact that women are not equal is seen, not as a question of difference, but as a matter of the unequal distribution of power: 'Gender ... is a matter of dominance, not difference ... The difference is that men have power and women do not' (MacKinnon 1987: 39).

Less concerned with the narrowness of legal doctrine and its inability to recognise difference, radical theories focus on the central issue of power. Thus, in an exchange with Gilligan, MacKinnon opines that women only value love and intimacy as this is what is required to keep us available to men: 'Difference is the velvet glove on the iron fist of domination. The problem ... is not that differences are not valued; the problem is that they are defined by power' (1987: 8).

These themes are brought out in her work in the areas of rape, domestic violence, pornography and sexual harassment. A reading of MacKinnon's work reveals the importance of her tie to Andrea Dworkin (1981, 1987) – an alliance which often focuses on the issue of pornography. Both writers were instrumental in the creation of the Indianapolis State Ordinance which, for the first time, created civil remedies for women harmed by pornography. It was soon after conception declared to be unconstitutional by the Supreme Court as being a violation of the first Amendment right to free speech (American Booksellers v Hadnut 475 US 1001 [1986]). MacKinnon (1987: 148) argues that this is another illustration of the law's role in maintaining pornography as 'an institution of gender inequality ... [which] like rape ... fuses the eroticisation of domination and submission with the social construction of male and female'. The relationship is reinforced, MacKinnon argues, by the First Amendment's protection of the right to free speech – which reimposes women's silent, victim position, reducing woman's sexuality to a projection of male fantasy.

Although wielding a considerable hold on the American academy and media,[2] MacKinnon is not without her critics, whose main concern is her overdetermining the power of law and the position of women (Brown 1995; Smart 1989; Cornell 1991). She over-privileges law to the extent that it is elevated to a position of being a 'barometer of the whole social world' (Smart 1989: 81). Smart, however, points out that all social relations are gendered, conceding that law is especially powerful (Smart 1989: 4–25). The problem is that the 'Power of Law' is reinforced when it is targeted as the main site for feminist politics which aim to raise women to the male standard. In her exchanges with Gilligan, MacKinnon clearly demonstrates her impatience with the promotion of the values of love, care and passion: 'Women's expressed desire is only an ideology' (Cornell 1991: 133), amounting to complicity in our own oppression. MacKinnon's recognition of the social construction of the gender divide has been described as a 'flirtation' (Brown 1995: 78), with most of her writing adopting a rhetorical style which has the effect of naturalising the subordinate and dominant position of the sexes. The gender-hierarchy, according to MacKinnon, defines what 'women' are; any affirmation of the feminine is simply to rattle ones chains and any pleasure spoken of is derided as being masochism. Her representations of male sexuality describe a transhistorical, undistorted reign – and never focus on its fragmentation, contradictions or its moments of crisis.[3] Drucilla Cornell states, however, that this presents 'an ideology of lesser expectation' (Cornell 1991: 139). She argues that we must look beyond this oppressive 'reality' or feminism loses its transformative character. The problem with MacKinnon's disregard of difference is that she treats the work of Gilligan and French writers, such as Luce Irigaray and Hélène Cixous, as one and the same. The latter are not attempting to define 'the' category of women but to use the power of the feminine to disrupt the gender hierarchy. The evocation of sexual difference (indebted to the writings of Luce Irigaray 1985, 1993) suggests a beyond to the present eroticised binary where we can only switch positions within the sado-masochistic scenario. Yet, in this scenario, it is the male position which MacKinnon desires; the ideal of human nature she adheres to is drawn from the masculine, the phallic values of self-assertion and integrity. Cornell illustrates this clearly by quoting from MacKinnon herself: 'I'm getting hard on this and am about to get harder … the way women reason morally is [not] in a "Different Voice" … it is morality in a higher register' (MacKinnon 1987: 39).

Cornell, however, drawing from the writing of Luce Irigaray, argues that affirmations of feminine desire can have a transformative effect. When we recognise multiplicity rather than MacKinnon's 'fantasy of symmetry' we can change the conflation of erotic desire from a win/lose equation. If we view the subject in the erotic relation as seeking intimacy rather than freedom, the body is transformed from being a barrier (stark, phallic wall) to representing a position of receptivity, affirming openness to the other. Thinking in these terms, rather than reaffirming the masculine ideal of assertion is more apt for many of our legal relationships (for example, to children), and it may also help us around political and legal feminists' 'problem with rights' (Kingdom 1991). Indeed such a post-modernist approach can have a powerful influence over the ways in which feminists theorise law more generally.

The Influence of Post-modernism

Post-modernism has had a revolutionary impact on the area of feminist jurisprudence, as in other areas. By proclaiming the death of the subject, the stability of both gender and law as unifying categories has been undermined. This challenges the very idea of a feminist jurisprudence – if there is no absolute truth and no fixed category woman, then an all-encompassing account of law's subordination of women is impossible. However, it is important to notice that jurisprudence has always shown itself to be a rather strange bed-fellow for feminists; engagement has at times produced work which has replicated the inadequacies of masculine theory. Yet there is a need to maintain the distinctiveness of feminist theory in the discourse of law, especially in light of the implications of post-modernism. The influence of post-modernism has impacted on feminist theories of law to highlight the following insights:

1. *Jurisprudence is at odds with deconstructive emphases within feminist theory.*
Feminist theory attacks abstract, universal theories about the social world.

Jurisprudence, which is often referred to as 'the' epistemology of law, 'the' science of law or 'the' theory of law, must clearly be a target. Yet many have attempted to offer a feminist version; MacKinnon's 'Quest for a Feminist Jurisprudence' repeats the mistakes of marxism and liberalism in offering a theory as a scientific and objective truth. The effect is another totality: 'Radical feminism is feminism' (MacKinnon 1989: 117). This attempt to construct a whole theory of women's oppression is riddled with the same 'reductionist, totalizing, inadequately nuanced, valorizing of gender difference, unconsciously racist and elitist' characteristics of masculine theory (Bordo 1990: 663).

2. *Jurisprudence presumes an identifiable unity of law.*
The discipline of jurisprudence has given law 'assumed fictional solidity and permanence' (Jackson 1993: 398) – some mythic source outside social construction so that principles like justice, rights and equality have an almost pre-given quality. Post-modern theory sees law as a set of symbols and norma (Derrida 1990) which people recreate in their own lives. The structure of legal thought is contingent and law is always partial and circumscribed by the social field. Writers such as Derrida (1990) and Foucault (1979) focus attention on the social processes and forms that law and legal power take in social relations showing that change occurs only in relation to localised and particularised contests. These are enacted by historical agents whose strategies are both authorised and circumscribed by legal conventions. Indeed Bower comments that the failure of legal decisions can create a cultural space for political mobilisation: 'Law limits the expression of individual group aspirations and claims and simultaneously provides powerful resources for marginalised groups to assert their interests, to articulate rights claims and to refigure their identities' (Bower 1994: 1,009).

If we recognise law as a field of ongoing struggle, we must ensure 'women' can take part. This leads us back, once again, to the ways in which law both operates as a barrier to and a facilitator of participation in law.

3. *Fallacy of the legal subject.*
The very concept of the liberal subject – the notion of the meaning-giving agent, distinct from social structures and linguistic conventions – has been deconstructed as liberal structures are themselves dereified. Feminists have joined these deconstructive expeditions by pointing out that what has been paraded as the universal lessons of man is merely the male in disguise, and by suggesting that 'all theories of the subject have been appropriated to the side of the masculine' (Irigaray in Marks and de Courtivron 1984: 99, 104). The category 'woman', like others, is culturally constructed. These subjects have multiple realities including features such as class, race and sexual orientation. However, a feminism claiming a fractured narrative, which lacks coherence and rationality, is easier to ignore. This has led some writers to distrust post-modern theories: 'Somehow it seems

highly suspicious ... that just at the moment when so many of us who have been silenced begin to demand the right to name ourselves, to act as subjects rather than objects of history, that just then the concept of subjecthood becomes problematic?' (Harstock 1990: 163).

However, as Smart notes, 'Feminist work has a growing affinity with the idea of analysing the micro-politics of power' (Smart 1989: 68). Moreover, critics of postmodernism fail to recognise that feminism has only been able to avoid fragmentation through the process of exclusion. She points to MacKinnon's work where difference is either condemned or assimilated. Nonetheless, there remains the need to recognise that these multiple persons enter into social relations where certain forms of power are present. Kimberley Crenshaw, for example, argues that to account for the experience of blacks under the legal system one must recognise the historical and continual narrative of hegemonic racism (Crenshaw 1988: 133). Yet we can recognise this narrative without naturalising the social category 'black' which surely only exists in a racist society. In a similar sense the category 'woman' is part of the process of fixing gender and sex. The work of Judith Butler is vital here (Butler 1990, 1993). Butler disputes the common view of gender as a cultural overlay to the naturalised sex; rather, sex is an artefact of the on-going process of gendering. It is not *a priori* given. Law is seen as a practice which makes women feminine *and* biologically female. The effect of this is that we can't expect a utopian reversal but we can take part in the ongoing process of negotiating human and sexual relations. We must, however, recognise the barriers which exclude women from negotiating their place in the law and society. To do so we must refer to the work of Drucilla Cornell.

Cornell recognises that such ideals of personhood must at present be constrained in order to make a coherent claim to law. Previously, any engagement has implied an exhausting contestation of imposed definitions of woman. Cornell disputes the notion that personhood can be defined by law, but rather sees it as a process of working through – re-imagining. This aspiration is characterised by the 'feminine' – that which is outside the current gender hierarchy. However, to be marked as a 'woman' is not to be allowed the chance for such imagining. If we think of representations of women in the legal system, they are invariably degrading and stereotypical. Smart, for example, describes the process of fixing 'womanhood' as 'rapable, vulnerable and victimizable' which sanctions regulation and control. Cornell, in her quest to affirm the 'feminine' beyond what currently masquerades for femininity, does see a role for law in facilitating this move.

In her most recent work, *The Imaginary Domain*, Cornell advocates a distinction between law as a coercive set of rules and justice which must be maintained so that 'justice cannot be reduced to another power seeking ideology' (Levinas 1981). The law, as coercive order, should be used, according to Cornell, to guarantee minimum conditions. These will allow women 'the equivalent chance to undertake the struggle to become a person'. Minimum conditions include: bodily integrity, protection of imaginary domain and sufficient access to linguistic resources to facilitate this project of becoming a person. Thus the harms presently suffered by women, for example, by pornography, sexual violence, battery and so on, are addressed but don't operate to paralyse or victimise. They do not turn on gender comparison between men and women (this is one of the major problems with the rights discourse) but rather recognise equality for each of us as sexuate beings.

Cornell's perspective, which draws upon a history of problematic feminist engagements with law, has much to offer future work in this area. Although complexities and power struggles remain, it forms part of a growing body of work which means that we can face law with our eyes open. Recognising the ways in which law has operated to stifle difference – so that claims made by women have had to be equated to a male standard or comply with accepted notions of femininity – does not mean abandoning law. Cornell shows that legal solutions can assist a project of diversity by guaranteeing minimum conditions to ensure participation. Thus in going to law in this first sense we must recognise the importance and history of gender for women. It is only once we have entered the power struggle to gain these minimum political rights that we can enjoy the luxury of embracing fully any notions of 'non-identity' as advocated by some writers in the fast developing area of queer theory (see Bower 1994; Herman and Stychin 1995). To do so would be to depoliticise gender, although this must be our ultimate goal, our feminist vision.

Notes

1. It is important to note the distinction between this kind of cultural feminism and that of those French Feminists who advocate the need to affirm the feminine. This is not a reductive, essentialist argument but promotes feminine ways of thinking, based on the multiple and diffused experience of female sexual pleasure. This is often encapsulated by the term *jouissance* to describe this plurality which can serve to disrupt the binary structures of male 'phallogocentric' thought and offer the possibility of new conceptions and perhaps more radical ways of engaging with the legal system (see Cornell 1991: 17).
2. Wendy Brown (1995) analyses the rhetorical power of MacKinnon's work, which explains the apparent palatability of this 'radical' work.
3. Brown criticises MacKinnon's overdetermination of pornography which should be historically situated in a time of 'proliferation … and diffusion of sexuality in the late twentieth century' (Brown 1995: 87). MacKinnon, she argues, 'encodes the pornographic age as the truth … [she] fails to read the $10 billion a year porn industry as a "state of emergency" of a male dominant heterosexual regime' (Brown 1995: 88).

References

Bordo, S. (1990) 'Material Girl: the effacements of postmodern culture', *Michigan Quarterly Review*, Fall: 653–78.

Bower, L. (1994) 'Queer Acts and the Politics of "Direct Address": Rethinking Law, Culture and Community', *Law & Society Review*, 28, 5: 1,009–33.

Brown, W. (1995) *States of Injury; Power and Freedom in Late Modernity*, Princeton: Princeton University Press.

Bryson, V. (1992) *Feminist Political Theory*, London: Macmillan.

Butler, J. (1990) *Gender Trouble: Feminism and the Subversion of Identity*, New York: Routledge.

Butler, J. (1993) *Bodies that Matter*, New York: Routledge.

Chodorow, N. (1978) *The Reproduction of Mothering: Psychoanalysis and the Sociology of Gender*, Berkeley: University of California Press.

Cornell, D. (1991) *Beyond Accommodation: Ethical Feminism, Deconstruction and the Law*, London: Routledge.

Cornell, D. (1995) *The Imaginary Domain*, London: Routledge.

Crenshaw, K. (1988) 'Race, Reform and Retrenchment Transformation and Legitimation in Anti-Discrimination Law, *Harvard Law Review*, 101: 1,331.

Derrida, J. (1990) 'Force of Law: The "Mythical Foundation of Authority"', *Cardozo Law Review*, 11, 5–6.

Dinnerstein, D. (1987) *The Rocking of the Cradle and the Ruling of the World*, London: Women's Press.

Dworkin, A. (1981) *Pornography: Men Possessing Women*, London: Women's Press.

Dworkin, A. (1987) *Intercourse*, London: Arrow Books.

Foucault, M. (1979) *Discipline and Punish*, New York: Vintage Books.

Gilligan, C. (1982) *In a Different Voice: Psychological Theory and Women's Development*, Cambridge: Harvard University Press.

Harstock, N. (1990) 'Foucault on Power', in Linda J. Nicholson (ed.) *Feminism/Postmodernism*, London: Routledge.

Herman, D. and C. Stychin (eds) (1995) *Legal Inversions: Lesbians, Gay Men and the Politics of Law*, Philadelphia: Temple University Press.

Irigaray, L. (1985) *Speculum of the Other Woman*, trans. G. Gill, Ithaca: Cornell University Press.

Irigaray, L. (1993) *An Ethics of Sexual Difference*, trans. C. Burke and G. Gill, Ithaca: Cornell University Press.

Jackson, E. (1993) 'Contradictions and Coherence in Feminist Responses to Law', *Journal of Law and Society*, 20, 4: 398.

Kingdom, E. (1991) *What's Wrong with Rights?: Problems for Feminist Politics of Law*, Edinburgh: Edinburgh University Press.

Lacey, N. (1993) 'Theory into Practice? Pornography and the Public/Private Dichotomy', *Journal of Law and Society*, 93–113.

Levinas, E. (1981) *Otherwise Than Being or Beyond Essence*, The Hague: Martinus Nijhoff Publishers.

MacKinnon, C. (1952) 'Feminism, Marxism, Method and the State', *Signs: Journal of Women in Culture and Society*, 7, 3: 515–44.

MacKinnon, C. (1987) *Feminism Unmodified. Discourses on Life and Law*, Cambridge: Harvard University Press.

MacKinnon, C. (1989) *Towards a Feminist Theory of the State*, Cambridge: Harvard University Press.

Marks, Elaine and Isabelle de Courtivron (eds) (1984), *New French Feminisms*, Brighton: Harvester Press.

Reaume, D. (1996) 'What's Distinctive About Feminist Analysis of Law?', *Legal Theory*, 2: 265–99.

Scales, A. (1986) 'The Emergence of Feminist Jurisprudence: an Essay', *Yale Law Journal*, 95: 1373–403.

Smart, Carol (1989) *Feminism and the Power of Law*, London: Routledge.

West, R. (1988) 'Jurisprudence and Gender', *University of Chicago Law Review*, 55: 14.

Further Reading

Introductions

Olsen, F. (1995a) *Feminist Legal Theory – Foundations and Outlooks*, Aldershot: Dartmouth.

Olsen, F. (1995b) *Feminist Legal Theory – Positioning Feminist Theory Within the Law*, Aldershot: Dartmouth.

Weisberg, D. (1993) *Feminist Legal Theory: Foundations*, Philadelphia: Temple University Press.

Supplementary Texts

Bottomley, A. (ed.) (1996) *Feminist Perspectives on the Foundational Subjects of Law*, London: Cavendish.

Brophy, J. and C. Smart (eds) (1985) *Women and the Law*, London: Routledge & Kegan Paul.

Edwards, S. (1981) *Female Sexuality and the Law*, Oxford: Martin Robertson.

Kennedy, H. (1992) *Eve was Framed: Women and British Justice*, London: Chatto & Windus.

O'Donovan, K. (1985) *Sexual Divisions in the Law*, London: Weidenfeld & Nicolson.

Okin, S. (1989) *Justice, Gender and the Family*, New York: Basic Books.

West, R. (1993) *Narrative, Authority and Law*, Unviersity of Michigan Press.

Chapter 6

Feminism and Anthropology

Penelope Harvey

Feminist anthropology is a problematic union, for some a contradiction in terms, for others the challenge that motivates their scholarship. This essay will outline some of the difficulties entailed in attempting to forge an alliance between these approaches and consider the possibilities for feminist anthropology that have emerged in recent years. Despite difficulties and much critique, feminism has made a difference to the practice of anthropology and anthropology in turn has made a contribution to feminist thinking. As the diversity within both feminist and anthropological thinking is increasingly recognised and made explicit, the mutual influences become harder to trace, yet the evidence of a productive relationship appears more tangible. My account will thus trace the history of a relationship, that has become more complex, more critical and yet more creative as it has become more self-aware.

An Awkward Relationship

Anthropology, the comparative study of human cultural experience and social life, necessarily involves a critical engagement with western science and social theory. Even those anthropologists who study 'at home', draw on the disciplinary attention to alternative ways of being in order to locate the specificity of western practice.

> One important first-stage point in anthropology is that there is no culturally innocent (or culture-free) reality. Any claims to have a privileged handle on reality, to be able to perceive an extra-cultural reality, are in themselves cultural. (…) In stark heuristic terms, the real world is not simply 'out there' waiting to be discovered, raw and in culture-free innocence, by science; rather, science is actively constructing reality, and has persuasive means to assert what is to count as 'real'.
>
> (McDonald 1994: 12)

Despite the apparent convergence with feminist interests in the critique of scientific objectivity, anthropology's focus on cultural difference presents a problem for many feminist approaches to the study of social life. The problem centres on the implications of the political commitment(s) that distinguish feminist

73

thinking. In their ethnographic accounts of cultural practices which differ, often quite radically, from the experiences of a relatively homogeneous, university-educated western readership, anthropologists often fail to provide what many feminist scholars are seeking in their work; the evidence of links and similarities through which to develop a politics of solidarity and connection. Indeed, 'from a feminist perspective, the political implications of moral relativism are potentially reactionary, as they preclude the definition of either oppression or liberation' (Bell 1993: 61).

However, the problem works both ways. For anthropologists, the feminist focus on cross-cultural similarities frequently perpetuates the ethnocentric bias of western researchers which anthropological attention to difference seeks to challenge. Hence the awkward relationship (Strathern 1987). The awkwardness does not simply arise from the fact that anthropological and feminist scholarship have not focused on the same political systems of difference, but that the investigator's relationship to their subject matter has engendered two very different, even incompatible, forms of radicalism. The feminist self exists through an extensive identification of the female subject and an antagonistic separation from the male Other. Anthropological knowledge by contrast is constituted in attempts to establish close relations with the cultural Other while seeking radical separation from habitual cultural assumptions. This paradoxical relationship between the feminist and the anthropologist can, of course, be embodied in one scholar.

Let me take an example from my own experience as a fieldworker in an Andean village where I found it was quite common for men to beat their wives. I was far more horrified by these beatings than the people with whom I was living. The women with whom I talked expected that sexual relationships would involve some degree of confrontation and when talking about other people and even about themselves in retrospect, they could find it quite funny. Such expectation was not accompanied by an attitude of resignation however. Women always actively contested such violence. They fought back, complained loud and hard and did not experience the shame and isolation that so often characterises domestic violence in western cultures.

The ethnographic treatment of such issues is problematic (Harvey 1994). Anthropologists project otherness through the mere selection of their research topics and to focus on wife-beating implies dissociation and a sense of separation between observer and observed that can all too easily be used to strengthen racist attitudes. One response to this problem within Andean studies has been to simply not write about these aspects of peoples' lives. Another standard response has been to dissociate drunken violence from indigenous culture and attribute it to the negative influences of westernised *mestizo* lifestyle. The problem with both these responses, however, is that they treat the relationship between wife-beating and drunkenness as entirely familiar and recognisable. Cross-cultural comparison is thus rendered unproblematic on an *epistemological* level despite the difficulties it produces on the political level.

To what extent might the anthropologist profitably draw on the *feminist* literature which seeks to understand the dynamics of violent confrontation? These writings are explicitly produced in order to find ways to mitigate the effects of such violence. The stance is interventionist, the aim to reveal hidden oppression, to objectify practice and to create a sense of support and visibility for those concerned, and to foster the social conditions required for those effected to achieve a moral distance from the violence that others perpetrate. However, as an anthropologist it is difficult to embrace these interventionist aims. Do we know what we are dealing with? It might look like domestic violence, but what does it mean to those involved? Much depends on how we conceptualise relationships between persons and particularly those characterised as relationships of sexual difference.

In the Andean region a focus on sexual difference distracts attention from the more specific distinction between consanguineal and affinal kin, that is, between kinds of relatives. The cases of 'domestic violence' which I tried to comprehend seemed to be more meaningfully understood as confrontations between husbands and wives than between men and women. The important point to make here is simply that in our attempts as anthropologists to write about issues which have a high profile on the feminist political agenda we are caught in the dilemma of both *knowing* what is involved and why we disapprove and *knowing that we do not know* exactly what we are dealing with as we try to respect the cultural differences which confront and confound us. Similar dilemmas can occur for those who do anthropology within their own cultural environments as the detailed knowledge of each case, which anthropological fieldwork brings to the fore, generates precisely the kind of complexity which anthropologists are loath to gloss over. The balance is hard to strike and often fiercely debated.

Ethnographic studies are central to this endeavour and offer a source of information which can be used in contrasting ways, depending on the interests of the ethnographer. Thus while ethnographies can serve on the one hand as case studies within a general comparative approach to the study of hierarchical gender relations, they also provide the opportunity to reflect on the basic cultural concepts through which we experience and attempt to deal with gender inequality. Such reflection is not concerned to produce examples of utopian alternatives, but rather to act on the belief that any political project which aims to effect social change entails a responsibility to try and make sense of how those involved understand their circumstances. Political advocacy of any kind becomes a highly complex affair once there is an awareness that commonplace notions of inequality and oppression have emerged from a very particular history of western social relations. Of particular importance to the feminist debates in this regard are the concepts such as autonomy, possession and commodification through which contemporary western understandings of oppression are habitually expressed (Strathern 1988, 1996).

Feminist Anthropology in the 1970s

The bases for contemporary feminist anthropology are somewhat different to those that were available in the 1970s when anthropology and feminism had a much closer and less problematic relationship. During a period of wide-spread political activism feminist anthropologists were working to reveal and correct the male bias in the discipline by paying attention to the position of women (e.g. Weiner 1976), focusing on what women did and said in studies that sought to highlight the autonomous agency of women in western and non-western cultures alike. These studies were integral to the feminist discussion at the time concerning the extent and nature of women's subordination. Anthropology had considerable influence in these debates, both in providing evidence for the universal subordination of women and in generating explanatory frameworks for this inequality. Ortner (1974) emphasised the symbolic association of women and men with what most readers understood at that time as an unproblematic hierarchical distinction between nature and culture. Women were universally devalued through their systematic association with the devalued domain of nature. Rosaldo (1974), in similar vein, posited a universal and hierarchical distinction between the public and the private domains of social life in which women were overwhelmingly associated with the less prestigious private sphere.

These theories were important and insightful in many respects. They emphasised that gender constructs expressed value and could symbolise relationships other than those between men and women, that meanings were arbitrary and that gender is intrinsically relational and requires attention to the activities and values associated with both men and women (Ortner and Whitehead 1981). This work resonated with that of scholars such as Reiter (1975) and Sacks (1974) who sought to develop economic explanations of social and cultural phenomena. Indeed the common focus on the subordination of women helped to break down barriers between symbolic and materialist analyses. However, there was much to be refined in their models. They were prone to conflating 'women' with 'mothers' and were uncritical of the extent to which the nature/culture dichotomy was embedded in the social paradigms of modernity, which also underwrite the sex/gender distinction with its implicit appeal to biological foundationalism. Subsequent anthropological critique established that the reproductive body was not necessarily equated with a domain of 'nature', or even with a specifically female capacity, nor were 'culture' and 'nature' necessarily understood as mutually exclusive domains of practice or signification (MacCormack and Strathern 1980).

The Cultural Construction of Gender Difference

By the 1980s, ethnographers had more or less turned away from attempts to generate universalising explanatory theories and began to look instead at the specific social and cultural processes through which men and women are distinguished in different times and places. Those who still worked with a sex/gender distinction would look at the cultural construction of male and female gendered identities, often continuing the project to describe and value the lives of women across cultures (Caplan 1987). Indeed it is interesting that there was a strong mutual interest in the notion of 'the cultural construct' among western scholars generally which has been sustained in the associated critical activity of deconstruction.

In 1987 Collier and Yanagisako edited an influential collection of essays on gender and kinship which began to look at the centrality of the concept of 'reproduction' in the cultural constructionist debates and at the implicit appeal to the non-cultural biological foundationalism so characteristic of modern social thought. It was pointed out that western social theorists have found it important to distinguish the production of people from the production of things. This distinction supports an understanding of reproduction as being primarily about persons, and requiring a radical (biological) distinction between men and women, and of production as concerned primarily with things. Such production rests on a cultural rather than a biological distinction between men and women. However, when these ideas are compared with other ethnographic possibilities it is clear that the relationships involved in the reproduction of human persons are generally deemed more complex than that. The *particular* differences in the reproductive biologies of men and women rarely function as the *basis* for the social differences between men and women, or for cultural understandings of gender difference (Moore 1993). And, in fact, this is the case for both western and non-western peoples (Laqueur 1990; Martin 1987). The warning is, that if we fail to understand other cultural possibilities, we will simply reproduce images (even stereotypes) of ourselves when wc look at others.

As important, and perhaps more germane to feminist concerns, was the way in which this work also led to a resurgence of interest in the analysis of western cultural institutions and practices, that invoked ideas of natural connections, such as those through which the family is constituted (Thorne and Yalom 1992). The critique of biological foundationalism has been particularly productive in the literature on the new reproductive technologies which have, as a focus of public controversy, made explicit many western foundational assumptions about gender, bodies, ownership, as well as the more abstract concepts of personhood and relatedness (see Edwards et al. 1993; Strathern 1992).

This anthropological interest in the workings of kinship within the context of contemporary western cultures has opened up new possibilities for feminist anthropology. The work on the new reproductive technologies identified, for example, important links between anthropological interests in kinship and feminist approaches to technoscience. Similar questions have been raised concerning the nature of hybrids, the effects of literalisation, the cultural politics of biology,

and the naturalisation of power in the context of the processes of commodification and globalisation which characterise contemporary capitalism (see
Franklin 1995).

Furthermore, it is interesting to note that to a large extent these approaches
also came up against the limits of gender as a heuristic concept for the analysis
of such relationships. Within anthropology, the study of gender no longer implies
an engagement with feminist concerns. 'Gender' as a subject of inquiry, was
incorporated into the anthropological mainstream with no tangible political
effect beyond the reiteration that everyday, common-sense understandings of the
differences between men and women were not given in nature or biology. This
was due, in part, to the easy assimilation of social constructivism to an 'invisible'
liberal politics that simply embraces pluralism and does not focus on either the
political origins or the consequences of difference. By the mid-1980s feminist
scholarship and anthropology seemed quite distant from each other in many
ways. Feminism was concerned with asymmetrical power relations, not gender
difference *per se*, while anthropological interests in gender did not necessarily
assume asymmetry, nor did the study of power imply oppression.

The recognition of the limits of gender for feminist purposes marked a new
convergence between feminism and anthropology, for feminist scholarship was
also fully engaged in the critical deconstruction of the category 'woman'. Thus,
while gender can no longer be treated as a self-evident basis for identity politics,
the new context of explicit attention to the complexity of subjectivity and to the
cultural and social dimensions of the research process itself, has enabled old
questions to be raised in new ways. Sexual politics is still on the agenda although
the dynamics and effects of power are no longer assumed, but taken as the focus
of attention. Ginsburg and Rapp, for example, in an exemplary collection, focus
on the difference it makes to put reproduction at the centre of social theory:

> Clearly, questions of culture, politics, and biology are impossible to disentangle around the
> topic of reproduction, as they often involve transnational processes that link local and global
> interests. Our goal is to keep the tension among these domains, while recognizing that our
> very categories – biological, global, and local – are also subject to interrogation.
>
> (Ginsburg and Rapp 1995: 3)

The Body

This focus on the politics of reproduction is one aspect of another field of
contemporary convergence between feminism and anthropology, the body
and the concept of embodiment. This focus on the body is related to a
reconsideration of the relationship between sex and gender. Ethnographic
studies have become more attentive to the ways in which it is not simply gender
difference but also sex difference that varies cross-culturally. The implications are
important. The assumption that culturally variable notions of gender are con-

structed on the basis of universal understandings of sex difference becomes untenable and the foundationalism of western biological categories is challenged (Moore 1994).

The challenge has been taken up in various ways. A new literature on third sex, on androgyny and hermaphrodism has appeared, with some fascinating contributions (see, for example, Herdt 1994). Some continue with the constructionist approach, arguing simply that distinct cultures model gender on their own particular understandings of sexual difference. More radical are those who question the extent to which sex (as defined by material bodily characteristics) makes a difference to understandings of gender (as defined by symbolic social characteristics) (see, for example, Moore 1994). A re-reading of the ethnographic literature on bodies, gender and sex difference, reveals that for many peoples these differences between the material and the symbolic can only be sustained through comparison with a western notion of biology. If local understandings are treated on their own terms, this distinction between the material and the symbolic becomes untenable, for gender difference is tangible and material and exists as much within bodies as between bodies. Bodies frequently contain both male and female substances, substances which furthermore are often transferable between bodies during a life-time. Thus while men and women might be distinguished according to genital classes, the gender of these men and women depends on their bodily state in relation to gendered substance, and is thus more importantly related to age and reproductive history than to reproductive biology (Meigs 1990).

Since Bourdieu theorised the relationship between discourse and social action through an appeal to bodily praxis as a mode of knowledge (Bourdieu 1977), anthropologists have been interested in embodiment as a process of practical enactment. Feminist attention to the embodied nature of subjectivity has been influential in moving the discussion from a sociological to a more psychoanalytic domain and exploring the implications of the relationship between the body, sexual identity and the subjectivity of researcher and researched alike. The shift has been important in redirecting the attention of the ethnographer to the non-spoken or non-discursive aspects of social practice, and to the fact that a focus on genital sex is very reductive of the ways in which bodies gender relationships. In general, work on the body has reinforced the awareness of the differences within and between women, and of the limited explanatory force of an appeal to sexual difference, for the male/female dichotomy is not understood universally as either natural or explanatory of social difference.

Complex Subjectivity

Work on the embodied nature of subjectivity is directly related to the developing common interest among anthropologists and feminist scholars in working through the implications of placing a more complex notion of the subject at the centre of our social theories. These common interests in the exploration of complexity have made possible a new alliance between feminism and anthropology. Sameness and difference no longer necessarily constitute the awkward hiatus between feminism and anthropology. Complex subjectivity is relational and these relations provide the possibilities for both similarity and difference to emerge. It is now widely recognised that difference need not preclude similarity, particularly when the global aspects of local interactions are brought into play and consideration is given to the ways in which cultural practices develop in a dynamic relationship with outside forces (Cowan 1996).

For many the way forward in this respect is to focus explicitly on relationships of both similarity and difference, as produced in western theoretical practice and in people's daily lives. There is a return here to the preoccupation with knowledge and its effects, particularly the ways in which knowledges naturalise power. It is defamiliarisation rather than deconstruction that is proposed, undoing connections of kind, increasing awareness of the ways in which domain specific practice (difference) is produced and sustained and looking for ways to blur boundaries (Yanagisako and Delaney 1995). In terms of this agenda the analytical enterprise is itself constituted as political practice and is for many a point of resolution between feminist politics and anthropology, particularly noticeable in the turn towards the study of how western science operates as domain-specific knowledge (e.g. Traweek 1988; Suchman 1987; Franklin 1995), and of how political entities such as nation states naturalise and gender territories and citizens in particular strategies of inclusion and exclusion (Mosse 1985; Stolcke 1995; Williams 1995).

This approach also offers a fruitful point of overlap between those who are inclined to the anthropology of women, looking at the lives of women cross-culturally, and those who are more inclined to look at how gender as a system of difference relates to structures of social inequality. The latter offers a more inclusive approach, but the focus on how similarities and differences are produced in practice (including gender differences) would require that attention be paid to those social situations in which gender differences are highly salient. Thus while in some ways the insistence among certain feminist ethnographers on paying particular attention to the domain of women's practice might appear to mark a return to the essentialist distinctions of previous decades, it is important to acknowledge that attention to the gendered nature of fieldwork, and to the situatedness of knowledge, might require the fieldworker to produce an ethnography of this kind. Among Australian aboriginal peoples, for example, 'women's knowledge' is a distinctive and autonomous domain of expertise (Bell 1993). Such knowledge is now recognised by the white Australian judicial authorities as an essential element of local understandings of land rights despite the fact that such knowledge can only be repeated to other women (with subsequent problems for many establishment male lawyers). A focus on women's practice in a context of this kind should not preclude the question of what gender is doing, how it is produced and sustained.

Thus despite the fact that anthropology has a nervous politics of a kind not easily accepted by activists, there is an increasing interest within the discipline to explore the positive outcomes afforded by the contradictions that a feminist anthropologist is forced to confront. Abu-Lughod remarks in her discussion of the possibilities for developing a new feminist ethnography, that there has been little acknowledgement within anthropology of the ambiguous, in-between status of many persons, researchers and researched alike, for 'built into anthropology was the assumption that we stood outside' (Abu-Lughod 1990: 27). Anthropologists, interested above all in comparative theories of knowledge, are increasingly working with more complex notions of the (knowing) subject, enabled in part through engagement with the contemporary feminist focus on the politics of knowledge.

Feminist Ethnography

Feminist ethnography is an increasingly visible genre of writing, which has usefully been distinguished from the 'anthropology of women', the effort to understand the lives of women across cultures, and the 'feminist anthropology' that is concerned with 'the social and political ramifications of women as the second sex' (Behar 1996: 14). Feminist ethnographers seek to reveal the problematic nature of the authorial 'I', by bringing together contrasting accounts, audiences, and fields of expertise so as to emphasise the processual and partial nature of all ethnographic writing (e.g. Wolf 1992). The field is contentious (see Gordon 1996). Some argue that women's literary and political creativity has gone unrecognised in a particular male genealogy of new experimental writing which has proved very influential in the past decade. Others feel that feminist anthropologists should be wary of experimental post-modern ethnography. They argue that the genre masks the careerism of a group of men, already secure in the academic hierarchy, blind to the politics of difference which they pretend to address, and comforting themselves with an inflated assessment of the real world effects of their experiments (see Mascia-Lees, Sharpe and Cohen 1989; Stacey 1988).

Nevertheless, the focus on writing and the politics of authorship and of reading has become an established concern. Implicit in these concerns is the recognisable feminist preoccupation with the ways in which the canon of the discipline is established and reproduced (Lutz 1996). The writings of women denied professional status, ignored classics – often written by the wives of 'great men' – are being recovered. There is also more attention paid to the work of Third World writers and of women of colour, attention made possible as Visweswaran has argued (following Alarcon 1990), by 'unsettling the (feminist) logic of identification by displacing gender from the center of feminist theory, and starting from a consideration of how race, class or sexuality determines the positioning of a subject' (Visweswaran 1994: 75).

Conclusion

The focus on situated knowledge has produced ethnographies which study relationships between domains of practice, and which can thus embrace difference and similarity, span global and local interests and question in effect how any difference ever emerges as such.

The domains that an anthropological attention bring into view are not necessarily different in kind from those that might appear through other disciplinary lenses. There is cross-disciplinary concern, for example, with concepts of the person and of agency. What anthropology has to offer, above all, is the comparative perspective. Anthropology can show how, for example, it is only in particular western models of personhood that fragmentation appears to be disempowering. In the 1990s, in an intellectual environment where it is possible to conceive of a feminist practice that no longer depends on the exclusionary categories of gender difference, many new possibilities have emerged. The self-styled 'diasporic feminists', working with notions of a 'transnational, translational subjectivity that has developed through the mediation and dissolution of boundaries' (Ong 1996: 366), offer new paradigms for thinking about the relationship between identity and place, between representation, experience and political economy. Through their work we can find ways to imagine how it is possible to maintain the space to think about difference, while not losing sight of the fact that difference appears in the same social contexts in which connections are forged.

References

Abu-Lughod, L. (1990) 'Can There be a Feminist Ethnography?', *Women and Performance*, 18: 7–27.
Alarcón, N. (1990) 'The Theoretical Subject(s) of *This Bridge Called My Back* and Anglo-American Feminism', in G. Anzaldua (ed.) *Making Face, Making Soul: Haciendo Caras*, San Francisco: Aunt Lute, 356–69.
Behar, R. (1996) 'Introduction: Out of Exile', in R. Behar and D. Gordon (eds) *Women Writing Culture*, Berkeley: University of California Press, 1–32.
Bell, D. (1993) 'Yes Virginia, there is a feminist ethnography: reflections from three Australian fields', in D. Bell, P. Caplan and W. J. Karim (eds) *Gendered Fields: Women, Men and Ethnography*, London: Routledge.
Bourdieu, P. (1977) *Outline of a Theory of Practice*, Cambridge: Cambridge University Press.
Caplan, P. (ed.) (1987) *The Cultural Construction of Sexuality*, London: Tavistock.
Collier, J. and S. Yanagisako (1987) *Gender and Kinship: Essays Toward a Unified Analysis*,

Stanford: Stanford University Press.

Cowan, J. (1996) 'Being a Feminist in Contemporary Greece: Similarity and Difference Reconsidered', in N. Charles and F. Hughes-Freeland (eds) *Practising Feminism: Identity, Difference, Power*, London: Routledge, 61–85.

Edwards, J. et al. (1993) *Technologies of Procreation: Kinship in the Age of Assisted Conception*, Manchester: Manchester University Press.

Franklin, S. (1995) 'Science as Culture, Cultures of Science', *Annual Review of Anthropology*, 24: 163–84.

Ginsburg, F. and R. Rapp (1995) *Conceiving the New World Order: The Global Politics of Reproduction*, Berkeley: University of California Press.

Gordon, D. (1996) 'Conclusion: Culture Writing Women: Inscribing Feminist Anthropology', in R. Behar and D. Gordon (eds) *Women Writing Culture*, Berkeley: University of California Press, 429–41.

Harvey, P. (1994) 'Domestic Violence in the Peruvian Andes', in P. Harvey and P. Gow (eds) *Sex and Violence: Issues in Representation and Experience*, London: Routledge, 66–89.

Herdt, G. (ed.) (1994) *Third Sex, Third Gender: Beyond Sexual Dimorphism in Culture and History*, New York: Zone Books.

Laqueur, T. (1990) *Making Sex: Body and Gender from the Greeks to Freud*, Cambridge, Mass.: Harvard University Press.

Lutz, C. (1996) 'The Gender of Theory', in R. Behar and D. Gordon (eds) *Women Writing Culture*, Berkeley: University of California Press, 249–66.

MacCormack, C. and M. Strathern (eds) (1980) *Nature, Culture and Gender*, Cambridge: Cambridge University Press.

Martin, E. (1987) *The Woman in the Body: A Cultural Analysis of Reproduction*, Boston: Beacon.

Mascia-Lees, F., P. Sharpe and C. Cohen (1989) 'The Postmodernist Turn in Anthropology: Cautions from a Feminist Perspective', *Signs*, 15 (1): 7–33.

McDonald, M. (ed.) (1994) 'Introduction: A Social-Anthropological View of Gender, Drink and Drugs', in *Gender, Drink and Drugs*, Oxford: Berg, 1–31.

Meigs, A. (1990) 'Multiple Gender Ideologies and Statuses', in P. Reeves Sanday and R. Goodenough (eds) *Beyond the Second Sex: New Directions in the Anthropology of Gender*, Philadelphia: University of Pennsylvania Press, 101–12.

Moore, H. (1933) 'The Differences Within and the Differences Between', in T. del Valle (ed.) *Gendered Anthropology*, London: Routledge, 193–204.

Moore, H. (1994) *A Passion for Difference*, Oxford: Polity.

Mosse, G. (1985) *Nationalism and Sexuality*, New York: Howard Fertig.

Ong, A. (1996) 'Women Out of China: Traveling Tales and Traveling Theories in Postcolonial Feminism', in R. Behar and D. Gordon (eds) *Women Writing Culture*, Berkeley: University of California Press.

Ortner, S. (1974) 'Is Female to Male as Nature is to Culture?', in M. Rosaldo and L. Lamphere (eds) *Woman, Culture and Society*, Stanford: Stanford University Press, 67–88.

Ortner, S. and H. Whitehead (eds) (1981) *Sexual Meanings: The Cultural Construction of Gender and Sexuality*, Cambridge: Cambridge University Press.

Reiter, R. (ed.) (1975) *Toward an Anthropology of Women*, New York: Monthly Review Press.

Rosaldo, M. (1974) 'Women, Culture and Society: a Theoretical Overview', in M. Rosaldo and L. Lamphere (eds) *Woman, Culture and Society*, Stanford: Stanford University Press, 67–88.

Sacks, K. (1974) 'Engels Revisited: Women, the Organization of Production and Private Property', in M. Rosaldo and L. Lamphere (eds) *Woman, Culture and Society*, Stanford: Stanford University Press, 207–22.

Stacey, J. (1988) 'Can There Be a Feminist Ethnography?', *Women's Studies International Forum* 11 (1): 21–7.

Stolcke, V. (1995) 'Talking Culture: New Boundaries, New Rhetorics of Exclusion in Europe', *Current Anthropology*, 36: 1–24.

Strathern, M. (1987) 'An Awkward Relationship: the Case of Feminism and Anthropology', *Signs*, 12 (2): 276–92.

Strathern, M. (1988) *The Gender of the Gift*, Berkeley: University of California Press.

Strathern, M. (1992) *Reproducing the Future: Anthropology, Kinship and the New Reproductive Technologies*, Manchester: Manchester University Press.

Strathern, M. (1996) 'Gender: Division or Comparison?', in N. Charles and F. Hughes-Freeland (eds) *Practising Feminism: Identity, Difference, Power*, London: Routledge, 38–60.

Suchman, L. (1987) *Plans and Situated Actions: The Problems of Human-Machine Communication*, Cambridge: Cambridge University Press.

Thorne, B. and M. Yalom (eds) (1992) *Rethinking the Family: Some Feminist Questions*, Boston: Northeastern University Press.

Traweek, S. (1988) *Beamtimes and Lifetimes*, Cambridge: Harvard University Press.

Visweswaran, K. (1994) *Fictions of Feminist Ethnography*, Minneapolis: University of Minnesota Press.

Weiner, A. (1976) *Women of Value, Men of Renown*, Austin: University of Texas Press.

Williams, B. (1995) 'Classification Systems Revisited: Kinship, Caste, Race and Nationality as the Flow of Blood and the Spread of Rights', in S. Yanagisako and C. Delaney (eds) *Naturalizing Power: Essays in Feminist Cultural Analysis*, London: Routledge, 201–36.

Wolf, M. (1992) *A Thrice-Told Tale: Feminism, Postmodernism, and Ethnographic Responsibility*, Stanford: Stanford University Press.

Yanagisako, S. and C. Delaney (1995) *Naturalizing Power: Essays in Feminist Cultural Analysis*, London: Routledge.

Further Reading

Atkinson, J. and S. Errington (eds) (1990) *Power and Difference: Gender in Island S.E. Asia*, Stanford: Stanford University Press.

Boddy, J. (1989) *Wombs and Alien Spirits: Women, Men and the Zar Cult in Northern Sudan*, Madison: University of Wisconsin Press.

Cornwall, A. and N. Lindisfarne (1994) *Dislocating Masculinity: Comparative Ethnographies*, London: Routledge.

di Leonardo, M. (1991) *Gender at the Crossroads of Knowledge: Feminist Anthropology in the Postmodern Era*, Berkeley: University of California Press.

Ginsburg, F. (1989) *Contested Lives: The Abortion Debate in an American Community*, Berkeley: University of California Press.

Ginsburg, F. and A. Tsing (1990) *Uncertain Terms: Negotiating Gender in American Culture*, Boston: Beacon Press.

Green, S. (1997) *Urban Amazons*, London: Macmillan.

Martin, E. (1994) *Flexible Bodies: Tracking Immunity in American Culture – From the Days of Polio to the Age of AIDS*, Boston: Beacon.

Moore, H. (1988) *Feminism and Anthropology*, Cambridge: Polity Press.

Scheper-Hughes, N. (1992) *Death Without Weeping: The Violence of Everyday Life in Brazil*, Berkeley: University of California Press.

Strathern, M. (ed.) (1987) *Dealing with Inequality: Analysing Gender Relations in Melanesia and Beyond*, Cambridge: Cambridge University Press.

Tsing, A. (1993) *In the Realm of the Diamond Queen: Marginality In an Out of the Way Place*, Princeton: Princeton University Press.

Chapter 7

Black Feminisms

Kadiatu Kanneh

The very possibility of a chapter entitled 'Black Feminisms' is reliant on particular theoretical and political histories. These recent and contentious histories have developed from debates within Black politics, cultural studies, 'Third World' nationalisms, feminist activism and theories. The aim of this chapter is to pick up a possible narrative thread between and through these histories of identity and debate, examining the meanings and difficulties of Black feminisms and their relationship to cultural and national identities.

The term 'Black' is radically unstable and is applied to various, related political positions. An attempt to trace the meanings that surround and inform this term involves an engagement with its geographical, cultural and political indeterminacies, with its reliance on context and time. As a locus of antagonisms and conflicts, Black feminism distinguishes itself from White or 'First World' feminisms, and is at once involved in cultural or national ideologies, in ways which have become increasingly complex. In order to locate and identify a phenomenon such as 'Black feminism', the contexts of academic convention, cultural domination and cultural currency become determinate factors. Any analysis of the recent emergence of an identifiable field of Black feminist criticism, or Black feminist politics, has to include a keen sensitivity to the marked inscriptions of difference and specificity, of connection and visibility *within* the field.

A major polarity in Western Black feminist thought, particularly for the British context, is that between the terminology and politics of the United States and Britain. For the purposes of United States politics, 'Black' is a term referring to the African-American population, whereas Asian-Americans (meaning both South Asians and, for example, Chinese, Korean, Filipina descendants), Latinas and Native Americans are categorised as 'people of colour'. In Britain, 'Black' is a political category often describing Asians (referring to people of the sub-continent), Africans and Afro-Caribbeans, with often a wider inclusion of 'non-White' people.

The current US preference for racial categorisation based on country or continent of origin or descent, hyphenated with national identity (as in 'African-

American') over the politicised term 'Black', as well as the retaining of the term 'Third World' for North American 'people of colour', at once blurs and begs the distinction between *national* and *cultural* identities. The attempt, in the British context, to sub-categorise 'Black' into 'more accurate' sections, as in the 1991 Census[1] can result in a de-politicising of the term and a further obfuscation/ exclusion of various 'Black' identities under a spuriously scientific 'comprehensiveness'. The titles, 'Black Other', or 'Any other ethnic group' marks the bearer as '*more* other than Black'.

The shifting meanings of 'Black' as a racial, cultural, national or political term has implications for the development and meanings of Black feminisms. The relationship between the terms 'Black' and 'feminism' allows for a sustained critique, both of the feminist movement and identities, and of Black politics.

Beginning with an anthology initially conceived in 1979, the rawness and violence of new articulations and new alliances can be traced. Moraga and Anzaldúa's *This Bridge Called My Back* (1983) is a text of crucial importance for the staking out of what can now be acknowledged as oppositional territory. Its subtitle, 'Writings By Radical Women of Color' immediately shifts these alliances into a political space that allows for connections 'capable of spanning borders of nation and ethnicity'.[2] What this means for an anthology emerging from United States feminist radicalism in the late 1970s and early 1980s is a reconfiguration of identity politics around 'Third World' immigrant women and African-American women. The internationalism of the text, its insistence that both connections and contentions with the United States will form the basis of 'political necessity',[3] is one that is still, in 1983, a fraught and uneasy alliance of differences.

The 'Third World' dimensions of the political arguments in this anthology, based around issues in, for example, Central and South America, in the Caribbean and in South Africa, are primarily contained within the politics of the feminist movement. Toni Cade Bambara's Foreword (Moraga and Anzaldúa 1983) points to 'the initial motive' behind several of the pieces included being a need to 'protest, complain or explain to white feminist would-be allies that there are other ties and visions that bind'. Immediately following this, White feminism becomes secondary, even superfluous: 'the process of examining that would-be alliance awakens us to new tasks' (1983: vi).

Moraga's original Preface supports Bambara's sentiments with a reference to White feminists as 'so-called sisters' (1983: xiii). The prevalent conflicts that emerge from her Introduction are reflected by other writers in the anthology and attest to the complications of both feminist movement and cultural affiliation. Moraga's lesbian identity presents itself, crucially, as an exclusionary threat to her identification with women *and* men of colour. Drawing attention to a continuing political thread throughout the text, Moraga launches an attack on separatism as the luxury of White feminism and the unacceptable sacrifice of feminists of colour: 'But the deepest political tragedy I have experienced is how with such grace, such blind faith, this commitment to women in the feminist movement grew to be exclusive and reactionary. *I call my white sisters on this*' (1983: xiv).

The direct challenge to a White-dominated feminism and the continual calls for a more broad-based movement that allows for *different* cultural/racial communities and politics are significant aspects of *This Bridge Called My Back*. The concentration on relationships *between* women offers a scrutiny of class, race and cultural issues that promises to assault any notion of feminism as a stable place to usher in others.

Otherness, however, is equally not a *stable* place on which to build mutual identifications or communities of recognition. Many of the writers bear witness to misunderstandings and divisions between women of colour themselves. As a political grouping that amalgamates African-American, Asian-American, Latina and Native American women, 'Women of Colour' broaches and re-evaluates the notion of *Black* feminism and necessarily includes within itself urgent questions of cultural, racial and *social* affiliation. Brought into political visibility out of conflict with a predominantly White feminist movement, 'Women of Colour' do not become the automatic site of resolution.

These recognitions of difference and of conflict within difference in the context of feminism makes *This Bridge* an important milestone in Black feminist writing. The introduction of 'Third World' alongside African-American feminisms allows for a discussion of racial, economic *and* national issues that act as critical points of tension in defining Black feminism. The statement of Chrystos, as a Native American, that: 'I am afraid of white people' (1983: 68), a statement aimed at (White) feminist collectives, can be read alongside Moraga's anxiety – as a Chicana – about Black lesbians: 'Black dykes ... I felt ignored me, wrote me off because I looked white' (1983: xvii). If to be a 'Woman of Colour' is not (necessarily) a matter of *physical* visibility, the emphasis in the text slides between cultural, economic and social issues, negotiating and questioning the limits and meanings of *racial* identities. Black American women are represented here as *another ethnicity* within a larger 'Third World' movement, which *also* incorporates Japanese Americans. That Black Americans are *not* 'Third World' peoples or *new* immigrants allows the text to indirectly highlight the *differences* between *African-American* and *Black* feminisms and to insist on the *non*-comprehensiveness of African-American feminisms for theories and politics of race, culture or class.

Each chapter in the anthology is a self-categorisation within these limits. The repeated, 'I stand here as ... I am a ...', calls attention to a late twentieth-century preoccupation with dual or sub-national categories and with difference. Looked at from one angle the anthology bristles with conflict, with the *splintering* of feminism into disjointed and violently delineated groups (or individuals). Looked at again, the 'poor women, black and third-world women, and lesbians' (Audre Lorde, in Moraga and Anzaldúa 1983: 98) allow for coalitions, for fluidity and change. The temporary nature of these *un*-easy alliances and identities – spoken with such desperation and tension in 1979 – remain as one of the most significant challenges for Black feminism to date.

This Bridge is a useful point of departure for a chapter about late twentieth-century Black feminisms because it reveals the difficulties and complexities that accrue to both Black *and* feminist identities. Moraga, in her 1983 Foreword, claims that the original conception of *This Bridge* is now showing its age. Erupting primarily within and against mainstream (White) feminist movement, the 1979 preoccupations did not include detailed discussion of relationships between women and *men* of colour. Solidarity as *non-White* women creates a focus on feminism and Black/White divisions. The differences *between* women of different ethnicities, and different cultural backgrounds, pushes to one side any *concentrated* discussion of families or communities. They become what is different *from*, excluded *by*, hidden *behind*.

The difficulties of an alliance that places *visible* against *felt*, remembered or hidden difference presents a problematic unity in the anthology, revealing itself particularly in certain writings by Women of Colour who do not identity (unproblematically) as *Black*. Rosario Morales, for example, who accounts for herself as 'indian bones … spanish sounds', also describes an ambiguous social position: 'what I do remember is to walk in straight and white into the store and say good morning in my see how white how upper class how refined and kind voice all crisp with consonants bristling with syllables' (1983: 108).

Here, the confusion of racial identity with class identity, both of which are revealed as indicative of each other, succeeds in assessing 'true' Black identity as being at odds with an ambiguous, invisible identity that is, nevertheless, Black, or 'of colour'. The accepted community of Black women in other sections of the text is here disrupted with the anxiety, 'you don't belong' (1983: 108). This anguished ambiguity sits uncomfortably alongside the *Black Feminist Statement* from the 'Combahee River Collective' that very clearly and coherently sets out the agenda, meaning, genesis and beliefs of Black feminist organisation, stating that the Black feminist is what is distinguishable from and between Black (male) liberation movements and the White left (1983: 211).

The consistently oppositional stance of the essays and ideas in the anthology, defining non-White female identity continually in terms of difference *from* (community, collective, the visible, the obvious, or the White, the male …) creates a volume that presents the rage and violence of identities *in the process* of self-definition. Placing a range of histories, familial and cultural subjectivities under the difficult banner of 'Women of Color' ushers in an assault on feminist politics from a range of positions. Feminist identification becomes a matter of uneasy alliances, of negotiating difference, of interpreting the meaning and validity of sexuality, class, heritage, culture and even *race*. The spiritual visions underpinning many of the literary and political statements attest to the dedication to alternative self-definitions that the volume attempts to represent. Gloria Anzaldúa's reading of the Tarot (1983: 246), Cherríe Moraga's belief in astrology (1983: 248), and the final piece of the volume, by Chrystos, direct themselves to a search for other ways of living beyond North American capitalism. Chrystos's claim that 'We have lost touch with the sacred' (1983: 244) adds a kind of final vision to the book's presentation of 'alternative' values.

This 'alternative', spiritual re-definition of self emerges in the writing of Alice Walker – a Black feminist, or 'Womanist' – whose contribution to Black feminist criticism and politics in the United States and beyond has been critical. Alice Walker's rejection of the term 'feminist' for Black women in favour of 'Womanist' in her 1983 collection of essays is a response to cultural difference and the specificities of her own (Black, Southern) sense of community. With references to histories of slavery and sassiness, gardens of flowers, food and 'the Folk', Walker creates an essentially 'home-grown' vision of the Black feminist who '*Loves* the Spirit' (1984: xii).[4]

In Search of Our Mothers' Gardens, with essays written from 1970 to the early 1980s, is a collection that emphasises the significance of 'home', loyalty and roots. The South is the place of 'the people' who provide the emotional energy of the writing: 'I see the same faces, hear the same soft voices, take a nip, once in a while, of the same rich mellow corn, or wine' (1971: 138). Looking to the South for 'wholeness' (1975: 48) and for 'continuity' (1976: 13), Walker's sense of herself as a 'Black revolutionary artist' (1971: 130) is linked indissolubly to her sense of origins and to her sense of connection with a Southern Black community and identity: 'And when I write about the people there, in the strangest way it is as if I am not writing about them at all, but about myself. The artist then is the voice of the people, but she is also The People' (1971: 138).

This certainty about belonging, identity and *speaking for* a definable 'people' contrasts Walker with the conflictual, emergent and divided subjectivities that present themselves in *This Bridge*. Walker's re-discovery and popularisation of Black Renaissance writers like Zora Neale Hurston have, for her, the logic of unearthing a family. In her title essay, 'In Search of Our Mothers' Gardens', Walker's eulogy to her mother's un-famous artistry becomes witness not only to an American, but to a long *African* heritage (1974: 243). This acknowledgement of community beyond the United States and the Southern states becomes a central point of Walker's writing, and her sense of herself as *spokesperson* for the community becomes a larger and more problematic claim in the context of international, or other Black feminisms.

With the publication of her novel, *Possessing the Secret of Joy* (1992), Walker's presentation of 'African' culture (in general) under American feminist judgement, reveals the difficulties of her position as spokesperson for *all* Black women. Her loyal allegiance to the United States in terms of 'freedom' and escape allows her to represent the 'barbarity' of African practices (including the undifferentiated practices of clitoridectomy, excision and infibulation) as part of a larger state of cultural unfreedom. Africa as victim *needing* American feminism – an Africa to which Walker makes unhesitating claim – points towards the dangers of *internationalist* Black feminism within the United States. The dimension in her previous writing of spiritual communion with her foremothers becomes a difficulty when applied *over* cultural and national borders. The complicated and uncertain union between the 'Third World' perspective and Black feminism in *This Bridge* can be recalled here both as a proviso and a corrective.

The institutionalisation of Black feminism in the United States becomes solidified through collections such as *Home Girls: A Black Feminist Anthology* (1983). *Home Girls* sets out to promote Black feminism as distinct from both a White-dominated feminist movement and the exclusive concerns of Black men. Barbara Smith is then able to state, in 1983, that 'we have a movement of our own' (1983: xxxi). The choice of anthology as a form for representing Black feminisms is an important one, allowing, as in *This Bridge*, a range of political ideas, concerns and approaches to exist together, and giving the impression of a field *in the making*. As Barbara Smith puts it in her Introduction to *Home Girls*: 'anthologies which bring together many voices seem particularly suited to the multiplicity of issues of concern to women of color' (1983: xlix). This multiplicity of issues covers subjects such as lesbianism, Black women artists, the family, culture and feminist organisation.

The significance of the concept of 'home' in the title – one of the concepts that is central to Alice Walker's ideas – lies in the longing for, or realisation of, a place from which to speak. This place of self and recognition is also a place to *claim* and to *own*. It provides the possibility of being an *insider*: 'Home has always meant a lot to people who are ostracized as racial outsiders in the public sphere. It is above all a place to be ourselves' (1983: li).

The conflation of Black women with 'Third World' women in the Introduction points to a difficulty that also hovers over the language of *This Bridge*. Merging the identity of racial outsider with *national* outsider, and therefore identifying *unproblematically* with women of the 'Third World' (particularly African women) confuses the theoretical positions of United States Black feminists. The identity of 'home' becomes, in this formulation, a widening and elastic metaphor of possession.

However, the final piece in the collection and, in many ways, the most significant, addresses precisely this issue of home, belonging and possession. Bernice Johnson Reagon's 'Coalition Politics: Turning the Century' approaches the difficulties, dangers and necessities of feminist coalition by continually examining the meaning of 'home'. If 'home' is cultural and racial *security*, the certainty of naming and defining, then coalition has nothing to do with 'home'. For Reagon, speaking from a background of Black Civil Rights, the idea of feminist coalition involves the *incursion* of *different* women into feminism, its constant re-definition through conflict and flexibility. It does not, for her, involve the comfortable embracing of similar women into a safe place: 'In a coalition you have to give, and it is different from your home. You can't stay there all the time' (1983: 359).

Barbara Smith's later article, 'Between a Rock and a Hard Place: Relationships Between Black and Jewish Women' (1984) continues with the issue of coalition and self-examination by exploring relationships between African-American and Jewish women, particularly within the feminist movement. Her clear statement: 'I am anti-Semitic' (1984: 69), does not leave her with a safe place from which to speak and allows her to discuss honestly the possibilities of alliance and conflict – even competition – between Jewish and Black women. Refusing the temptation of 'ranking ... oppressions' (1984: 75), Smith's essay considers the connections as well as the mistrust between the two groups, emphasising (with references to Reagon's earlier piece) the positive and vital nature of coalition politics. Referring to Black women as 'Third World' throughout the piece allows for a clear-cut argument between two apparently internally undifferentiated groups. The category 'Black', then, however, operates *indistinctly across* national and cultural boundaries.

Carole Boyce Davies's recent text *Black Women, Writing and Identity* (1994) addresses this tendency to homogenise and delimit Blackness and Black womanhood to one particular location or cultural experience. Taking the experiences of Black women (im-)migrants as her primary example, Boyce Davies insists on the continual re-negotiation of Black women's identity *between* places and nations. In this way, Black womanhood and therefore Black feminism cannot become stratified to one particular history or set of preoccupations. Boyce Davies's emphasis on 'migratory subjectivity existing in multiple locations' (1994: 4) points *also* to the imperative to name, place and historicise where one is speaking *from* and *to* whom. Her identification of the United States as primary signifier and therefore *definer* of Black feminism through publication and cultural strength is significant here: 'Thus to identify Black women's writing primarily with United States writing is to identify with US hegemony' (1994: 4).

The debates throughout the 1980s in Britain around the identity of Blackness – who is to be included and who ruled out – took place in the context of a conscious political movement to locate Blackness within a *range* of communities who were excluded in particular, racialised ways, from *Britishness*. Blackness as the identity of non-White others – including, for example, Afro-Caribbeans, Africans, Asians, Chinese – placed issues of race above issues of culture, religion or origins, and created a broadbased, collective identification around racial difference:

> In Britain in the 1980s, this shared sense of objectification was articulated when the racialized disempowered and fragmented sought empowerment in a gesture of politicized collective action. In naming the shared space of marginalization as 'black', postcolonial migrants of different languages, religions, cultures and classes consciously constructed a

political identity shaped by the shared experience of racialization and its consequences.

(1997: 3)

Heidi Safia Mirza's Reader, *Black British Feminism* (1997), is organised around this inclusive interpretation of 'Black' as a term that operates similarly to 'Black', 'Women of Colour' and 'Third World Women' in the US.

The different histories behind Black feminist writing in Britain and in African countries provide different conditions for political identities. For Afro-Caribbean, Asian and African British feminists, the link with a 'Third World' subjectivity is nuanced, generally, by more direct familial experience than is common in Black feminist writing from the United States. The relatively short history of Black feminism in Britain, due to the more recent settlement of postcolonial migrants[5] (although the history of Black people in Britain, particularly in the port cities of Cardiff, Liverpool, Bristol, London, spans colonial history – see Fryer 1984) is inexorably tied to issues of migration, re-location, 'origins' and cultural differ-ence. The cultural stake in the nation of Britain is frequently problematised as well as energised by personal or familial memories of arrival.

The anthology, *Motherlands* (1991), emphasises the powerful influence of 'Third World' origins on the writing of British feminists. The term 'motherlands' is linked with histories of exile, longing and displacement, and the editor, Susheila Nasta's stated aim in the Introduction, to 'generate a cross-cultural dialogue between critics and writers whether in "First" or "Third" worlds' (1991: xviii), reveals the intention of the book to remain sensitive to national/cultural speci-ficities. The third section of the text, 'Absent and Adopted Mother(land)s', under-lines the project's concern with connections, with the liminalities of nations and homes, and with the continual re-negotiation of racial and cultural identities. 'Home Girls', particularly in this section, gains a complicated and layered set of meanings, analysing the writing of immigrants and migrants whose home is both present and elsewhere.

The reading of African, Caribbean and Asian novels primarily explores the 'universal' issues and themes of motherhood, native language (or 'mother-tongue') and the self-expression of women within the institutions of family, nation, community. The role of colonial institutions – with their imposition of gendered or national identities – places the criticism of these texts within a wider problematic of 'First/Third' world politics and power. The criticism of these texts also introduces the question of the politics of 'First World' criticism of 'Third World' texts. The difficulties of writing about (explaining, analysing) fiction from one (social/cultural) context out of another can itself risk the dynamics of im-perialist encounter. The reading of Black women's writing from the West or the 'Third World' has, then, to remain aware of the insights of Black *and* 'Third World' feminisms.

A text that is discussed more than once in the collection is Ama Ata Aidoo's novel, *Our Sister Killjoy* (1977). As a narrative that charts the experiences of a

Ghanaian woman in Europe, the text acts as a locus for exploring the difficulties of dialogue between White/Western and African women. Histories of imperialism and the realities of racism and exploitation underlie Sissie's analysis of inter-continental migration and inter-racial friendship between women. The peculiarities of this text, besides its blending of poetry and prose, of letter-form, autobiographical address and third person narrative, are the simultaneous recognition of the oppression of Africa and the violence of racism, and the representation of a relationship between two women that curiously *reverses* the expected power structure. The merging of genres and the shift in authorial address places attention on narrative voice and expression – on the importance of narrative control. In this way, the relationship between Sissie and Marija is related from a position of *knowledge*, with Sissie taking up a 'masculine' position against Marija's emotional *dependence*.

The effect of this is a narrative that promotes African subjectivity to the place of observer, definer and historical judge. Reversing dominant perspectives, African female subjectivity presents European history, landscape, people and language as ethnographically strange, with Marija's German English placed at a similar expressive disadvantage as pidgin in European ethnographies/novels. The feminism of the text is, then, deliberately and inescapably placed within specific cultural locations, at the point of conflict between dominant and subordinate national identities. 'Black feminism', in relation to this text, is both a re-evaluation of African femininity in respect of African communities and men, and a re-examination of racial and cultural differences between women.

The letter that moves towards the conclusion of the novel emphasises Sissie's 'anti-western neurosis', and her fear of the loss of African identity – particularly African femininity. As a letter addressed to an African man, the text refuses a direct engagement with the politics or feminisms of 'the West' and yearns instead for the autonomy of definition 'That is why, above all, we have to have our secret language. We must create this language ... So that we shall make love with words and not fear of being overheard' (1977: 116).

However, the 'authenticity' of origins, of cultural identity, of race, prevail as issues within the politics of Black feminisms. Identity politics and debates over 'mixed race' identity, forms of racism and class complicate the broad terrain of 'racial difference' on which 'Blackness' is identified. It is here that the impact of postmodernism on Black feminisms has been, in some ways, enabling. Its corrective against identity politics, against the 'authenticity' of Blackness, allows for multiple Black female identities to be expressed, recognised and valorised:

> A postmodern black feminist identity ... is not just based on racism and oppression but on recognizing the fluidity and fragmented nature of racialized and gendered identities. In this sense we can reclaim subjectivity from the cul de sac of identity politics and reinstate it in terms of a powerful, conscious form of political agency.
>
> (Mirza 1997: 13)

bell hooks's essay, 'Postmodern Blackness', explores the relevance of post-modernist theories for Black politics. Her recognition of the *threat* that post-modernism imposes on Black politics is significant and exposes the difficulties and dangers of postmodernist thinking for Black feminisms. As a critique of identity politics, potmodernism can be seen to threaten the formation and sus-taining of an oppositional voice against the reality of racist society and insti-tutions. As Pratibha Parmar claims:

> To assert an individual and collective identity as a black woman has been a necessary historical process, both empowering and strengthening. To organize self-consciously as black women was and continues to be important; that form of organization is not arbitrary, but is based on a political analysis of our common economic and cultural oppressions.
>
> (Parmar 1987: 68)

However, postmodernism's deconstruction of 'the subject', including 'the Black subject', or 'the Black female subject' can *also* be seen as liberating the diversity of Black lived experience and subjectivities: 'Such a critique allows us to affirm multiple black identities, varied black experience. It also challenges colonial imperialist paradigms of black identity which represent blackness one-dimen-sionally in ways that reinforce and sustain white supremacy' (hooks 1991: 28).

The autonomy of definition is a major issue within Black feminisms. However, this issue has a range of dimensions, as this brief 'narrative' of Black feminisms reveals. The layering of antagonisms, of conflicts and struggles that Black femin-isms have undergone, whether within the general feminist movement, within cultural/racial communities, and, finally, between continents and cultures, defies any easy definition of a politics or an identity. The insistent need for an awareness of global inequalities and cultural difference, initially called for by Black femin-isms, is a difficulty and an ongoing project within and between Black feminisms. In conclusion, the novel, *Our Sister Killjoy*, provides a useful and telling comment on the pitfalls and dangers of defining ourselves and others: 'I know everyone calls you Sissie, but what is your name?' (Aidoo 1977: 131).

Notes

1. 'After consultation with the Commission for Racial Equality, among others, nine separate categories – White, Black Caribbean, Black African, Black Other, Indian, Pakistani, Bangladeshi, Chinese, Any other ethnic group – were decided upon' (Ang-Lygate 1995: 18).
2. Cherríe Moraga, 'Refugees of a World On Fire', Foreword to the second edition, Cherríe Moraga and Gloria Anzaldúa (eds) *This Bridge Called My Back*.
3. Ibid.
4. *In Search of Our Mothers' Gardens*, published in Britain by The Women's Press, 1984; first published by Harcourt Brace Jovanovich in 1983, xii.

5. 'However, if genealogies span centuries, can we undertake a genealogy of Black British feminism when the immediate history of concerted black feminist activity in Britain reaches back only over the last 50 years, over the relatively short time of postcolonial migration and settlement here?' Heidi Safia Mirza (1997: 6).

References

Aidoo, Ama Ata (1977) *Our Sister Killjoy*, Harlow: Longman.

Ang-Lygate, Magdalene (1995) 'Shades of Meaning', *Trouble and Strife* 31: 15–20.

Boyce Davies, Carole (1994) *Black Women, Writing and Identity: Migrations of the Subject*, London: Routledge.

Fryer, Peter (1984) *Staying Power: The History of Black People in Britain*, London: Pluto.

hooks, bell (1991) 'Postmodern Blackness', in *Yearning: Race, Gender and Cultural Politics*, London: Turnaround.

Mirza, Heidi Safia (1997) *Black British Feminism: A Reader*, London: Routledge.

Moraga, Cherríe and Gloria Anzaldúa (eds) (1983) *This Bridge Called My Back*, New York: Kitchen Table: Women of Color Press.

Nasta, Susheila (ed.) (1991) *Motherlands: Black Women's Writings from Africa, the Caribbean and South Asia*, London: The Women's Press.

Parmar, Pratibha (1997) 'Other Kinds of Dreams', in Heidi Safia Mirza (1997). First published in *Feminist Review*, Special issue, 'The Past Before Us: Twenty Years of Feminism', no. 31, Spring 1989: 55–65.

Smith, Barbara (ed.) (1983) *Home Girls: A Black Feminist Anthology*, New York: Kitchen Table: Women of Color Press.

Smith, Barbara (1984) 'Between a Rock and a Hard Place: Relationships Between Black and Jewish Women', in Elly Bulkin, Minnie Bruce Pratt and Barbara Smith (eds), *Yours in Struggle: Three Perspectives on Anti-Semitism and Racism*, New York: Long Haul Press.

Walker, Alice (1984) *In Search of our Mothers' Gardens*, London: The Women's Press.

Walker, Alice (1992) *Possessing the Secret of Joy*, London: Jonathan Cape.

Further Reading

Cannon, Katie G. (1995) *Katie's Canon: Womanism and the Soul of the Black Community*, New York: Continuum.

Carby, Hazel (1987) *Reconstructing Womanhood: The Emergence of the Afro-American Woman Novelist*, New York; Oxford: Oxford University Press.

Cobham and Collins (eds) (1990) *Watchers and Seekers: Creative Writing By Black Women in Britain*, Cambridge: Cambridge University Press.

Collins, Patricia Hill (1990) *Black Feminist Thought: Knowledge, Consciousness and the Politics of Empowerment*, London: Unwin Hyman.

hooks, bell (1982) *Ain't I a Woman: Black Women and Feminism*, London and Sydney: Pluto Press.

hooks, bell (1984) *Feminist Theory: From Margin to Center*, Boston: South End Press.

hooks, bell (1992) *Black Looks: Race and Representation*, Boston: South End Press.

hooks, bell (1993) *Sisters of the Yam: Black Women and Self-Recovery*, Boston: South End Press.

Hull, Gloria T., Patricia Bell Scott and Barbara Smith (eds) (1992) *All the Women Are White, All the Blacks Are Men, but Some of Us Are Brave: Black Women's Studies*, New York: Feminist Press.

James, Stanlie M. and Abena P. A. Busia (eds) (1993) *Theorizing Black Feminisms: The Visionary Pragmatism of Black Women*, London: Routledge.

Stratton, Florence (1994) *African Literature and the Politics of Gender*, London and New York: Routledge.

Tate, Claudia (1985) *Black Women Writers at Work*, Harpenden, Herts: Oldcastle Books.

Williams, Patricia J. (1993) *The Alchemy of Race and Rights*, London: Virago; originally published Harvard University Press, 1991.

Chapter 8

Post-colonial Feminist Theory

Sara Mills

Before trying to encompass the concerns of post-colonial feminist theory, it is necessary first to describe mainstream post-colonial theory. Post-colonial theory developed, in essence, from the work of the colonial discourse theorist Edward Said, particularly his books *Orientalism* (1978) and *Culture and Imperialism* (1993). Said analysed the way that Europe in the nineteenth century represented many of the cultures with which it came into contact through imperial expansion; he argued that the West produced these other cultures as an Other to a Western norm. For example, travellers and scholars represented these other cultures as not only different from British culture, but also as negatively different. Thus, for Said, other peoples were described as lazy, degenerate, uncivilised, barbaric – as Other to the civilised, hard-working British. Post-colonial theory has developed in the last ten years, both building on Said's work and reacting to some of its globalising tendencies (see Ahmad 1993). It is concerned to analyse and theorise the enduring impact of nineteenth-century European colonialism, both in those countries, such as India and Africa, which were colonised and in those, such as Britain and France, which colonised. Post-colonial theorists consider that there were a range of different colonial and imperial relations during the nineteenth century which still have a major effect on the way that cultures see themselves.[1] It is this concern with the present-day legacy of imperialism which is the fundamental focus of post-colonial theory. Whilst post-colonial theory covers a very wide range of theoretical concerns, it is broadly focused not only on the analysis of economic and political structures, but also on the examination of the development of particular structures of thinking and behaviour.

Feminist post-colonial theorists are not a unified group. However, they can be said to be those feminists who have reacted against the lack of address to gender issues in mainstream post-colonial theory and also against the universalising tendencies within Western feminist thought. Post-colonial feminist theory has been extremely influential in the following ways: firstly, it has brought about a 'worlding' of mainstream feminist theory; feminist theory has moved from a rather parochial concern with white, middle-class English-speaking women, to a focus on women in different national and cultural contexts. It has also forced a

argues that the obsessive cleanliness of the Victorians, which centred on the management of women's labour within the household, produced a particular type of domesticity which was very labour-intensive. Within the Victorian period, the number of household tasks increased because of this concern with cleanliness, and within the colonial sphere, the role of the British female was as a manager of numerous servants employed to maintain the colonial household as an epitome of this type of 'civilised' domestic management. McClintock is thus able to tie in gender ideologies and power hierarchies with those of imperialism. She states that imperialism was 'a violent encounter with pre-existing hierarchies of power that took shape not as an unfolding of its own inner destiny but as an untidy, opportunistic interference with other regimes of power' (McClintock 1995: 6). The operation of patriarchy within the Home context was one of those pre-existing hierarchies of power. What she terms the 'cult of domesticity' was a central feature of the assertion of colonial rule over other countries and in fact British colonial domestic management became a central part of the 'education' of 'native' subjects within the mission system: 'the mission station became a threshold institution for transforming domesticity rooted in European class and gender roles into domesticity as controlling a colonized people' (McClintock 1995: 35). The way homes were managed within the colonial context by British women was taken to be an exemplar for the 'natives', and there were numerous conduct books and household management manuals to help achieve this exemplary status. These texts were influential in surveying and constraining British females almost as much as they were in giving guidelines on how servants should be controlled (see Mills 1996). The texts themselves openly draw attention to the fact that if the colonial household is managed well, and presents itself as clean and well-organised, so will the rest of the empire. Thus, women's domestic labour (both that of the British woman and the female and male servants she controlled) was an integral part of the underpinning of imperial rule.

Rajeswari Sunder Rajan has contributed to this debate on the role of the representation of women within the colonial context in her focus on the image of Indian women, within both the colonial and the post-colonial context. In the same way as many of the critics in Sangari and Vaid's (1996) collection of essays, *Re-casting Women: Essays in Colonial History*, Rajan stresses that the parameters of post-colonial female subjectivity are mapped out both by colonial and anti-colonial forces, and that the boundaries and content of femininity, at a symbolic level, are often where issues relating to national identity are worked out. Thus, when there are discussions on how Indian women are treated, this is often a question of national importance, concerning the way that present-day cultures relate to tradition and to Western influence. However, rather than seeing this as a restrictive process, as many critics have, describing the state of agentlessness which indigenous females are attributed, Rajan sees that it is possible to 'explore ... the historically victimized ... female subject as the site for the constitution of alternative subjectivities' (Rajan 1993: 11). Rather than taking on board uncritically the colonial representations of Indian females as passive victims lacking in agency, she seeks to 'displace the traditional construction of the "sati" (the widow who dies upon her husband's funeral pyre) in terms of one who chooses to die/is forced to die, first on to the questions of the embodied subject (the subject of pain) and then onto (precolonial) literary and historical representations of the widow who chooses to *live*' (Rajan 1993: 11). This does not mean that she glorifies the burning of widows, but that she explores from a variety of different perspectives the possibilities of subject-position which are mapped out for these women and with which they then negotiate. Like Gayatri Spivak's more recent work, Rajan is thus concerned to rethink agency particularly as it relates to indigenous females (Spivak 1993b). Thus, whilst much Western feminist theory has been concerned to be critical of essentialism (that is, the notion that there is an essence of 'woman' which all women, regardless of nationality and culture, possess), post-colonial feminist theory has been moving in a more productive direction. The critique of essentialism has involved Western feminists in the adoption of a position whereby it is difficult to posit agency or a voice from which to speak to/for other women. If the notion of 'woman' is questioned, then the fundamental base on which feminism is founded seems to be undermined. Post-colonial feminism, because of this concern to move away from a simplistic Western individualistic analysis of agency, which does not 'fit' models of indigenous female behaviour, has tried to develop new ways of describing and theorising agency. They are also concerned to try to move away from the notion, often implicit in Western feminist writings, that 'third-world' women are all the same, that is, that they share some sort of essence. Gayatri Spivak has argued for the adoption of a strategic essentialism, that is, rather than assuming that one *is* a particular type of subject and thus a particular type of essence, she suggests that there may be certain circumstances, particularly in resistance movements, where it is necessary to adopt a particular type of role and hence subject-position strategically. Despite the contradictions inherent in this position, it does entail a position of agency; as Spivak puts it: 'I don't want a theory of essences' – what she wants is a theory of agency and strategy (1993b: 15).

British Women's Involvement in Colonialism

There has been a great deal of debate within post-colonial feminist theory about how to interpret the actions of British women within colonialism. As I mentioned above, post-colonial theory characterises the colonial period as one where British men were the main actors and where British women only played a subsidiary role. In historical accounts of the empire, British women were often portrayed as causing the downfall of the empire by creating distance between the colonisers and their colonial subjects. For example, it has been asserted that the memsahibs in India, because they brought to an end easy sexual relations between British males and their Indian concubines, brought in a period of greater distance between the colonial subjects and their rulers. Early feminist work in this area set about rewriting this history; it centred on recovering the history of women within the British empire, portraying them in a positive light, uninvolved with the oppression of colonialism, and in many cases trying to resist colonial rule. Jane Haggis has been very critical of some of this work, arguing that this focus on white women serves both to silence colonised women and to represent colonised people as ungendered (Haggis 1990). However, more recent work has tried to move away from the tendency to eulogise British women and has concentrated on try-ing to analyse the complexity of their positions, both as part of and distant from the power structures of the colonial state (Ware 1992; Mills 1991; Chaudhuri and Strobel 1992). This has involved the development of a more theoretically based form of interpretation which does not focus on value and judgement. Chaudhuri and Strobel's collection of essays, *Western Women and Imperialism: Complicity and Resistance*, in particular, is focused on the need to examine the way in which British women in India and Africa constituted themselves as subjects in the process of, for example, campaigning for 'equal rights' for those women whom they saw as oppressed because of practices such as clitoridectomy, sati, child marriage and the harem/polygamy. In the process of campaigning for women whom they considered to be more badly treated than themselves, British women carved out for themselves both a political voice and also a position from which they could view themselves as relatively privileged. British women were very in-volved in campaigns for women's rights in the colonial context, for example they campaigned against the Contagious Diseases Acts in India, for world temper-ance, against slavery, against the killing of twins, all of which were often explicitly focused on the alleviation of suffering amongst 'native' women. But this cam-paigning was more a fundamental element in British women achieving a political voice for themselves. This resulted in women in other countries becoming a vehicle whereby Western women could achieve a subject position for themselves, often at the expense of indigenous women's subject-position and sense of agency. Gayatri Spivak has been especially critical of this process whereby Western women speak for a universal female subject, when in fact it is the voices of the 'other' female subjects and the variety and range of those voices which are occluded. The essays in the Chaudhuri and Strobel collection both describe in some detail the range of activities in which British women were engaged within the colonial sphere, challenging the notion that it was primarily a male space, and also examine the way in which British women both resisted and were com-plicit with colonial ideologies and colonial rule. In this way, it is now possible to analyse British's women's activities without feeling that it is necessary to reclaim and revalue them.

Subaltern Subjects

Chandra Talpade Mohanty was instrumental in questioning the production of the 'Third World woman' as a homogeneous category in Western feminist texts. She considers the ways in which certain feminist texts produce the 'third world' woman as someone who 'leads an essentially truncated life based on her feminine gender (read: sexually constrained) and being "third world" (read: ignorant, poor, uneducated, tradition-bound, domestic, family-oriented, victimized, etc.)' (1984: 337). In much the same way as the nineteenth-century British women discussed above carved out for themselves a political voice through their focus on what they saw as the 'plight' of women in India and Africa, so Western feminists today often present themselves as modern, educated, controlling their sexuality and their bodies, in stark contrast to their image of the 'third world' woman. It is not simply a question of representation, but also a question of the political agendas which are assumed: Mohanty argues that certain Western feminists in their theoretical work have focused on an '(implicitly consensual) priority of issues around which apparently all women are to organise' (Mohanty 1984: 334). She goes on to argue against the type of universalising which some Western feminists have advanced, assuming that women are 'an already constituted, coherent group with identical interests and desires, regardless of class, ethnic or racial location or contradictions' and this 'implies a notion of gender or sexual difference or even patriarchy ... which can be applied universally and cross-culturally' (1984: 337). This type of theorising, which focuses on the oppression of women globally, has the effect of constituting women as powerless, mistaking 'the discursively consensual homogeneity of "women" as a group ... for the historically specific material reality of groups of women' (1984: 338). Mohanty's critique of Western feminism has been central to a rethinking of the essential bases of feminist thought: what the terms 'woman' or 'women' refer to, and so on. Together with the type of critique mounted on essentialist thinking, which I mentioned above, post-colonial feminist theory has brought questions of who is speaking for whom and to what end into the forefront of discussion (Fuss 1989; Butler 1990).

Gayatri Spivak has also developed a critique of this homogenising tendency within Western discourse when discussing the 'third world'; however, Spivak tries to isolate the emphasis on certain types of colonised subject rather than others by Western theorists (Spivak 1993a). She discusses the extent to which certain elite indigenous subjects within the colonial period were complicit with the colonial authorities, and it is this subject whom she locates as the one who most approximates to colonial notions of what the Third World is like. By contrast, the subaltern, the non-elite colonial subject, is 'irretrievably heterogeneous' (1993a: 79). Spivak stresses that the subaltern subject was often involved in insurrections against the colonial authorities but should not be considered to be outside the sway of colonial determinants and does not therefore constitute a 'pure form of consciousness' (1993a: 81). When discussing the subaltern female subject she notes that 'both as object of colonialist historiography and as subject of insurgency, the ideological construction of gender keeps the male dominant. If, in the context of colonial production, the subaltern has no history, and cannot speak, the subaltern as female is even more deeply in shadow' (1993a: 83). In order to speak of this subaltern female subject the Western feminist critic therefore has to 'unlearn female privilege' (1993a: 91), in the sense that she has to think about the history of her position in relation to the subaltern.

In her article 'Three women's texts and a critique of imperialism', Spivak significantly reorients post-colonial feminist criticism in forcing a re-examination of some of the key literary texts in women's studies, so that, rather than analysing them as 'the psychobiography of a militant female subject' as many Western feminists have done, and charting the development of an autonomous female psyche, one is forced to 'wrench oneself away from the mesmerising focus on the "subject-constitution" of the female individualist' (1985: 245). If feminists focus on the white, central female characters in texts such as *Jane Eyre* and *Wide Sargasso Sea*, then in some senses, they are caught up in the text's own logic which is determined by its production within the colonial context. Thus, in this type of individualistically focused type of reading, feminists would be unable to examine the production of other subject-positions, or even perhaps more importantly, the marginalising of other subject-positions. Particularly in her analysis of Jean Rhys's *Wide Sargasso Sea*, Spivak demonstrates that by close textual analysis it is possible to trace the way that certain characters are made marginal to the text. In this text, Christophine the Martiniquan maid is tangential to the narrative: 'she cannot be contained by a novel which rewrites a canonical English text within the European novelistic tradition in the interest of the white Creole rather than the native' (1985: 253). Thus although Rhys' text rewrites *Jane Eyre* so that 'the woman from the colonies is not sacrificed as an insane animal for her sister's consolidation' (Spivak 1985: 251), it is necessary to see that this novel is still written from the perspective of the coloniser. The very form of the novel, with its focus on a highly individualised subject, cannot be significantly revised to cope with diversity and other subject-positions. Firdous Azim has found this of particular interest when she has described the development of the novel form in relation to colonialism, and she, like Spivak, is convinced that the novel is a colonial form, in that the development of extreme forms of individualism served colonial ends, representing a particular type of subjectivity which was implicitly contrasted to undifferentiated 'native' subjects (Azim 1993). Not only is this important in terms of the development of certain kinds of cultural production, but it is also important in terms of the types of sensibility which are produced within a culture, and which are taken to be self-evident.

Chela Sandoval has named a particular type of theorising within this field as

'US Third World feminism' to describe a form of feminist theory which sets itself in opposition to the dominant or hegemonic feminism of white, middle-class Anglo-Americans. She argues that in some senses a position of a third gender is being developed in US Third World feminist writings in their insistence on their inability to fit into the categorisation of gender which Western feminists have formulated, and she suggests that 'women of color somehow exist in the interstices between the legitimated categories of the social order' (Sandoval 1991: 4). She maintains that rather than responding to this 'differential consciousness' of US Third World feminism, 'hegemonic feminists' or mainstream Western feminists, have in fact characterised it as a problem to be solved through theories of difference. She focuses in particular on the history of feminism which white feminists have written: 'these constructed typologies have fast become the official stories by which the white women's movement understands itself and its interventions in history' (1991: 5). However, she shows how in fact they present themselves as all-embracing, covering all elements of feminist praxis and in that process of seeming inclusiveness they 'systematically curtail the forms of experiential and theoretical articulations permitted US third world feminism' (1991: 6). They thus erase the activities of Black American feminist theorists over the past thirty years, except in terms of their critique of white feminist thought.

In a close textual analysis of certain white feminist theorists, she shows the way in which Black American feminists are seen to have 'forced' white feminists to consider race issues, but their activities in other areas are downplayed. Sandoval, by contrast, rewrites the history of the development of 'oppositional consciousness' in the United States, within which she locates US Third World feminist theory; thus, these Third World feminist thinkers were both active within the women's movement as a whole, which they conceived of as the white women's movement, but they were also perhaps more fundamentally actively involved in the movements which worked on issues of civil rights. Sandoval identifies this weaving to and fro between different movements as a 'differential' consciousness which 'represents the variant, emerging out of correlations, intensities, junctures, crises' (1991: 14). She cites Chicana theorist Aida Hurtado's statement that 'women of color's fighting capabilities are often neither understood by middle-class feminists nor leftist activists in general, and up until now, these fighting capabilities have not been codified anywhere for them to learn' (cited in Sandoval 1991: 15). US Third World feminists do not see themselves as a homogeneous group but neither do they see their differences in opposition to one another. Sandoval's analysis of differential consciousness enables a new position of fluid identities:

> differential consciousness requires grace, flexibility and strength; enough strength to confidently commit to a well-defined structure of identity for one hour, day, week, month, year; enough flexibility to self-consciously transform that identity according to the requisites of

another oppositional ideological tactic if reading of power's formation require it; enough grace to recognise alliance with others committed to egalitarian social relations and race, gender and class justice, when their readings of power call for oppositional stands.

(1991: 15)

Thus, differential consciousness should not be seen as a pressure which 'forces' white feminists to admit to their own implicit racism; it is a productive way of thinking through the changes necessary for more recognition of difference without forcing difference into a static and oppositional categorisation. Trinh T. Minh-ha's work adds to the 'third-world' feminist theorist's stance of not wanting to play the marginal role of critique, and not wanting to be only the subject of the 'special issue' in feminist journals. She puts it bluntly in the following way: 'It is as if everywhere we go, we become Someone's private zoo' (1989: 80). Mitsuye Yamada comments on this situation of being positioned as a minority: 'It must be odd/to be a minority/he was saying./I looked around/and didn't see any./So I said/Yeah/it must be' (cited in Trinh 1989: 79). In this sense, post-colonial feminism has managed to define a position from which to theorise, which does not simply involve critique, but which has implicit within it a set of key concerns and methodologies, and which will enable it to map out alternative positions of subjectivity.

Futures

In some senses, at least, much post-colonial feminist theory has been in the past of necessity concerned with critique. In the future, it is clearly the case that post-colonial feminist theory will further build on the type of productive work mentioned above, concerned with developing new forms of analysis. For example, in examining the role of white women in the colonial context, it may be possible to more clearly delimit the ways in which these stereotypes have played a part in the construction of the parameters for subject-positions circulating in Britain in the present day. Whilst this type of work has been undertaken in terms of analysing post-colonial identity in ex-colonies such as India and Australia, it has not been fully explored in relation to Britain. It may also be possible to explore the socio-economic and cultural factors which lead to questions of national identity being symbolised through the representation of women. But perhaps the most important area in which post-colonial feminism can develop is in the theorising of difference, whereby women can speak across national and cultural barriers, not to assume that their contexts or concerns are the same, but rather to develop a set of theoretical principles of 'translation', so that alliances can be formed in spite of, and perhaps (paradoxically) because of, differences in power and differences in culture. This is not to re-assert some simplistic notion of sisterhood, but rather to work with a far more complex notion developed within Italian feminist thought of entrustment (*affidamento*), whereby women become acutely aware of their socio-economic and cultural privileges in relation to one another (see de Lauretis 1994). This will involve Western post-colonial feminists in more analytical work on their own social and cultural past and present, and it will involve more critical work on the concerns of the types of feminism that they have developed.

Notes

1. Those countries which were invaded and settled by Europeans arc said to have been colonised (e.g. India, and also the so-called 'white' colonies like Canada and Australia). There were, however, a wide range of other relations of domination by Europe, for example, relations of domination through trade, or through Christianity being imposed – these relations are generally termed imperial. The distinction between imperial and colonial relations, however, is not a clear cut one, since all imperial relations changed over time, because of economic and political factors. Because of this, I will be using the terms almost interchangeably throughout the chapter; I will make clear where I am only referring to one type of context.
2. I use the term subject-position to suggest that subjectivity, or even individuality, is temporary and often scarcely achieved. We take up a range of subject-positions which shift and are modified over time and due to changes in context; these subject-positions together make up the sense of who we are at any particular moment, but they are largely determined by external factors, such as, in this case, whether one is a colonial representative and thus whether one has power over others.

References

Ahmad, Aijaz (1993) *In Theory: Classes, Nations, Literatures*, London: Verso.

Azim, Firdous (1993) *The Colonial Rise of the Novel*, London: Routledge.

Bhabha, Homi (1994) *The Location of Culture*, London: Routledge.

Butler, Judith (1990) *Gender Trouble: Feminism and the Subversion of Identity*, London: Routledge.

Chaudhuri, Nupur and Margaret Strobel (eds) (1992) *Western Women and Imperialism: Complicity and Resistance*, Bloomington and Indianapolis: Indiana University Press.

de Lauretis, Teresa (1994) 'The essence of the triangle, or taking the risk of essentialism seriously: feminist theory in Italy, the US and Britain', in Naomi Schor and Elizabeth Weed (eds), *The Essential Difference*, Bloomington and Indianapolis: Indiana University Press.

Fuss, Diana (1989) *Essentially Speaking: Feminism, Nature and Difference*, London: Routledge.

Haggis, Jane (1990) 'Gendering colonialism or colonising gender: recent women's studies approaches to white women and the history of British colonialism', in *Women's Studies International Forum*, vol. 13, no. 1/2.

Hyam, Ronald (1990) *Empire and Sexuality: The British Experience*, Manchester: Manchester University Press.

Innes, Lyn (1994) 'Virgin territories and motherlands: colonial and nationalist represen-tations of Africa and Ireland', in *Feminist Review*, no. 47: 1–14.

Lewis, Reina (1996) *Gendering Orientalism: Race, Femininity and Representation*, London: Routledge.

McClintock, Anne (1995) *Imperial Leather: Race, Gender and Sexuality in the Imperial Contest*, London: Routledge.

Mills, Sara (1991) *Discourses of Difference: Women's Travel Writing and Colonialism*, London: Routledge.

Mills, Sara (1996) 'Colonial domestic space', in *Renaissance and Modern Studies*, special issue on space, vol. 39: 46–61.

Mohanty, Chandra Talpade (1985) 'Under Western eyes: feminist scholarship and colonial discourses', *Boundary 2*, vol. 3: 333–58.

Rajan, Rajeswari Sunder (1993) *Real and Imagined Women: Gender, Culture and Postcolonialism*, London: Routledge.

Said, Edward (1978) *Orientalism*, Harmondsworth: Penguin.

Said, Edward (1993) *Culture and Imperialism*, London: Chatto and Windus.

Sandoval Chela (1991) 'US third world feminism: the theory and method of oppositional consciousness in the postmodern world', *Genders*, no. 10, Spring: 1–24.

Sangari, Kumkum and Sudesh Vaid (eds) (1986) *Recasting Women: Essays in Colonial History*, New Delhi: Kali for Women.

Sharpe, Jenny (1993) *Allegories of Empire: The Figure of Woman in the Colonial Text*, Minnea-polis: University of Minnesota Press.

Sinha, Mrinalini (1995) *Colonial Masculinity: The 'Manly' Englishman and the 'Effeminate Bengali' in the late Nineteenth Century*, Manchester: Manchester University Press.

Spivak, Gayatri Chakravorty (1985) 'Three women's texts and a critique of imperialism', in *Critical Inquiry*, 12, Autumn: 243–62.

Spivak, Gayatri Chakravorty (1987) *In Other Worlds: Essays in Cultural Politics*, London: Routledge.

Spivak, Gayatri Chakravorty (1993a) 'Can the subaltern speak?', reprinted in Patrick Williams and Laura Chrisman (eds) *Colonial Discourse and Post-colonial Theory*, Hemel Hempstead: Harvester Wheatsheaf.

Spivak, Gayatri Chakravorty (1993b) *Outside in the Teaching Machine*, London: Routledge.

Stoler, Ann Laura (1989) 'Rethinking colonial categories: European communities and the boundaries of rule', in *Comparative Studies in Society and History*, vol. 31: 134–61.

Trinh T. Minh-ha (1989) *Woman Native Other: Writing Postcoloniality and Feminism*, Bloom-ington and Indianapolis: Indiana University Press.

Ware, Vron (1992) *Beyond the Pale: White Women, Racism and History*, London: Verso.

Williams, Patrick (1996) 'Colonial discourse and post-colonial theory', *Year's Work in Critical and Cultural Theory*, no. 2, English Association/Blackwell: 138–53.

Young, Robert (1995) *Colonial Desire: Hybridity in Theory, Culture and Race*, London: Rout-ledge.

Further Reading

Ashcroft, Bill, Gareth Griffiths and Helen Tiffin (1994) *The Post-Colonial Studies Reader*, London: Routledge.

Brah, Avtar (1996) *Cartographies of Diaspora*, London: Routledge.

Donaldson, Laura (1993) *Decolonializing Feminisms*, London: Routledge.

Frankenberg, Ruth (1993) *White Women, Race Matters*, London: Routledge.

Mills, Sara (1996) 'Post-colonial feminist theory', Chapter 8 in Sara Mills and Lynne Pearce (eds) *Feminist Readings/Feminists Reading*, 2nd edition, Hemel Hempstead: Harvester Wheatsheaf.

Mohanty, Chandra Talpade, Ann Russo and Lourdes Torres (eds) (1991) *Third World Women and the Politics of Feminism*, Bloomington: Indiana University Press.

Parker, Andrew, Mary Russo, Doris Sommer and Patricia Yaeger (eds) (1992) *Nationalisms and Sexualities*, London: Routledge.

Trinh T. Minh-ha (1988) 'Not you, like you: post-colonial women and the interlocking questions of identity and difference', in *Inscriptions: Feminism and the Critique of Colonial Discourse*, University of California at Santa Cruz, no. 3/4: 71–9.

Chapter 9

Lesbian Theory

Caroline Gonda

> Theory – the seeing of patterns, showing the forest as well as the trees – theory can be a dew that rises from the earth and collects in the rain cloud and returns to earth over and over. But if it doesn't smell of the earth, it isn't good for the earth.
>
> (Rich 1986: 213–14)

Adrienne Rich's remarks, in 'Notes toward a Politics of Location', are particularly apposite for a discussion of lesbian theory. Although many recent developments have come from academics trained in deconstruction and post-structuralism, the roots of lesbian theory lie in direct, personal and polemical writing: the language may have changed, but the debates show continuity. This chapter will revolve around three preoccupations which have remained central to lesbian theory: identity, sexuality and community. Separately or in conjunction, those concerns prompt a whole range of lesbian theoretical writings: from the 1960s to the 1990s; from grass-roots pamphlets to high-academic monographs; and across disciplines from anthropology, ethics, history, philosophy, politics, psychology or sociology to literary criticism, film studies, cultural studies, rhetoric or pure theory. (Though, of course, like Wilde's truth, theory is never pure and rarely simple.) Following Rich's metaphor, we might say that identity, sexuality and community are the earth to which lesbian theory returns.

In saying all this, however, I have already perpetrated a number of assumptions which need to be questioned. When *does* 'lesbian theory' start, and what *are* its 'roots'? The first question can't be answered till we have agreed on the second. One of my main objectives in this chapter is to re-open the question of what we do or don't recognise as 'theory'. I want to suggest not only that 'theory' need not emerge from, or remain bounded by, academic disciplines or institutions, but also that polemic is not the only alternative form theory may take. In the last thirty years, lesbian theory has often most fruitfully been worked out and exemplified in fiction and poetry, a point I shall return to at the end of this chapter. But lesbian theory – in the sense of lesbians' attempts to make sense of sexual desire, identity, ethics and politics – goes much further back than three decades. Where to begin? With the letters pages of the British magazine, *Arena 3*, in the early

1960s, for example, debating issues of biological essentialism versus choice, the place of politics in lesbian lives, the questions of what we would now call roleplay or stereotyping? With its US equivalent, *The Ladder*, conducting similar debates in the 1950s? With the many arguments about same-sex desire, and its place in the individual's life and in society, voiced in that early British publication, *The Freewoman* (1909 onwards)? Or with the female 'case histories' cited in Havelock Ellis's *Sexual Inversion* (1897), women whose sense of the nature and origin of their desire for other women is often very well theorised?

These are not, perhaps, the places we might expect to search for the origins of theory: in the letters pages of monthly magazines or the female appendices to male-authored scientific studies. Yet that incongruity is more apparent than real. Both the correspondence columns and the case histories might be excluded from conventional notions of what constitutes theory on the grounds that they are 'anecdotal' or 'just personal', as if these qualities were not only out of keeping with 'theory' but actually inimical to it. The polarisation of 'empirical' versus 'theoretical' has itself become a straw doll (see Belsey 1980, ch. 1); the answer is not, however, to reject one side or the other but to reinstate a better sense of how the empirical fits into and informs the theoretical. What is true for feminists in general is truer still for lesbians: the personal is not only political, it is where the theory has to start. It is through reflecting on personal, lived experience that lesbians move towards 'theory' in Rich's sense of the word: 'the seeing of patterns, showing the forest as well as the trees'. Crucially, in these early examples, theory is also a collective endeavour. For the magazine correspondents and for the female contributors to Ellis's study, the personal is directed to communal ends: these women are defining and (re)creating identity, helping something to come into being that is more than the sum of the individual women's stories.

An additional barrier to recognising these earlier works as 'lesbian theory' is thrown up by the question of *naming*. Late nineteenth- and early twentieth-century writers speak of women's same-sex desire in terms of 'female sexual inversion' or 'female homosexuality'; but do these different names suggest that what they describe is not the same as something called 'lesbianism'? There's a danger here that we fall victim to a crude form of nominalism – nobody's talking about 'lesbianism', so lesbianism doesn't exist, can't be seen to be theorised. Even those critics and historians who do see continuity between 'inversion', 'female homosexuality' and 'lesbianism' (Faderman 1991 and Newton 1989) still tend to see lesbian consciousness as at best a late nineteenth-century phenomenon: no lesbian consciousness before the 'sexologists' and their theories, because how can you be conscious of what you are if you don't have a word for it? (Faderman 1991).

As Emma Donoghue's work has shown, however, it is anyway simply not true that earlier centuries did not 'have a word for it': a woman might not choose to identify herself by terms such as 'tommy' or 'sapphist', but the names were there, for better or worse (Donoghue 1993). Beginnings are necessarily arbitrary: Donoghue's book goes back to the late seventeenth century, and that's just the Early Modern West! As the term 'sapphist' itself should remind us, there's a good case for starting with the ancient Greeks (Sappho of Lesbos wasn't the only woman-loving female poet of the ancient world). My own arbitrary beginning, however, is set much later: I take as my starting point another term which is in itself problematic, 'second-wave feminism', and begin with the late 1960s and early 1970s.

A recurring feature of lesbian theoretical writings of the last thirty years on identity, sexuality, and community is the (self-) definition of lesbian(s) and/or lesbianism(s) in relation to other identities, groups, or movements. This relation is characteristically an oppositional one, whether the opposition is to heterosexual feminism, gay liberation, or, more recently, queer politics. Yet it begins from a vantage point of lesbians who have sought inclusion within the political movements they now chastise. Lesbians reflect on their exclusion from, or silencing within, those movements, and on the causes of that silencing and exclusion. Gene Damon (the pen-name of Barbara Grier), editor of *The Ladder*, notes that 'many of the women's rights groups shun and fear Lesbians because of the "brand" they fear they will receive' (Damon 1970: 341). Martha Shelley's 'Notes of a Radical Lesbian' recounts heterosexual women's reactions to a self-declared lesbian at a feminist meeting: 'many women avoided her. Others told her to keep her mouth shut, for fear she would endanger the cause' (Shelley 1969, 1970: 345). For Shelley, 'Lesbianism is one road to freedom – freedom from oppression by men'; men's hostility to the lesbian is fuelled by her independence, 'a terrible threat to male supremacy' (1969: 343, 345). This independence has its penalties, however: exclusion from child-rearing; discrimination in the job market; and extreme 'social contempt and ridicule' (1969: 345). Lesbians are labelled as mentally sick because of their assumed hostility to men; but, Shelley argues, given the oppressive nature of male-dominated society, 'If hostility to men causes Lesbianism ... Lesbianism is a sign of mental health' (1969: 346). She sees heterosexual feminists' rejection of lesbians as based on fear and resentment: 'Straight women fear Lesbians because of the Lesbian inside them, because we represent an alternative ... They are angry at us because we have a way out that they are afraid to take' (1969: 347).

The implication of Shelley's remarks is that (in the words of Alix Dobkin's song) 'any woman can be a lesbian', but that heterosexual women repress 'the Lesbian inside them' through fear. Gene Damon's article, on the other hand, seems to suggest that lesbians are born, not made; that they don't have a choice about belonging to 'the last totally persecuted minority group in this United States', that is, homosexuals. Lesbians are even more disadvantaged than male homosexuals, however: 'As Lesbians, we are even lower in the sand hole; we are women (itself a majority/minority status) and we are Lesbians: the last half of the least noticed, most disadvantaged, minority' (Damon 1970: 342–3). Feminists may be ridiculed for demanding women's rights, Damon argues, but lesbians are constantly at risk of losing their jobs or even being jailed because of their 'sexual preferences', whether they engage in political activism or not: 'We have been much closer to the fire and brimstone than most of you' (Damon 1970: 340).

Damon's article brings into play the central notion of lesbians as doubly oppressed: sharing the oppression of women, the oppression of gay men, but experiencing it as a double(d) burden. That sentiment is echoed in the intro-duction to the Women's Issue of *Come Together*, the British newspaper of the Gay Liberation Front (GLF), published in July 1971:

> We share the experiences of our gay brothers but as women we have endured them differ-ently. Whereas the men in GLF partake of the privileges of the male – you have been allowed to organise, talk and dominate – we have been taught not to believe in ourselves, in our judgement, but to act dumb and wait for a man to make the decision. As lesbians, 'women without men', we have always been the lowest of the low.
>
> (Walter 1980: 89)

Lesbians appear here as victims of both sexes' social conditioning, in contrast to Shelley's notion of lesbians as women who perforce have already had to *overcome* female socialisation. As Aubrey Walter notes, however, this stage of lesbians' history in the GLF was short lived. Once GLF lesbians had succeeded in forcing lesbianism on to the agenda of the Women's Liberation Movement (at the second WLM conference in Skegness, October 1971 [reported in Walter 1980: 150–54]), the pattern of identification by which they had seen themselves as 'gay first and women second' was disrupted. GLF's failure to give equal space to lesbian politics and issues led to a formal split in February 1972 (Walter 1990: 30–32), and to many lesbians' diverting their political energies into the women's move-ment. The wheel would come full circle with the rise and fall of queer politics in the 1990s.

The place of lesbianism within the women's movement, meanwhile, remained a vexed question. Lesbians had been variously represented as a threat (Betty Friedan's notorious 'lavendar menace' accusation), as an irrelevance (or 'lavendar herring'), or as the heroines and vanguard of the WLM because of their refusal to relate sexually to men. Radicalesbians' pamphlet, 'The Woman Identified Woman' (1970), which defined a lesbian as 'the rage of all women condensed to the point of explosion' (Radicalesbians 1970, 1988: 17), veered between praising lesbians as exemplary for their 'woman identification' and lamenting the existence of 'lesbian' as a male-defined sexual category. Come the revolution, would 'lesbians' no longer exist? Some writers, such as Ti-Grace Atkinson, were suggesting that fully committed feminists were '"lesbians" in the political sense', even if they had 'never had sexual relations with other women'; or that all feminists should sport badges proclaiming 'I am a Lesbian' (Douglas 1990:

143). Political lesbianism, in this early incarnation, had everything to do with politics but as little as possible to do with sex. If any woman could be a lesbian, did that mean every woman should? And what would 'being a lesbian' mean, within that framework?

'We do think that all feminists can and should be political lesbians', the Leeds Revolutionary Feminists stated in 1979. 'Our definition of a political lesbian is a woman-identified woman who does not fuck men. It does not mean compulsory sexual activity with women' (Onlywomen 1981: 5). The Leeds manifesto, appropriately subtitled 'The Case Against Heterosexuality', argued fiercely that 'The heterosexual couple is the basic unit of the political structure of male supremacy ... Heterosexual women are collaborators with the enemy ... Every woman who lives with or fucks a man helps to maintain the oppression of our sisters and hinders our struggle' (Onlywomen 1981: 6–7). As one participant in the ensuing, furious debate noted, 'those ideas [had] been hanging around for years but [had] never been stated so baldly before' (Onlywomen 1981: 11). Throughout the 1970s radical critiques of heterosexuality had argued that 'political lesbianism' – withdrawing one's sexual services from men and devoting all one's energies to women – was the duty of every serious feminist. While women reserved their sexual energies for men, writers argued, they also cast women as second-class citizens, unworthy of that ultimate commitment (Douglas 1990: 144–5). Lesbianism, Ginny Berson argued in 1975, 'is not a matter of sexual preference, but rather one of political choice which every woman must make if she is to become woman-identified and thereby end male supremacy' (Douglas 1990: 148). Critiques of heterosexuality tacitly or explicitly assumed that there was nothing natural about 'sexual preference', and that sexual practice could and should be determined by 'political choice'.

The 'political lesbianism' argument, as formulated by the Leeds manifesto, raises more questions than it answers about sex, identity and politics. The main problem is one of definition: what is the role of sexual desire and/or sexual practice in defining 'lesbian'? It is not clear, for example, why heterosexual women's renunciation of sex with men should be labelled 'political lesbianism'. Some lesbian contributors to the debate rejected the Leeds definition both as falsely including heterosexual celibacy within 'lesbianism' and as occluding the specificity of lesbian experience. One lesbian feminist wrote that this notion of political lesbianism

> displaces the political importance which feminists have always attached to the sexual area of our lives. In particular it ignores the importance of women's sexual relations with other women whilst making the question of whether women have sexual relations with men central to the whole definition of political lesbianism.
>
> (Onlywomen 1981: 34)

'Political lesbianism', here, ironically, seems to *depoliticise* lesbianism; as other debaters complained, it also desexes it. (It's not about whom you do go to bed with, but whom you don't.) The notion of lesbianism as a positive *sexual* choice is wholly subsumed in the insistence on political necessity: 'political lesbianism' might be a duty, but perish the thought that lesbianism might be a pleasure! (At best, it's presented as laying to rest political conflicts and contradictions in one's private life – a view some lesbians greeted with wry amusement or angry despair.) In this stark outline of 'political lesbianism', female same-sex desire seems to have become an irrelevance. As Dorothy Allison writes, while acknowledging the tactical usefulness of the term 'political lesbian', 'Political lesbians made the concepts of lust, sexual need, and passionate desire more and more detached from the definition of lesbian' (Allison 1995: 140).

'Political lesbianism' was not, however, the only strand of lesbian theory to argue against a wholly or primarily sexual definition of 'lesbian'. Adrienne Rich's celebrated and controversial essay, 'Compulsory Heterosexuality and Lesbian Existence' (1980), not only emphasised the ideological and practical forces by which heterosexuality is socially imposed and maintained (including the endless assertion of its 'naturalness' and the erasure of 'lesbian existence' from historical record); it also proposed an expanded sense of what 'lesbian existence' might mean – the 'lesbian continuum'. 'I mean the term *lesbian continuum* to include a range – through each woman's life and throughout history – of woman-identified experience, not simply the fact that a woman has had or consciously desired genital sexual experience with another woman', she wrote. 'If we consider the possibility that all women – from the infant suckling at her mother's breast ... to the woman dying at ninety, touched and handled by women – exist on a lesbian continuum, we can see ourselves as moving in and out of this continuum, whether we identify as lesbian or not' (Rich 1980, 1986: 51, 54).

Rich's theory had certain obvious advantages for lesbian historians bedevilled by questions of women's 'genital sexual experience' with each other in previous centuries (questions summarised in Sheila Jeffreys' appropriately titled 'Does It Matter If They Did It?' [Lesbian History Group, 1988]): on Rich's 'continuum', women's 'romantic friendships' (Faderman 1981) and/or 'marriage resistance' and 'gyn/affection' (Raymond 1986) would count as signs of 'lesbian existence'. Clinical definitions of 'lesbianism' according to sexual practice are not only unnecessarily restrictive but unreliable, Rich suggests: they obscure the vital continuities between all kinds of shared female experience. We have moved from the idea that any woman *can* be a lesbian, or that every woman *should* be a (political) lesbian, to the theory that every woman *is* on the lesbian continuum at one time or another – whatever her own sense of identity or identification may be.

Criticisms of Rich's 'continuum' model predictably overlapped with criticisms of 'political lesbianism': Rich herself later expressed concern that women who had never questioned 'the privileges and solipsisms of heterosexuality' were using 'lesbian continuum' as 'a safe way to describe their felt connections with women, without having to share in the risks and threats of lesbian existence' (Rich 1986: 73). The complexities of the continuum, she suggested, were being oversimplified into a kind of 'lifestyle shopping' (Rich 1986: 73). Other lesbians protested that once again the specificity of lesbian experience was being blurred: where was the sense of lesbianism as an erotic 'commitment of skin, blood, breast and bone' (Stimpson 1982: 244)?

Both 'political lesbianism' and the 'lesbian continuum' had emphasised actual or potential similarities between lesbian and nonlesbian women: the lesbians in these theories were very much 'women first and gay second' (if at all). Both theories either played down or ignored commonalities between gay male and lesbian experience. Gender identification took precedence over (homo)sexual identification. For Monique Wittig, however, this gender identification was a false move: 'it would be incorrect to say that lesbians associate, make love, live with women, for "woman" has meaning only in heterosexual systems of thought and heterosexual economic systems. Lesbians are not women' (Wittig 1980, 1992: 32).

Here, lesbians' (homo)sexuality places them outside conventional categories of gender – categories which, Wittig argues, are not natural, but economically, historically and socially created. Wittig's theory would find many adherents among the academic theorists of the 1990s.

In the early 1980s, meanwhile, it was perhaps inevitable that the 'de-sexing' of lesbian theory would prompt a backlash (though the word 'backlash' may be in questionable taste in this context). Amber Hollibaugh was not the only lesbian to accuse feminism of censoring lesbian sexuality: 'it became this really repressive movement, where you didn't talk dirty and you didn't want dirty ... So after meetings, we *ran* to the bars. You couldn't talk about wanting a woman, except very loftily' (Hollibaugh and Moraga 1981, 1983: 411). When lesbians did begin to 'talk dirty', with the Lesbian Sex Mafia's planned speakout on 'politically incorrect sex' at the 1982 Barnard College conference on sexuality, anti-pornography groups targeted the conference in protest; an event seen in retro-spect as the beginning of the 'Lesbian Sex Wars' (Allison 1995: 105–8). On one side were women variously described as 'pro-sex', as 'anti-censorship' (forming the Feminist Anti-Censorship Taskforce, or FACT, in the wake of the Barnard Conference), or, latterly, as 'sex radicals'; on the other, women who claimed the name of 'lesbian-feminists' for themselves and argued passionately that their opponents' views were incompatible with feminism.

Both sides in the Sex Wars also argued that they (unlike the opposition) were the 'real lesbians'. The 'sex radicals' proclaimed the joys of sadomasochism, 'butch/femme' roleplaying, fetishism, sex toys and more, characterising those who recoiled, disapproved, or just weren't interested, as cowards, killjoys, or 'vanilla' lesbians. (Probably only in a culture of extreme culinary deprivation and ignorance could 'vanilla' have been used as a synonym for 'bland or flavourless'!)

'Lesbian-feminists', meanwhile, saw in both 'butch/femme' roleplay and sado-masochistic 'top/bottom' dynamics a pattern of dominance and submission reflecting heterosexual structures. The 'sex radicals', they argued, were either acting out heterosexual 'false consciousness' or misguidedly adopting gay male sexual practices. 'Real lesbians' just don't *do* such things. Nor, according to the more extreme lesbian-feminist views, should they engage in 'reactionary' or 'male' sexual behaviour such as 'objectifying' (seeing women as sexual objects), possessiveness (including monogamy), penetration of any kind, sexual language denoting any of the foregoing (we don't talk about fucking), or 'goal-orientated' sex (it's very *male* to see orgasm, hers or yours, as the point of making love). As one lesbian sardonically commented, 'some people's ideal of lesbianism is that we all dance around in a circle holding hands and then fall down on the ground AND GO TO SLEEP' (Roberts, in a conversation with Alison Hennegan, c. 1983). The choice between the literal restrictions of s/M bondage and the ideological restrictions of correct lesbian-feminist sex must often have seemed unappealing. (The truth, one suspects, is that the middle ground of lesbianism went on living and loving much as before, in defiance of edicts from both sides.)

Though much of the Lesbian Sex Wars was fought out in journals and anthologies – the sadomasochistic *Coming To Power* (Samois 1982) countered by *Against Sadomasochism* (Linden et al., 1982), for example – the battles were not entirely or exclusively verbal. Both sides' accounts stress the unacceptable violence of the opposition's behaviour. Sheila Jeffreys, noting some sadomasochists' adoption of fascist regalia, argues that 's/M scenarios re-enact the torture of gays by fascists as well as the torture of blacks by whites, Jews by Nazis, women by men, slaves by slave-owners'; she styles sadomasochism 'the erotic cult of fascism' (Jeffreys 1986, 1993: 210). Reviewing Jeffreys' *The Lesbian Heresy* (1993), Roz Kaveney accuses lesbian-feminists of being the real perpetrators of violence against women, citing as evidence for this the attack by 'a group of women, disguised with ski-masks, [who] smashed up Chain Reaction (the lesbian s/M London night club) with crowbars and injured the women who got in their way – in the name of opposing violence against women' (Kaveney 1994: 94). As Jeffreys notes, lesbian-feminists themselves have been accused by the s/M lobby of fascism: lesbian-feminists holding a meeting to 'challenge the promotion of s/M were 'accused of being "just like the National Front"' (Jeffreys 1986, 1993: 216). Meanwhile, she claims, the US group Samois harassed and intimidated 'feminist bookstores which would not display their promotional literature prominently' (1986: 231–2).

It is not surprising to find lesbian-feminist theorists pointing to continuities between the violence inherent in s/M scenarios and the violent conduct of the s/M lobby; what is perhaps more surprising is the way in which lesbian sadomasochists present themselves as victims of lesbian-feminists' ruffianly behaviour. One minute sadomasochists revel in being sexual outlaws, breaching taboos and transgressing boundaries; the next, it seems, they're just nice girls who'd play quietly together if those nasty rough feminists didn't keep spoiling the game. The ideology of s/M (including lesbian s/M) reveals similar contradictions: so much talk of power and danger on the one hand, so much insistence on safety and consent as the framework for them on the other. As Alison Hennegan notes, consent is the one shibboleth which must never be questioned: sexual outlawry has its limits, danger is kept safe (Hennegan 1993). (How different, how very different, from the home life of our own dear Divine Marquis de Sade.)

I have already suggested that lesbian theory is not only to be found in academic or polemical writings, and lesbian 'sex radical' theories offer a further illustration of this. While academic theorists constructed 'a butch-femme aesthetic' (Case 1988) or explored the 'mother-daughter dynamics' of lesbian-feminism versus sadomasochism (Creet 1991), s/M theory was also emerging in more indirect ways, particularly in the creation and circulation of photographic images. The work of photographers such as Della Grace, Tessa Boffin and Jean Fraser, offered consumable images of s/M and butch/femme roleplay, a new sexual iconography – or, critics maintained, a return to harmful pornographic stereotypes of lesbian sexuality (Grace 1991; Boffin and Fraser 1991). Despite feminist opposition, these images increasingly came to be taken for granted as part of 'lesbian culture': by the editors of gay and lesbian magazine and television programmes (e.g. Grace's s/M sequences in Channel 4's 'Lesbians Unclothed' programme); and indeed by shapers and purveyors of mainstream culture. Witness, for example, the cover image of *The Penguin Book of Lesbian Short Stories* (Reynolds, ed. 1993): a butch/femme full-frontal pose of two women whose skeletal thinness and cadaverous flesh tones both recall the horrors of concentration-camp images and perpetrate that old 'neurasthenic' myth of lesbians as dead from the waist down.

These proliferating images (and their watered-down imitators) make their own, supposedly informed statements about what lesbians are, how lesbians live, what lesbians want – or should want. As Gillian Hanscombe suggests, in the 'market forces' ideology behind the production and consumption of 'lesbian erotica', it's but a short step from saying lesbians want this (so it must be right) to saying 'If this isn't what lesbians want, then they ought to want it, or they're not real lesbians' (Hanscombe 1991: 217–18). In the increasingly consumerist ideology of sexual 'lifestyle shopping', as in the creation and circulation of s/M images and icons, lesbians were following the lead of gay male theory and culture. For lesbian-feminists such as Jeffreys, lesbian culture had taken a wrong turning, becoming 'a pale version of the male' (Jeffreys 1993: 142, quoting Weeks 1977).

What Jeffreys saw as a false or dangerous merging of lesbian and gay male identity and culture was, however, only one facet of the larger problem of identity politics in the 1980s and early 1990s. Like the Women's Liberation Movement, the 'Lesbian Nation' (Johnston 1973) found itself under strain, and at times under attack, in the areas of race and class. In 1977, the Combahee River Collective's 'Black Feminist Statement' had rejected

> the fractionalization that white women who are separatists demand. Our situation as Black people demands that we have solidarity around the fact of race, which white women of course do not need to have with white men, unless it is their negative solidarity as oppressors.
>
> (Combahee 1977, 1982: 16)

The statement also criticised the 'biological determinism' of lesbian separatist views, and questioned 'whether lesbian separatism is an adequate and progressive political analysis and strategy, even for those who practice it, since it so completely denies any but the sexual sources of women's oppression, negating the facts of class and race' (1977, 1982: 17).

Moreover, as Audre Lorde argued in 'An Open Letter to Mary Daly', denying or ignoring the racial dimension of oppression produces a distorted sense of what is at stake in resisting that oppression: 'The white women with hoods on in Ohio handing out KKK literature on the street may not like what you have to say, but they will shoot me on sight' (Lorde 1979, 1984: 70).

Black lesbians, meanwhile, also came under attack from sections of the Black community who regarded lesbianism as 'the whites' disease' or as 'racial suicide'; Cherríe Moraga found that Chicana lesbians were similarly portrayed as traitors to their own kind for failing to dedicate themselves to the embattled Chicano male, already oppressed by the white man (Moraga 1983: 112–14). Meanwhile, Moraga suggests, the culture and theory of white lesbians offered only the illusion of an alternative: '"Womon's history", "wommin's music", "womyn's spirituality", "wymyn's language", abounded – all with the "white" modifier implied and unstated. In truth, there was/is a huge amount of denial going on in the name of female separatism' (1983: 127). Third World women in particular, Moraga argues, cannot afford to throw out 'the entire business of racial/ethnic culture' in response to the fact that 'some aspects of that culture are indeed oppressive' (1983: 127). Being lesbian and being Chicana are 'two inseparable facts of my life. I can't talk or write about one without the other' (1983: 142).

'What I know for sure is that class, gender, sexual preference, and racial prejudice form an intricate lattice that both restricts and shapes our lives, and that resistance to that hatred is not a simple act', Dorothy Allison writes. 'Claiming your identity in the caldron of hatred and resistance to hatred is more than complicated; it is almost unexplainable' (Allison 1993: 143). For Allison, traditional feminist theory 'has had a limited understanding of class differences or of how sexuality and self are shaped by both desire and denial'; a monolithic notion of patriarchy as the root of all social evils is unhelpfully simplistic. 'The ideology implies that we are all sisters who should turn our anger and suspicion only on the world outside the lesbian community' (1993: 142); but Allison's experience of telling and living the truth about class within that community has been a bitter one. Irena Klepfisz's twenty-five years of office work and feminist activism lead her to contemplate not the connections but 'The Distances Between Us': the 'extraordinary arrogance and ignorance concerning working-class people' among feminists: 'To most middle-class feminists, as to most middle-class non-feminists, working-class women remain mysterious creatures to be "reached out to" in some abstract way. No connection. No solidarity' (Klepfisz 1985, 1991: 192).

'Identity politics at its best is about making connections between people and groups not normally perceived as related', writes Lisa Kahaleole Chang Hall; all too often, however,

> the pressure comes from all sides to choose, choose. Pick a singular identity and then fit in: a lesbian identity that ignores cultural, racial, and class differences, a racial identity that represses sexual differences and multiracial histories, a gender identity that conflates it all. But our lives are infinitely more complex than the way we present them.
>
> (Hall 1993: 220, 222)

With so many different identities clamouring to be chosen, the dream of the Lesbian Nation – or even of *a* lesbian community – seemed less and less likely to become a reality. Arlene Stein, editor of *Sisters, Sexperts, Queers: Beyond the Lesbian Nation*, often found herself

> speaking of 'lesbian culture' or 'lesbian politics', knowing full well that the vast diversity of class, race, ethnicity, geography, and even sexuality among us makes describing such coherent entities difficult, if not impossible. To paraphrase Gertrude Stein, I found myself reflecting on whether there is really a 'we' there.
>
> (Stein 1993: xvi)

Even 'a gender identity that conflates it all' is no longer so simple to establish. Wittig's 'lesbians are not women' continues to reverberate (Calhoun 1994), while the doyenne of gender theory, Judith Butler, argues that gender is a performance, or '*a kind of imitation for which there is no original*' (Butler 1991: 21). Even biological sex, Butler has recently argued, is socially constructed through repetitive performance, from that founding moment of 'interpellation' ('It's a girl!') on down (Butler 1993). The 1991 retrospective celebrating twenty-one years of the lesbian journal *Trivia* finds the original editor reflecting anxiously on the recent inclusion of writing by a male-to-female transsexual who identifies as lesbian: what is, or what should be, the place of 'transgendered' individuals in lesbian culture?

Academic proponents of lesbian and gay studies (attacked by Jeffreys as the falsely homogenising 'lesbianandgay theory' [Jeffreys 1993: 97]) and 'queer theory' have added to the confusion. Camille Paglia, who is lesbian, and Eve Kosofsky Sedgwick (dubbed 'the soft-spoken queen of gay studies' by *Rolling*

Stone), who isn't, both identify as gay men. (Paglia, giving a twist to the old 'inversion' model, calls herself 'a gay man trapped in a woman's body'.) Sedgwick's book *Tendencies* celebrates 'queer' as something 'multiply transitive' – across genders, across sexualities, across perversions (Sedgwick 1994: xii). According to Teresa de Lauretis, in the *differences* special issue which launched the notion of 'queer theory', 'queer' is intended to counteract or question the false inclusiveness of 'lesbian and gay' while making it clear what we do all have in common (de Lauretis 1991). The problem with 'queer' – and therefore with 'queer theory' – is, however, that its definition becomes so broad as to encompass any deviation from white, middle-class, heterosexual, monogamous, missionary-position (and probably procreative) sex: anyone who feels at odds with social or sexual convention can claim the label 'queer', including, presumably, heterosexual men. This is an inclusiveness beyond even Rich's 'lesbian continuum' but with even more danger of degenerating from political consciousness into 'lifestyle shopping'.

The 'queer moment' celebrated by Sedgwick may represent new possibilities for alliance and coalition between lesbians, gay men and others; it may threaten a return to 'lesbian invisibility'; or it may already have passed. 'Look, X, don't you realize nobody except academics calls themselves "queer" any more?', a friend of mine asked a male academic. He thought a moment and then said sadly (having just edited a volume on 'queer politics'), 'Oh dear, it's true.' The story reflects more than the passing of 'queer', however: as lesbian and gay theory becomes more entrenched in academia, is it losing touch with the politics that once fuelled it?

Lesbian theory, as I said at the outset, has spread across a whole range of academic disciplines now. Lesbian and Gay Studies itself is flourishing both as an academic subject (particularly in the US) and as an area of academic publishing. But the costs of this academic respectability may have been too high. Judith Butler, expressing her willingness to 'appear at political occasions under the sign of lesbian', adds the rider that she 'would like to have it permanently unclear what that sign signifies' (Butler 1991: 14). Lesbian theory in academia often reads as if its aim is to keep the meaning of 'lesbian' 'permanently unclear' – or to avoid what Catherine Belsey calls 'the tyranny of lucidity' (Belsey 1980: 4). I don't believe lucidity need be tyrannical (apart from anything else, the notion is insulting to readers); nor is lesbian theory which only a tiny minority of readers already fluent in the language of poststructuralism can understand likely to serve any useful political purpose. And while I'm not a 'political lesbian' (or 'head first lesbian', as Gillian Hanscombe calls them [Hanscombe 1995: 16]), I do believe that lesbian theory must be political or it is worthless. As Susan Wolfe and Julia Penelope suggest, however, it may be more pernicious than that: it seems too great a coincidence that at the moment in history when oppressed groups – women, blacks, gays – were beginning to demand that their subjectivity be attended to, a school of theory emerged which proclaimed the death of subjectivity (Wolfe and Penelope 1993)!

If high-academic lesbian theory is, as I'm arguing, often 'not good for the earth', what does the future of lesbian theory hold? The relentless play of postmodernism may produce a self-referential world of academic discourse in which lesbian theory need never leave 'theory', but I hope not. I hope, too, that the institutionalisation of lesbian studies and lesbian theory won't lead to the processing and constricting of lesbian ideas to produce neat course packages or institutionally acceptable, bleached-out 'career lesbians'. 'Lesbian academic' is another model of identity on offer to us, but one to be approached with caution.

Jeffner Allen's *Lesbian Philosophies and Cultures* (Allen, ed. 1990) and Betsy Warland's *InVersions: Writings by Dykes, Queers, and Lesbians* (Warland, ed. 1991) offer a sense of the variety and excitement which lesbian theory can boast; they do so partly because their scope is not exclusively academic, but includes work by writers of fiction and poetry. As I suggested earlier, these other genres have been fruitful ground for lesbian theory in the last thirty years: from card-carrying novels of ideas such as Hanscombe's *Between Friends* and *Figments of a Murder* (1982, 1995), Sara Maitland's *Virgin Territory* (1984) or Michèle Roberts's *A Piece of the Night* (1978), to experiments with language such as June Arnold's *The Cook and the Carpenter* (1973) with its gender-neutral pronouns, or with literary form – Christine Crow's deconstruction of the 'coming-out novel' in *Miss X, or the Wolf Woman* (1990). Questions of lesbian identity, sexuality and community have been debated and explored in poetry and prose: Rich's *Twenty-One Love Poems* (1978), Maureen Duffy's *Lyrics for the Dog Hour* (1968) and her novels *The Microcosm* (1966) and *Love Child* (1971), Anna Livia's story of the Lesbian Sex Wars, 'Lust and the Other Half' (1990), Hanscombe and Suniti Namjoshi's collaborative sequence, *Flesh and Paper* (1986). Poetic sequences such as Michelle Cliff's *Claiming An Identity They Taught Me To Despise* (1980) and Jackie Kay's *The Adoption Papers* (1991) have explored racial differences and identity formation; utopias by Sally Gearhart (1978), Joanna Russ (1975), and Monique Wittig (1969) have worked out alternative models of lesbian life and community.

In the vicissitudes of British feminist publishing over the last few years, lesbian writing outside the academy has had to fight for survival. Plenty of books on 'lesbian chic' and its variants (more than we need) still appear, but many of the openings for lesbian *literature* have been closed down, as feminist houses go under, redefine their market, or cut back to the bone in order to survive. It may now be easier to be published abroad than it is in Britain. Another possibility (for those who can afford it or who have institutional facilities available) is electronic publishing, the world of the Internet. Lesbian theory is being developed in 'cyberspace', via e-mail and discussion lists; lesbian literature, too, can be made available to some readers, on the 'home pages' of individuals or publishers. Not all writers and readers have access to this electronic world, however, and academics in particular need to be wary of careless assumptions about resources – assumptions which can silence or disenfranchise lesbians outside academic institutions. (The brief for one major lesbian academic project recently assumed that all contributors had e-mail facilities, could produce work on disk in the latest software programmes, or could afford to make transatlantic phone calls to the editor if that weren't the case!) Cyberspace, then, can be at best only part of the answer. Conventional publishing (including perhaps an increase in self-publishing) will remain an important factor in the continuing life of lesbian theory.

One final assumption of my own so far remains to be questioned. I have spoken of 'opening up' our ideas of what constitutes theory, but throughout this chapter have confined my remarks to what appears in print, on book jackets, on television, on computer screens – to 'theory' as something which must be published in order to qualify (even if 'publication' means not a book or an article but a duplicated newsletter or a photographic exhibition). Yet 'lesbian theory', un-published and unsung, has gone on happening all the time in the oldest tradition of all – by word of mouth. In discussion groups and at conferences, in seminars and at political meetings, lesbian theory continues to draw strength from our collective endeavour. Always in process, questioning and changing, lesbian theory is alive in all these places; and in the conversations between friends that go on late into the night.

References

Abel, Elizabeth (ed.) (1982) *Writing and Sexual Difference*, Brighton: Harvester Press.

Abelove, Henry, Michèle Aina Barale and David Halperin (eds) (1993) *The Lesbian and Gay Studies Reader*, New York and London: Routledge.

Allen, Jeffner (ed.) (1990) *Lesbian Philosophies and Cultures*, Albany, New York: SUNY Press.

Allison, Dorothy (1993) 'A Question of Class', in Stein (ed.) *Sisters, Sexperts, Queers*.

Allison, Dorothy (1995) *Skin: Talking About Sex, Class and Literature*, London: Pandora.

Arnold, June (1973) *The Cook and the Carpenter: A Novel by the Carpenter*, Plainfield, Vermont: Daughters, Inc.

Barrington, Judith (ed.) (1991) *An Intimate Wilderness: Lesbian Writers on Sexuality*, Portland, Oregon: Eighth Mountain Press.

Belsey, Catherine (1980) *Critical Practice*, London: Methuen.

Boffin, Tessa and Jean Fraser (eds) (1991) *Stolen Glances: Lesbians Take Photographs*, London: Pandora Press.

Butler, Judith (1991) 'Imitation and Gender Insubordination', in Diana Fuss (ed.) *Inside/Out*.

Butler, Judith (1993) *Bodies That Matter: On the Discursive Limits of 'Sex'*, New York and London: Routledge.

Calhoun, Cheshire (1994) 'Separating Lesbian Theory from Feminist Theory', *Ethics*, vol. 104, April: 558–81.

Case, Sue-Ellen (1988) 'Toward a Butch-Femme Aesthetic', revised version in Abelove et al. (eds) (1993) *The Lesbian and Gay Studies Reader*.

Cliff, Michelle (1980) *Claiming An Identity They Taught Me To Despise*, Watertown, Massachusetts: Persephone Press.

Combahee River Collective (1977) 'A Black Feminist Statement', reprinted in Gloria T. Hull et al. (eds) (1982) *But Some Of Us Are Brave*.

Creet, Julia (1991) 'Daughter of the Movement: The Psychodynamics of Lesbian s/m Fantasy', *differences: A Journal of Feminist Cultural Studies. Queer Theory Issue*, vol. 3, Summer.

Crow, Christine (1990) *Miss X, or the Wolf Woman*, London: The Women's Press.

Damon, Gene (pseud. for Barbara Grier) (1970) 'The Least of These: The Minority Whose Screams Haven't Yet Been Heard', in Robin Morgan (ed.) *Sisterhood is Powerful*.

de Lauretis, Teresa (1991) 'Queer Theory: Lesbian and Gay Sexualities. An Introduction', *differences: A Journal of Feminist Cultural Studies. Queer Theory Issue*, vol. 3, Summer.

Donoghue, Emma (1993) *Passions Between Women: British Lesbian Culture, 1668–1801*, London: Scarlet Press.

Douglas, Carol Anne (1990) *Love and Politics: Radical Feminist and Lesbian Theories*, San Francisco, California: Ism Press.

Duberman, Martin Bauml, Martha Vicinus and George Chauncey Jr (eds) (1989) *Hidden from History: Reclaiming the Gay and Lesbian Past*, New York: New American Library; published in the UK by Penguin Books, 1991.

Duffy, Maureen (1966) *The Microcosm*, London: Hutchinson and Co. Ltd.

Duffy, Maureen (1968) *Lyrics for the Dog Hour*, London: Hutchinson and Co. Ltd.

Duffy, Maureen (1971) *Love Child*, London: Weidenfeld and Nicolson.

Ellis, Havelock (1897) *Sexual Inversion*.

Faderman, Lillian (1981) *Surpassing the Love of Men: Romantic Friendship and Love Between Women from the Renaissance to the Present*, New York: Quill.

Faderman, Lillian (1991) *Odd Girls and Twilight Lovers: A History of Lesbian Life in Twentieth-Century America*, New York: Columbia University Press.

Fuss, Diana (ed.) (1991) *Inside/Out: Lesbian Theories, Gay Theories*, New York and London: Routledge.

Gearhart, Sally (1978) *The Wanderground*, Watertown, Massachusetts: Persephone Press.

Grace, Della (1991) *Love Bites*, London: Gay Men's Press.

Grier, Barbara and Coletta Reid (eds) (1976) *The Lavender Herring: Lesbian Essays from 'The Ladder'*, Baltimore, Maryland: Diana Press.

Hall, Lisa Kahaleole Chang (1993) 'Bitches in Solitude: Identity Politics and Lesbian Community', in Stein (ed.) *Sisters, Sexperts, Queers*.

Hanscombe, Gillian (1982) *Between Friends*, Boston, Massachusetts: Alyson Press.

Hanscombe, Gillian (1991) 'In Among the Market Forces', in Judith Barrington (ed.) *An Intimate Wilderness*.

Hanscombe, Gillian (1995) *Figments of a Murder*, Melbourne, Victoria, Australia: Spinifex Press.

Hennegan, Alison (1993) 'Death of a Nation?', *The Women's Review of Books*, vol. XI, no. 2, November 1993: 12–13.

Hoagland, Sarah Lucia and Julia Penelope (eds) (1988) *For Lesbians Only: A Separatist*

Anthology, London: Onlywomen Press.

Hollibaugh, Amber and Cherríe Moraga (1981) 'What We're Rollin Around In Bed With: Sexual Silences in Feminism'; reprinted in Ann Snitow, Christine Stansell and Sharon Thompson (eds) (1983) *Powers of Desire: The Politics of Sexuality*, New York: Monthly Review Press.

Hull, Gloria T., Patricia Bell Scott and Barbara Smith (1982) *All The Women Are White, All The Blacks Are Men, But Some Of Us Are Brave: Black Women's Studies*, New York: The Feminist Press at the City University of New York.

Jeffreys, Sheila (1986) 'Sadomasochism: The Erotic Cult of Fascism', reprinted in Sheila Jeffreys (1993) *The Lesbian Heresy*.

Jeffreys, Sheila (1988) 'Does It Matter If They Did It?', revised version of earlier (1984) article, in Lesbian History Group, *Not A Passing Phase*.

Jeffreys, Sheila (1993) *The Lesbian Heresy: A Feminist Perspective on the Lesbian Sexual Revolution*, Melbourne, Victoria, Australia: Spinifex Press.

Johnston, Jill (1973) *Lesbian Nation: The Feminist Solution*, New York: Simon and Schuster.

Kay, Jackie (1991) *The Adoption Papers*, Newcastle upon Tyne: Bloodaxe Books.

Kaveney, Roz (1994) Review of Sheila Jeffreys, *The Lesbian Heresy*, in *Perversions*, vol. 2, Summer, 92–8.

Klepfisz, Irena (1985) 'The Distances Between Us', reprinted in McEwen and O'Sullivan (eds) (1991) *Out the Other Side*.

Lesbian History Group (1988) *Not A Passing Phase: Lesbians In History 1840–1985*, London: The Women's Press.

Linden, Robin Ruth, Darlene R. Pagano, Diana E. H. Russell and Susan Leigh Starr (eds) (1982) *Against Sadomasochism: A Radical Feminist Analysis*, East Palo Alto, California: Frog in the Well.

Livia, Anna (1990) 'Lust and the Other Half', reprinted in Judith Barrington (ed.) (1991) *An Intimate Wilderness*.

Lorde, Audre (1979) 'An Open Letter to Mary Daly', reprinted in Audre Lorde (1984) *Sister Outsider: Essays and Speeches by Audre Lorde*, Freedom, California: The Crossing Press.

Maitland, Sara (1984) *Virgin Territory*, London: Michael Joseph.

McEwen, Christian and Sue O'Sullivan (eds) (1991) *Out the Other Side: Contemporary Lesbian Writing*, London: Virago Press.

Moraga, Cherríe (1993) *Loving in the War Years: Lo Que Nunca Pasó Por Sus Labios*, Boston, Massachusetts: South End Press.

Morgan, Robin (ed.) (1970) *Sisterhood is Powerful: An Anthology of Writings from the Women's Liberation Movement*, New York: Vintage Books.

Namjoshi, Suniti and Gillian Hanscombe (1986) *Flesh and Paper*, Seaton, Devon: Jezebel Tapes and Books.

Newton, Esther (1989) 'The Mythic Mannish Lesbian: Radclyffe Hall and the New Woman', revised version of earlier (1984) article; in Duberman et al. (eds) *Hidden from History*.

Onlywomen (eds) (1981) *Love Your Enemy? The Debate Between Heterosexual Feminism and Political Lesbianism*, London: Onlywomen Press.

Radicalesbians (1970) *The Woman Identified Woman*, reprinted in Hoagland and Penelope (eds) (1988) *For Lesbians Only*.

Raymond, Janice (1986) *A Passion for Friends: Toward a Philosophy of Female Affection*, Boston, Massachusetts: Beacon Press.

Reynolds, Margaret (ed.) (1993) *The Penguin Book of Lesbian Short Stories*, London: Penguin Books.

Rich, Adrienne (1978) *Twenty-One Love Poems*, New York and London: W. W. Norton & Co.

Rich, Adrienne (1980) 'Compulsory Heterosexuality and Lesbian Existence', reprinted in Adrienne Rich (1986) *Blood, Bread, and Poetry*.

Rich, Adrienne (1986) *Blood, Bread, and Poetry: Selected Prose, 1979–1985*, New York and London: W. W. Norton and Co.

Roberts, Michèle (1978) *A Piece of the Night*, London: The Women's Press.

Russ, Joanna (1975) *The Female Man*, New York: Bantam Books.

Samois (eds) (1982) *Coming to Power*, Boston, Massachusetts: Alyson Publications.

Sedgwick, Eve Kosofsky (1994) *Tendencies*, London: Routledge.

Shelley, Martha (1969) 'Notes of a Radical Lesbian', reprinted in Robin Morgan (ed.) (1970) *Sisterhood is Powerful*.

Stein, Arlene (ed.) (1993) *Sisters, Sexperts, Queers: Beyond the Lesbian Nation*, New York: Plume (Penguin Books).

Stimpson, Catharine R. (1982) 'Zero Degree Deviancy: The Lesbian Novel in English', in Elizabeth Abel (ed.) *Writing and Sexual Difference*.

Walter, Aubrey (ed.) (1980) *Come Together: The Years of Gay Liberation 1970–73*, London: Gay Men's Press.

Warland, Betsy (ed.) (1991) *InVersions: Writings by Dykes, Queers, and Lesbians*, Vancouver: Pressgang Publishers.

Weeks, Jeffrey (1977) *Coming Out: Homosexual Politics in Britain from the Nineteenth Century to the Present*, London: Quartet Books.

Wittig, Monique (1969) *Les Guérillères*, Paris: Les Editions de Minuit; translated by David Le Vay as *The Guérillères* (1971), London: Peter Owen.

Wittig, Monique (1980) 'The Straight Mind', reprinted in Monique Wittig (1992) *The Straight Mind and Other Essays*.

Wittig, Monique (1992) *The Straight Mind and Other Essays*, Hemel Hempstead: Harvester Wheatsheaf.

Wolfe, Susan and Julia Penelope (eds) (1993) *Sexual Practice, Textual Theory: Lesbian Cultural Criticism*, Cambridge, Massachusetts and Oxford: Blackwell Publishers.

Further Reading

Abelove, Henry, Michèle Barale and David Halperin (eds) (1993) *The Lesbian and Gay Studies Reader*, London: Routledge.

Bristow, Joseph and Angelia Wilson (eds) (1993) *Activating Theory: Lesbian, Gay, Bisexual Politics*, London: Lawrence and Wishart.

differences (1991) volume 3 (1), special issue, 'Queer Theory: Lesbian and Gay Sexualities'.

differences (1994) volume 6 (2/3), special issue, 'More Gender Trouble: Feminism Meets Queer Theory'.

Fuss, Diana (ed.) (1991) *Inside/Out: Lesbian Theories, Gay Theories*, New York: Routledge.

Jeffreys, Sheila (1994) *The Lesbian Heresy: A Feminist Perspective on the Lesbian Sexual Revolution*, London: The Women's Press.

Munt, Sally (ed.) (1992) *New Lesbian Criticism: Literary and Cultural Readings*, Brighton: Harvester Press.

Palmer, Paulina (1993) *Contemporary Lesbian Writing: Dreams, Desire, Difference*, Buckingham: Open University Press.

Rich, Adrienne (1986) 'Compulsory heterosexuality and lesbian existence', in her *Blood, Bread and Poetry*, New York: W. W. Norton.

Smyth, Cherry (1992) *Lesbians Talk Queer Notions*, London: Scarlet Press.

Stein, Arlene (ed.) (1993) *Sisters, Sexperts, Queers: Beyond the Lesbian Nation*, New York: Plume.

Chapter 10

Theorising Gender and Sexuality

Stevi Jackson

Gender and sexuality are among feminism's most central concepts, yet there is no consensus on how to define them or how to theorise their interrelationship. The term gender has been used since the early 1970s to denote culturally constructed femininity and masculinity as opposed to biological sex differences. Sexuality – erotic identities, desires and practices – is usually conceptualised as distinct from, but related to, gender. The concepts of gender and sexuality both take 'sex', a highly ambiguous term, as a point of reference. In the English language the word 'sex' can denote either the distinction between male and female (as 'two sexes') or sex as an erotic activity (to 'have sex'). Similarly 'sexual' can refer to the different activities or attributes of men and women, as in such phrases as 'the sexual division of labour', or it can refer to the erotic sphere of life, for example, to 'sexual fantasies'. Moreover the term 'sex' can be used – more commonly in French, but sometimes in English – to name sexual organs which are simultaneously erogenous zones and the body parts which distinguish male from female.

This linguistic confusion is not a mere accident, but tells us something about the male-dominated and heterosexist culture in which we live. It is commonly assumed that being born with a particular set of genitals (sex organs) defines one as of a particular sex (female or male), which means that one will normally become 'properly' feminine or masculine (the appropriate gender) and will desire and engage in erotic activity with 'the other sex', with someone possessing a different set of sex organs from one's own. This circular and deterministic reasoning has served to justify women's subordination and to define heterosexuality as the only fully 'natural' and legitimate form of sexuality. Hence it is politically important for feminists to challenge this way of thinking, to break the patriarchal chain which binds sex, gender and sexuality together as if they were inseparable and unchangeable.

A first step is to separate out the three terms sex, gender and sexuality in order to explore how they are interrelated. Distinguishing 'sex' from 'gender' not only serves to emphasise the social and cultural origins of differences between women and men, but can also help to resolve the ambiguity of the word 'sex'. If gender

131

is used to refer to the distinction between women and men, the terms 'sex' and 'sexuality' can be reserved for erotic activities, desires, practices and identities. However, these working definitions are not always easy to sustain and not all feminists would endorse them. For example, psychoanalytic theorists have long disliked the sex–gender distinction, seeing sex, gender and sexuality as too closely bound together to be easily disentangled, and they frequently use the term 'sexuality' to encompass what other feminists would call gender (see Mitchell 1982). The term 'gender' itself has an Anglo-American heritage and is more often used by English speakers; in France, for example, the word sex is still preferred, or sometimes social sex' (see Mathieu 1995). Some dislike the term 'gender' because it leaves the concept of 'sex' untheorised (Wittig 1992), while others make use of the concept of gender while also calling 'sex' into question (Delphy 1984, 1993; Butler 1990, 1993). There are also those who resist the imposition of the term gender in the name of 'sexual difference', which they see as irreducible to either biological sex or sociocultural gender (Braidotti 1994).

There are, then, theoretical differences underlying these terminological dis-agreements. Since this chapter is concerned with gender and its relationship with sexuality, I will focus primarily on those theorists who have developed and elab-orated the concept of gender, although I will take note of those who are sceptical about the whole enterprise. Those who accept the utility of the concept of gender are by no means a homogenous group, but include feminists with very different points of view. In the course of the chapter I will chart the development of feminist thinking on gender and its interrelationship with sexuality and identify some of the key differences of perspective which have emerged. For simplicity I will deal first with the concept of gender, before moving on to sexuality.

The Concept of Gender

Although the concept of gender did not become current among feminists until the 1970s, the idea that it encapsulates – that differences between men and women are not wholly determined by biology – has a longer history. This was summed up by Simone de Beauvoir, writing in the 1940s: 'One is not born a woman but becomes one'. The contention that women are made rather than born has been central to the development of theories of gender. Another, and crucial, feature of feminist perspectives is that gender is conceptualised as hierarchical: we are not dealing with a symmetrical difference between women and men but an asymmetrical, unequal relationship. However, the term gender is sometimes used, in the context of 'gender studies', to displace women as the central object of analysis in favour of a purportedly more 'inclusive' focus on both genders.

Ann Oakley (1972) was among the first to make the distinction between the sex we are born with and the gender we acquire. Oakley did not invent the distinction between sex and gender, but borrowed it from Robert Stoller, a psychologist who had worked with individuals born with ambiguous genitalia. Stoller found the distinction useful in describing the situation of people whose biological sex was found to be at variance with the gender category in which they had been placed at birth and in which they located themselves. Following Stoller, Oakley suggested that gender is not a direct product of biological sex. She defined sex as the anatomical and physiological characteristics which signify biological maleness and femaleness and gender as socially constructed masculinity and femininity. Masculinity and femininity are defined not by biology but by social, cultural and psychological attributes which are acquired through becoming a man or a woman in a particular society at a particular time.

Another influential account of gender was produced by Gayle Rubin, in a now classic article: 'The traffic in women: notes on the "political economy" of sex' (1975). Whereas Oakley distinguished gender from biological sex, Rubin related gender to reproductive sexuality, encapsulating the two in the term 'sex/gender system' (a formulation she later revised, see Rubin 1984). According to Rubin, every society 'has a sex/gender system – a set of arrangements by which the biological raw material of human sex and procreation is shaped by human, social intervention' (1975: 165). These arrangements are culturally variable conventional ways of organising human sexual relations, particularly through the structures of kinship and marriage. Gender itself is defined as 'a socially imposed division of the sexes' and is 'a product of the social relations of sexuality' (Rubin 1975: 179).

Oakley and Rubin, along with other feminists writing at that time, contributed to an emerging critique of what is now called 'essentialism': the mode of thinking which treats social phenomena like gender and sexuality as if they exist prior to and outside the social and cultural discourses, practices and structures which give rise to them. These early formulations made it possible to think of masculinity and femininity as historically and culturally variable rather than fixed by nature. Moreover, what it means to be a woman or a man also varies within any given society at one time, reflecting differences which cut across those of gender such as class or 'race'. For example, the dominant nineteenth-century conception of women as fragile, delicate creatures requiring protection from chivalrous, virile men was flatly contested by the Black ex-slave and suffrage campaigner Sojourner Truth:

> That man over there says women need to be helped into carriages and lifted over ditches and to have the best places. No-one ever helped me into carriages over ditches or gave me the best place – and ain't I a woman? Look at me! Look at my arm ... I have ploughed, and planted, and gathered into barns and no man could head me – and ain't I a woman? I could work as much as any man ... and bear the lash as well and ain't I a woman?
>
> (Quoted in Carby 1982)

Problematising the Sex–Gender Distinction

Although Rubin and Oakley emphasised the cultural construction of gender, both assumed a biological basis on which this distinction was founded: in Oakley's case, anatomical sex differences; in Rubin's, procreative sexual activity. In so doing, both left us with problems which have continued to be debated. Rubin's work raises the issue of the relationship between sexuality and gender, in particular whether they are as inextricably tied together as she originally implied. I will return to this issue later, in the light of her subsequent modification of her position. For now I want to concentrate on the problematic legacy of Oakley's sex–gender distinction. The question feminists have asked here is this: is it the case that biological sex differences mark a natural division onto which the social distinction of gender is mapped, or is the relationship between the two more complex?

For some time feminists have argued, from a variety of perspectives, that the opposition between sex and gender should be questioned. Some have argued that it is not in the interests of feminism to replicate and perpetuate the dualism between culture and nature which pervades our culture. For example, Moira Gatens (1983) points to the origin of the term outside feminism and questions whether this distinction can actually serve feminists in understanding women's embodied experience. Somer Brodribb goes further, suggesting that we are dealing not merely with a dualistic opposition between nature and culture, but a patriarchal ideology which privileges culture over nature. She sees the emphasis on social 'gender' to the exclusion of biological differences as a refusal of the female body which, she says, 'is sexism not liberation' (Brodribb 1992). 'Sexual difference' theorists such as Rosi Braidotti (1991, 1994) also see the concept of gender as insufficient to capture the interplay between the specificity of women's embodiment and the social and cultural definition of women as a devalued 'other'.

On the other hand there are those who question the sex-gender distinction on the grounds that its challenge to essentialism does not go far enough since it still assumes a natural sex onto which gender is grafted. If gender is social, it is argued, we should consider how it shapes our ideas about biological sex. We should question the very existence of gender categories themselves and ask why and how the social world is divided into the two groups we call 'women' and 'men'. This position is often associated with recent writings by poststructuralists and postmodernists, such as Judith Butler (1990), and Denise Riley (1988), but it began to be developed by French materialist feminists in the 1970s.[1] These writers, associated in the late 1970s with the journal *Questions Féministes* (*QF*), include Christine Delphy, Monique Wittig, Colette Guillaumin and Nicole-Claude Mathieu (see Adkins and Leonard 1996). Materialist feminists have continued to elaborate on their theories of gender or 'social sex' (Mathieu 1995) and, along with postmodern feminists, have done much to further our analysis of gender.

Materialist and Postmodern Perspectives on Gender

Materialist and postmodern feminists bring the existence of gender categories themselves into question, arguing that 'women' and 'men' are social categories defined in relation to each other rather than on the basis of a pre-social biological essence. While sharing this radically anti-essentialist position, they differ in their mode of analysis. Materialist feminists emphasise social structural relations, treating men and women as social groups founded upon unequal, exploitative relationships, while postmodern feminists emphasise cultural explanations, seeing 'men' and 'women' as discursively constructed categories. In this section I will explore these two perspectives further, taking Christine Delphy and Judith Butler as exemplars of each.

The materialist feminist position on gender follows from the conceptualisation of men and women as existing in a class-like relationship (see Chapter 1). Patriarchal domination is not based upon pre-existing sex differences, rather gender exists as a social division because of patriarchal domination. Hence hierarchy precedes division. As Delphy and Leonard put it: 'For us "men" and "women" are not two naturally given groups who at some time fell into a hierarchical relationship. Rather the reason the two groups are distinguished socially is because one dominates the other' (Delphy and Leonard 1992: 258).

This argument is in keeping with a Marxist method of analysis. For Marxists classes only exist in relation to one another: conceptually and empirically there can be no bourgeoisie without the proletariat and vice-versa. Similarly 'men' and 'women' exist as socially significant categories because of the exploitative relationship which both binds them together and sets them apart from each other. Conceptually there could be no 'women' without the opposing category 'men', and vice-versa. As Monique Wittig says, 'there are no slaves without masters' (1992: 15).

The implications of treating 'men' and 'women' as social categories were outlined in the editorial to the first issue of *Questions Féministes*, in which the collective's critique of naturalistic explanations of sexual difference was established as a basic tenet of their radical feminist stance. They opposed the ideas of 'sexual difference' feminists, arguing that the idea of feminine 'difference' derives from patriarchal reasoning and has served to justify and conceal our exploitation. In order to counter this ideology, they argue, radical feminism must refuse any notion of 'woman' that is unrelated to social context:

> The corollary of this refusal is our effort to deconstruct the notion of 'sex differences' which gives a shape and a base to the concept of 'woman' and is an integral part of naturalist

ideology. The social mode of being of men and of women is in no way linked to their nature as males and females nor with the shape of their sex organs.

(1981: 214–15)

Just as class struggle seeks to do away with classes, so feminist struggle should aim to do away with sex differences. In a non-patriarchal society there would be no social distinctions between men and women. This does not mean women becoming like men, since 'men' as we know them would no longer exist: 'for at the same time as we destroy the idea of the generic "Woman", we also destroy the idea of "Man"' (1981: 215).[2] As Delphy later put it: 'If women were the equals of men, men would no longer equal themselves' (Delphy 1993: 8).

The materialist feminist perspective treats 'sex' – what is usually seen as the 'obvious', natural distinction between men and women – as itself the product of society and culture. This is clearest in the work of Christine Delphy, who is unusual among the French materialist feminists in using the term gender. Delphy reversed the usual logic of the sex-gender distinction, suggesting that rather than gender being built upon the foundation of biological sex difference, 'sex has become a pertinent fact, hence a perceived category, because of the existence of gender' (Delphy 1984: 144). Gender creates anatomical sex 'in the sense that the hierarchical division of humanity into two transforms an anatomical difference (which is itself devoid of social implications) into a relevant distinction for social practice' (Delphy 1984: 144).

In her more recent work Delphy has elaborated on the idea that sex itself is socially constructed. She argues that rather than the difference between men and women being a self-evident anatomical fact, recognising that difference is itself a social act. The potential of the idea of 'gender' for Delphy is not just that it denaturalises differences between women and men, but that it focuses our attention on the very existence of the division of humanity into two gender categories. It is not enough, she argues, to treat the content of gender as variable, while assuming that the container (the category woman or 'man') is unchangeable. Rather, we should treat the container itself as a social product (Delphy 1993).

This radical questioning of the gender divide can also be found in the writings of Judith Butler. In *Gender Trouble* Butler points out that if gender does not follow automatically from sex then there is no reason to believe that there are inevitably only two genders: 'The presumption of a binary gender system implicitly retains the belief in a mimetic relation of gender to sex whereby gender mimics sex or is otherwise restricted by it' (Butler 1990: 6).

Once we begin to question the linkage in this way, we must also begin to ask whether sex itself might not be a fact of nature but a product of particular scientific discourses. If the immutability of sex is contested then, Butler suggests, 'this construct called "sex" is as culturally constructed as gender; indeed perhaps it was always already gender' (1990: 7).

That Butler's postmodern deconstruction of sex echoes Delphy's materialist account is no accident. The link between the two is the work of another materialist feminist, Monique Wittig, who developed her perspective from foundations laid down by Delphy, Guillaumin and others, and whose unique contribution was to identify the category of sex as 'the political category that founds society as heterosexual' (Wittig 1992: 5). Butler draws on Wittig in analysing the 'heterosexual matrix', the compulsory order of sex/gender/desire' that ties sex and gender into normative heterosexuality (Butler 1990). Butler, however, reads Wittig in isolation from other materialist feminist work and filters out Wittig's materialist emphasis on structural inequalities.[3] We are thus left with the impression that Wittig 'understands "sex" to be discursively produced and circulated by a system of significations oppressive to women, gays and lesbians' (Butler 1990: 113). Wittig's work is thus shaped to fit Butler's own contention that gender is a 'regulatory fiction'.

For Butler, both gender and sex are fictive in the sense that they are constructed through discursive and non-discursive practices. If sex, as well as gender, is a construct then it follows that the body does not have a pre-given essential sex. Rather, bodies are rendered intelligible through gender and 'cannot be said to have a signifiable existence prior to the mark of their gender' (Butler 1990: 8). Bodies become gendered through the continual performance of gender. Hence gender, rather than being part of our inner essence, is performative; to be feminine is to perform femininity. A central means through which Butler explains this is through her analysis of drag which she sees as mocking the idea that 'being feminine' expresses some inner, true gender identity. When a man performs in drag, dressing and acting like a woman, he is usually seen as mimicking or parodying an 'original' model, a 'real' woman. Butler's point is that, given that gender is a construction, there is no original. 'The parody is *of* the very notion of an original' (1990: 138). Drag de-naturalises gender, takes apart its performative elements and displays the fictionality of their coherence and reveals 'the imitative structure of gender itself' (1990: 137).

In conceptualising gender as performative, Butler is not saying that gender is something you 'put on' in the morning and discard at will (see Butler 1993: x). In her later book, *Bodies that Matter*, she makes it clear that we are constrained into gender. In response to those critics who accuse her of denying the materiality of the body, Butler argues that materiality is an effect of power and that sexed bodies are forcibly materialised through time.[4] Rather than thinking of the 'performative' as a performance, Butler turns to a notion of 'performativity' deriving from linguistics. Linguistic performatives are forms of speech which, by their utterance, bring what they name into being; for example, when a priest or registry office official says 'I pronounce you man and wife'.

Performativity is effective because it is 'citational': it entails citing past practices, referring to existing conventions, reiterating known norms. In this sense the pronouncement 'it's a girl', made at an infant's birth, brings a girl into being, begins the process, as Butler puts it, of 'girling the girl'. The process works because the phrase 'it's a girl' draws on the authority of the conventions which establish what a girl is. In naming sex, the norms of sex are being cited. Sex is materialised, according to Butler, through a complex of such citational practices which are both normative and regulative – and hence coercive and constraining (if never totally effective). In her emphasis on the normative and regulatory effects of performativity, Butler seems to be reaching towards some notion of a socially ordered world, but the social eludes her grasp. As Caroline Ramazanoglu points out, the question of where these norms come from or why they 'so often produce "heterosexual hegemony", male dominance, or any other imbalance of power does not appear to be an appropriate question to be asked within the logic of her theory' (1995: 37).

Butler's perspective on sex and gender entails a view of 'women' as a construct with no reality or unity prior to discourse. Butler is not alone in this project: it is a common feature of much postmodern feminism. Denise Riley, for example, characterises 'women' as erratic, inconstant and unstable; as a 'fluctuating identity' and a 'volatile collectivity' (1988: 1–2). This position is substantiated not only by the idea that 'women' is a discursive construct, but also by invoking differences among women. Thus the category 'women', for whom feminists claim to speak, is deemed exclusionary, representative only of some (white, privileged) women. Yet, while taking account of differences among women, the postmodern perspective also destabilises other identities such as 'lesbian' or 'black'. It leaves women with no position to speak from *as* women, or as Black women or as lesbian women, no position around which to mobilise politically (Stanley 1990).

Postmodernists are not unaware of these problems, hence they often talk of the strategic necessity of 'risking' essentialism (see, for example, Fuss 1989; Spivak and Rooney 1994). The 'risk' exists because it is assumed that the only alternative to postmodern deconstruction is to posit some essential difference between women and men and some essential unity to 'women' as a collectivity. But this is not the only alternative; materialist feminists bring the category 'women' into question without denying the material existence of women as a social group defined not by their 'essence' but by their location within the hierarchy of gender. Such a perspective also allows us to take account of the diversity which exists among women in terms of their materially differing locations in terms of class, sexuality, nationality, ethnicity and so on.[5]

The association of this deconstruction of gender with postmodernism and the disappearance of 'women' explains some feminists' resistance to it. If women and men are treated as a disembodied set of cultural categories, the reality of women's experience vanishes from view (Brodribb 1992). Furthermore, if gender is treated merely as a cultural distinction, or as a neutral term denoting social differences, the concept then serves to depoliticise feminist insights on male supremacy

(Thompson 1989; de Groot and Maynard 1993). These are not, however, necessary consequences of using the concept of gender. From a materialist feminist perspective gender is not simply a difference but a hierarchical division analogous to class, founded on material oppression and exploitation.

Gender and Sexuality

From my discussion of Butler's work it should be evident that these perspectives on gender also have implications for the ways in which we view sexuality, and in particular the distinction between heterosexuality and homosexuality. The assumption that gender rests on biological difference or procreative sex can all too easily lead to the assumption that heterosexual relations between anatomical males and anatomical females belong in the realm of nature. Sexuality is an area of social life which is particularly susceptible to essentialist arguments, the reduction of all the complexities of human sexual desires and practices to procreative heterosexuality and the survival of the human species. This reduction of heterosexuality to a reproductive imperative is closely tied to naturalistic ideas about gender. Hence it is commonly assumed that differences between women and men are directly explicable by reproductive biology. Moreover, sexuality validates gender: 'femininity' equates with attractiveness to men; sexual conquest of women confirms masculinity. It is then assumed that sexual difference is essential to sexual desire, that 'opposites' attract; hence heterosexuality is defined as 'normal' through what Tamsin Wilton (1996) has called 'heteropolarity'.

Hence feminists have an interest in challenging essentialist ideas on sexuality, as well as naturalistic accounts of differences between women and men. Clearly species survival does not demand that everyone engages in procreative sex to the exclusion of all other practices. Nor can we think of sexuality as a pre-given drive or essence which is 'repressed' or controlled by social forces. This common conception of sexuality rests on the unknowable: a hypothesised 'natural' sexuality uncontaminated by social influences. It cannot account for cultural and historical variations in sexuality nor for differences between men's and women's sexuality, except as products of nature or differential repression – and the 'unrepressed' sexuality envisaged is usually represented as the heterosexual male norm. Finally this 'drive reduction' model conceptualises the social regulation of sexuality as a negative force and does not allow for the productive deployment of power, the social *construction* of sexuality. Human sexual relations are social relations and hence meaningful to participants and shaped by the social contexts in which they occur.

In searching for alternatives to essentialism some feminists have turned to psychoanalytic accounts. However, even those forms of psychoanalysis which do not endorse the view that biology is destiny often rely on notions of pre-social drives and treat gender and sexuality as so intertwined that it is difficult to conceptualise lesbian and gay sexualities in any positive way. More potentially productive for feminism are the interactionist conceptualisation of 'sexual scripts' (Gagnon and Simon 1974) and Foucault's (1981) analysis of sexuality as discursively constituted. While deriving from very different theoretical traditions, these two perspectives share common assumptions. Both offer a critique of the idea of repression and suggest that there is no pre-given sexuality separable from its social or cultural construction. Both suggest that the various practices, identities, desires and body parts brought together under the heading of sexuality achieve their unity only through the scripts and discourses which constitute them *as* sexual. Sex, in Foucault's terms, is a 'regulatory ideal'. Both, potentially at least, suggest that the interrelationship between gender and sexuality is not pre-determined but is a product of particular historical and social contexts.[6] Of the two perspectives it is Foucault's which has been more influential among feminists and queer theorists.

One feminist much influenced by Foucault is Gayle Rubin, who drew on his work in uncoupling her conceptualisation of the sex/gender system (Rubin 1984, 1994). In revising her earlier (1975) view, Rubin argues that gender and sexuality should not only be treated as analytically distinct, but that they should constitute separate areas of critical analysis (Rubin 1984). In particular, she argued that in focusing on gender relations, on women's oppression, feminists ignore the separate oppression suffered by sexual 'minorities'. Most feminists would accept the need for an analytical distinction between gender and sexuality, without which we cannot explore their intersections, and most agree with Rubin that we should not over-privilege sexuality since this decides the issue of how they intersect in advance. Most, however, would still see sexuality and gender as connected. In particular, feminists have been interested in the relationship between the hierarchical division between women and men and the institutionalisation of heterosexuality.

In Judith Butler's work, as we have seen, the construction of gender and of sexed bodies interconnects with the normative, hegemonic status of heterosexuality. The materialist feminist perspective sees the binary divide between hetero and homo sexualities as deriving from gender. In a world without gender 'the distinction between homo and heterosexuality will be meaningless (*QF* 1981: 215). It is from these foundations that Wittig argues that lesbians, as fugitives from the heterosexual contract, 'are not women' (1992: 32). Other materialist feminists, notably Delphy, are critical of the essentialism implied by treating lesbianism as lying outside the cultural construction and regulation of gender and sexuality (see Jackson 1996), as are Fuss (1989) and Butler (1990). Sexual categories and identities, whether lesbian or heterosexual, depend on the prior existence of gender, on the possibility of desiring 'the same sex' or 'the opposite sex' (Jackson 1995).

In these accounts gender is apparently given causal priority over sexuality, but this is not the only way of thinking about their interrelationship. Psychoanalysis, in establishing the object of desire as central to the process of becoming a gendered subject, prioritises sexuality. Some radical feminists, from a very different perspective, also accord determining power to sexuality. For Catharine MacKinnon, for example, sexuality 'is that process which creates, organizes, expresses and directs desire, creating the social beings we know as women and men' (1982: 516). The division of gender is founded on 'the social requirements of heterosexuality, which institutionalises male sexual dominance and female sexual submission' (1982: 533). The problem with analyses such as MacKinnon's is that they reduce gender to sexuality, ignoring other, non-sexual, components of gender and of women's subordination.

Whatever perspective feminists take, most are aware that the boundaries of 'proper' gender identifications and of heterosexuality are policed in a variety of ways, that those who step outside these boundaries are usually stigmatised and often punished. Compulsory heterosexuality (Rich 1980) entails both keeping women *down*, as the subordinate gender, and in keeping them *in*, within the confines of relationships with men. Where the policing of these boundaries are concerned, gender divisions and normative heterosexuality are mutually reinforcing. As Tamsin Wilton points out, lesbians and gay men are stigmatised by calling their gender into question (they are not 'real men' or 'real women'); conversely men are coerced into being masculine by the threat of being labelled 'queer' and women who are 'unfeminine' are stigmatised as lesbians (Wilton 1996).

Queer, Gender Transgression and the Body

The interrelationship between gender and sexuality is, as we approach the millennium, a central issue within feminist debates. There is a renewed interest in the critique of heterosexuality and a revitalisation of debates between and among lesbian and heterosexual feminists (Wilkinson and Kitzinger 1993; Richardson 1996; Jackson 1988). At the same time we have witnessed the development of 'Queer theory', which has its feminist variants in the work of Judith Butler and others, but which has a life of its own outside feminist debate. Both feminism and Queer entail questioning binary divisions and both seek to dislodge heterosexuality from its hegemonic, normative status. Beyond this, their emphases differ. Whereas feminists take the oppression of women as their point of departure, Queer developed from gay political and theoretical priorities. Feminists are concerned both with heteronormativity, the ways in which heterosexuality's normative status is reinforced, and with what some have called 'heteropatriarchy' (Kitzinger and Wilkinson 1993): the ways in which compulsory heterosexuality is implicated in the subordination of women. These concerns imply a view of gender as hierarchical. Queer theorists, on the other hand, are more centrally preoccupied with heteronormativity and more rarely take account of women's subordination. Hence, while Queer takes gender seriously, seeing it as implicated in the maintenance of heterosexual hegemony, it does not necessarily conceptualise it as hierarchical.

Some feminists are highly critical of Queer theory since it ultimately displaces patriarchal gender hierarchy in favour of heterosexuality as the primary regulatory system and has the effect of 'disappearing' lesbians (Jeffreys 1994). Other feminists, however, welcome the inclusiveness of queer and actively engage with it (Wilton 1996; Smart 1996). At the time of writing, these debates are ongoing and are currently shaping discussions of the interrelationship between gender and sexuality (see Richardson 1996; Jackson 1998). There is also, as part of these debates, a growing interest in forms of gender transgression, from camp and drag through to post-operative transsexuality (see, for example, Garber 1992; Herdt 1994). These phenomena, too, are the subject of much debate. Queer theorists tend to see them as potentially subverting the binary divide of gender whereas some radical feminists argue that they reinforce gender (Jeffreys 1996). Interestingly, debates around heterosexuality and gender transgression are drawing in both feminist and gay male theorists; the heat generated may in part result from a history of the tensions between lesbian and gay politics and theory (see Jackson 1988).

The other central issue of the moment is 'the body'. It is through our embodiment that we recognise each other as gendered beings and engage in sexual practices. Ideas about the body have, at least implicitly, always underpinned feminist debates on gender and sexuality, and the body is increasingly becoming the terrain on which these debates are fought out. The idea of the 'natural' body has been questioned from a variety of perspectives and, once again, Queer and postmodern theorists have often been at the forefront of this trend (Butler 1993; Grosz 1995). Those with a stake in the project of sexual difference, however, have asserted 'the specificity of the lived, female bodily experience' (Braidotti 1994: 40). Feminism certainly cannot afford to leave the body untheorised as simply the inert matter on which gender is inscribed. On the other hand, much existing theorising treats the body as an abstraction which occludes 'the lived, fleshy, experienced matter of (womanly) bodies' (Hughes and Witz 1997). With the body increasingly becoming a focal point of feminist debate we should consider how everyday understandings of gender and sexuality are mediated through embodied experience – and there is some work which does this (see, e.g., Bartky 1990; Scott and Morgan 1993; MacSween 1993; Holland et al. 1994; Ramazanoglu 1995). While continning to question the naturalness of the body, we need to ground our analysis in material social relations and practices, giving attention to bodies in interaction and bodies as socially located. We may then produce analyses which speak to the lived and varied actualities of gendered and sexual embodiment.

Notes

1. The foundations for postmodernist work were also laid by earlier writers influenced by structural anthropology, linguistics and psychoanalysis, such as those involved in the British journal *m/f*, for whom the question of how women are produced as a category was central (see Chapter 2 and Adams and Cowie 1990). Gayle Rubin had also suggested that 'men' and 'women' are social, rather than natural categories, products of systems of marriage and kinship (Rubin 1975: 179).

2. This point, made in a section of the editorial co-written by Christine Delphy and Monique Plaza, was later made, in almost the same words, by Monique Wittig (see Wittig 1992: xx).

3. Instead, Butler locates Wittig within a form of 'French Feminism' invented by Anglo-American writers, a category which exludes most French feminists except a chosen few such as Kristeva and Irigaray and includes many male French theorists such as Lacan, Derrida and Foucault. For a discussion of this imperialist silencing of French feminism, see Delphy 1995; for a more detailed discussion of Butler's misrepresentation of Wittig, see Jackson 1996.

4. In shifting her focus to the materialisation of sexed bodies, gender as a social division is displaced from centre stage (see Hughes and Witz 1997).

5. Some, more sociologically informed, postmodern theorists suggest a middle ground which does not deny the material contexts of women's lives, but which advocates a view of 'women' as provisional, contextual and contested, and which allows for the differing locations from which the concept of women is mobilised (see, for example, Nicholson 1994). Another analysis, drawing on Sartre, is Iris Marion Young's conceptualisation of gender as seriality and women as a serial collectivity, a loose unity of those socially defined as women but also differentially located within other social divisions and hierarchies. The category 'women' thus has a social reality, but a diverse and complex one (Young 1994).

6. There is not the space here for a discussion of the differences between these perspectives. For a good discussion of this, see Connell and Dowsett 1992.

References

Adams, Parveen and Elizabeth Cowie (eds) (1990) *The Woman in Question*, London: Verso.

Adkins, Lisa and Diana Leonard (eds) (1996) *Sex in Question: French Materialist Feminism*, London: Taylor & Francis.

Bartky, Sandra (1990) *Femininity and Domination*, New York: Routledge.

Braidotti, Rosi (1991) *Patterns of Dissonance*, Cambridge: Polity; New York: Routledge.

Braidotti, Rosi (1994) 'Feminism by any other name' (interview), *differences*, 6 (2/3): 27–61.

Brodribb, Somer (1992) *Nothing Mat(t)ers: A Feminist Critique of Postmodernism*, Melbourne: Spinifex.

Butler, Judith (1990) *Gender Trouble: Feminism and the Subversion of Identity*, New York: Routledge.

Butler, Judith (1993) *Bodies that Matter*, New York: Routledge.

Butler, Judith (1994) 'Against proper objects', *differences*, 6 (2/3): 1–26.

Carby, Hazel (1982) 'White women listen', in Centre for Contemporary Cultural Studies (eds) *The Empire Strikes Back*, London: Hutchinson.

Connell, Robert W. and Gary W. Dowsett (1992) ' "The unclean motion of the generative parts": frameworks in Western thought on sexuality', in R. W. Connell and G. W. Dowsett (eds) *Rethinking Sex*, Melbourne: University of Melbourne Press.

de Groot, Joanna and Mary Maynard (1993) 'Facing the nineties: problems and possibilities for women's studies', in J. de Groot and M. Maynard (eds) *Women's Studies in the 1990s*, Basingstoke: Macmillan.

Delphy, Christine (1984) *Close to Home: A Materialist Analysis of Women's Oppression*, London: Hutchinson.

Delphy, Christine (1993) 'Rethinking sex and gender', *Women's Studies International Forum*, 16 (1): 1–9.

Delphy, Christine (1995) 'The invention of French feminism: an essential move', *Yale French Studies*, 87: 190–221.

Delphy, Christine and Diana Leonard (1992) *Familiar Exploitation: A New Analysis of Marriage in Contemporary Western Societies*, Oxford: Polity.

Foucault, Michel (1981) *The History of Sexuality, Volume One*, Harmondsworth: Penguin.

Fuss, Diana (ed.) (1989) *Essentially Speaking*, New York: Routledge.

Gagnon, John and William Simon (1974) *Sexual Conduct*, London: Hutchinson.

Garber, Marjorie (1992) *Vested Interests: Cross-Dressing and Cultural Anxiety*, London: Routledge.

Gatens, Moira (1983) 'A critique of the sex/gender distinction', in J. Allen and P. Patton (eds) *Beyond Marxism?*, New South Wales: Intervention Publications. Reprinted in her *Imaginary Bodies*, London: Routledge 1996.

Grosz, Elizabeth (1995) *Space, Time and Perversion*, London: Routledge.

Herdt, Gilbert (ed.) (1994) *Third Sex, Third Gender: Beyond Sexual Dimorphism in Culture and History*, New York: Zone Books.

Holland, Janet, Caroline Ramazanoglu, Sue Sharpe and Rachel Thomson (1994) 'Power and desire: the embodiment of female sexuality', *Feminist Review*, 46: 21–38.

Hughes, Alex and Anne Witz (1997) 'Feminism and the matter of bodies: from de Beauvoir to Butler', *Body and Society*, 3 (1): 47–60.

Jackson, Stevi (1992) 'The amazing deconstructing woman: the perils of postmodern feminism', *Trouble and Strife*, 25: 25–311.

Jackson, Stevi (1995) 'Gender and heterosexuality: a materialist feminist analysis', in M. Maynard and J. Purvis (eds) *(Hetero)sexual Politics*, London: Taylor & Francis.

Jackson, Stevi (1996) *Christine Delphy*, London: Sage.

Jackson, Stevi (1998) *Concerning Heterosexuality*, London: Sage.

Jeffreys, Sheila (1994) 'The queer disappearance of lesbians: sexuality in the academy', *Women's Studies International Forum*, 17 (5): 459–72.

Jeffreys, Sheila (1996) 'Heterosexuality and the desire for Gender', in D. Richardson (ed.) *Theorising Heterosexuality: Telling it Straight*, Buckingham: Open University Press.

Kitzinger, Celia and Sue Wilkinson (1993) 'Theorizing heterosexuality', in S. Wilkinson and C. Kitzinger (eds) *Heterosexuality: A 'Feminism and Psychology' Reader*, London: Sage.

MacKinnon, Catharine (1982) 'Feminism, Marxism, method and the state: an agenda for theory', *Signs*, 7 (2): 515–44.

MacSween, Morag (1993) *Anorexic Bodies*, London: Routledge.

Mathieu, Nicole-Claude (1995) 'Sexual, sexed and sex-class identities', in L. Adkins and D. Leonard (eds) *Sex in Question: French Materialist Feminism*, London: Taylor & Francis.

Mitchell, Juliet (1982) 'Introduction I', in J. Mitchell and J. Rose (eds) *Feminine Sexuality: Jacques Lacan and the Ecole Freudienne*, London: Macmillan.

Nicholson, Linda (1994) 'Interpreting *Gender*', *Signs*, 20 (1): 79–105.

Oakley, Anne (1972) *Sex, Gender and Society*, Oxford: Martin Robertson.

Questions Féministes Collective (1981) 'Variations on a common theme', in E. Marks and I. de Courtivron (eds) *New French Feminisms*, Brighton: Harvester.

Ramazanoglu, Caroline (1995) 'Back to basics: heterosexuality, biology and why men stay on top', in M. Maynard and J. Purvis (eds) *(Hetero)sexual Politics*, London: Taylor & Francis.

Rich, Adrienne (1980) 'Compulsory heterosexuality and lesbian existence', *Signs*, 5 (4): 631–60.

Richardson, Diane (ed.) (1996) *Theorising Heterosexuality: Telling it Straight*, Buckingham: Open University Press.

Riley, Denise (1988) *'Am I That Name?' Feminism and the Category of 'Women' in History*, London: Macmillan.

Rubin, Gayle (1975) 'The traffic in women', in R. Reiter (ed.) *Toward an Anthropology of Women*, New York: Monthly Review Press.

Rubin, Gayle (1984) 'Thinking sex: notes for a radical theory of the politics of sexuality', in C. Vance (ed.) *Pleasure and Danger*, London: Routledge.

Rubin, Gayle (1994) 'Sexual traffic' (interview with Judith Butler) in *differences*, 6 (2/3): 62–99.

Scott, Sue and David Morgan (eds) (1993) *Body Matters*, London: Falmer.

Smart, Carol (1996) 'Collusion, collaboration and confession: on moving beyond the heterosexuality debate', in D. Richardson (ed.) *Theorising Heterosexuality: Telling it Straight*, Buckingham: Open University Press.

Spivak, Gayatri Chakravorty and Ellen Rooney (1994) 'In a Word', interview in N. Schor and E. Weed (eds) *The Essential Difference*, Bloomington: Indiana University Press.

Stanley, Liz (1990) 'Recovering "women" in history from historical deconstructionism', *Women's Studies International Forum*, 13 (1/2): 153–5.

Thompson (1989) 'The sex/gender distinction: a reconsideration', *Australian Feminist Studies*, 10: 23–31.

Wilkinson, Sue and Celia Kitzinger (eds) (1993) *Heterosexuality: A 'Feminism and Psychology' Reader*, London: Sage.

Wilton, T. (1996) 'Which one's the man? The heterosexualisation of lesbian sex', in D. Richardson (ed.) *Theorising Heterosexuality: Telling it Straight*, Buckingham: Open University Press.

Wittig, Monique (1992) *The Straight Mind and Other Essays*, Hemel Hempstead: Harvester Wheatsheaf.

Young, Iris Marion (1994) 'Gender as seriality: thinking about women as a social collective', *Signs*, 19 (3): 713–38.

Further Reading

Adkins, Lisa and Diana Leonard (1995) *Sex in Question: French Materialist Feminism*, London: Taylor & Francis.

Butler, Judith (1990) *Gender Trouble: Feminism and the Subversion of Identity*, New York: Routledge.

Butler, Judith (1993) *Bodies that Matter*, New York: Routledge.

Butler, Judith (ed.) (1994) *More Gender Trouble: Feminism Meets Queer Theory*, special issue of *differences*, vol. 6, no. 3/4, Bloomington: Indiana University Press.

Fuss, Diana (ed.) (1991) *Inside/Out: Lesbian Theories, Gay Theories*, New York: Routledge.

Haraway, Donna (1991) 'Gender for a Marxist dictionary', in her *Simians, Cyborgs and Women*, London: Free Association Books.

Jackson, Stevi and Sue Scott (1996) *Feminism and Sexuality: A Reader*, Edinburgh: Edinburgh University Press.

Jackson, Stevi (1998) *Concerning Heterosexuality*, London: Sage.

Oakley, Ann (1972) *Sex, Gender and Society*, Oxford: Martin Robertson; reprinted in 1984 by Blackwell.

Richardson, Diane (1996) *Theorising Heterosexuality: Telling it Straight*, Buckingham: Open University Press.

Rubin, Gayle (1975) 'The traffic in women', in R. Reiter (ed.) *Toward an Anthropology of Women*, New York: Monthly Review Press.

Rubin, Gayle (1989) 'Thinking sex: notes for a radical theory of the politics of sexuality', in C. Vance (ed.) *Pleasure and Danger*, London: Pandora.

Schor, Naomi and Elizabeth Weed (eds) (1996) *The Essential Difference*, Bloomington: Indiana University Press.

Chapter 11

Feminist Linguistic Theories

Deborah Cameron

In a book about contemporary feminist theories, the case of feminist *linguistic* theory is something of an anomaly. Language figures prominently in the theorising of feminists working in other academic disciplines, but in linguistics, the discipline that takes language as its specific object of study, there is no such thing as a fully elaborated feminist theory of language. The psychoanalytic and post-structuralist currents discussed in Chapters 12 and 13 might claim to have such a theory; but a linguist must have reservations about what is meant by 'language' in the work of people like Hélène Cixous, Luce Irigaray and Julia Kristeva, whose claims about language and gender can only be interpreted metaphorically, not literally.

For instance, take the claim that women are 'excluded' from symbolic language: as a metaphor it is resonant and powerful, but it cannot be literally true if you believe (as virtually all linguists do) that the capacity for language is innate in humans – it's like saying that women are excluded from walking upright. Just as men and women can both walk (unless prevented by injury or disability), but for social reasons they may be distinguishable by the *way* they walk, it is only in their learned ways of *using* a given language that gender groups are differentiated. Mindful of this important distinction, feminists within linguistics have stopped short of claiming to have a distinctive theory of language *per se* and have pursued instead a series of debates on various aspects of the relationship between gender and language *use*.

Here, though, I do not want to survey the field from the perspective of main-stream linguistics; rather I will adopt the perspective of feminism. Nor does that mean exclusively *academic* feminism. The political importance of analysing and intervening in language was emphasised from the first by grass-roots feminist activists. As Liz Kelly comments:

One of the most powerful things feminism has done, and must continue to do, is to create new language and meanings which provide women with ways of naming and under-standing their own experience. ... It was our experience of language as a form of power – the power to name and define – which made it such a key issue from the beginnings of this wave of feminism. We didn't need linguistic or semiotic theory to understand how basic and fundamental an issue this was. It still is.

(Kelly 1994: 48)

The 'power to name and define' can be understood in two senses: *our* power, as feminists, to (re)name and (re)define our own realities, but conversely also the power of dominant groups to name and define reality for everyone. Since our lives and relationships are carried on to a large extent through language, since our knowledge of the world is mediated through language, the power to name and define is an important arena for reproducing or challenging oppressive social relations.

Liz Kelly notes that '[feminists] didn't need linguistic or semiotic theory' to arrive at this insight. It was arrived at by way of experience and practical political struggle (more than twenty years on it is hard to remember how many things feminists urgently needed to 'name and define': sex discrimination, domestic labour, sexual harassment, child sexual abuse, reproductive rights …). But it would not be true to say that feminists had no interest in more abstract theoretical questions. In Britain the extent of their interest was underlined when Dale Spender published *Man Made Language* (1980), an accessible synthesis of ideas about language and gender. This book was read and discussed in many women's groups.

From the point of view of many linguists Dale Spender oversimplified the issues. Nevertheless it should be acknowledged that *Man Made Language* had a positive effect, in that it opened up a space (in the movement, not just the academy) for certain questions to be addressed more explicitly. It challenged feminist linguists who disagreed with Spender to come up with more complex arguments, which might contribute to a more effective feminist linguistic practice as well as theory.

Below I will consider the results of this 'opening up' of theoretical questions, asking what contribution feminist linguists have made to feminists' understanding of 'language as a form of power'. I will organise this survey under two main headings: one which is concerned with the question of 'sexist language', how gender is represented in linguistic systems and how those representations can be challenged or changed; and one which is concerned with the way women and men actually use language, that is, with a form of social behaviour.

Sexist Language

The 'power to name and define' depends on having certain linguistic resources available to you (or being able to create new ones). In principle, language is an infinite resource, and linguistic creativity is the birthright of everyone who speaks, signs or writes. In practice, however, our inherited linguistic resources[1] have an inbuilt gender bias, and many obstacles stand in the way of those who would like to challenge it.

If we take English as our example, the first thing to notice is that it provides many resources simply for drawing attention to gender. Males and females are given gender-specific names, are commonly addressed using gender-marked titles (*sir, Mr X, Miss, darling*), are sometimes described using different words (for example, a man cannot be 'pretty' unless you specifically want to imply he is effeminate), and are almost always referred to using gender-marked pronouns like *he* and *she*. It is difficult, in English, to say something about a specific individual without making their gender explicit. That is not true of all languages; not all mark gender in the same way and to the same extent (Finnish and Turkish, for instance, have no equivalents of *he* and *she*).[2] But when children learn a language like English, they also learn that gender is a highly salient factor in talking about human beings. The distinction is built into our vocabulary and built into our grammar. In some areas of language, gender-marking is optional (for example, it is unconventional but not impossible to give a child a 'genderless' name); in other areas, such as pronoun usage, the rules of English require it.

The second thing to notice is that these rules embody a number of implicit assumptions about relations between men and women. In English (and many other languages), the 'unmarked' or default gender is masculine. Traditionally, the masculine pronouns *he, him(self), his* are used for 'generic' cases ('an artist must be true to his vision'; 'talk to your client before you give him advice'). The same principle dictates that a number of common words referring to persons have an unmarked form for male persons and a special, 'marked' form for female persons. Thus we get pairs like *manager* and *manageress* or *actor* and *actress*, which 'mark' feminine gender by adding a feminine suffix. In these cases, too, the masculine form doubles as the generic form. Equity is always described as 'the actors' union', not 'the actors' and actresses' union'. One of the most important points made by feminists is that the 'unmarked' status of the masculine gender in English and many other languages is not arbitrary, or purely a question of grammar (a point that emerges clearly if we look at the history of the English generic masculine: see Bodine 1975). Another implicit assumption found in some areas of language is that women are fundamentally *sexual* beings: applied to them, apparently neutral words take on sexual connotations (compare 'an honest man' and 'an honest woman'). Sexual connotations are frequently slurs: English provides a large number of negative terms describing women as prostitutes (*prostitute*, along with *nurse*, is the only occupational term in English where the unmarked form refers to women and the masculine form (*male prostitute*) is marked).

All this is well known, and it is also well known that feminists during the past two decades have made organised efforts to change the conventions of English (particularly the 'unmarked masculine' rule) and to coin or popularise new terms (such as 'unwaged' rather than 'non-working' for women who do not have a job outside their homes). But what are the *theoretical* implications of this feminist struggle to 'name and define'? *Why* are languages like English so androcentric (male-centred) and sexist? What is the social and psychological effect of their androcentrism? And how can it be challenged effectively?

Feminist discussion of these questions has often made use of 'the Sapir–Whorf hypothesis'. Sapir (1949) and Whorf (1976) were linguists who suggested that our worldview is determined by the structures of the particular native language we happen to speak: when we categorise reality, we unconsciously use the categories of our own grammar as a guide to what matters. For example, Whorf suggested that whether you think of 'fire' as a process or an object depends heavily on whether it is a verb or a noun in your language. Scientifically-speaking it *is* a process, but in English it is a noun, so this perception does not come naturally to English-speakers.

Feminists in the 1970s applied this kind of argument to gender, suggesting that languages which mark gender assiduously in their grammars, and treat the masculine as the unmarked gender, will lead their speakers to perceive the world in gender-polarised and androcentric ways. It was also suggested that the reason this happened was that languages had been shaped from the perspective of men – it was men, not women, who had historically generated the linguistic representations, and men who continued to control them.

This argument, and the Sapir–Whorf hypothesis, became familiar to a wide feminist audience through the popular work of Dale Spender. It also inspired the linguist and science fiction writer Suzette Haden Elgin to invent a 'woman's language' named Ladaan, whose creation and subsequent herstory are narrated in a novel-trilogy, *Native Tongue*, *The Judas Rose* and *Native Tongue III* (Elgin 1985, 1987, 1994). Outside fiction, however, we should be cautious about taking the Sapir–Whorf argument too literally or framing it too crudely.

To begin with, it seems likely that Sapir and Whorf overstated their case. They were writing at a time before the Second World War when linguists believed that languages could vary without limit, and their objective was to discredit the racist myth that non-European groups spoke 'primitive' languages. Today it is generally agreed that the differences among languages are trivial compared to the overall structural similarities. There is a basic blueprint for human language, which most linguists believe is innate.

That does not rule out the possibility of language and culture mutually influencing one another (though it should make us pause before suggesting that men – or anybody else – 'made' language). But when we consider the question of linguistic influences on our perception we need to bear in mind that the ideas of Sapir and Whorf have often been presented as much more crudely deterministic than they really were. Dale Spender adopted an extremely 'strong' version of the hypothesis, which was not only crude in its rendering of the original but also puzzling in the light of feminist language practices which Spender was well aware of and presumably approved of. If language determined perception absolutely, how could we explain the fact that feminists in the past twenty years *have* challenged the androcentrism of English, and that they *have* coined new terms to describe old and new realities? There is a basic contradiction in Spender's argument that 'man made language' constrains our perceptions in accordance with a 'male' worldview. If this were so, how could Spender herself ever have come up with the argument? At the very least, feminists who maintain that language affects perception must shift to a weaker form of the Sapir–Whorf hypothesis if their claims are to be credible.

There is, moreover, an important distinction between the influence of *words* on mental categorisation and the influence of *grammar*: words can be consciously reflected on, we constantly create new ones and alter or eliminate old ones, but grammatical categories are more fixed and their implications more likely to remain invisible to us. Whorfian examples that dwell on vocabulary – such as the observation that Eskimos have a lot of words for snow – are not very significant theoretically, even where they are accurate.[3] No-one would take the statement that 'printers have a lot of terms for type fonts' or 'surfers have words for many different kinds of waves' as implying that printers and surfers think differently from other people; nor would it be self-evident that the words enabled the printers/surfers to distinguish the fonts/waves rather than vice-versa. The argument about Eskimos and snow is tainted by a form of racism which falsely exoticises cultures remote from one's own.

Bearing this in mind, let us look more closely at the specific problem of gender-marking in English grammar, which is, potentially, a Whorfian phenomenon – a case where a social distinction is not merely *lexicalised* (encoded in words) but *grammaticised*, built into the rules for constructing well-formed sentences. So, does it determine, or less strongly, does it influence, the way we perceive the world?

A number of studies which investigate how English speakers actually interpret generic masculine terms have come to the conclusion that 'masculine' takes precedence over generic' (see Silveira 1980). However, it is difficult to separate the effects of language from the effects of common-sense assumptions about the world that words refer to. For example, one way to test perceptions of gender in English is to ask people to fill in blanks where they will have to use a third-person singular pronoun, for example, 'when a nurse comes off the night shift, ＿＿ may have trouble adjusting to a normal sleeping pattern'. Although 'a nurse' here is generic, most people will choose the pronoun *she* to fill the blank. This might be taken as evidence that *he* is not a true generic: if it were, then people should find nothing unnatural in using it in this context. But people doing this sort of task inevitably draw on social scripts and stereotypes according to which a 'typical' nurse is a woman. This does not mean, however, they are unaware of the existence of male nurses, and equally it need not imply that *he* could never be used as a true generic. In other words, context is at least as important to perception as the surface form of words.

Other examples might also lead us to question how far linguistic form in itself is the main influence on our thinking. For instance, statements made in the media are not infrequently androcentric and sexist *though the words they use are not formally gender-marked* – like the report on a Birmingham man who went on trial for attacking his *next door neighbour's wife* with a machete (Cameron 1992). Where did this unfortunate woman live, if not next door to her attacker? There is no explicit gender-marking on the word *neighbour* (it is not like *actress*), nothing that prevents us from using it in relation to either sex, and (unlike the case of *nurse*) no clear cultural stereotype associating the role of 'neighbour' with one sex more than the other. Yet the author of the sentence quoted above uses *neighbour* as if it could only refer to men. This is sexism, and it is made manifest in language; but it is not what feminist reformers usually mean when they talk about 'sexist language', and a set of formal guidelines prescribing gender-neutral terms would leave it untouched.

I do not want to give the impression I think there is no problem of sexist language. But it does no good to locate this at a 'global' level (men made language and language determines thought) where the arguments are unconvincing, the evidence is mixed, and finding solutions is logically impossible. I would identify three errors in the 'orthodox' feminist approach. One is a tendency to over-emphasise *language*, to portray it as the root cause of everything else, and to separate it out too much from all the other things it works in conjunction with. The second error is to suppose that language only matters if it has demonstrable effects on *thinking*, and if no such effects can be shown then there is no reason to intervene in it (hence the need to exaggerate its influence on thought). I am sceptical of the argument that we should change things like generic *he* and *man* because they are 'confusing' and 'inaccurate'. Like every other competent speaker of English, I know perfectly well that a banner saying 'all men are equal' is meant to be generic, and a sign on a toilet door saying 'men' is not. But this does not mean the generic masculine is acceptable. It may not be confusing but it is symbolically insulting: as the philosopher Janice Moulton once remarked (1981), it's like the way we say 'Kleenex' for all tissues, or (in Britain) 'hoover' for all vacuum cleaners. In English, male human beings are constantly presented as the leading brand. This symbolic affirmation of male superiority is reason enough for feminists to argue for change.

The third mistake is to fixate on particular linguistic items (like *he, man* or other single words), as opposed to larger patterns of *discourse*. Even when one cannot point to a single unequivocally offensive word, sexism can appear more subtly, in the way words are combined to favour a sexist interpretation. For instance, Kate Clark (1992) has investigated the language of reports on sexual violence against women in *The Sun*. She looks at headlines like GIRL, 7, MURDERED WHILE MUM

DRANK IN THE PUB, and points out that what is *not* said is as important as what is, and the interpretation is produced by an interaction of the two. The choice of a passive – '[was] murdered' – allows the headline writer to avoid mentioning the agent of the action' (the murderer, a man). The next human agent mentioned in the headline is 'Mum', who is said to have been drinking in the pub at the time her daughter was murdered. This is likely to trigger an inference by the reader that the mother's negligence is to blame for the girl's death.

For feminists it is important to recognise and understand this kind of complexity. The commonest (and in mainstream terms, most successful) line of resistance to sexist language has been to produce non-sexist language guidelines which essentially involve substitutions of single terms – neutral forms for biased or offensive ones. But this 'literal translation' approach will not catch cases like the *Sun* headline, or sexist uses of gender-neutral words like *neighbour*. In addition, the approach can be over-mechanical, pointlessly translating words into a 'neutral' or 'inclusive' form without asking if the result is *conceptually* an improvement. One recent guide (Doyle 1995) proposes 'parental instinct' for 'maternal instinct': this is a meaningless gesture of inclusiveness, since the very idea of such an instinct can only arise or make any sense within a framework of sexist assumptions about female biology and motherhood.

Our aim in reforming language cannot be simply to change surface linguistic forms, but must be to change the *meanings* underlying them. The struggle to create new meanings is more difficult, but also much more important, than the struggle to eliminate a finite number of sexist linguistic forms. To put it in the terms Liz Kelly uses (see above), we have to recognise that you can rename reality without actually redefining it; and that is a hollow victory, which can sometimes rebound on feminists.

Consider, for instance, what has happened to terms like 'sexism', 'sexual harassment', 'sexual violence'. As they have moved into mainstream usage – which is something their feminist originators wanted – they have often acquired a kind of liberal, 'equal opportunities' meaning which is at odds with more radical feminist understandings. Thus 'sexism' for instance often means just 'treating either sex unfairly by comparison with the other'. For feminists, by contrast, sexism is a systemic structural relation in which women are subordinated. Any disadvantage experienced by men *as men* (for example, the norm that they should be emotionally inexpressive) is not so much sexism *against men* as it is an aspect of the larger system which allows men to dominate (and must therefore discourage individual men from adopting subordinate 'feminine' roles).

To think of language as a code, a set of words with fixed definitions, underestimates the active creativity of language-users: a creativity which makes change possible, but equally makes possible *resistance* to change (the reinterpretation of feminist terms like 'sexism is an example). An adequate feminist theory of language and meaning must recognise the complexity of the task we are engaged in, and not suggest either that we are powerless in the face of a man-made language, or that simply by creating new usages we can automatically impose new meanings on the speech community as a whole. Precisely because meaning is *not* fixed, there is no end to the struggle over 'the power to name and define'.

Women and Men Speaking

If the 'power to name and define' requires linguistic resources, it also requires the means and opportunity to use them. One of the ways in which women have been kept in a subordinate place is through a denial of our right to be equal linguistic actors. Women are 'silenced': whether explicitly, through restrictions on the contexts and roles in which they may speak (for example, the nineteenth-century ban on women speaking in public to a mixed audience); or implicitly through less formal social practices which effectively restrict women in many everyday contexts: disparagement of our ability to tell jokes, refusal to recognise our contributions in discussions, disapproval of girls who are not 'quiet' and 'good listeners'.

But to see women's linguistic inequality only in terms of 'silence' oversimplifies the issue. Women's linguistic activity in some contexts can be seen as a species of domestic labour whose benefits men appropriate (see Fishman 1983). It is common in western societies for women to be restricted linguistically in the public sphere, but to talk *more* than men in the private sphere: it tends to be women who oil the wheels of social and familial interaction, who channel information within a household and who perform – largely through speaking and listening – the demanding but invisible work of emotional maintenance for other family members.

Although I have begun by postulating a gender *inequality* (following the principle that this survey takes feminism, not linguistics, as its starting point), observations of gendered speech behaviour have been framed on the whole within a context of social scientific research into sex or gender *differences* – that is, linguists define what they are doing as investigating empirically the differing speech-styles of women and men. One could question whether this kind of research is necessarily feminist, or of use to feminism. Merely drawing attention to male-female differences can be a reactionary move, and in this case sometimes has been.

Research on gender differences in language use has gone through three major 'phases', though these have overlapped chronologically rather than proceeding in a neat linear sequence. The pioneering piece of work was Robin Lakoff's essay *Language and Woman's Place* (1975), which represents what I will term a 'deficit model'. According to Lakoff, women have been socialised to display their femininity in a language whose main characteristic is ineffectualness or lack of force. Just as little girls don't learn to throw the kind of punch that will actually hurt anyone, or if they do learn it they are discouraged from ever using this skill, so they learn by imitation and reinforcement to use a style of speaking that is designed to earn approval rather than to exert authority. Lakoff regards this style as a deficiency, imposed socially on women (it is not our 'fault', it is 'society's' – but still, it makes us inferior speakers). The same argument underpins 'assertiveness training', whose feminist variant also dates from the mid 1970s – see Cameron 1994 and 1995).

Other feminists took issue with this model, preferring to interpret the gender differences Lakoff cited as signs of women's subordinate status. Proponents of this 'dominance model' differed from Lakoff on three counts. First, they questioned whether the key variable is gender/femininity, or whether it is power/low status; some behaviours associated with women may be typical of subordinate speakers more generally – confusion occurs because women outnumber men in low-status positions (see O'Barr and Atkins 1980). Second, and following on from this, they rejected Lakoff's suggestion that gendered linguistic behaviour is the 'global' consequence of early socialisation rather than a response to the 'local' demands of particular contexts. Finally, dominance theorists disagreed with Lakoff's evaluation of women as ineffectual speakers. They argued that, on the contrary, women show both skill and rationality in adopting certain strategies to minimise male hostility and maximise male co-operation. In other words, if you are objectively powerless, your 'least worst' option may well be to display a lack of assertiveness. What's wrong is not women's language, but the subordinate positioning to which this language is appropriate.

In the 1980s, a third model gained influence, the 'cultural difference' model whose best-known representative is Deborah Tannen (1990). This returns to Lakoff's emphasis on socialisation, though it stresses the peer group rather than the family. It proposes that girls and boys, socialising largely with others of their own sex in groups that are typically organised in very different ways (large hierarchical boys' groups and small intimate girls' groups), develop orientations to linguistic interaction as different as those of different cultures (for example, France and Japan). Boys learn to use interaction primarily to gain and maintain status, whereas girls learn that its main purpose is to foster closeness and connection. This leads the sexes both to behave differently and, when they form relationships later on, to misunderstand one another's meanings and intentions to a degree that causes serious conflict – like intercultural conflict, but in some ways worse, since few people are aware how profound gender differences are.

Tannen, however, would not wish to return to Lakoff's negative view of women's language-use, or conversely to the dominance model critique of men's behaviour in mixed-sex interaction. 'Difference' theorists are cultural relativists in the tradition of 'different but equal', and what they advocate is not that either sex should change but that both should learn mutual understanding and tolerance. Then again, some of the feminists who have expressed enthusiasm for Tannen's work may find support in it for the view that women are not just different-but-equal but actually 'better' conversationalists, meaning more open, caring and co-operative, than men. This is in some ways an appealing thought, but there are intellectual and political objections to it. Intellectually, the objection is that the 'women are better' thesis is simplistic and essentialist (it takes for granted gender differences which require explanation, and it lumps all women together). Politically, one might object that if the root cause of a situation is inequality and exploitation, then a celebratory response is not appropriate.

Language and gender researchers have been preoccupied in the 1990s by arguments between supporters of the 'dominance' and 'difference' models. What is at stake in these arguments is not so much facts about language-use as conceptions of gender itself. Many researchers (myself included) find it alarming that the field seems to be returning to an old-fashioned model of gender 'complementarity', as if it made sense to talk about microsocial arrangements in boys' and girls' peer groups in total isolation from macrosocial questions about the sex/gender system and the power relations it reproduces. (Why are boys and girls different in just these ways? And why is the result of cross-sex 'misunderstanding' almost always to the disadvantage of women?) We are surely dealing not with random difference, but with a linguistic version of the sexual division of labour. The objection to Tannen is put well in the title of a critical article – 'When "difference" *is* "dominance"' (Uchida 1992 [my emphasis]; see also Troemel-Ploetz 1991 and Cameron 1995).

Yet few feminist linguists advocate a simple return to the 'dominance' approach, for it is clear that this model – and indeed all the three models I have outlined – suffers from an essentialism that is not compatible with the most sophisticated current feminist thinking. By 'essentialism' here I do not mean biologism, but a way of thinking which treats gender divisions as given in advance and 'women' as a static and homogeneous category. Gender divisions should not be used as the ultimate explanation of other social phenomena, because they are themselves social phenomena in need of explanation. And like other social phenomena, they are variable in time and space.

Feminist linguistics has sometimes been guilty of treating the behaviour of a minority as if it represented women's condition universally. While there is evidence that gender-related differences in linguistic behaviour occur very widely across cultures (see Sherzer 1987 for a survey), they are not always the same differences, and do not necessarily give rise to the same political problems. For example, even within western Anglophone communities, many Black (also Jewish and working-class white) women do not identify with the standard picture of women speakers as weak and unassertive (or as some would prefer to see it, especially caring and egalitarian). Their traditional problem is being seen as too 'strong': stereotyped as pushy loudmouths or tyrannical matriarchs. Some have encountered these prejudices less within their own communities than among middle-class white feminists.

Such women may put a different construction from their more privileged sisters on behaviours which the latter regard as 'feminist'. Penelope Eckert and Sally McConnell-Ginet (1992) give the example that it may be very important to a working-class cleaning woman to be addressed by her middle-class employer as 'Mrs Smith' rather than 'Shirley', though to the middle-class woman this preference connotes (a) a formality she is uncomfortable with ('we're both women, after all') and (b) a distressing lack of feminist consciousness ('why does she want to proclaim her status as someone's wife?'). In cases like this we have to recognise that the same linguistic convention which subordinates Sarah Smythe may be experienced as empowering by Shirley Smith. This is not (as a 'difference' theorist might argue) because the two women come from separate backgrounds and do not understand one another's ways of speaking: it is because they are differently (hierarchically) positioned. The middle-class woman has an interest in glossing over this, but the working-class woman is very much aware of it, and wants her employer to deal with it by making an explicit gesture of respect rather than an empty gesture of (imaginary) solidarity. The situation is, in fact, another instance of conflict (in this case between women) over 'the power to name and define' women's realities.

Conclusion: Thinking Globally, Acting Locally

The idea of a shared, authentic, post-patriarchal 'women's language' as propounded by Suzette Haden Elgin and hinted at by Dale Spender is not only utopian (in the sense of 'impossible'), it has also been criticised for making the essentialist and even imperialist assumption that all women are the same. And in this case I believe the argument is not just trendy postmodernist posturing (or self-righteous identity politics, though it can occasionally shade into that): it is of tremendous *practical* political importance that feminists develop a linguistic practice which is neither exclusionary nor completely relativistic; a way of interacting that does not assume we cannot communicate across difference, but equally does not fall into the trap of supposing that because we are women, or indeed feminists, we will automatically share a common language.

Language is inherently two-sided. We have it because we are social animals whose way of life demands we operate as part of a group; but we need it because we are also individuals, with no unmediated access to one another's internal thought processes. When we talk, therefore, we are both affirming something which is shared (minimally, our capacity for linguistic communication) and investigating something which is not (the experiences of another person). Feminist linguistic theory must pay due attention both to what we share (not only as women speakers, but as human speakers) and to what divides us.

So what is the way forward for feminist linguistic theory and practice? The conclusion I draw from the points made above is that in future our ways of thinking about language and gender must become less 'global' and more 'local' (for a more elaborate argument on this point, see Eckert and McConnell-Ginet 1992). Women's relation to language is certainly affected in material ways by the social relations of gender that obtain in their societies. The construction of 'women' and 'men' includes their construction as linguistic actors with differing rights and responsibilities; in learning their 'shared' language, too, both sexes will learn a particular set of cultural meanings to do with gender. These are the 'global' points. But it is only by analysing the specifics of their 'local' operation – which is not always and everywhere the same – that feminists will be able to act politically, in a way that leads to practical results.

What linguistic theory has to contribute to feminists' understanding of 'language as a form of power' is a sense of the complexity of the issues. While I agree with Liz Kelly that 'we didn't need linguistic or semiotic theory to understand how basic and fundamental an issue [language] was', that does not mean a theory of language is unnecessary. Implicitly, we always have a theory. If we are to build on our successes in 'creating new language and meanings' and avoid repeating our failures (such as superficial, 'inclusive' terms or essentialist accounts of so-called 'women's language'), then we feminists – activists as well as academics – must continue to develop theory and practice together.

Notes

1. 'Our' here implicitly means 'English-speakers'. This discussion will take the English language as its main source of examples, but it is very important to keep in mind that English is not the only language in the world, and not all languages work in the same way English does.
2. There is some evidence that this does affect the speed at which children acquire the concept of gender initially – Finnish-speaking children are slower than English-speaking children, who are slower than children acquiring Hebrew, a language where all pronouns are gender-marked (i.e. 'I', 'you', 'we', 'they' as well as 'he/she'). On the other hand there is no evidence that end result is any different, and it certainly cannot be said that Finnish or Turkish women live in a feminist paradise because of their genderless language – which is a point against crude versions of linguistic determinism (see the discussion below of the Sapir–Whorf hypothesis).
3. Geoff Pullum (1991) claims in an article titled 'The Great Eskimo Vocabulary Hoax', that the extensive snow-vocabulary of the Eskimos is actually a myth. The argument reproduced below that in any case the Whorfian interpretation is racist is also Pullum's.

References

Bodine, Ann (1975) 'Androcentrism in prescriptive grammar', reprinted in Cameron 1990.

Cameron, Deborah (ed.) (1990) *The Feminist Critique of Language: A Reader*, London: Routledge.

Cameron, Deborah (1992) *Feminism and Linguistic Theory*, 2nd edn, London: Macmillan.

Cameron, Deborah (1994) 'Just say no: the empire of assertiveness', *Trouble and Strife* 29/30, Winter.

Cameron, Deborah (1995) *Verbal Hygiene*, London: Routledge.

Clark, Kate (1992) 'The linguistics of blame', in Michael Toolan (ed.) *Language, Text and Context*, London: Routledge.

Doyle, Margaret (1995) *The A–Z of Non-Sexist Language*, London: Women's Press.

Eckert, Penelope and Sally McConnell-Ginet (1992) 'Communities of practice: where language, gender and power all live', in Kira Hall, Mary Buchholz and Birch Moonwomon (eds) *Locating Power*, Berkeley, CA: Berkeley Women and Language Group.

Elgin, Suzette Haden (1985) *Native Tongue*, London: Women's Press.

Elgin, Suzette Haden (1987) *The Judas Rose*, London: Women's Press.

Elgin, Suzette Haden (1994) *Native Tongue III*, London: Women's Press.

Fishman, Pamela (1983) 'Interaction: the work women do', in Barrie Thorne, Cheris Kramarae and Nancy Henley (eds) *Language, Gender and Society*, Rowley, MA: Newbury House.

Kelly, Liz (1994) 'Stuck in the middle', *Trouble and Strife* 29/30, Winter.

Lakoff, Robin (1975) *Language and Woman's Place*, New York: Harper & Row.

Moulton, Janice (1981) 'The myth of the neutral "man"', in Mary Vetterling-Braggin (ed.) *Sexist Language*, New York: Rowman and Littlefield.

O'Barr, William and Bowman Atkins (1980) '"Women's language" or "powerless language"?, in Sally McConnell-Ginet, Ruth Borker and Nelly Furman (eds) *Women and Language in Literature and Society*, New York: Praeger.

Pullum, Geoff (1991) *The Great Eskimo Vocabulary Hoax, and Other Irreverent Essays on the Study of Language*, Chicago: University of Chicago Press.

Sapir, Edward (1949) *Selected Writings on Language, Culture and Personality*, Berkeley: University of California Press.

Sherzer, Joel (1987) 'A diversity of voices: women's and men's speech in ethnographic perspective', in Susan Phillips, Susan Steel and Christine Tanz (eds) *Language, gender and sex in comparative perspective*, New York: Oxford University Press.

Silveira, Jeannette (1980) 'Generic masculine words and thinking', *Women's Studies International Quarterly*, vol. 3, pp. 165–78.

Spender, Dale (1980) *Man Made Language*, London: Routledge & Kegan Paul.

Tannen, Deborah (1990) *You Just Don't Understand: Women and Men in Conversation*, New York: Morrow.

Troemel-Ploetz, Senta (1991) 'Selling the apolitical', *Discourse and Society*, vol. 2, no. 4: 489–502.

Uchida, Aki (1992) 'When "difference" is "dominance": a critique of the "anti-power-based" cultural approach to sex differences', *Language in Society*, vol. 21, no. 4: 547–68.

Whorf, Benjamin Lee (1976) *Language, Thought and Reality: Selected Writings*, Cambridge, Mass: MIT Press.

Further Reading

Cameron, Deborah (ed.) (1998) *The Feminist Critique of Language: A Reader*, London: Routledge.

Cameron, Deborah (1992) *Feminism and Linguistic Theory*, 2nd edn, London: Macmillan.

Clark, Kate (1992) 'The linguistics of blame', in Michael Toolan (ed.) *Language, Text and Context*, London: Routledge and repr. in Cameron 1998.

Coates, Jennifer (1986) *Women, Men and Language*, London: Longman.

Coates, Jennifer (ed.) (1998) *Language and Gender: A Reader*, Oxford: Blackwell.

Coates, Jennifer and Deborah Cameron (eds) (1988) *Women in their Speech Communities*, London: Longman.

Crawford, Mary (1995) *Talking Difference*, London: Sage.

Eckert, Penelope and Sally McConnell-Ginet (1992) 'Think practically and look locally: language and gender as community-based practice', *Annual Review of Anthropology*, 21: 461–90.

Fishman, Pamela (1983) 'Interaction: the work women do', in Barrie Thorne, Cheris Kramarae and Nancy Henley (eds) *Language, Gender and Society*, Rowley, MA: Newbury House.

Freed, Alice, Victoria Bergvall and Janet Bing (eds) (1997) *Language and Gender: Theory and Research*, London: Longman.

Gal, Susan (1991) 'Between speech and silence: the problematics of research on language and gender', in M. di Leonardo (ed.) *Gender at the Crossroads of Knowledge*, Berkeley, CA: University of California Press, pp. 175–203.

Goodwin, Marjorie H. (1990) *He-said-she-said*, Bloomington, IN: Indiana University Press.

Hall, Kira and Mary Buchholz (eds) (1995) *Gender Articulated: Language and the Socially-Constructed Self*, London: Routledge.

Johnson, Sally and Ulrike Meinhof (eds) (1996) *Language and Masculinity*, London: Longman.

Lakoff, Robin (1975) *Language and Woman's Place*, New York: Harper & Row.

Livia, Anna and Kira Hall (eds) (1997) *Queerly Phrased*, New York: Oxford University Press.

McConnell-Ginet, Sally (1990) 'Language and gender', in F. Newmeyer (ed.) *Linguistics: The Cambridge Survey, Vol. IV: The Sociocultural Context*, Cambridge: Cambridge University Press.

Maltz, Daniel and Ruth Borker (1982) 'A cultural approach to male-female misunderstanding', in John J. Gumperz (ed.) *Language and Social Identity*, Cambridge: Cambridge University Press.

Penelope, Julia (1990) *Speaking Freely*, New York: Pergamon.

Sherzer, Joel (1987) 'A diversity of voices: women's and men's speech in ethnographic perspective', in Susan Phillips, Susan Steele and Christine Tanz (eds) *Language, Gender and Sex in Comparative Perspective*, New York: Oxford University Press.

Spender, Dale (1980) *Man Made Language*, London: Routledge & Kegan Paul.

Swann, Joan (1992) *Girls, Boys and Language*, Oxford: Blackwell.

Tannen, Deborah (1990) *You Just Don't Understand: Women and Men in Conversation*, New York: Morrow.

Tannen, Deborah (ed.) (1992) *Gender and Conversational Interaction*, Oxford: Oxford University Press.

Troemel-Ploetz, Senta (1991) 'Selling the apolitical', *Discourse and Society*, 2.4: 489–502.

Uchida, Aki (1992) 'When "difference" is "dominance": a critique of the "anti-power-based" cultural approach to sex differences', *Language in Society*, 21.4: 547–68.

Wodak, Ruth (ed.) (1997) *Gender and Discourse*, London: Sage.

Chapter 12

Psychoanalytic Feminist Theory

Sue Vice

As the term 'psychoanalysis' suggests, its concern is to offer an account, or analysis, of the mind's – the psyche's – structure and its relation to the body, and use that as the basis for treating certain kinds of sickness. Psychoanalysis is popularly known as the 'talking cure'; it is often represented in films or novels in scenes where a bearded, European-accented older man sits behind a couch, on which lies his patient, often a woman, who progresses towards self-knowledge by telling the analyst her life-history, which he must interpret. This scenario is almost as commonplace in twentieth-century culture as some of psychoanalysis' central concepts: penis envy, the Oedipus complex, the phallic symbol. As these terms suggest, psychoanalysis is closely concerned with gender, sexuality, familial relations, and, as we shall see, the fact that their expression and construction are not always available to the conscious mind. Clearly these areas are also those of central interest to feminism. These particular terms also show, however, where feminist disquiet with psychoanalysis comes from. Its Freudian legacy means that the masculine is taken as the norm, the feminine seen simply as a lesser, 'castrated' version of that norm. Far from being a tool to analyse the oppression of women, psychoanalysis has been seen by some feminist writers as another weapon in the armoury of patriarchy. To enlist on behalf of feminism the insights of psychoanalysis, in particular the concept of the unconscious, and the idea that gender is a psychic and not a biological identity, post-Freudian writers have focused on the very early pre-Oedipal stages of a child's life, and mothering. These writers have for the most part fallen into two groups: the Anglo-American object-relations school, and French feminist theory.

How the relationship between psychoanalysis and feminism has functioned, and why, is the concern of this chapter, which will start with a summary of Freud's role in the origins of psychoanalysis. It will then move on to consider post-Freudian theorists Melanie Klein and Jacques Lacan; then some feminist theorists whose work has been informed by psychoanalysis, particularly in relation to the body, language, sexual difference and orientation, motherhood, and cultural production such as film.

Freud and Psychoanalysis

Sigmund Freud was born in the Austro-Hungarian Empire in 1856, and died in London in 1939, having fled Vienna, where he lived and worked, after the Nazis invaded Austria. He described psychoanalysis as a phenomenon of the twentieth century (*The Interpretation of Dreams* was published in 1900), but also acknowledged the nineteenth-century precursors whose work he synthesised in producing his central concepts, particularly that of the unconscious. Freud first practised as a neurologist; in 1885 he went to Paris to work with the famous Jean-Martin Charcot, at Charcot's Salpêtrière clinic for nervous diseases. Charcot was involved in treating hysteria – varieties of debilitating physical symptoms affecting women, with no clear organic cause.

On his return to Vienna in 1887, Freud continued his investigation of the mind by taking up the theory of his colleague Josef Breuer that 'hysteria was the product of a physical trauma which had been forgotten by the patient' (Strachey 1955: 14). Together, they wrote *Studies on Hysteria* (1895), a collection of five case histories of women 'suffering from reminiscences' (Freud 1962: 39). The women's fears and phobias (of train journeys, fog, lifts, Red Indians, worms), hallucinations (Miss Lucy R. suffered a recurrent olfactory hallucination, the smell of burnt pudding), and physical symptoms (including amnesia, asthma, feeling cold, neck-cramps, squints and stammers) all turned out to have their origins in repressed memories. One of these women, Anna O., actually coined the phrase the 'talking cure' (ibid.: 83) for the relief she obtained by discussing her hallucinations with Breuer. Breuer admits that this strange fact – the disappearance of symptoms once they had been given verbal utterance – took him by surprise, and only later became a therapeutic technique (102). Elaine Showalter suggests that one of Anna O.'s symptoms, which included anorexia and speech disorders, her phantom pregnancy, was closely related to her therapeutic insights. As well as representing her love for Breuer, it signified the birth of their shared psychoanalytic method. Psychoanalytic therapy depends on the transference and countertransference which take place between analyst and analysand, in which each sees their childhood relationships re-enacted in the person of the other. Showalter sees the move from Charcot's habit of exhibiting and photographing his female patients, to the dialogue of the 'talking cure', as one absolutely in women's interests:

> Because Breuer respected the intelligence of his hysterical female patient, encouraged her to speak, and then listened carefully to what she said, he was able to translate the body language and the female antilanguage of hysteria into a psychoanalytic theory of the unconscious.
>
> (Showalter 1985: 157)

The 'relation between symptoms and ... psychical traumas' (Freud 1962: 51), made clear by hysteria, suggested that there were parts of the mind unavailable either to the subject her- or himself, or to an observer; these parts are what Freud was to call 'the unconscious'. During his self-analysis, Freud established three principles which he elaborated upon for the rest of his career, as James Strachey points out (Strachey 1955: 18–21). The unconscious, argued Freud, consists of the activity of primary sexual and destructive instincts, which are in conflict with internal forces of self-preservation, and external social forces. Second, the analysis of dreams proved invaluable in accessing the unconscious; as did, thirdly, Freud's working out of the relationship between primary (unconscious) and secondary (conscious) thought processes. Later, he divided the psyche into the more familiar realms of the id (the repository of unstructured instincts), the ego (the realistic element) and the super-ego (the internalised parental function, moral and critical).

Between 1893 and 1895 Freud developed his theory of the Oedipus complex and infantile sexuality. In the former, the small boy loves his mother and experiences a jealous hatred of his father. His complex is resolved by the 'castration complex': the father steps in to forbid the boy access to the mother, on pain of losing his organ, and the boy, in obeying, identifies with the father and the power he wields. Freud makes the little boy the model for both sexes, and describes the little girl as a deficient version of him: she 'extends her judgement of inferiority from her stunted penis to her whole self', as he puts it (Freud 1962: 193). Because she is already 'castrated', in not possessing a penis, the little girl's Oedipus complex is not resolved but initiated by the castration complex. In her case, according to Freud, she now loves her father and hates the betraying mother, who has 'sent her into the world so insufficiently equipped' (ibid.). It is clear from these comments of Freud's why the Oedipus complex is problematic for feminist psychoanalysis, as it constructs women as the inferior 'second sex', in Simone de Beauvoir's phrase. Post-Freudians have made modifications to this apparent prescriptiveness: Lacan emphasised the power-symbolism of the phallus, which can theoretically be appropriated by either sex; Klein argued that the Oedipus complex occurs much earlier than Freud suggests, and the infant's drives focus not on the father and his anatomy, but on the mother and hers.

Freud and Women

The ambivalent relationship feminist thought has had with Freudian psychoanalysis and what has been called its 'phallic conceit and paternal authority' (Flieger 1989: 191) can be traced back to Freud and Breuer's *Studies on Hysteria*. On the one hand, work was begun in *Studies* on concepts which have determined the course of twentieth-century thought in general. As we have seen, the hysterical phenomenon of bodily symptoms with a psychic rather than a simply organic cause suggested to Freud a psyche divided between conscious and unconscious realms; and as the psychic origin of these symptoms was to be found in the sexual arena, the idea of a libido which is unlikely to find any simple satisfaction was also born. On the other hand, Freud was a part of the problems he identified. Neither here, nor in his infamous 'Fragment of an Analysis of a Case of Hysteria', the case history of Dora (1905), did he produce a sustained commentary on the social oppression suffered by women, even when this was germane to the illness suffered. Eighteen-year-old Dora had recently written a suicide note, after repelling the advances of an elderly family friend; Freud accepts that she was sent to him to persuade her she should accept the older man, so that her father could continue his affair with the man's wife. Not only did Freud fail in his mission to persuade Dora of this, he was unable to find out how she gathered her own sophisticated sexual knowledge, or keep her as a patient: she abruptly terminated the analysis after a few months. His case history has been seen as a kind of revenge on a lively and intelligent young girl, who would not submit to him as either 'older man' or analyst, and who was unable to follow the path of her brother, who became a prominent politician (see Bernheimer and Kahane 1985). Equally, Showalter points out that for Breuer's patient Anna O., 'hysteria was a "creative" escape from the boredom and futility of her everyday life' as a young woman in a restrictive nineteenth-century orthodox Jewish family (Showalter 1985: 156).

Freud only produced writings on feminine identity and female sexuality itself late in his career (for instance, Freud 1925, 1931, 1933). As we have seen, his central concepts took the male child as a model, so that the female seemed like an imperfect version. Luce Irigaray has fascinatingly analysed the scattered writings of Freud on femininity and concluded that his definition of its nature is strikingly similar to that of melancholia, or depression (Freud 1915). Like the melancholic, a woman prefers affection to passion; has little interest in the outside world; and has suffered a primordial disappointment – castration, in the woman's case. In other words, female sexuality is necessarily pathological, as melancholia is in men (Irigaray 1985).

Juliet Mitchell claims that feminist objections to Freud, including his ignoring the social position of the women he wrote about (not just his analysands, but the governesses, mistresses and mothers who turn up in his case histories and other papers), take too literal a view of the relation between external and internal realities (Mitchell 1975: 12). Her argument is that Freud is describing, and not prescribing, the nature of the symbolic order. Freud is always at pains to point out, Mitchell says, that 'so-called "normality" is only relative' (ibid.), and has neither a personal stake in advocating the status quo, nor in simply silencing those women whose hysteria might be seen as bodily protest at the contradictions of patriarchy, as was the case with Anna O.

Almost despite itself, Freudian psychoanalysis offered to feminism a useful synthesis of earlier work on the idea of the unconscious, and a discourse about the body and sexuality. Later critical work on Freud's writing revealed its lacunae: the fact that the little boy is taken as the norm for human development, and that at a crucial moment Freud's account of the Oedipus complex in the little girl falters: he cannot account for the fact that, having hated the mother for failing to provide her with a penis, the little girl ends up identifying with her again when she is an adult woman. Further, Freud's attitude to his male and female analysands was materially different; his writings on female sexuality are often inconsistent, and construct femininity as pathological. For discussions particularly of the demonising of the mother in Freud's Oedipal formulation, see Benjamin (1990); of the prescriptiveness of his theories, Millett (1969). These specific objections should be set against the use feminists have been able to make of Freud's concepts in different contexts from his own, and how they have constructed a model of femininity different from the 'castrated' one of Freudian psychoanalysis.

Klein and the Maternal

Melanie Klein, who left her native Austria for Britain before the Second World War, revised and extended several Freudian categories in the light of her child analysis during the 1940s and 1950s. She most notably contested the idea of a pre-Oedipal realm – the child is Oedipal much earlier than Freud suggests, according to Klein. She also emphasised the mixed feelings of mother and child for each other; and offered an alternative to the Freudian view of the maternal body as one which is superseded by the 'superior' paternal law, and is only a site for regressive feelings in later life. In their book *Freud's Women*, Lisa Appignanesi and John Forrester (1992: 442) make a clear distinction between the 'phallocentric' (a term coined by Ernest Jones, meaning centred on masculine privilege and assertion) Freudian position on gender difference, and the apparently more feminine-friendly stance of the followers of Klein (including Ernest Jones 1950 and Karen Horney 1973). Whereas Freud posited a single, phallic sex which takes up the positions of masculine and feminine according to different reactions to the threat of castration, the Kleinian argument is that there are two original sexes, male and female (Appignanesi and Forrester 1992: 442). Interestingly, Freud's theory seems to allow for greater fluidity of gender position, at least in theory; he points out that humans could have ended up divided into more than two sexes, perhaps following the drives such as urethral, voyeuristic, oral and anal (quoted in Appignanesi and Forrester 1992: 442; Sayers 1992: 4). Klein, on the other hand, argues that children have a very early knowledge of the mother's vagina as well as the father's penis, and so the division into two sexes is inevitable.

Despite the fact that Klein's concept of sexual difference appears more rigid than Freud's, she has also made a great impact on feminist theory, and particularly since the early 1980s there has been much debate on the idea of a 'return to Klein' (see the Klein Special Issue of *Women: A Cultural Review* 1990). This is partly due to Klein's emphasis on the importance of the maternal, in contrast to Freud's on the role of the father, and Freud's habit of writing out the mother in his case histories. Klein was also distinctive in giving priority to interpersonal relations over individual instinct; her analysis of hysteria, for instance, was based on the idea that its symptoms symbolized not only bodily memories, as Freud asserted, but relations with others.

Klein's theories, with their emphasis on the maternal, have elements in common with Kristeva's (Doane and Hodges 1992). Klein argues that the infant feels envy not for the paternal penis, but for maternal plenitude, that state of being united with the mother; Kristeva, that creativity is a way of expressing the maternal semiotic realm, to which all subjects have access, within the symbolic. Kristeva suggests that the pre-linguistic realm (the semiotic), which is characterised by bodily rhythms and pulsions, appears to be superseded by the realm of law and language (the symbolic), but continues to exert pressure on it from within. This pressure is particularly evident in certain artistic forms, such as poetry, and mental states, such as psychosis. Klein and Kristeva differ in their views of the nature of gender, however; while Klein sees femininity as an innate drive, Kristeva sees it as a non-essential attribute, a position which changes as social circumstances change (Moi 1985: 163–7).

As Nancy Fraser implies in the introduction to *Revaluing French Feminism* (Fraser and Bartky 1992), the publication of the influential anthology *New French Feminisms*, edited by Elaine Marks and Isabelle de Courtivron (1985), coincided with the reissue of a landmark of Anglo-American object-relations theory, Dorothy Dinnerstein's *The Rocking of the Cradle and the Ruling of the World* (1987), often coupled with Nancy Chodorow's *The Reproduction of Mothering: Psychoanalysis and the Sociology of Gender* (1978). *New French Feminisms* introduced French feminist theory to the English-speaking world whereas *Revaluing French Feminism* attempts to evaluate the legacy of the anthology and the era of thought it ushered in, and its particular impact on feminist psychoanalysis as well as cultural theory. Object-relations theory, a Kleinian-influenced school of psychoanalytic thought, concentrates on the first year of the infant's life, and its formative relations with a range of objects, real and fantasied, bodily parts and whole persons (Wright 1992: 284). In her book, Dinnerstein offers a Kleinian view of the toll taken socially and environmentally by humans' inability effectively to mourn the loss of the initial oneness with the mother: a oneness arising from current child-care arrangements, divided according to gender. Dinnerstein argues that the only difference between men and women is biological, so women have a responsibility to establish the reasons for their 'compliance' in a division of labour where they 'rock the cradle', and rule over childhood, while men 'rule the world', and exert public dominance (1987: 160). She claims that contemporary 'abuses', including nuclear proliferation and the drift towards despotism, are the inevitable result of female-dominated child-care (1987: xxv). Both men and women fear the female power they remember from infancy, and work together to restrain it in adult, social life. Dinnerstein, while regarding Freud's legacy as potentially revolutionary, distances herself from the inevitability he sees in the construction of gender difference. One of her solutions, which seems almost laughably simple, is shared child-care arrangements.

Like Dinnerstein's, Chodorow's work has been more influential in the social sciences than in psychoanalytic thought (Wright 1992: 46); she has argued that the division between the sexes is reproduced because women currently have total responsibility for mothering, and invariably produce distinctive, asymmetric responses in their children according to gender. Chodorow argued that mothering by women generates in men a defensive masculinity, 'and a compensatory psychology and ideology of masculine superiority [which] sustained male dominance' (1989: 1). She has more recently altered her emphasis on women's mothering as the sole reason for male dominance, and sees it as one important factor contributing to patriarchal fear and suppression of women (1989: 6).

Although both writers follow the Kleinian urge to redress Freudian negativity towards the maternal, these two books are also critical of motherhood. As the quotations from both suggest, there is an element of blaming the maternal, implicit in their accounts of patriarchal dominance. Critics say that Chodorow and Dinnerstein get the equation the wrong way round: psychical reality forms the social, not vice versa (Brennan 1989: 8). However, their emphasis is on particular social structures rather than timeless psychic mechanisms, and their assumption that altering the former can change the latter makes their claims forward-looking and optimistic, if rather limited in scope.

Jacques Lacan

The very influential French theorist Lacan trained as a psychiatrist, and his 1932 doctoral thesis on paranoia and language attracted the interest of surrealists living in France, including Salvador Dalí (Sarup 1992: 21). From 1953, for twenty-six years, Lacan held weekly public seminars on Freud's writings on psychoanalytic technique, and in 1964, having been expelled from more orthodox bodies, established his own school, L'Ecole Freudienne de Paris. He died in 1981, having dissolved the EFP a year earlier.

Lacan inaugurated a 'return to Freud' in his seminars and writings, bringing structuralist and post-structuralist theories of language to bear on Freud's central concepts of the unconscious, the construction of gender, and his model of the subject's development. Lacan's great innovation was to emphasise the simultaneous acquisition of language and concept of one's self at the moment of the Oedipal crisis. The child is catapulted at once into the symbolic world of language, law and sexual difference. Lacan argues that this catapulting is not without cost, and the regret every subject feels for lost unity with the mother in the pre-Oedipal imaginary realm is what constitutes the unconscious (Lacan 1977). In his well-known slogan, Lacan claims that the unconscious is structured like a language, although others have pointed out that this is to over-simplify (Benveniste 1971: 136). He means by this that as language works by a system based on lack (each word, or signifier, stands in for a missing object, or signified), so does the subject's unconscious: its existence commemorates the 'lack' of the mother.

The big issue for feminist approaches to Lacan is the role of what he calls 'the phallus' in his theory of language and the subject. Lacan claims that this is a neutral 'third term', a signifier of lack: the child is separated from its mother by the intervention of the father, who is the 'bearer of the phallus', the one whose law must be obeyed. Thus the phallus reminds the child of loss of the maternal; the child also sees that the mother desires the father, and imagines that if only s/he possessed the phallus, that badge of power, s/he could have the mother's undivided love. Feminist critics of Lacan point out how hard it is to separate the phallus from the literal organ, the penis, if only because of verbal and visual coincidence (Brennan 1989: 4). If the phallus symbolises difference and the lack that makes language-use possible, there may be a danger of return to the Freudian idea that women only exist as imperfect men, and that they will be less able to use language. Feminist proponents of Lacan point out that his theory is non-biological and non-essentialist, as the feminine position is open to both men and women, although Brennan says that nonetheless it 'implicates' biology (1989: 7).

French Feminist Theory: Irigaray and Kristeva

The appeal of French feminist psychoanalytic theory is its effort to make femininity its central concern, directed against the perception that the symbolic order is a patriarchal monolith. Although there are many French feminists writing in this area, as Nancy Fraser points out, for the English-speaking world this theory has become identified with Julia Kristeva, Irigaray and Hélène Cixous almost exclusively (Fraser and Bartky 1992: 1). At first glance, the former two seem clearly differentiated on the grounds of 'essentialism', the doctrine that characteristics are inborn, biological and definitional, and are not subject to historical change (see Wright 1992: 77–83). While Kristeva advocates a positional, or 'nominal' (Alcoff 1988) conception of gender, which is not based on biological difference, Irigaray's interest in reversing traditional psychoanalytic views of the feminine has led her to be accused of precisely this biologism. However, the two estimates can be turned around. Kristeva's emphasis on the maternal, and her apparent consignment of lesbianism to the realms of the psychotic, has led some critics to find in her work an advocacy of 'compulsory motherhood' (Judith Butler, in Fraser and Bartky 1992); and appreciation of Irigaray's reliance on metaphor, as much as on bodily reality, has become much more widespread (Whitford 1991). The particular metaphor Irigaray has adopted as the basis of her representational system is that of two lips speaking together (Irigaray 1985). This acts both as a counter to the unified, rigid phallic metaphor of Lacanian psychoanalysis, if the lips are read as vaginal, and as a figure for women's relationship to language and utterance, if they are taken to be oral.

Those in support of Irigaray's project see the charge of essentialism as the result of over-simplification. Diana J. Fuss points out that Irigaray's reliance on the form of the female body is a rhetorical ploy, and asks, 'What might be at stake in the deployment of essentialism for strategic purposes?' (in Fraser and Bartky 1992: 94). Elizabeth Grosz (1989) argues that the '"two lips" is not a truthful image of female anatomy but a new emblem by which female sexuality can be positively *represented*' (1989: 111, 116).

What may look like excessive reliance on biology in Irigaray's case is an insistence on the role of representation in constructing even 'the phenomenology of bodily experience' (Grosz 1989: 111). This is the reason for Irigaray's validation of feminine nature, in her recent book *je, tu, nous*, where she appears to be praising pre-existent, 'natural' virtue: '[Women's] choices tend more toward maintaining peace, a clean environment, goods we really need in life, humanitarian options' (1993: 12). Again, it is rather the case that Irigaray is pointing to the result of patriarchal social relations, not to an innately good female nature which need only be released, or given equal status with the male, for its benefits to be shared. Equality is not on Irigaray's agenda: 'women's exploitation is based upon sexual difference; its solution will come only through sexual difference', she writes (1993: 12, 13).

Margaret Whitford points out that Irigaray is drawing upon the way in which women are symbolised in western culture, precisely as natural and ahistorical, in order to combat it, making it particularly ironic that she is accused of doing exactly what she is criticising (Whitford 1991: 60). Irigaray's strategy is a 'ruse' to expose philosophy's essentialism, and the maternal-feminine on which it depends.

Kristeva is also concerned with the nature of the feminine, and has become somewhat notorious for polemical statements such as the following, from a 1974 interview: 'a woman cannot "be"' (in Marks and de Courtivron 1985: 137). This is because 'woman' is a social rather than a natural construct, and the fight to dissolve the bourgeois humanist conception of identities must include sexual identities (ibid.: 138). Kristeva argues that 'the women's struggle cannot be divorced from revolutionary struggle, class struggle, or anti-imperialism' (ibid.: 140), which is a long-debated question among socialist feminists.

As Moi points out, the benefit of Kristeva's analysis for feminism in particular is that it defines the feminine in a non-biologistic way, as that which is marginal to the symbolic order (Moi 1985: 166). At the moment women are marginal to that order, as are various other groups, including intellectuals, the working class and blacks (although race is not an issue directly addressed by Kristeva). What these marginalised groups have in common, therefore, is their greater access to the semiotic, which is also marginal to the symbolic. Repressed memories of the maternal semiotic exert disruptive pressure on the symbolic order. In political terms, such marginality, according to Kristeva, affords these groups great revolutionary potential. Moi points out that this observation represents an inaccurate conflation of groups whose relations to patriarchy's modes of production are quite different; while women and workers have an essential role to play in (re)production which they could exploit in a revolutionary manner, intellectuals do not (Moi 1985: 171).

Nancy Fraser interestingly points out that the one opinion the writers in *Revaluing French Feminism* share is the rejection of compulsory motherhood (Fraser and Bartky 1992: 18). As we have seen in relation to Klein, Dinnerstein, Chodorow, Irigaray and Kristeva, the maternal forms the pressure point of their theories, uniting questions of the body, biology, language and feminine identity.

Masquerade and Performance

Psychoanalytic feminist thought has also followed another route, perhaps more closely connected to the 'nominalism' mentioned above, and which has had its greatest impact in the area of cultural criticism. More recently, queer theory – which concentrates on the potential for bi- and homosexual identifications to upset traditional dual, fixed structures of meaning – has also followed this path. This is the area of masquerade, or gender as a performative strategy. Joan Riviere was a disciple of the Kleinian Ernest Jones, and her 1929 essay, 'Womanliness as a Masquerade' has had a significant influence on writers concerned with the nature of femininity and with representations of it. The essay's importance lies in its denial of any fixed, essential feminine nature, and it has also been influential for studies of transvestism, dressing up and the subversion of sartorially coded gender identities in general (see Copjec 1989; Gaines and Herzog 1990).

In her essay, Riviere discusses three case studies, which have in common the fact that, according to Riviere, 'women who wish for masculinity may put on a mask of womanliness to avert anxiety and the retribution feared from men' (Riviere 1966: 210). The most extensively treated case is that of a successful American woman who nonetheless has a problematic relation to public speaking and language. Riviere describes this woman's habit of seeking reassurance after a public lecture from 'unmistakable father-figures', often through the sexualised activity of flirtation, in an act of 'propriation' which was, however, merely an act of 'masquerading as guiltless and innocent' (Riviere 1966: 213). This behaviour marks the woman's anxiety in relation to both her parents: she identifies with the father and 'takes his place, so she can "restore" him' (Riviere 1966: 217) as an appeasing gift to the mother who is both feared and hated. The father also needs appeasing in case he tries to extract punishment for his daughter's hatred (and perhaps destruction) of the mother, by a counter-masquerade as, again, feminine.

The passage where Riviere attempts to answer the question whether masquerade is 'normal' or pathological is frequently quoted as the central part of her argument:

> Womanliness therefore could be assumed and worn as a mask, both to hide the possession of masculinity and to avert the reprisals expected if she was found to possess it – much as a thief will turn out his pockets and ask to be searched to prove that he has not the stolen goods. The reader may now ask how I define womanliness or where I draw the line between genuine womanliness and the 'masquerade'. My suggestion is not, however, that there is any such difference: whether radical or superficial, they are the same thing.
>
> (Riviere 1966: 213)

Opponents of claims that the idea of masquerade is liberatory point to its apolitical implications. Judith Butler asks whether masquerade necessarily transforms aggression and fear of reprisal into seduction and flirtation, as it appears to here (Butler 1990: 48).

Essential Femininity

The topic of masquerade raises the question of what it is to be a woman; is it a question of essences, biological or otherwise, or of the Kristevan notion of non-essential positions – in this case the positionality of surfaces? As Marjorie Garber puts it in *Vested Interests*, 'if "woman" is culturally constructed, and if female impersonators are *conscious* constructors of artificial and artifactual femininity, how does a "female impersonator" differ from a "woman"?' (Garber 1993: 354).

The potential that masquerade offers is a deconstruction of the idea of biological determinism, of 'the "real" woman not yet disfigured by patriarchal social relations' (Doane 1988: 219). It suggests that the woman can play the woman or not as she pleases. Jane Gaines claims that gender confusion and ambiguity are 'a female fabrication that is profoundly distressing to patriarchal culture' (Gaines and Herzog 1990: 28). The central issue concerns the nature of what is masked in the masquerade: is there any femininity prior to the mimicry, or indeed outside language? Butler quotes two rival positions on this question: Irigaray attempts to theorise the feminine outside the phallic economy, while Jacqueline Rose assumes the Lacanian position of claiming that 'there is no pre-discursive reality … no place prior to the law which is available and can be retrieved' (Butler 1990: 55).

The concept and language of masquerade have often been used to discuss the position of the female film spectator, whose gaze is not accommodated, according to some theorists, within classical cinema. Laura Mulvey's influential and psycho-analytically based essay 'Visual Pleasure and Narrative Cinema' (1975) suggests that the three gazes – of audience, camera and characters – in film are all mas-culine. Mulvey (1981) goes on to argue that the only position a female spectator can take up, therefore, is a masochistic one. Some critics have suggested rather that the exclusion of the female gaze means that the female spectator (that is, the spectator in a feminine position) has a greater gender mobility than the male (Penley 1989). In order to be the voyeur which film constructs the spectator as, the woman 'puts on the sexual guise of the male, effecting a trans-sex iden-tification', as Jane Gaines puts it (Gaines and Herzog 1990: 24); this is a trans-vestite spectatorship, rather than a masochistic or non-existent one.

Masquerade has also been used to analyse not just the female spectator, but the very possibility of the representation of the female body on screen. Using the theories of Riviere, Irigaray and Michèle Montrelay, Mary Ann Doane points out that woman is evicted equally from psychoanalysis and cinema, two dis-courses 'purportedly about her', and that 'historically, there has always been a certain imbrication of the cinematic image and the representation of women' (Doane 1991: 20).

Masquerade, especially on screen, can provide women with the necessary dis-tance – an ironic awareness of the pose and clothes – for signification. Judith Butler points out that, in Riviere's essay, this desire for access to sign-production may underlie the fact that the woman in the case history experiences Oedipal rivalry with the father, not over the love of the mother, but with the father as a public speaker, 'that is, as a user of signs rather than a sign-object, an item of exchange' (Butler 1990: 51).

Conclusions

The future of psychoanalytic theory within feminism seems very rich. As well as the 'return to Klein', signalled for instance by the establishment of the Women's Therapy Centre in London (Wright 1992: 457–61), psychoanalytic feminism underlies recent developments in lesbian theory, gender studies and queer theory. The latter in particular has benefited from the long-standing debate in feminist psychoanalysis between signifier and signified, body and language, literal and metaphorical, as Caroline Evans and Lorraine Gamman suggest in *A Queer Romance*: 'some representations, what we call "queer" representations, seem to share ... the capacity to disturb stable definitions' (Burston and Richardson 1995: 46). New work is beginning, although rather slowly, on psychoanalysis and 'race'; as psychoanalysis has been a discourse about, but not of, women, it has been neither about, nor of, people of colour. It is interesting to speculate whether issues of Oedipalisation, gender construction, and transference, in particular, will be revitalised by the incorporation of racial difference. To return to Freud's idea that it is only accidental that there are two sexes, and there could just as easily have been four drive-based positions instead, it may turn out to be the case that the Law of the Father is the Law of the White Supremacist Father specifically (Stephanie Munro, forthcoming work on Irigaray and race), while other fathers may have other laws.

References

Alcoff, Lisa (1988) 'Cultural Feminism Versus Poststructuralism: The Identity Crisis in Feminist Theory', *Signs* 13 (3): 405–36.

Appignanesi, Lisa and John Forrester (1992) *Freud's Women*, London: Weidenfeld and Nicolson.

Benjamin, Jessica (1990) *The Bonds of Love*, London: Virago.

Benveniste, Emile (1971) *Problems in General Linguistics*, Miami: Miami University Press.

Bernheimer, Charles and Claire Kahane (eds) (1985) *In Dora's Case*, London: Virago.

Brennan, Teresa (ed.) (1989) *Between Feminism and Psychoanalysis*, London: Routledge.

Burston, Paul and Colin Richardson (eds) (1995) *A Queer Romance: Lesbians, Gay Men and Popular Culture*, London: Routledge.

Butler, Judith (1990) *Gender Trouble: Feminism and the Subversion of Identity*, New York: Routledge.

Chodorow, Nancy (1978) *The Reproduction of Mothering: Psychoanalysis and the Sociology of Gender*, Berkeley: University of California Press.

Chodorow, Nancy (1989) *Feminism and Psychoanalytic Theory*, Cambridge: Polity Press.

Copjec, Joan (1989) 'The sartorial superego', *October* 50.

Dinnerstein, Dorothy (1987) [1976] *The Rocking of the Cradle and the Ruling of the World*, London: The Women's Press.

Doane, Janice and Devon Hodges (1992) *From Klein to Kristeva: Psychoanalytic Feminism and the Search for the 'Good Enough' Mother*, University of Michigan Press, Ann Arbor.

Doane, Mary Ann (1988) 'Woman's Stake: Filming the Female Body', in C. Penley (ed.) *Feminism and Film Theory*, London: Routledge.

Doane, Mary Ann (1991) 'Film and the Masquerade: Theorizing the Female Spectator', *Femmes Fatales*, London: Routledge.

Flieger, Jerry Aline (1989) 'Entertaining the Ménage à Trois: Psychoanalysis, Feminism, and Literature', in Richard Feldstein and Judith Roof (eds) *Feminism and Psychoanalysis*, Ithaca and London: Cornell University Press.

Fraser, Nancy and Sandra Lee Bartky (eds) (1992) *Revaluing French Feminism: Critical Essays on Difference, Agency, and Culture*, Bloomington: Indiana University Press.

Freud, Sigmund, *The Standard Edition of the Complete Psychological Works of Sigmund Freud*, 24 vols, trans. and ed. James Strachey, London: the Hogarth Press and the Institute of Psycho-Analysis 1953–73 [abbreviated below as *SE*].

Freud, Sigmund (1905) 'Fragment of an analysis of a Case of Hysteria', *SE* 7: 1–122.

Freud, Sigmund (1915) 'Mourning and melancholia', *SE* 14: 239–385.

Freud, Sigmund (1925) 'Some psychical consequences of the anatomical distinction between the sexes', *SE* 19: 241–60.

Freud, Sigmund (1931) 'Female sexuality', *SE* 21: 223–46.

Freud, Sigmund (1933) 'Femininity', *SE* 22: 112–35.

Freud, Sigmund (1962 [1910]) 'Five Lectures on Psychoanalysis', in *Two Short Accounts of Psycho-Analysis*, Harmondsworth: Penguin; *SE* 11.

Freud, Sigmund (1986 [1924]) 'A Short Account of Psychoanalysis', in Albert Dickson (ed.) *Historical and Expository Works*, Harmondsworth: Penguin; *SE* 19.

Freud, Sigmund and Josef Breuer (1974 [1895]) *Studies in Hysteria*, Harmondsworth: Penguin; *SE* 2: 37–59.

Gaines, Jane and Charlotte Herzog (eds) (1990) *Fabrications: Costume and the Female Body*, London: Routledge.

Garber, Marjorie (1993) *Vested Interests: Cross-Dressing and Cultural Anxiety*, London: Penguin.

Grosz, Elizabeth (1989) *Jacques Lacan: A Feminist Introduction*, London: Routledge.

Horney, Karen (1973) 'The Denial of the Vagina', in Harold Kelman (ed.) *Feminine Psychology*, New York: Norton.

Irigaray Luce (1985) [1974], *Speculum of the Other Woman*, trans. Gillian C. Gill, Ithaca, NY: Cornell University Press.

Irigaray, Luce (1993) *je, tu, nous*, London: Routledge.

Jones, Ernest (1950) *Papers on Psycho-Analysis*, London: Baillière, Tindall & Cox.

Klein, Melanie (1990) [1975] *The Writings of Melanie Klein*, 4 vols. Vol. 1: *Love, Guilt and Reparation*; vol. 2: *The Psycho-Analysis of the Child*; vol. 3: *Envy and Gratitude*; vol. 4: *Narrative of a Child Analysis*, London: Virago.

Klein, Melanie (1990a) [1946] 'Notes on Some Schizoid Mechanisms', reprinted in Klein (1990), vol. 3.

Lacan, Jacques (1977) *Ecrits: A Selection*, trans. Alan Sheridan, London: Tavistock.

Lacan, Jacques [1958] 'The meaning of the phallus', in Juliet Mitchell and Jacqueline Rose (eds) (1982) *Feminine Sexuality: Jacques Lacan and the Ecole Freudienne*, London: Macmillan.

Marks, Elaine and Isabelle de Courtivron (eds) (1981) *New French Feminisms*, Brighton: Harvester.

Millett, Kate (1969) *Sexual Politics*, London: Virago.

Mitchell, Juliet (1975) *Psychoanalysis and Feminism*, Harmondsworth: Penguin.

Moi, Toril (1985) *Sexual/Textual Politics: Feminist Literary Theory*, London: Methuen.

Mulvey, Laura (1975) 'Visual Pleasure and Narrative Cinema', *Screen* 16 (3), Autumn.

Mulvey, Laura (1981) 'Afterthoughts on "Visual Pleasure and Narrative Cinema" inspired by *Duel in the Sun*', *Framework* 6, summer: 15–17.

Munro, Stephanie, from an ongoing Ph.D.

Penley, Constance (1989) '"A certain refusal of difference"', in *The Future of an Illusion: Film, Feminism, and Psychoanalysis*, London: Routledge.

Riviere, Joan (1966) [1929] 'Womanliness as a masquerade', in H. Ruitenbeek (ed.) *Feminine Sexuality*, New Haven: College and UP.

Sarup, Madan (1992) *Jacques Lacan*, Hemel Hempstead: Harvester.

Sayers, Janet (1992) *Mothering Psychoanalysis: Hélène Deutsch, Karen Horney, Anna Freud, Melanie Klein*, London: Penguin.

Showalter, Elaine (1985) *The Female Malady: Women, Madness and English Culture, 1830–1980*, Harmondsworth: Penguin.

Strachey, James (1955) 'Sigmund Freud: A Sketch of His Life and Ideas', in Freud and
Breuer (1974).

Whitford, Margaret (1991) *Luce Irigaray: Philosophy in the Feminine*, London: Routledge.

Women: A Cultural Review, 1 (2), summer 1990.

Wright, Elizabeth (1992) (ed.) *Feminism and Psychoanalysis: A Critical Dictionary*, Oxford:
Blackwell.

Further Reading

Brennan, Teresa (1989) *Between Feminism and Psychoanalysis*, London: Routledge.

Chodorow, Nancy (1994) *Femininities, Masculinities, Sexualities: Freud and Beyond*, London:
Free Association Books.

de Lauretis, Teresa (1994) *The Practice of Love: Lesbian Sexuality and Perverse Desire*, Bloomington: Indiana University Press.

Freud, Sigmund (1977) *On Sexuality*, The Penguin Freud Library, Volume 7, Harmondsworth: Penguin.

Freud, Sigmund (1977) *Case Studies I: 'Dora' and 'Little Hans'*, The Penguin Freud Library,
Volume 8, Harmondsworth: Penguin.

Macey, David (1988) *Lacan in Contexts*, London: Verso.

Moi, Toril (ed.) (1991) *The Kristeva Reader*, Oxford: Blackwell.

Mitchell, Juliet and Jacqueline Rose (1982) *Feminine Sexuality: Jacques Lacan and the Ecole
Freudienne*, Basingstoke: Macmillan.

Screen (ed.) *The Sexual Subject: A Screen Reader on Sexuality*, London: Routledge.

Whitford, Margaret (ed.) (1991) *The Irigaray Reader*, Oxford: Blackwell.

Chapter 13

Postmodernism and Feminism

Patricia Waugh

The term postmodernism has come to seem definitive of our end-of-millennium consciousness, along with all the other 'post-' phenomena which emerged in the 1970s and 1980s: post-industrialism, post-Marxism, post-humanism and, of course, so-called 'post-feminism'. The term exerts an enormous grip upon our intellectual climate and upon contemporary debates within feminism. A crucial problem in trying to assess the relations between postmodernism and feminism is that, although feminism can be broadly defined as a political movement whose objectives are ultimately emancipatory, postmodernism cannot be described so easily. The term 'postmodernism' has now come to designate a bewilderingly diverse array of cultural practices, writers, artists, thinkers and theoretical accounts of late modernity. It also refers to a more general sense of radical change in the ways of thinking we have inherited from the eighteenth-century European Enlightenment.

The Enlightenment has been characterised as a project definitively committed to 'develop objective science, universal morality and law, and autonomous art according to their own inner logic' (Habermas 1981: 9). Postmodernists, however, have argued that science, ethics and art are or no longer should be seen as separable. Hence postmodernism denies the possibility of an 'objective' science discovering the laws of an independently existing reality; it repudiates the pursuit of universal and rational ethical principles; it rejects the existence of a separate category of the 'aesthetic' which is removed from the realms of science, ethics or everyday cultural practice.

Many feminists remain sceptical about the likely political consequences of a total abandonment of the Enlightenment project. Yet feminism has been drawn into that postmodern critique which accuses Enlightenment thinkers of setting up so-called 'universal' categories of knowledge and value which actually exclude entire communities or groups of people, and of claiming 'objectivity' for knowledge which actually reflects vested interests. Feminism has in fact always contributed its own critique of the Enlightenment, arguing that the notion of a universal rational Subject is implicitly masculine, as is its understanding of history as a grand narrative of progress. By the same token, the idea that knowledge was an objective reflection of an independently existing world fell by the wayside. Recently, feminist theory has come to manifest a number of overt postmodern symptoms: an infatuation with such concepts as the sublime, with the idea of radical alterity (otherness) or the possibility of a feminine 'space' outside of rationality and patriarchal hierarchies, and a fondness for images suggestive of fluidity or hybridity such as the cyborg or the nomad.

Postmodernism and Feminism: A Brief History

The term 'postmodernism' was first used in the 1950s by critics concerned to describe what they perceived to be new kinds of literary experiment arising out of but moving beyond those of cultural modernism. By the early eighties, however, the term shifts from the description of a range of aesthetic practices involving playful irony, parody, self-consciousness and fragmentation, to a use which encompasses a more general shift in thought and seems to register a pervasive cynicism about the progressivist ideals of the Enlightenment. 'Postmodernism' is now used to designate a new cultural epoch in which capitalism, in its latest consumerist phase, invades everything, leaving no remaining oppositional space (Jameson 1991). Postmodernism thus comes to encompass a constellation of preoccupations involving repudiations of foundationalism (the idea that knowledge can be grounded in secure *a priori* principles), a range of aesthetic practices which disrupt the modernist concept of artistic autonomy, and a variety of attempts to describe the present cultural mood or condition. The term is now variously used to describe both the contemporary cultural condition *per se* and a diverse range of intellectual responses which appear in part actually to construct that condition.

Perhaps postmodernism is best thought of as a 'mood' arising out of a sense of the collapse of all those foundations of modern thought which seemed to guarantee a reasonably stable sense of Truth, Knowledge, Self and Value. The refusal to separate domains of knowledge has, in fact, absorbed both knowledge and experience into the realm of the aesthetic. Even scientific knowledge becomes a fiction: there are no objective 'facts', for 'facts' too are produced through forms of observation and discourse determined by theoretical (fictional) frames. Indeed, Jean Baudrillard has described postmodernism as a condition of hyperinflation of the aesthetic, for 'art is everywhere, since artifice is at the very heart of reality' (Baudrillard 1983: 151).

Ihab Hassan has usefully offered an epochal definition of postmodernism as an: 'antinomian movement that assumes a vast unmaking of the Western mind' (in Wellmer 1985: 338). He uses the term 'unmaking', to cover terms such as deconstruction, decentring, demystification, discontinuity and difference, which feature prominently in postmodern discourse. These terms assume or imply a rejection of the idea of a rational coherent subject, and the end of 'grand narratives' of universal truth or of ideas such as Marx's theory of the progressive development of productive forces. If the search for universal truth requires confidence in the ability of the rational enquirer to arrive at fundamental, generally applicable knowledge, then it would seem that the demise of the rational subject also entails the collapse of the notion of 'Truth'. Similarly, therefore (the argument runs), without a foundation in universal and objective knowledge, there cannot be a political project of universal emancipation through the rational pursuit of such knowledge because no such knowledge is achievable.

For some, particularly those influenced by the thought of Michel Foucault, to continue to believe in the Enlightenment project is either to ignore everything which it excludes, or to be guilty of perpetrating totalitarian violences under the banner of freedom and progress. The crisis in knowledge – the idea that all knowledge is constructed and reflects relations of power – is seen to entail a crisis in the political orientation of the Enlightenment. With the rejection of Descartes' move to found Reason in individual subjectivity comes the argument that individual subjectivity is not a basis, but a result of historically variable discursive operations. Consequently, the focus shifts towards an emphasis on relativity, and a receptiveness to ideas of 'difference', plurality, fragmentation, non-totality, aesthetic self-fashioning, contingency and 'language games'.

Postmodernism thus entails a pervasive crisis in the modern understanding of selfhood as founded upon a unitary coherent subjectivity. Much of this 'crisis' was actually formulated within the discourse of modernity. For example, the Marxist critique of individualism had already anticipated much of this argument. It was later extended by post-structuralist thinkers such as Althusser, Lacan and Derrida through an engagement with Saussure's structural linguistics. Here language 'far from reflecting an already given social reality, constitutes social reality for us' (Weedon 1987: 22). This approach has implications for subjectivity. Against the idea of subjectivity as 'an essence at the heart of each individual which is unique, fixed and coherent', poststructuralism 'proposes a subjectivity which is precarious, contradictory and in process, constantly being reconstituted in discourse every time we think or speak' (1987: 32–3).

The crisis in the understanding of selfhood and knowledge has produced a radical uncertainty which has infected feminism as much as any other emancipatory movement. Historically, the rise of second-wave feminism coincided with a growing incredulity towards universal truth-claims. Yet feminism has, to some extent, always been 'postmodern'. Feminists have shown how Enlightenment discourses universalise white, Western, middle-class male experience and have thus exposed the buried strategies of domination implicit in the ideal of objective knowledge. Feminists as well as postmodernists have long recognised the need for a new ethics responsive to technological changes and shifts in the understanding between the relations of power and knowledge. Feminism has provided its own critique of essentialist and foundationalist assumptions, arguing, for example, that gender is not a consequence of anatomy and that social institutions do not reflect universal truths about human nature. Simply in articulating issues of sexual difference, feminist discourse weakens the rootedness of Enlightenment thought in the principle of ungendered sameness and universalism. Once knowledge is regarded as constructed and situated, as produced within a specific context, then, so the argument goes, Truth can no longer be envisaged as discoverable by objective, rational thought.

Both critiques suggest that earlier models of knowledge may have been complicit with those very forms of oppression they were designed to supplant (Foucault 1981; Butler 1990). Indeed, some feminists have argued that Enlightenment discourses of emancipation have functioned as much to oppress as to liberate women. Contemporary feminists have analysed the ways in which 'universal' principles were always contradicted by the Enlightenment's construction of a public/private split – which consigned women to the 'private' realm of embodiment and domesticity in order to demarcate a public realm of reason and subjective sovereignty as essentially abstract, disinterested and, above all, male. In recent years, debates on identity and 'difference', the recognition that there is no universal 'woman' for whom feminism can speak, also resonate with the radical uncertainty of postmodernism.

Yet feminist ideas clearly arise out of and are made possible by those of modernity and its models of reason, justice and autonomous subjectivity. Feminists have fought for the extension of Enlightenment discourses and sovereign rights to women as full human subjects. Feminist critics of postmodernism have cautioned against an unthinking acceptance of an epistemological critique which might amount to no more than a revolt of secure but ungrateful bourgeois sons against their more authoritarian Enlightenment fathers. It seems unlikely that feminism can sustain itself as a political and emancipatory movement unless it continues to acknowledge and to interrogate its relation to the discourses of Enlightenment. At the risk of sounding essentialist, I would still argue that, never having experienced the kind of subjective sovereignty and political security of the average white, Western, male postmodernist, it would seem that feminists may have more to lose in a premature renunciation of the goals and methods of Enlightenment thought. For, to accept the arguments of strong postmodernism is to raise uncertainty even about the existence of a specifically female subject and inevitably, therefore, about the very possibility of political agency for women.

The crucial question in the relations between feminism and postmodernism would seem to be whether it is possible to preserve the emancipatory ideals of modernity which seem necessary to the very endeavour of feminism, whilst dispensing with those absolute epistemological foundations which have been so thoroughly and variously challenged. Alternatively, how far is it possible to modify those foundations rather than urging their total abandonment? As a political practice, surely feminism must continue to posit some belief in the

notion of effective human agency, the necessity for historical continuity in for-
mulating identity and a belief in some kind of historical progress. All along it
would seem that feminism has been engaged in an effort to reconcile context-
specific difference or situatedness with universal political aims: to modify the Enlightenment in the context of late modernity and according to the specific needs
and perspectives of women, but not to capitulate to the nihilistic and ultra-
relativist positions of postmodernism as a celebration of the disembodied 'view
from everywhere' (Bordo 1990: 133).

Feminists, like other commentators on postmodernism, remain deeply divided:
most are either for it or against it. Some feminists dismiss postmodernism as
mystificatory academic pretentiousness, while others see it as the only viable
future for a rejuvenated political philosophy:

> feminism and postmodernism are the only contemporary theories that present a truly
> radical critique of the Enlightenment legacy of modernism. No other approaches on the
> contemporary intellectual scene offer a means of displacing and transforming the mas-
> culinist epistemology of modernity.
>
> (Hekman 1990: 189)

Evaluations of postmodern art and literature tend to line up in similarly polarised
camps. Terry Eagleton (1985), for example, dismisses postmodernism as a perversion of the radical energies of an earlier avant-garde, and sees it as a cultural
practice which merely reflects the superficiality of late capitalist consumer
society. Linda Hutcheon (1989), on the other hand, sees in the postmodern the
only possibility of critique and opposition from the margins which gives a voice
to feminists, post-colonials, ethnic, racial and sexual minorities. According to
some critics, such as Fredric Jameson (1991), this tendency to praise or condemn
postmodernism is simply beside the point: for we are *in* the condition of postmodernity and simply have no choice but to resign ourselves to that condition.
For Jameson, therefore, postmodernism is best thought of as a periodising concept which serves to correlate the formal and stylistic features of contemporary
culture with the underlying economic structures of late consumer capitalism.

A Map of the Postmodern

If we are to begin to map the relations between feminism and postmodernism,
we need to break down the global version of the postmodern condition into more
analytically manageable categories and units. For the moment I will propose that
we maintain a distinction between postmodernism as an aesthetic practice and
postmodernism as a critique of knowledge. I shall argue that one way in which
to begin to disentangle the relations between feminism and postmodernism (as
theoretical critiques and cultural practices) is to view postmodernism as existing
in two generic varieties; one I shall refer to as 'strong' and the other 'weak', and

then to see both varieties in turn operating in 'reconstructive' and 'decon-structive' modes. Broadly, deconstructive modes tend to be more concerned with a critique of the legacy of the Enlightenment and in their strong forms to recommend its entire abandonment; reconstructive modes are more concerned with imagining alternative futures which either transform or attempt to break entirely with those of modernity, again depending on whether the vision is what I have called 'weak' or 'strong'.

If we break down postmodernism in this way, we may discover that a particular form of the postmodern which has been productive for feminism in the aesthetic sphere may be problematic for feminist critiques of knowledge and for feminist politics. This suggests, contrary to globalising accounts of the postmodern condition, that feminism is free to take a strategic stance on postmodernism, selecting those aspects which might be useful to a particular goal at a particular time.

Strong Postmodernism

'Strong' deconstructive postmodernism probably begins with Nietzsche's critique of metaphysics. In a famous statement in *The Genealogy of Morals*, he declared that 'there is only a perspectival knowing' (Nietzsche 1969: 111, 3). He suggests that we are deluded in our belief that we can find universal meta-narratives which may ground knowledge or ethics. Following this, strong post-modernism tends to champion perspectivism and thus 'difference' (which is potentially endless); exhibits, therefore, a tendency towards nominalism – refusing the idea that there is 'a reality', out in the real world, to which 'concepts' actually refer, assuming that 'concepts' construct and even produce the reality they pretend to describe. Postmodernism, furthermore, tends towards a preference for performance and rhetoric over intrinsic or universal truth or right, towards models of dissensus rather than consensus as the basis for political action, and calls for an acknowledgement of the incommensurability of the various language games, or 'little narratives', which reflect the specific perspectives and interests of particular groups in society. Strong postmodernists reject any claim to knowledge which makes 'an explicit appeal to some grand narrative, such as the dialectic of the Spirit, the hermeneutic of meaning, the emancipation of the rational or working subject or the creation of wealth' (Lyotard 1984: xxiii). Such claims are regarded as disguised manifestations of a totalising will-to-power where 'man', seeking his destiny in the conquest of nature, has sought to impose his ideal blueprints on the rest of the human race and, in so doing, has produced the violences, wars, totalitarianisms and pogroms of the last two hundred or so years. On the one hand, this kind of critique has exposed the gendered exclusiveness of the so-called 'universal' narratives of progressive modernity, but, on the other, it seems to entail the view that feminism has no more legitimacy than any other political language game. Within the terms of 'strong' postmodernism one could not even make an unconditional claim that it is wrong to oppress women. Indeed, for postmodern feminists such as Judith Butler (1990), the term 'woman' is merely a signifier with no substance, referring to nothing, simply a token in the particular language game in which it happens to be deployed.

Strong reconstructive postmodernism begins with similar premises to the deconstructive variety, but produces a number of 'aestheticised' and sometimes utopian accounts of knowledge and culture. One of the best-known is that of Richard Rorty. Though Rorty's project of cultural reconstruction requires the centrality of notions of consensus, his version of 'little narratives' suggests that political and social solidarity do not require universal epistemological foundations or 'grand' and monocausal narratives and that progress is actually impeded by the continued search for such absolute guarantees: 'solidarity has to be constructed out of little pieces, rather than found already waiting' (Rorty 1989: 94). What makes Rorty 'strong' in his postmodernism, however, is his insistence that society can only be transformed without violence through *vocabularies*. Rather than searching for scientific proof or metaphysical certainty, or a structural analysis of economic or social inequality, we should now recognise that the way to understand and to change our world is through the artificial mutation and manipulation of vocabularies. There is no truth awaiting our discovery, only 'truths' to be invented through the creative uses of language. For Rorty, the Enlightenment represents an adherence to an outmoded scientism which should now give way to a post-Nietzschean cultural aestheticism in which 'the method is to redescribe lots and lots of things in new ways, until you have created a pattern of linguistic behaviour which will tempt the rising generation to adopt it, thereby causing them to look for appropriate forms of non-linguistic behaviour' (1989: 9). Rorty's project is another example of what might be called strong linguistic determinism. Once everything is conceived in terms of language, here 'vocabularies', then the revolution of the word is claimed to be inseparable from revolution in the world: only irony can save us.

That such a position raises enormous difficulties for any emancipatory collective movement concerned with profound economic and social inequalities is immediately obvious. But perhaps even more problematic for feminists (though paradoxically more seductive) is a pervasive rhetoric of the 'sublime' which I would also categorise as another aestheticist version of strong reconstructive postmodernism. Rhetorics of the sublime usually take the form of positing a utopian 'space' outside of rationality, consciousness or language, to be set against a world conceived in the terms of linguistic determinism. If we cannot step outside of our systems of signification, not even to criticise one language game from within the terms of another, then there is no empirical means of comparing linguistic systems, of evaluating them or of understanding one from the perspective of another. Once this incommensurability thesis is accepted, then it is not surprising that so many postmodernists have invoked some version of the sublime as a space of the 'other' outside of publicly available modes of discourse or knowledge, opaque to rational methodologies. There was a dangerous tendency in the various postmodern critiques of reason which circulated in the 1980s, to regard alterity as a sublime space outside the law, recoverable through madness, hysteria, or some metaphorised return to the body. If physical space could not be politically transformed, the power of the imaginary or a new supra-rational sublime must be heightened and politicised. Indeed the work of French feminists such as Luce Irigaray was quickly appropriated for this postmodern reading of the sublime (see, for example, Deleuze and Guattari 1983). But analogy may all too easily be mistaken for causality and a revolutionary political significance claimed for a semi-mystical notion of otherness. This space was often designated 'feminine', but in the hands of male theorists rarely had very much to do with actual women and even threatened, in continuing to identify femininity with a mysterious, irrational and unrepresentable 'otherness', to keep real women locked in a prisonhouse of (postmodern) language: a condition which might seem disturbingly similar to that earlier state of eternal femininity challenged by the entire tradition of modern (i.e. Enlightened) feminism.

Strong Postmodern Feminism: From Lyotard to Haraway

Contemporary 'strong' postmodernism, in both its deconstructive and reconstructive modes, owes much to Jean-François Lyotard's *The Postmodern Condition* (1984). This has been the most influential text in establishing the antifoundationalist thrust of the strong postmodern critique of knowledge in its axiomatic assumption of the exhaustion of Enlightenment metanarratives and of the so-called emancipatory project of modernity. In this section, I wish to examine its significance for feminists and to examine the work of one 'strong' postmodern feminist, Donna Haraway, whose critique of science and politics bears many resemblances to Lyotard's position.

Lyotard's argument is that the commitment of post-Enlightenment thinkers to the instrumental uses of science and technology in the cause of social justice, and to the pursuit of objective knowledge as the foundation of social progress, is no longer a viable or desirable objective: 'the society of the future falls less within the province of a Newtonian anthropology (such as structuralism or systems theory) than a pragmatics of language particles. There are many different language games – a heterogeneity of elements' (Lyotard 1984: xxiv).

Lyotard claims that there can be no objective grounds for truth, because science and philosophy are discourses whose 'truths' make sense only in terms of their own internal organisation; there is no external truth to which they refer. He is saying, therefore, that rationalism fails because it cannot ground its own rational procedures and requires another kind of discourse, narrative knowledge or 'customary' knowledge, in order to achieve a sense of grounding. In the post-modern world, however, this customary knowledge has now fragmented into a multiplicity of heterogeneous language games with their own internal rules.

There can no longer be belief, therefore, in privileged meta-discourses such as Nature, History, Spirit or Pure Reason which transcend local and contingent conditions and in which truth can be grounded. What follows from this, for feminism, is that gender, like class, or race, or ethnicity, can no longer be regarded as an essential or even a stable category, nor can it be used to explain the practices of human societies as a whole. It is no longer legitimate to appeal to the category 'women' to ground a metanarrative of political practice – even in the name of emancipation.

According to the logic of Lyotard's argument, therefore, the continued adher-ence to metanarratives of gender must necessarily blind feminist theorists to the oppressive ethnocentricity and heterocentricity lurking in all essentialist truth claims about the nature of 'woman' or feminine experience. Moreover, Lyotard's argument implies that any recourse to trans-historical structures as a means of explaining political oppression will simply re-enact those forms of oppression in reverse mode. Political communities founded on the solidarity of shared experi-ence might only exist legitimately in local, provisional and attenuated forms. Indeed, the publication of Lyotard's book coincided with a shift within feminism itself to an assault on essentialism and a problematisation of the notion of difference.

Lyotard's strong deconstructive critique has certainly been valuable in alerting feminists to essentialism and ethnocentrism in their own thought and his notion of heterogeneity does seem to hold out some possibility of pragmatic 'dialogue' across groups (see Fraser and Nicholson 1988). We might wish to contest the pro-claimed 'openness' of Lyotard's thought, however, for his thesis contains its own (hidden) authoritarian structures of legitimation. This impinges very directly on my chosen example of strong postmodern feminism: Haraway's (1990) work on the cyborg. Lyotard, like all strong postmodernists insists the pre-emptive Doubt of Cartesianism (Decartes' idea that we should doubt everything until reason delivers certainty) should be renounced for an ever open-ended postmodern Uncertainty. What follows is that first, the dialectical pursuit of truth through rational critique, must therefore give way to endless postmodern 'dialogue'; and, second, that the assumptions underpinning classic scientific methodology – that the truth of a hypothesis can be verified by testing it against observable phenom-ena – must be abandoned for the acceptance of fictionality and indeterminacy. But the very examples used to proclaim that the legitimacy of scientific method is now exhausted, are simultaneously mobilised to provide the scientific legit-imacy of Lyotard's own position.

He achieves this by substituting a model of knowledge derived from the New Science for the supposedly discredited epistemologies of classic realist science.

He highlights those aspects of the New Science (particularly quantum physics' attempts to describe and formulate the nature of sub-atomic particles) which appear to exist in the manner of aesthetic objects: as indeterminate structures given realisation through the act of an intentional consciousness (the Uncertainty Principle). Scientific knowledge thus becomes indistinguishable from aesthetic knowing: science is used to deny the hegemony of science. Where once Enlightenment thought produced a scientised world, now postmodernism offers a thoroughly aestheticised one. Lyotard achieves this sleight of hand by representing New Science so that it corresponds with his postmodernist argument. He emphasises its concern with 'undecidables', with a radically uncertain world characterised as 'discontinuous, catastrophic, non-rectifiable and paradoxical (Lyotard 1984: 60). Curiously enough, the New Science comes to share the postmodern condition in all its details of undecideability and indeterminacy. Uncertainty is not simply a consequence of the limitations on us as knowers, but is the very condition of the universe itself and inherent in the structure of matter. Moreover, this condition now becomes paradoxically reassuring. Once we recognise that materialism is dead: we can give up the painful and searching condition of modern Doubt and re-identify ourselves in a world where cells and stars, consciousness and matter, are similarly constituted, open-ended, radically Uncertain.

In Donna Haraway's 'Manifesto for Cyborgs' we see a similar conflation of the organic and the inorganic, of science with art and of fictionality with fact, in a strong reconstructive postmodern feminist version of Lyotard's reading of science. For Donna Haraway the cyborg is an answer to the question of what might fill the void left by postmodern feminists' necessary sense of exile from all those (masculinist) Utopian dreams of Enlightenment which sought to return to an original wholeness, an ultimate reconciliation of cosmos and consciousness. Haraway informs us that 'a cyborg is a cybernetic organism, a hybrid of machine and organism, a creature of social reality as well as a creature of fiction' (1990: 191). More pertinently, for feminism, a cyborg is 'a creature in a postgender world; it has no truck with bisexuality, pre-Oedipal symbiosis, unalienated labour, or other seductions to organic wholeness through a final appropriation of all the powers of the parts into a higher unity ... The cyborg skips the step of original unity, of identification with nature in the Western sense' (Haraway 1990: 192).

The myth which, according to Haraway, is refuted by the image of the cyborg is nothing less than the founding myth of modernity: the search for reconciliation, in the absence of belief in a transcendent Deity, of all those dualisms, of mind and body, consciousness and cosmos, art and science, custom and reason, associated with the Enlightenment. For the very moment which brought modern science to birth also delivered its twin: a redemptive humanist aesthetic which might compensate for all that science would abstract from the world, disenchanting its inhabitants, disembedding them from a unified lifeworld, offering the cold comfort of spectatorship at a world picture of pure mechanical design. Haraway, however, will have no truck with such notions of the machine in the garden. In her postmodern landscape of urban technological and post-industrial space, 'machine is us, our processes, an aspect of our embodiment' (1990: 222), open to the possibility of regeneration but not rebirth, collapsing the myth of the two realms of science and humanistic culture, cutting across the fundamental distinctions which differentiate human from machine, man from woman, nature from nurture.

The cyborg is offered as a way out of the dualisms of modernity in which women have always discovered themselves on the weaker or negated side. The cyborg is intended to explode the delusions of the Cartesian rational subject in its search for a bedrock of knowledge located in an autonomous and unitary consciousness, which turns out to be nothing more than an endless, fictional projection. Yet, in a peculiar way, and as with Lyotard's image of Uncertainty, the cyborg promises ultimate reconciliation in a postmodernist and post-humanist world. The cyborg offers a different kind of radical fictionality: that there is no truth to discover, no unitary consciousness to which we might return; there is only endless fictionality, endless construction of shifting subjectivities, technological productiveness, only an absolute condition of Uncertainty. The cyborg, too, is science as art, machine as human, a hybrid and unstable constellation of fact and fiction which denies any privileged epistemological status to biologism *or* mentalism.

Haraway thus exhorts us to renounce our nostalgia for the old myths of wholeness (much as Lyotard insists we give up the pursuit of 'grand narratives' and our aching for totality), and recognise that the shift from organic to industrial to postindustrial society carries with it the liberatory potential of the postmodern, polymorphously perverse information systems to explode concepts of subjectivity and truth which have functioned within the paradigms of modernity to oppress women. Her argument, of course, is fraught with all those problems about ethics and agency which have already been rehearsed during the course of this chapter. The cyborg is another image of the postmodern sublime, of a radical alterity which seduces with utopian promise yet presents enormous problems for a feminist politics. Not the least of these problems is its tendency to romanticise the marginal as unrepresentable and therefore to repeat as a gesture of liberation those very patriarchal discourses which have been used to control women in the first place: biologically fixed Woman might now become technologically (and infinitely) manipulable Woman.

Indeed, the cyborg is a concretised image of that impossible 'view from everywhere', of partial, multiple, floating subjectivities, which is advocated by some postmodernists as an alternative to a discredited 'view from nowhere' (the idea of an 'objective' point of reference from which to view the world). What they share, of course, is a sublime dis-embodiment: the idea of a disembodied 'knower' is replaced in the postmodern version by the 'body-in-bits', the protean being whose negative capability extends to an ability to occupy numerous subject positions. Haraway shares with Lyotard the postmodern retreat from the regulative ideal of a unified rational subjectivity whose capacity to generate a view from nowhere becomes the guarantee of an 'objective' knowing, and she too substitutes a perspectival constructivism claimed to be ethically superior in its refusal of the violences of 'totalising' knowledge. Yet, as I have already suggested, this 'view from everywhere' bears no relation to the constraints imposed on our actual being in the world. Moreover, without the capacity to stand back, to believe in the view from nowhere as a kind of regulative principle underpinning our attempts to know and judge, we would be unable to discriminate amongst different points of view. Postmodern hybridity, nomadism, fragmentation and endless fictionality may seem to offer an escape route from biological, social and cosmic determinism. However, if they preclude the possibility of discrimination between, and negotiation across, multiple positions and discourses, then it is difficult to see how such a radical or strong postmodernism could form the basis for any kind of politics, ethics or epistemology which assumes the necessity for personal and collective agency and responsibility.

Weak Postmodernism

At this point (or impasse?), I will turn to examine some examples of 'weak postmodernism' and consider what, if anything, they may offer feminists reluctant to embrace strong postmodernism in either or both its aesthetic and philosophical modes. Unlike strong postmodernism, the weak version may accept the human need to invest in grand narratives, though its proponents would reject monocausal varieties and insist that all knowledge is embedded or situated in particular cultures or cultural traditions. According to weak postmodernism, understanding arises through the practices, customs, traditions and textures of a particular culture and we may arrive at a shared structure of values, a sense of personal significance, and the possibility of belief in historical progress through collective engagements which do not require foundations of truth or value. In some versions of 'weak postmodernism', however, the ideal of objectivity or the impulse toward the 'view from nowhere' is to be preserved but is brought to earth and combined with the perspective of the culturally situated and embodied subject. In this way, weak postmodernism resists the utopian seductiveness of the strong postmodern 'view from everywhere' and the fluid, disembodied and centreless subject which underpins it.

The starting point for weak postmodernism is Martin Heidegger and the tradition of hermeneutic theory. For Heidegger, modernity is characterised by a denial or disavowal of being-in-the-world. A detached subjectivity has come to stand over an inert nature, looking, speculating, fixing and judging; its instrumental rationalism radically distanced from the world it surveys, distorted into the shape of its own fictionally projected ends. But, says Heidegger, 'in clarifying being-in-the-world we have shown that a bare subject without a world never … is … given' (Heidegger 1962: 152). Heidegger's influence on weak deconstructive postmodernism is most obviously felt in the work of Hans-Georg Gadamer. The central thesis of Gadamer's *Truth and Method* (1960) is that there can be no Archimedean point outside of culture from which to achieve 'objective knowledge', for understanding exists only in relation to the perspectives (or 'prejudice' as he calls it) provided for us through our cultural traditions and these perspectives can never be brought to full rational consciousness.

Though seemingly close to Heidegger's position, Gadamer's version of being-in-the-world does allow for greater intervention and agency, for though we can never achieve full knowledge, we may become aware of our prejudices and therefore begin to modify them through exposure to experiences of truth which seem to contradict our own – though neither self nor world can ever be rationally conceptualised in any final sense. However, if strong postmodernism seems not to anchor subjectivity at all, raising all the problems for feminism of ethical accountability and political agency, weak postmodernism may seem to raise the same difficulties through the provision of too much anchorage. Yet, Gadamer's elaboration of 'embodied' knowledge does function to remove the gendered polarities of mind and body written into the history of modernist philosophy. Gadamer's work suggests the extent to which *all* human understanding is actually rooted and embodied in profound cultural relations and traditions: we can neither separate 'reason' from 'custom', nor should we seek to do so.

The varieties of reconstructive postmodernism which have emerged from the hermeneutic critique may be regarded as 'weak' in that they never entirely abandon the importance of agency, of the need to experience the self as a coherent and consistent, if revisable entity, nor do they dispute the assumption that ethics requires a subject. Some of the more recent communitarian versions of this model of self and society, however, may seem as 'strong' as the centreless worlds of the cyborg. So Alasdair MacIntyre's (1985) work, for example, has in common with strong postmodernism, an insistence that truth and value are only ever internal to the conditions of particular communities or enclosed institutional frameworks.

MacIntyre advocates an ethical system based on a return to a pre-modern model of virtue and practical wisdom, but tempered by a modern, aesthetic sense of how we might reformulate and rewrite the scripts of tradition. In such a world, we would not be subjected to stagnatory anchorage, but neither would we float dangerously adrift. MacIntyre tends to conceive of culture in homogenous terms and to ignore the fact that most of us move daily between multiple groups and communities each with different preoccupations and often non-complementary goals, values and aims. There are elements of MacIntyre's work which have appealed to feminists, but it remains to be seen whether it is possible to reconcile this kind of contextualism with the modern imperatives of freedom, emancipation and the desire, simply, to change the script. MacIntyre does allow that we may become authors (or active agents) but, like those postmodernists who emphasise existing culture, or language, or biology, as final determinants of our being in the world, he too seems to offer only a script which has finally already been written.

Feminism and Weak Postmodernism

In its communitarian aspects, 'weak' postmodernism is becoming increasingly attractive to feminism as a way of dealing with the impasses of postmodernism in its 'strong' forms. The work of Seyla Benhabib (1992) represents the most forceful recent feminist attempt to come to terms with postmodernism whilst resisting the implications and the Uncertainty of its 'strong' versions. Indeed, she has explicitly argued that strong postmodernism threatens the entire identity of feminism as a politics and tries to discredit the emancipatory ideals which have guided it in the past. Whilst recommending a contextualist theory of knowledge or understanding, she nevertheless insists on the need to sustain a commitment to Enlightenment models of rationality as a regulative principle guiding our enquiries and beliefs. She argues for the need also to continue to envisage the possibility of Utopia (and therefore progress) as an inspiration for political practice and has put forward a persuasive case that social critics cannot afford to abandon the philosophical ideal of 'objectivity', for we need to able to detach ourselves from immediate contexts, to stand back, reflect upon, compare, and analyse cross-culturally. For this, we need at times to inhabit the detached stance of the rationalist philosopher:

> social criticism needs philosophy precisely because the narratives of our culture are so conflictual and irreconcilable that, even when one appeals to them, a certain ordering of one's normative priorities, a statement of the methodological assumptions guiding one's choice of narratives, and a clarification of those principles in the name of which one speaks is unavoidable.
>
> (Benhabib 1992: 226)

Benhabib seems to suggest that we need both a contextual sense of our perspective from the place in the world where we find ourselves, but also the discipline of imagining that world from outside but with ourselves inside it: an attenuated version of the View from Nowhere.

Of course, Nowhere is not just an image for a regulative ideal governing rationalist thought; it may also suggest No-place as Utopia. The 'View from Nowhere' is our capacity to imagine otherwise, to project an ideal beyond what is. Strong deconstructive postmodernism bears witness to an historical retreat from such utopian visions, and to a disillusionment with the Enlightenment hopes for rational planning of the perfect society. However, substituted in their place is the 'Nowhere' of its own strong reconstructive mode, a non-rationalist space of the sublime filled with cyborgs and nomads, chaos and catastrophe. It is assumed here that because we cannot arrive at absolute knowledge, there is nothing out there to know except the spectral shapes of our own projected fictional constructions.

In presenting my own account of postmodernism, I do not wish to deny the importance of both the 'Nowhere' of fictional space and the 'Nowhere' of rational thought as modes which enable the projection of ourselves beyond our own immediate preoccupations, but I would argue against the tendency of strong postmodernism to regard the two as identical procedures. Surely, in the 'Nowhere' of aesthetic fictions there is no responsibility for accurate depiction of historical reality, whereas in the 'Nowhere' of the ideal realm of objective knowledge, the aim is to describe and explain material realities. Strong postmodernism would deny that there is any distinction to be made between these ways of knowing, but my own argument has been that feminism may discover a viable relation with postmodernism only if wary of such 'strong' readings.

It would seem that the appropriate place for sublime fantasy, for the imagination of a No-Place unencumbered by physical or biological or historical limitation, is in works of fiction. In novels by Jeanette Winterson, Toni Morrison and Angela Carter, for example, history may be deconstructed as an endless regress of mirrors or reinvented in fantastic form. In Winterson's novel *Sexing the Cherry* (1989), for instance, ideas and images from postmodern science are used imaginatively to develop the theme of division and its overcoming: divisions which are directly presented as a consequence of Cartesian dualism and Newtonian science and which separate mind and matter, man and woman, feeling and reason. Set at the moment of the beheading of Charles I, the novel fantastically explores the beginnings of a historical and cultural divide where a feminised nature is transformed into a mechanical universe requiring dissection, demystification and naming of parts. The fictional universe of Winterson's novel postmodernistically breaks free of such determinism, however, in its narrative and formal re-enactment of the post-Einsteinian account of a universe where imaginative hypothesis and material reality are no longer opposed poles and where Nature becomes the flickering pictures of our relation to what must always exceed our conceptual categories. But all this takes place in the designated space of aesthetic fiction: as trial without the consequences of error. Such No-Places constitute one important kind of Utopianism. The Nowhere of the aesthetic, however, may provide imaginary visions, but only the Nowhere at the end of, and guiding rational thought, can attempt to determine the historical consequences of their actual realisation. For a feminist politics committed to the futures of actual women in the world, the rather more earth-bound and situated reason of weak postmodernism may complement the stronger postmodernist impulses at work in experimental art and literature.

In this chapter I have suggested that feminism can benefit from the post-modern, both in its cultural-aesthetic and in its epistemological modes, but that feminism should beware of their easy conflation and continue to explore the consequences of, and the alternatives to, the abandonment of the discourses of modernity. We do have choices and our relation to postmodernism is never one of necessary symbiosis, but always of strategic selection and a reasonable, if never purely rational, process of decision-making. If feminism, like some versions of the postmodern self, is an ever-revisable narrative project, then, like a good author, it needs a sense of the appropriate moment to stand back from its creations, to decide what is worth retaining and what has had its moment, what is of lasting value and what is simply pandering to fashion.

References

Baudrillard, J. (1983) *Simulations*, New York: Semiotext(e).

Benhabib, S. (1992) *Situating the Self*, Cambridge: Polity Press.

Bordo, S. (1990) 'Feminism, Postmodernism and Gender-Scepticism', in L. J. Nicholson (ed.) *Feminism/Postmodernism*, New York and London: Routledge.

Butler, J. (1990) *Gender Trouble*, New York: Routledge.

Deleuze, G. and F. Guattari (1983) *Anti-Oedipus*, Minneapolis: University of Minnesota Press.

Eagleton, T. (1985) 'Capitalism, Modernism and Postmodernism', *New Left Review* 152: 60–73.

Foucault, M. (1981) *The History of Sexuality. Volume 1: The Will to Truth*, Harmondsworth: Penguin.

Fraser, N. and L. Nicholson (1988) 'Social Criticism without Philosophy: an Encounter between Feminism and Postmodernism', *Theory, Culture and Society* 5, 2–3: 373–94.

Gadamer, H.-G. [1960] (1975) *Truth and Method*, in G. Barden and J. Cumming (eds), New York: Continuum.

Habermas, J. (1981) 'Modernity v. Postmodernity', *New German Critique*, 22.

Haraway, D. (1990) 'A Manifesto for Cyborgs: Science, Technology, and Socialist Feminism in the 1980s', in Nicholson (ed.).

Heidegger, M. (1962) *Being and Time*, New York: Harper and Row.

Hekman S. (1990) *Gender and Knowledge: Elements of a Postmodern Feminism*, Cambridge: Polity Press.

Hutcheon, L. (1988) *A Poetics of Postmodernism: History, Theory, Fiction*, London: Routledge.

Jameson, F. (1991) *Postmodernism*, London: Verso.

Lyotard, J.-F. (1984) *The Postmodern Condition: A Report on Knowledge*, Manchester: Manchester University Press.

MacIntyre, A. (1985) *After Virtue: A Study in Moral Theory*, London: Duckworth.

Nietzsche, F. (1969) *The Genealogy of Morals*, trans. W. Kaufmann, New York: Random House.

Rorty, R. (1989) *Contingency, Irony, Solidarity*, Cambridge: Cambridge University Press.

Weedon, C. (1987) *Feminist Practice and Poststructuralist Theory*, Oxford: Blackwell.

Wellmer, A. (1985) 'The Dialectic of Modernism and Postmodernism', *Praxis International* 4.

Winterson, J. (1989) *Sexing the Cherry*, London: Bloomsbury. Reprinted as Vintage paperback in 1990.

Further Reading

Flax, J. (1990) *Thinking Fragments: Psychoanalysis, Feminism and Postmodernism in the Contemporary West*, Berkeley: California University Press.

Huyssen, A. (1986) *After the Great Divide: Modernism, Mass Culture, Postmodernism*, London: Macmillan.

Jardine, A. (1985) *Gynesis: Configurations of Woman and Modernity*, Ithaca, New York: Cornell University Press.

Kaplan, E. A. (1983) *Postmodernism and its Discontents*, London: Verso.

Lovibond, S. (1990) 'Feminism and Postmodernism', in R. Boyne and A. Rattansi (eds) *Postmodernism and Society*, Basingstoke: Macmillan.

Morris, M. (1988) *The Pirate's Fiancée*, London: Verso.

Norris, C. (1990) *What's Wrong With Postmodernism?* Hemel Hempstead: Harvester Wheatsheaf.

Roberts, J. (1990) *Postmodernism, Politics and Art*, Manchester: Manchester University Press.

Waugh, P. (1992) *Practising Postmodernism/Reading Modernism*, London: Edward Arnold.

Chapter 14

Feminist Literary Theory

Maggie Humm

Introduction

Contemporary feminist literary theory moves across borders to recruit the energies of autobiography, social polemic and graphic poetry and is acutely experimental and exciting. Literary theory matters because all representations, literary or otherwise, are what make constructions of knowledge and subjectivity possible. Through representations we shape our identities and our worlds. The insights of feminist literary theory will help us, even require us, to think about cultural identities in new ways, and feminist border crossings are not simply metaphorical but grow out of a strong belief that criticism can help bring about a more equitable world.

Feminism is not simply an additive explanatory model alongside other political theories. To centralise women's experiences of sexuality, work and the family inevitably challenges traditional frameworks of knowledge. Feminism incorporates diverse ideas which share three major perceptions: that gender is a social construction which oppresses women more than men; that patriarchy shapes this construction; and that women's experiential knowledge is a basis for a future non-sexist society. These assumptions inform feminism's double agenda: the task of critique (attacking gender stereotypes) and the task of construction. Without this second task (sometimes called feminist praxis) feminism has no goal.

These themes give feminism a particular interest in *cultural* constructions of gender, including those in literature. The cultural practices of literature are pervasive in schools, higher education and in the media. Literature produces representations of gender difference which contribute to the social perception that men and women are of unequal value. Women often become feminists by becoming conscious of, and *criticising*, the power of symbolic misrepresentations of women.

If, as Audre Lorde argued, 'the master's tools will never dismantle the master's house', how do feminist literary theorists escape the patterns of thought and master-tools of the academy (Lorde 1984: 110)? My rather prosaic answer is to look at some key examples as well as key events which I think illustrate new literary principles and negotiations. My project is modest: to introduce and comment on the two main forms of 'border crossing' in contemporary feminist literary theory and on how these might help to reframe the Eurocentricism of literary studies. One of my foci is on feminist poet-criticism and on its open-sided associative intimacy with the reader which is hugely self-reflexive. As a new and unnamed area of literary feminism I am going to call this work *'gynographic criticism'* because it often entails an explicitly typographical 'performance' on the printed page. I also want to consider the 'deterritorialisation' of literature, to use Deleuze and Guattari's term, modelled by Asian and Black women and women of colour: women who have deftly and with some courage transformed the perceptual parameters of literary theory (Deleuze and Guattari 1986).

My premise is that critical analysis helps us to understand the cultural changes at work in these difficult times. Terry Eagleton claimed that the greatest English critics are frequently foreigners or outsiders to tradition, and my sense of current critical writing is that feminists, above all others, gamble the greatest stakes in this literary wager (Eagleton 1970).

Feminist Literary Theory from 1970 to the Present

The 1970s

Much of the most exciting recent work on gender and writing spins the term along paths that are not mapped in traditional literary theories. But in order to understand the genesis of that excitement we need to step back a moment to the publication of Kate Millett's *Sexual Politics* (1970) to recognise the telling fact that second-wave criticism *began* as a *spatial* construction, as border crossing, with its key theme 'the personal is political' linking two hitherto conceptually, separately spaced worlds. What feminist literary criticism uniquely offered, and why Millett's book is so generative, is a revolutionary *standpoint*, not simply, or not only, new critical tools. Yet in the 1970s feminist criticism was certainly beyond the border of the traditional academy, indeed it was invisible. The 1980 edition of the Modern Languages Association (MLA), *Introduction to Scholarship*, contains no mention of feminist criticism, and Margaret Drabble, in her plenary address to a recent conference, Literature: a Woman's Business, amusingly described Oxford University Press's shocked response to her suggestion that she include feminist criticism in her new edition of *The Oxford Companion to English Literature* published in 1985 (Gibaldi 1992). She did. Faced with this misogyny, feminist literary criticism in the 1970s tended to define space diachronically as *origin*, as the significance of male or female authorship, which was the key feature of feminist criticism at the time.

Second-wave feminism is often characterised as 'the break with the fathers' because critics such as Kate Millett, Germaine Greer and Mary Ellmann made revisionary readings of what Ellmann calls 'phallic' writing (Millett 1970; Greer 1971; Ellmann 1968). Critics focused on sexist vocabulary and gender stereotypes in the work of male authors and highlighted the ways in which these writers commonly ascribe particular features, such as 'hysteria' and 'passivity' only to women. Judith Fetterley's influential *The Resisting Reader* (1978) symbolised this new, politically informed, approach to literary criticism. In her book Fetterley attacks the writers whose works were 'canonised' in literary departments throughout America – Henry James, Hemingway, Fitzgerald and Faulkner.

Gynocriticism

In the 1970s feminist criticism grew into a new phase, often called gynocriticism or the study of women writers and women-identified themes. Critics, including Ellen Moers and Elaine Showalter, described women's literary expressions and 'sub-cultures' and defined and celebrated women's literary history as a progressive tradition (Moers 1976; Showalter 1977). Ellen Moers's *Literary Women* gave shape to a tradition of women's literature. Although it was attacked in the 1980s for its partial racism, homophobia and idiosyncratic choices, *Literary Women* was one of the first texts of feminist criticism to give women writers a history, describe women's choices of literary expression, and to make an identificatory celebration of the power of women writers: 'There is no point saying what women cannot do in literature, for history shows they have done it all' (Moers 1976: xiii).

A constant theme in feminist writing in this period is the issue of communication, as titles of several feminist books make clear: Tillie Olsen's *Silences* and Adrienne Rich's *The Dream of a Common Language*. The vital work of this decade was to explore a distinctive women's language and to establish a body of literary criticism. In 1975 the journal *Signs* was founded, with a review of literary criticism by Elaine Showalter. A similar debate developed outside the English-speaking world: the first programmatic discussion about 'Frauen Literature' took place in Germany in 1975–6; and the founding of the 'Frauenoffensive' publishing house and journal represented a common concern among German feminists to explore women's 'different' language and culture.

Elaine Showalter's *A Literature of Their Own* (1977) was an important contribution to this agenda. Reflecting on Woolf's *A Room of One's Own*, Showalter faced the similar issue of women's exclusion from the academy. Charting a long history of literary women, she brought attention to undervalued nineteenth-century writers such as Sarah Grand and George Egerton. Rather than defining a 'universal' woman's text, Showalter preferred to identify a female 'subculture' which created those texts. She replaced the traditional periods of literary history with an alternative three-stage process which she couched as a growth into consciousness – feminine, feminist and female. Cautioned by later critics for adopting a literary standard more applicable to the late twentieth century and for her resistance to theory, Showalter went on to develop her ideas in 'Toward a Feminist Poetics', 'Feminist Criticism in the Wilderness' and *The New Feminist Criticism* (1985). In these essays Showalter divided criticism into two distinct categories: the first type focused on the woman reader, a consumer of literature, and the second focused on the woman writer, a producer of textual meaning. Showalter described four models of gender difference – biological, linguistic, psychoanalytic and cultural – and claimed that these would be best addressed by a gynocentric model of feminist criticism.

From the hindsight of the 1990s this description of difference seems implicitly binary and is caught up in the notion that women's literature is in one category, the 'Other', in relation to the masculine tradition. Yet Showalter's work in this decade did offer a firm agenda for feminist criticism by describing a panoply of women's writing as a continuous and progressive narrative. Certainly gyno-criticism's stress on the significance of women's literary friendships held sway during the early 1980s, evident in the continuing popularity of Adrienne Rich's *Of Woman Born* (1976) and cultural feminism, for example, feminists (Davidson and Broner 1980) writing about the mother/daughter nexus, in *The Lost Tradition*. But it is the work of Sandra Gilbert and Susan Gubar (1988), above all, in the 1980s which created a feminist aesthetic from within the female literary tradition itself.

The 1980s

The Madwoman in the Attic (Gilbert and Gubar 1979) and their subsequent series of texts, *No Man's Land*, 3 vols (1988), focus on some of traditional criticism's most serious exclusions: the material and psychological controls over women; women's secret lives and culture; and anxieties of masculinity and femininity represented in literary metaphors of the frontier, the visual, the domestic and cross-dressing. Gilbert and Gubar built on Moers's and Showalter's acts of retrieval and, like those critics, are passionate about the oppositional function of women's writing. *The Madwoman in the Attic*, appearing nine years after Millett's *Sexual Politics*, is a compelling display of interwoven discourses. It includes a close textual analysis of the work of Jane Austen, the Brontës, Emily Dickinson and George Eliot, combined with psychohistory and medical and historical analyses. Like *Sexual Politics*, *Madwoman* is basically a revisionist history taking an existing model – the andro-centric paradigm described by Harold Bloom that literary sons suffer an anxiety of authorship and Oedipal struggle with male precursors – to show that women write in confrontation with culture and with themselves by creating an author's double: the madwoman in the attic.

In *No Man's Land*, Gilbert and Gubar moved on from *Madwoman*'s gynocritical focus which was in part shaped by a notion of patriarchal culture as a homo-genous and uniformly repressive entity. As the title suggests, all three volumes argue that twentieth-century literary history is a history of sexual conflict, and

Gilbert and Gubar's great achievement is to catalogue in full the repetitive sexual imagery (of rape and impotence) which dominates modernist writing by men. *No Man's Land* fosters a more pluralist feminist criticism than the singular psycho-analytic model of *Madwoman*. Gilbert and Gubar discuss how lesbian expatriates in Paris 'reinvented gender'; they explore the consumerism of the Gilded Age in an informed materialist analysis and describe the sexual imagery of imperialism. *No Man's Land* is sustained by a postmodern conviction that 'male' and 'female' are fictive constructs variously shaped by cultures.

One of the great achievements of Anglo-American feminist criticism in the 1980s was its ability to identify and conduct a very diverse gendered literary criticism. Feminist criticism proved firstly that literature was not simply a collection of great texts but was deeply structured by social/sexual ideologies, and secondly, that certain preoccupations and techniques predominate in women's writing in relation to those social structures. Of course, there were problems with the politics of pluralism. For example, lesbian, Third World and working-class critics attacked Annette Kolodny's prize-winning essay, 'Dancing Through the Minefield' (1980), arguing that pluralism covered over heterosexism and racism (Gardiner et al. 1982). Yet what is also clear now about that decade is the innovative and self-conscious *rapprochement* that was taking place between feminist criticism and feminist writing in the work of Audre Lorde, Alice Walker and Adrienne Rich. Feminist criticism was now married to feminist creative writing in a rich terrain of autobiographies, fictional narratives and poetic histories. And it is not insignificant for the future direction of feminist criticism in the late 1980s into theories of poststructuralism and postmodernism that Sandra Gilbert was the American editor of Hélène Cixous' and Cathérine Clément's *The Newly Born Woman* (1987).

Écriture féminine

In the 1980s Gilbert and Gubar's theme of a woman's anxiety of authorship was given shape in the first deconstructive text of feminist criticism, Toril Moi's *Sexual/Textual Politics* (1985). Only six years separate the publication of these works by Gilbert and Gubar and Moi but during that period the writings of the French feminists, the linguistic philosopher Jacques Derrida and poststructuralists had begun to inform Western feminist criticism. Moi gives a summary and analysis of the main kinds of Anglo-American and French criticism, but, ethnocentrically, did not consider Black writing.

The key feminist focus in this work of the late 1980s was on language. The challenge was, by interrogating the relation between gender identity and language, to refigure the powerful and sexually expressive relationships between language, literary forms and women's and men's psyches. French feminist critics adopted the term *écriture féminine* to describe a feminine style (which was equally available to both men and women). They discovered this 'style' in absences, ruptures and 'jouissances' in modernist writing. Cixous, in particular, argues that *écriture féminine* is to be found in metaphors of female sexuality and women's genital and libidinal differences.

French feminists' determination to break through patriarchal critical practices – by creating new forms of writing/thinking which could not be described as the 'other' half of male-defined rationality – inspired excitement and debate. Cixous and Irigaray (1974) laid claim to a repressed sexuality which created ways of thinking lying mute in patriarchy. Julia Kristeva identified this new feminine language as 'the semiotic' which she defines as the pre-Oedipal language of the mother and infants (see Humm 1994).

Deconstruction, in particular, appears a sophisticated and potentially revolutionary approach because it dismantled linguistic binary oppositions between men and women. However, a deconstructive approach can also evade the real practical and theoretical differences between white and Black feminists and white and Black lesbian feminists. Barbara Christian exposed the reactionary assumptions underlying the American academy's wholesale embrace of critical theory in the 1980s. The 'race for theory', she argued, further marginalised feminists outside the academy, frequently Black and/or lesbian women.

Black feminisms

From the mid-1980s racial difference became a key focus for feminist criticism as white feminists at last addressed the absences in their own processes of critical selection and commentary. It was Audre Lorde who posed the provocative view that we cannot create a useful feminist criticism with the methods and forms of language we inherit from 'the master's house' (Lorde 1984).

In addition, as Barbara Christian complained, Black women are 'tired of being asked to produce a Black feminist literary theory as if I were a mechanical man'. Christian pushed the theoretical debate further by pointing out that 'peoples of color have always theorized – but in forms quite different from our Western form of abstract logic ... in the stories we create, in riddles and proverbs' (1987: 53). The Black critical tradition that Christian describes began with Alice Walker's work in *Ms* (1974) and with Barbara Smith's groundbreaking essay 'Toward a Black Feminist Criticism' (1977). It continued in the first American anthology about Black women writers, *Sturdy Black Bridges* (Bell et al. 1979), as well as in collections co-edited by Smith: *But Some of Us Are Brave* (Hull et al. 1981), the first anthology of Black women's studies and *Home Girls* (Smith 1983), which focuses on Black lesbian writing. Several themes emerged in these texts: the ways in which extra-literary folk traditions and spirituality influence Black writing; the significance of mother/daughter relationships and varieties of female bonding in Black writing which are replicated in the close relationships between Black readers/critics/writers.

Building on this work, Black feminist criticism of the late 1980s and 1990s (for example, Marjorie Pryse and Hortense Spillers, eds, *Conjuring: Black Women, Fiction and the Literary Tradition* [1985] and Joanne Braxton and Andrée McLaughlin, eds, *Wild Women in the Whirlwind* [1990] began to create a Black aesthetic. These works and many others retrieved Black women's lost texts, placed them in history, described myths and women's traditions which proved that Black narratives, while not necessarily wanting to be *like* the texts of poststructuralism, could be said to be more akin in some of their textual features to poststructuralist texts than many white critical texts. In other words, Black criticism was not simply a self-naming, distinctive or essentially 'other' school or method *alongside* white criticism, but was permeating and transforming the whole agenda of feminist criticism.

Lesbian feminism and queer theory
Similar crucial and valuable feminist critiques at the end of the decade came from lesbian critics, white and Black. The critique of heterosexism in literary criticism, the recovery of lost lesbian writing and the search for a lesbian aesthetic, as well as the construction of queer theory, form the extensive work of critics such as Bonnie Zimmerman, Audre Lorde, Teresa de Lauretis and Adrienne Rich, among others. Lesbian feminist criticism challenges male-defined concepts of femininity and examines lesbian images and strategies in their historical and cultural moments. Queer theory is a discourse reversing homophobic categories to connect race, sexuality and activism.

The 1990s
The next step into the 1990s was perhaps predictable. The questions raised by the theoretical ferment of the 1980s and by the revelations of Black and lesbian critics led to a reshaping of critical identity which emerged as gender theory. This more recent development presented feminist criticism both with new possibilities and new problems. Elaine Showalter's career is a good example. Showalter moved on from providing forceful accounts of a women's literary tradition at the end of the 1980s to focusing on gender studies, with the publication of *Speaking of Gender* (1989), in which she claimed that feminist criticism had finished with her own gynocriticism and needed to focus on gender and sexual difference in texts by men as much as by women.

Gender studies opened up the possibility that feminist literary criticism could respond to gender theories in other disciplines – for example, in science (Evelyn Fox Keller 1985) or history (Joan Scott 1988), and could also retrieve homosexual literature from the margins of literary analysis. Eve Kosofsky Sedgwick's *Between Men* (1985) argued convincingly that representations of homosexuality could not be understood outside of their relation to women and to the gender system itself. Drawing on feminist theory of the 1980s, Sedgwick asked what theoretical framework could link sexual relations and power relations. Her answer was to recruit 'the representational finesse of deconstructive feminism' (Sedgwick 1985: 12). For example, Sedgwick treats representations of homophobia as tools for understanding the gender system as a whole. While Sedgwick's work challenged feminist criticism to explore how constructions of homosexuality are conjoined with misogynist constructions in general, gender studies as a practice separated itself from what has to be a fundamental aim of any feminist cultural work: the contribution that literary criticism can make to *feminist* projects. As Tania Modleski incisively argues, such work in gender studies is based on two fundamental and totally fallacious assumptions: one a heterosexual 'presumption' and the second an assumption of the 'equality between men and women' (Modleski 1991: 6). In this respect the appropriations of gender theory seem a retrograde step into the 1990s. Yet, as Joan Kelly-Gadol has pointed out, women do not, unproblematically, fit into the decades of linear 'masculine' history (Kelly-Gadol 1992). For example, Italian feminist semioticians are currently engaged in a highly complex theoretical debate about women's language. The Milanese group, *Libreria delle donne* (Women's Bookshop), devotes itself to a systematic analysis of mothering discourse (Bono and Kemp 1991).

Finally, by focusing on autobiography and on themes of place and displacement, critics such as Gloria Anzaldúa and Gayatri Spivak brought feminist criticism into the post-colonial, postmodern world (Anzaldúa 1987; Spivak 1990). So how do we figure this continual movement out of the current safe enclave of traditional criticism into gynographic and postcolonial criticisms; this intense and constant desire to cross literary borders?

'Listen Drink': feminist gynographic criticism

One image might be 'listen drink'. The famous animal behaviourist Beatrix Gardener died in the week I was asked to write this chapter. Gardener was the first to cross the border of animal/human communication. In 1963 Gardener lived closely with Washoe, a ten-month-old female chimpanzee, and communicated with her, not through speech, but through ASL or American Sign Language. Gardener's exciting and revolutionary notion was that a *gestural* rather than a vocal language (for which chimps lack the necessary anatomical and physiological equipment) might provide the breakthrough to human–chimpanzee communication (Smith 1985). Forty months later Washoe could express 132 signs such as 'baby', 'banana', even 'you' and 'yours'; but what was most dramatic was Washoe's ability to *combine* signs, not necessarily in the right order, but then English is unique among human languages for insisting on correct word order.

Washoe could 'double sign', and created a host of original phrases such as 'open food drink' for refrigerator and, my favourite, 'listen drink' for Alka Seltzer. In spite of Steven Pinker's attack in *The Language Instinct* (1994) that 'ape trainers' are not scientific and that chimps did not *properly* sign, far more significant was

Jane Goodall's observation, in her visit to a similar project with a chimpanzee, Nim, that chimps moved continually *back and forth over the border* between natural repertoire and ASL. Even Pinker, in a revealing aside, notes that the chimps 'know that the trainers like them to sign and that signing often gets them what they want' but often the chimps 'blithely sign simultaneously with their partner, frequently off to the side' (Pinker 1994: 340).

Inventive gynographic critics also do not necessarily use words in the right order but use parentheses, blank spaces and hyphenated titles to dramatise the constraining border between conceptual systems that Gardener productively overcame. For example, by weaving images of the female body into their texts, gynographic critics emphasise the materiality of pleasures like 'listen drink'. The following examples of gynographic criticism are not identical; there are important differences in approach. For example, Mary Daly is a philosopher, Hélène Cixous is a key proponent of *écriture féminine*; others are poststructuralists (Alice Jardine) or write personal criticism (Nicole Ward Jouve, Nancy Miller, Diana Collecott). Yet common themes and ideas underpin their work, most notably their inventive graphic re-vision of critical writing.

One of the first, and still the most powerful, examples of gynographic criticism is Hélène Cixous's 'Sorties' from *The Newly Born Woman* (Cixous and Clément 1987). Hugely influential, Cixous describes the oppositional border between 'culture/nature' as an opposition between 'men' and 'women'. One of her strategies for transforming this border is to explore a feminine 'sign' language which depends on allusions, metaphor and the body.

In America, Mary Daly's *Gyn/Ecology* is one of the most notable and dramatic gynographic critiques to date. Daly changes syntax – the whole structure of sentences – not just vocabulary. We must, she claims, connect our language with our bodies to 'remember the dismembered body of our heritage' (Daly 1978: 23). To take on the issue of a sexualised language is not necessarily to 'surrender' to essentialism. Rather, to focus on a word's internal structure as well as syntactical order is a necessary start to understanding the larger system of language itself. Daly's technique is to fragment language into its parts, 'departments which depart from departments' (Daly 1978: xiv). *Gyn/Ecology*, Daly claims, 'is a gynocritic manifestation of the Intransitive Verb' (Daly 1978: 23). Changing nouns to verbs is more than a linguistic game. It emphasises the importance of action. Prefixes particularly interest Daly because, of course, one characteristic of prefixes is that they act to intensify nouns, so punning with prefixes and hyphens enables Daly to create new double forms, like 'crone-logical' – a wonderful 'listen drink'. One example of how Daly's ideas work in a literary context is the fiction of Jean Rhys, who deliberately disrupts her novels with ellipses to hint at alternative and gendered ways in which a particular scene might be interpreted.

Alice Jardine's *Gynesis* describes how women are usually portrayed as a *sign of excess* in male texts, particularly in French modernism (Jardine 1988a). In a sequel text (1988b), 'In the Name of the Modern: Feminist Questions *d'après Gynesis*' Jardine playfully puns with male texts, and Lyotard, Derrida, Foucault – along with Saint Thomas Aquinas and Dictionaries – all appear as characters with starring roles in Jardine's dramatic collage. First performed in September 1985, the tape-play is about borders in the academy – about 'otherness' in post-structuralist and postmodernist accounts of representation. The tape-play enacts and then transforms the absence of women through a collective process of feminist questioning which focuses on the cultural production of meaning in criticism. It ends in a utopian prediction: 'if the same "changed" … all the history, all the stories would be there to retell differently, the future would be incalculable' (Jardine 1988b: 182).

I am not arguing, of course, that the political importance of a text can be read off its form in some simple way, *nor* that experimental writing is more radical than realist writing, but this continual reworking of the borders *between* different uses of vocabulary which are power-inflected can subvert traditional literary theory. One major way in which feminism *has* reconstituted knowledge is precisely through changing aspects of the language with the invention of new terms such as 'sexism'. While experimental self-perceptions are not always politically progressive, they do help to depict a different critical map and take the emphasis off the current academic devotion to pseudo-philosophical theory. For example, Nicole Ward Jouve's *White Woman Speaks With Forked Tongue* sets in play a dizzying dialogue between Jouve's aunt and Simone de Beauvoir (Jouve 1991). De Beauvoir's *The Second Sex* apparently stopped the aunt from watering her horse chestnut trees because the book had triggered a family argument about whether women could piss standing up and the exasperated aunt was unable to hold a hose-pipe ever again! Crossing the boundary of literary theory into auto-biography takes many different forms, from Audre Lorde's 'biomythography', which describes the complex mother/myth/biographies of some lesbian identities, to Bernice Johnson Reagon of Sweet Honey in the Rock's 'cultural auto-biography' – a kind of autobiographical community – and Gayatri Spivak's 'regulative psychobiography' which is a form of multilayered cultural criticism (Lorde 1982; Reagon 1982; Spivak 1990).

Nancy Miller's gynographic *Getting Personal* braids elements from Woolf, Anzaldúa and Greek myth into a narrative which includes Miller's failure in French, the size of her apartment, even the size of her father's penis (Miller 1991). Miller deliberately stages her essays as a *graphic* performance, by questioning the traditional border between the public world of the academy and her private room through typographical contrasts between italics, bold and lower-case typography. Miller's choice of inferior and superior typography is very revealing in the disjunction between the self-deprecating autobiography of the conference critic '*to be sure, as the morning unfolded none of the speakers threw her paper away – I clung to mine for dear life – but rarely have I wished so intensely to jump ship and go home*' which is printed in hugely affirmative italics (Miller 1991: 94). But by crossing the boundary between traditional academic objectivity and her own emotions, Miller sharpens our sense of the absence of women's emotional discourses in traditional academic life. This strong investment in making graphic marks, particularly italics, ellipses and hyphens, acts as a powerful and exemplary tool of struggle and is very vivid in post-colonial and lesbian critiques.

One instructive example of lesbian gynographic criticism is Diana Collecott's essay on H. D. – Hilda Doolittle, the modernist poet. The essay juxtaposes poems of H. D., quotations from Woolf and Kristeva with Collecott's reflections on her early hysterectomy and moment of recovery back in the maternal home. The critical narrative is fragmented with a blank page haunted by Collecott's own newly 'blank' body space, 'not a big organ, the size of a grapefruit perhaps? (the surgeon's knowing smile): women always imagine the uterus is large' (Collecott 1987: 150). Elizabeth Grosz suggests that a surgically non-sexual body, in the reproductive sense, prevents sexual difference being tied to sexual identity and hence allows for fluidity (Grosz 1994). Collecott's textual shrapnel of quotation, comment and poetry is a particularly apposite way of reading H. D., whose own writing was intensely personal and multigeneric. Influenced by Sappho, Japanese Haiku, Troubadour lyrics, post-impressionist art and cinema, H. D.'s 'explicitly gendered discourse' relied on 'innovative musical rhythms' (Friedman 1990: 86). In spite of Ezra Pound's injunction that 'H. D. is all right but shouldn't write criticism', many of her experiments with language anticipate postmodernism. Not surprisingly, her *Borderline Pamphlet*, written to promote the film *Borderline* about white abuse of Blacks, in which she starred with Paul Robeson, portrays a generation of borderline personalities.

A spectacular postmodern exponent of gynographic criticism is the American poet Rachel Blau Du Plessis. Her early and startling essay 'For The Etruscans' is extraordinarily heterogenous, ranging over contemporary feminism's major concerns: educational discrimination and the power of women's language. It is a daring combination of poetry and diary excerpts together with literary criticism and Etruscan history (Du Plessis 1992). The Etruscans, like my 'listen drink', are a grand metaphor for the exclusion of women's meaning–making from the literary canon. The Etruscan script, like women's writing, is *known* in the sense that its vocabulary has been translated, but we lack knowledge about the social and private contexts which give it meaning.

I have to confess that my well-taught scepticism about the representative adequacy of any critic, even feminist critics, made me search for D. H. Lawrence's *Etruscan Places* last summer before revisiting Du Plessis. Long out of print since its first publication in 1932, the book describes Lawrence's working holiday to see Etruscan tombs. Like Du Plessis, Lawrence is intrigued by the 'language of the old aboriginals of Southern Etruria' but he draws a firm border between culture (or Lawrence) and nature (the Etruscans) who, not surprisingly, Lawrence feminises (Lawrence 1932: 43). Lawrence's masculine binary is at odds with Du Plessis's collage of women's productive, reproductive narratives. For example, in *The Pink Guitar* Du Plessis engages the semiotic theory of Kristeva (see Chapter 12 of this book) by means of her own daughter's semiotic babblings: 'week of 1–6 July, 17 months, words: mur mur mur (more), caow; m/MMoo; DIRTY; WWWride (ride) RRweh (wet); Bluhh (blueberries) (Du Plessis 1990: 99).

In each of these critical essays there is a doubling and splitting of time and space in the graphic organisation. Characterised by the non-linear multi-disciplinary mixing of diaries and historical accounts, gynographic criticism explores connections between gendered structures of feeling and 'public' historical events in an open-ended way, embodying momentum, a desire to create a dialogue with reader and subject, in a contingent openness to others.

Post-colonial feminist literary theory

The second flamboyant example of 'border creativity' comes from writers who have some personal and historical experience of colonial borders. Gloria Anzaldúa, the Chicana feminist poet-critic, places her multilingual criticism on the borders of Mexico and Texas where she was born. Her book *Borderlands/La Frontera* is a rich exploration of Chicano history, writing and myth (Anzaldúa 1987). The title refers both to the place and to the form of critical writing in a postmodern mixture of poetry and criticism. What Anzaldúa achieves here, and in her later anthology *Making Face, Making Soul*, is a performance of different identities – continually remaking the boundaries between these Tex Mex, lesbian and academic identities through a montage of poetry, myth, autobiography and history. As Anzaldúa suggests, the 'listener/reader is forced into participating in the making of meaning – she is forced to connect the dots' (Anzaldúa 1990: xviii).

The energy of Anzaldúa's border writing comes from the effort to map an autobiographical and critical journey from her life as a migrant farmworker to a Chicana lesbian-feminist academic, but also from her choice of a contrapuntal juxtaposition of the genres of poetry, myth and autobiography. She synchronises the two conceptually distinct worlds of magic and history. For example: 'my soul makes itself through the creative act. It is constantly remaking and giving birth to itself through my body. It is this learning to live with *la Coatlicue* that transforms living in the Borderlands from a nightmare into a numinous experience. It is always a path/state to something else' (Anzaldúa 1987: 73).

In Britain these energies are often to be found outside the academic realm. Akua Rugg's *Brickbats and Bouquets* was the first volume of criticism by a Black woman in Britain and sets a propulsive tone for the rhetorical potency which I am calling 'border crossing' (Rugg 1984). Rugg came to Britain from Lagos and the volume is a collection of her reviews for *Race Today*, written in an engaging personal voice with its Black slang 'rapping' (this in 1975). The scripto-centric focus of academic criticism is more energetically denied by Ogundipe-Leslie in her special edition of *Research in African Literature*, 'Women as Oral Artists' (Ogundipe-Leslie and Boyce Davies 1994). Ogundipe-Leslie has taught in Nigeria and American universities and argues that criticism must cross the borders of literature to look at culture as 'the total product of a people's "being"' (Ogundipe-Leslie 1984: 81).

The anthology focuses on feminine forms, for example, birth songs and the popular Kiganda radio songs. Ogundipe-Leslie debunks two major assumptions of traditional criticism: that men dominate African significations, and that African women did not have a voice or space until they began writing in Roman script (Ogundipe-Leslie and Boyce Davies 1994). In her own earlier and fabulous example of critical border crossing, Ogundipe-Leslie attacks traditional criticism even more directly by writing 'The Nigerian Literary Scene' as a long poem, in the style of Pope's heroic couplets, chronicling the misogynist teaching of literature in Nigeria:

> Things fall apart
> And lecturers are the most adept
> at hurling the arrow of God
> into the river between.
> (Ogundipe-Leslie 1980: 6)

Other collections, for example, *Ngambika*, a reclamation of African women's writing, and *Out of the Kumbla: Caribbean Women and Literature* (both co-edited by Carole Boyce Davies in 1986 and 1990) also privilege diversity and heterogeneity by considering children's literature alongside adult. Other experimental border crossings by Asian feminist critics – for example, the collection *Women Writing in India* – points to the significance of retellings of the classics by Asian women writers (Tharu and Lalita 1993). Notable examples include Vaidehi's deconstruction of the fifth-century *Shakuntala*. This is a retelling of the myth from Shakuntala's point of view in order to highlight women's friendship and Sashi Deshpanda's subversion of the story of Gandheri who was married off to a blind man without her knowledge.

In her introduction to *We Sinful Women: Contemporary Urdu Feminist Poetry*, the critic Rukhsana Ahman points out that a decade ago British Asian writing had no critical attention but now, after years of creative achievement, Asian writing necessarily involves a border crossing of languages and cultures (Ahman 1990). What the feminist critic Uma Parameswaran calls 'native aliens' are subverting the flowery traditional Urdu and Bengali poetry and 'have assimilated in 30 years what it has taken the West 10 times that number of years to create' (Jena 1993: 5).

The post-colonial critic and filmmaker Trinh T. Minh-ha argues that walking on the edges can be hazardous (Trinh 1991). There are additional hazards for a white critic, not simply the paucity of material on South Asian and Black literature in public and university libraries. As the Afro-American feminist Valerie Smith pointedly suggests, 'the black woman as critic ... is often invoked when Anglo-American feminists and male Afro-Americanists begin to re-materialize their discourse' (Smith 1989: 44). Smith argues that 'this association of black women with re-embodiment resembles rather closely the association, in classic Western philosophy and in nineteenth century cultural constructions of womanhood, of women of colour with the body' (Smith 1989: 5).

Of course, according to the Asian-American writer Maxine Hong Kingston, because I am white I could be considered to be merely a teaching ghost like the white American Garbage Ghosts and Meter Reading Ghosts of *The Woman Warrior* (Hong Kingston 1976). A less immobilising vantage point is offered by Pat Parker in 'For the White Person Who Wants to Know How to be My Friend': 'The first thing you do is to forget that I'm Black. Second, you must never forget that I'm Black' (Abel 1993: 495).

A further issue is to question how far border crossing might be indispensably caught up in that romantic notion of the 'artist outsider' common to *fin de siècle* moments. As Elaine Showalter suggests in *Sexual Anarchy*, at the turn of the last century women were perceived to be figures of disorder, and 'social or cultural marginality seems to place them on the borderlines of the symbolic order' in a society longing for strict border controls around the definition of gender (Showalter 1992: 8) . One current and optimistic resistance to that scenario lies in the one key difference between the 1890s and the 1990s. Whereas, after 1890, women's writing entered a period of decline following George Eliot's death, currently feminist publishing, like women's studies, is booming.

Towards the millennium

In *Adam's Rib* Spencer Tracy says to Katharine Hepburn, 'You get cute when you get causey'. One of the many reasons I began to explore feminist literary theory was my very sad discovery that surprisingly few men seem to agree with Spencer Tracy. What feminism teaches you is that literary/critical languages, like any others, are not simply technologies of communication but intensely caught up in gender value judgements. This chapter offers an alternative by attempting to engage you in some very exciting contemporary critical journeys into what I hope will be a better critical future. None of us can predict what feminism will be like in one year, let alone in another century, but the future does have a habit of arriving.

Currently, the temptation to look towards the Millennium is irresistible. The beginning of a new age seems to invoke a state of mind preoccupied with meta-phoric changes as in 'New Labour'. Feminists involved in new literary *practices* rather than simply in metaphors are trying to understand the wider meanings of change. To point tentatively to some of their insights suggests alternative visions of the *purposes* of criticism: that critical evaluations can connect literary particulars with ethical concerns. The most generative feminist revisions focus on three key issues: politics, pedagogy/performance and positionality.

The first approach could be called 'political criticism'. This kind of writing has a clear personal presence which invites dialogue and yet is passionately a politics of difference. Such writing often begins with social and political judgements and evaluates texts with a partisan, self-reflexive vision. The pre-eminent example is Toni Morrison's dazzling *Playing in the Dark: Whiteness and the Literary Imagination* (Morrison 1992). Morrison's individual readings of classic American literature (Poe, Melville, Twain and Faulkner), by connecting racial realities with literary imaginations, decolonise literary theory itself in an eloquent, compelling revision of the American canon.

The second approach could be called 'pedagogic or performance criticism' which similarly tries to reach out to a wider audience. The question of *how* to study literature was not often posed at the beginning of second-wave literary feminism. Currently feminists are turning pedagogy itself into a process of cultural reconstruction while simultaneously deconstructing the canon. A good example is VéVé Clark's 'Talking Shop: A Comparative Feminist Approach to Caribbean Literature by Women', which utilises the Haitian *Marasa* principle, comparing dyadic texts to explore and *transform* binaries between these (Clark 1994). This kind of pedagogy searches out historical repetitions and paradoxes to help students and readers create their own dialectics of difference.

Finally, there is the issue of positionality which is addressed by border criticism. Border criticism, for example Mae Henderson's edited collection *Borders, Boundaries and Frames*, emphasises the different cultural codes and biconceptual realities often used by writers changing countries (geographical/spatial borders) or media (creative borders) (Henderson 1995). I find this approach particularly suggestive for my own work on Virginia Woolf's experiences of different media: her cinema-going, aesthetic essays, photography and fiction (Humm 1991 and forthcoming). In border criticism literature is only one among several signifying practices. For example, border criticism looks at gender performances dialectically through the visual *and* the literary to cut across the distinction between subjective and objective meanings.

By destroying the idea that literary theory is a bounded entity, feminist literary theorists move on from simply identifying the 'facts' of literary cultures to cultural transformations. 'For we (feminists) are in the unusual historical position of having come so far while the rest of society has been unable to move' (Schulman 1996: xii).

References

Abel, Elizabeth (1993) 'Black Writing, White Reading: Race and the Politics of Feminist Interpretation', *Critical Inquiry*, 19 (Spring): 470–98.

Ahman, Rukhsana (1990) *We Sinful Women: Contemporary Urdu Feminist Poetry*, London: The Women's Press.

Anzaldúa, Gloria (1987) *Borderlands / La Frontera: The New Mestiza*, San Francisco: Spinsters/Aunt Lute Book Company.

Anzaldúa, Gloria (1990) *Making Face, Making Soul*, San Francisco: Aunt Lute Foundation Books.

Bell, Roseann P., Bettye J. Parker and Beverley Guy Sheftall (eds) (1979) *Sturdy Black Bridges: Visions of Black Women in Literature*, New York: Anchor Books.

Bono, Paola and Sandra Kemp (eds) (1991) *Italian Feminist Thought*, Oxford: Blackwell.

Boyce Davies, Carole and Anne Graves (eds) (1986) *Ngambika: Studies of Women in African Literature*, Trenton NJ: Africa World Press.

Boyce Davies, Carole and Elaine Fido (eds) (1990) *Out of the Kumbla: Caribbean Women and Literature*, Trenton NJ: African World Press.

Braxton, Joanne and Andrée McLaughlin (eds) (1990) *Wild Women in the Whirlwind*, London: Serpent's Tail.

Christian, Barbara (1987) 'The Race for Theory', *Cultural Critique* 6 (Spring): 51–63.

Cixous, Hélène and Cathérine Clément (1987) *The Newly Born Woman*, Manchester: Manchester University Press.

Clark, VéVé A. (1994) 'Talking Shop: A Comparative Feminist Approach to Caribbean Literature by Women', in M. R. Higonnet (ed.) *Borderwork: Feminist Engagements with Comparative Literature*, Ithaca: Cornell University Press.

Collecott, Diana (1987) 'A Double Matrix: Re-Reading H. D.', in S. Roe (ed.) *Women Reading Women's Writing*, Brighton: Harvester Wheatsheaf.

Daly, Mary (1978) *Gyn/Ecology*, Boston: Beacon Press.

Davidson, C. N. and E. M. Broner (1980) *The Lost Tradition*, New York: Frederick Ungar.

Deleuze, Gilles and Félix Guattari (1986) 'What is a Minor Literature?', in D. Polan, trans., *Kafka: Towards a Minor Literature*, Minneapolis: University of Minnesota Press.

Du Plessis, Rachel Blau (1990) *The Pink Guitar: Writing as Feminist Practice*, London: Routledge.

Du Plessis, Rachel Blau (1992) 'For the Etruscans', in M. Humm (ed.) *Feminisms: A Reader*, Hemel Hempstead: Harvester Wheatsheaf.

Eagleton, Terry (1970) *Exiles and Emigrés: Studies in Modern Literature*, New York: Schocken Books.

Ellmann, Mary (1968) *Thinking About Women*, New York: Harcourt Brace Jovanovich.

Fetterley, Judith (1978) *The Resisting Reader*, Bloomington: Indiana University Press.

Friedman, Sandra S. (1990) 'H. D. Introduction', in B. K. Scott (ed.) *The Gender of Modernism*, Bloomington: Indiana University Press.

Gardiner, Judith et al. (1982) 'An Interchange on Feminist Criticism', *Feminist Studies*, 8 (Fall): 629–75.

Gibaldi, John (ed.) (1992) *Introduction to Scholarship in Modern Languages and Literatures 2/E*, New York: Modern Language Association.

Gilbert, Sandra and Susan Gubar (1979) *The Madwoman in the Attic: The Woman Writer and the Nineteenth Century Literary Imagination*, New Haven: Yale University Press.

Gilbert, Sandra and Susan Gubar (1988) *No Man's Land*, 3 vols, New Haven: Yale University Press.

Greer, Germaine (1971) *The Female Eunuch*, London: Paladin.

Grosz, Elizabeth (1994) *Volatile Bodies*, Bloomington: Indiana University Press.

Henderson, Mae (ed.) (1955) *Borders, Boundaries and Frames: Cultural Criticism and Cultural Studies*, London: Routledge.

Hong Kingston, Maxine (1976) *The Woman Warrior*, New York: Alfred A. Knopf.

Hull, Gloria T., Patricia Bell Scott and Barbara Smith (eds) (1981) *All the Women are White, All the Blacks are Men, But Some of Us Are Brave: Black Women's Studies*, New York: Feminist Press.

Humm, Maggie (1991) *Border Traffic: Strategies of Contemporary Women Writers*, Manchester: Manchester University Press.

Humm, Maggie (1994) *A Reader's Guide to Contemporary Feminist Literary Criticism*, Hemel Hempstead: Harvester Wheatsheaf.

Humm, Maggie (forthcoming) *Borderline*, Edinburgh: Edinburgh University Press.

Irigaray, Luce (1974) *Speculum de l'autre femme*, Paris: Editions Minuit.

Jardine, Alice (1988a) *Gynesis: Configurations of Woman and Modernity*, Ithaca: Cornell University Press.

Jardine, Alice (1988b) 'In the Name of the Modern: Feminist Questions *d'après Gynesis*', in S. Sheridan (ed.) *Grafts*, London: Verso.

Jena, Seema (1993) 'Editor's Note', *Daskhat*, 2 (Spring/Summer): 4–5.

Jouve, Nicole Ward (1991) *White Woman Speaks with Forked Tongue: Criticism as Autobiography*, London: Routledge.

Keller, Evelyn Fox (1985) *Reflections on Gender and Science*, New Haven, CT: Yale University Press.

Kelly-Gadol, Joan (1992) 'The Social Relation of the Sexes', in M. Humm (ed.) *Feminisms: A Reader*, Hemel Hempstead: Harvester Wheatsheaf.

Lawrence, David H. (1932) *Etruscan Places*, London: Martin Secker.

Lorde, Audre (1982) *Zami*, London: Sheba.

Lorde, Audre (1984) *Sister Outsider*, Trumansburg, NY: Crossing Press.

Miller, Nancy (1991) *Getting Personal*, London: Routledge.

Millett, Kate (1970) *Sexual Politics*, New York: Doubleday.

Modleski, Tania (1991) *Feminism Without Women*, London: Routledge.

Moers, Ellen (1976) *Literary Women*, New York: Doubleday.

Moi, Toril (1985) *Sexual/Textual Politics*, London: Methuen.

Morrison, Toni (1992) *Playing in the Dark: Whiteness and the Literary Imagination*, Cambridge: Harvard University Press.

Ogundipe-Leslie, Molara (1980) 'The Nigerian Literary Scene', *Kiabara*, 2: 3, pp. 6–10.

Ogundipe-Leslie, Molara (1984) 'African Woman, Culture and Another Development', *Journal of African Marxism*, 5: 77–92.

Ogundipe-Leslie, Molara and Carole Boyce Davies (1994) 'Special Issue: Women as Oral Artists', *Research in African Literature*, 25: 3 (Fall).

Pinker, Steven (1994) *The Language Instinct*, Harmondsworth: Penguin.

Pryse, Marjorie and Hortense Spillers (eds) (1985) *Conjuring: Black Women, Fiction and the Literary Tradition*, Bloomington: Indiana University Press.

Reagon, Bernice Johnson (1982) 'My Black Mothers and Sisters: Or On Beginning a Cultural Autobiography', *Feminist Studies*, 8 (Spring): 81–96.

Rich, Adrienne (1976) *Of Woman Born*, New York: W. W. Norton.

Rich, Adrienne (1980) 'When We Dead Awaken', in *On Lies, Secrets and Silence*, London: Virago.

Rugg, Akua (1984) *Brickbats and Bouquets: Black Women's Critique: Literature Theatre Film*, London: Race Today Publications.

Schulman, Sarah (1996) 'Introduction', in I. Zahara (ed.) *Feminism³: The Third Generation in Fiction*, Boulder: Westview Press.

Scott, Joan (1988) *Gender and the Politics of History*, New York: Columbia University Press.

Sedgwick, Eve Kosofsky (1985) *Between Men*, New York: Columbia University Press.

Showalter, Elaine (1977) *A Literature of Their Own*, Princeton: Princeton University Press.

Showalter, Elaine (ed.) (1985) *The New Feminist Criticism*, New York: Pantheon.

Showalter, Elaine (ed.) (1989) *Speaking of Gender*, London: Routledge.

Showalter, Elaine (1992) *Sexual Anarchy: Gender and Culture at the Fin de Siècle*, London: Virago.

Smith, A. (1985) 'Me Washoe, you Mother', *The Guardian*, 14 July: 12.

Smith, Barbara (1977) *Toward a Black Feminist Criticism*, Brooklyn, New York: Out and Out Books.

Smith, Barbara (ed.) (1983) *Home Girls: A Black Feminist Anthology*, New York: Kitchen Table Press.

Smith, Valerie (1989) 'Black Feminist Theory and the Representation of the "Other"', in C. A. Wall (ed.) *Changing Our Own Words*, New Brunswick: Rutgers University Press.

Spivak, Gayatri (1990) *The Post-Colonial Critic*, London: Routledge.

Tharu, Susie and K. Lalita (1993) *Women Writing in India Vol. 2: The Twentieth Century*, London: Pandora.

Trinh T. Minh-ha (1991) *Framer Framed*, Routledge: London.

Walker, Alice (1984) *In Search of Our Mothers' Gardens*, London: The Women's Press.

Further Reading

Feminist Theory

Benstock, Shari (ed.) (1987) *Feminist Issues in Literary Scholarship*, Bloomington: Indiana University Press.

Humm, Maggie (1995) *The Dictionary of Feminist Theory* 2/E, Hemel Hempstead: Harvester Wheatsheaf.

Moi, Toril (ed.) (1987) *French Feminist Thought*, Oxford: Blackwell.

Readers

Belsey, Catherine and Jane Moore (eds) (1989) *The Feminist Reader: Essays in Gender and the Politics of Literary Criticism*, London: Macmillan.

Eagleton, Mary (ed.) (1996) *Feminist Literary Criticism*, London: Longman.

Humm, Maggie (ed.) (1992) *Feminisms: A Reader*, Hemel Hempstead: Harvester Wheatsheaf.

Warhol, Robyn and Diane P. Herndl (eds) (1991) *Feminisms: An Anthology of Literary Theory and Criticism*, New Brunswick: Rutgers University Press.

Introductions

Braxton, Joanne and Andrée McLaughlin (eds) (1990) *Wild Women in the Whirlwind*, London: Serpent's Tail.

Humm, Maggie (1994) *A Reader's Guide to Contemporary Feminist Literary Criticism*, Hemel Hempstead: Harvester Wheatsheaf.

Humm, Maggie (1995) *Practising Feminist Criticism*, Hemel Hempstead: Harvester Wheatsheaf.

Jay, Karla and Joanne Glasgow (eds) (1990) *Lesbian Texts and Contexts*, New York: New York University Press.

Supplementary Texts

Smith, Sidonie and Julia Watson (eds) (1992) *De/Colonizing the Subject*, Minneapolis: University of Minnesota Press.

Chapter 15

Feminist Media and Film Theory

Sue Thornham

From its beginnings, writes Annette Kuhn, 'feminism has regarded ideas, language and images as crucial in shaping women's (and men's) lives'. The questions raised by such concerns are, she suggests, both political and theoretical, and crucial in the production of feminist knowledge:

> What relation, for instance, does spectatorship have to representations of women? What sort of activity is looking? What does looking have to do with sexuality? With masculinity and femininity? With power? With knowledge? How do images of women in particular, 'speak to' the spectator? Is the spectator addressed as male/female, masculine/feminine? Is femininity constructed in specific ways through representation? Why are images of women's bodies so prevalent in our society?
>
> (1985: 2, 6)

Media representations of women, then, were a central concern of the 'second wave' feminism of the 1960s and 1970s. Betty Friedan's (1963) *The Feminine Mystique* traced the post-war construction of the American ideal image of femininity (what Friedan called the 'happy housewife heroine') through media representations she found in women's magazines and advertising images. Demonstrations were organised against the 1968 Miss America contest and the Miss World competition in London the following year. And when the feminist journal *Women and Film* was launched in 1972, it saw its task as primarily a *political* one: 'taking up the struggle with women's image in film and women's roles in the film industry' (1972: 5). The concern was with media representations as false *images* of women, stereotypes which damage women's self-perceptions and limit their social roles.

'An anachronism we can ill afford'

This focus also characterised 1970s American academic feminist research on the media. A number of surveys of feminist media criticism/theory (Steeves 1987; Kaplan 1987; van Zoonen 1991) map the political differences within such work, drawing distinctions between liberal, radical and Marxist/socialist feminist approaches. But what is most apparent in these 1970s American studies is the similarity of the theoretical models on which they rely. Like Friedan's work, they concentrate on 'sex-role stereotyping' within media images, and to demonstrate it they apply the quantitative survey methods of mainstream American mass communication research.

The 1978 collection *Hearth and Home*, edited by Gaye Tuchman, provides an example of such work. Within the volume we can find a range of political perspectives. At one extreme is Carol Lopate's class-based analysis of the representation of Jackie Kennedy Onassis within women's magazines, which argues that such examples of the 'feminine mystique' function to obscure women's real role as a reserve labour force within capitalist society. At the other is the far from radical perspective of Sprafkin and Liebert's study of 'Sex-typing and Children's Television Preferences'. Its conclusion is that television's 'confining and out-moded sex roles' may *perhaps* undermine – or 'at least retard' – American society's inevitable progress towards the liberation of *both* sexes (1978: 239). But throughout the book, the dominant research methods, as in other contemporary 'sex-role research on the mass media' (Busby 1975), are the quantitative survey methods of 'content analysis' (measuring the frequency with which a particular image or word appears in media texts) and 'effects studies' (measuring the 'effects' of media messages through psychological tests or large-scale surveys). The theoretical assumptions underlying such research methods are outlined in Tuchman's introductory chapter. The media, she argues, firstly *reflect*, in the form of images or representations, society's dominant values. Hence content analyses reveal a predominance of traditional and stereotypical images of women across all media forms. Secondly, they act as agents of *socialisation*, transmitting stereotyped images of sex-roles, particularly to young people. Hence effects studies reveal that children exposed to such stereotypes have a more restricted view of appropriate sex-roles than those exposed to counter-stereotypical representations. Despite Tuchman's trenchant criticism of the media's treatment of women as 'symbolic annihilation', therefore, what she is condemning is a gap bridgeable within the existing social structure, a 'culture lag' between media images and the real roles of women in a changing society. Since 'the expansion of the American economy depends upon increasing the rate of female employment', such rigid stereotyping represents 'an anachronism we can ill afford' (Tuchman 1978: 37–8). In this last statement, the 'feminist' researcher aligns herself firmly with the dominant values of American society, for which the elimination of sexist stereotypes will, it seems, be wholly functional.

Woman as Sign

Griselda Pollock's (1977) 'What's Wrong with Images of Women?' addresses the inadequacy of this focus on media 'images' and stereotypes. The idea that 'images of women' merely *reflect* meanings which originate elsewhere (in the intentions of media producers, or in social structures),

> implies a juxtaposition of two separable elements – women as a gender or social group versus representations of women, or a real entity, women, opposed to falsified, distorted or male views of women. It is a common misconception to see images as merely a reflection, good or bad, and compare 'bad' images of women (glossy magazine photographs, fashion advertisements, etc.) to 'good' images of women ('realist' photographs, of women working, housewives, older women, etc.). This conception ... needs to be challenged and replaced by the notion of woman as a signifier in an ideological discourse.
>
> (Pollock 1977: 26)

Pollock's critique comes from an approach to the issue of media representations very different from the American model which we have been examining. It was an approach which was being developed in Britain in the 1970s within feminist art history (Betterton 1987; Williamson 1978) and, even more influentially, within feminist film theory. This view insists that representations are *not* merely reflections of reality, whether 'true' or distorted, but are rather the product of an active process of selecting and presenting, of structuring and shaping, of *making things mean* – of what came to be termed a 'signifying practice'. It therefore moves away from the examination of media images in terms of their degrees of 'truthfulness', and towards an analysis of the processes through which such images are made to carry particular meanings – in Pollock's words, the processes through which they become 'signifier[s] in an ideological discourse'.

This approach drew on emergent theories within European structuralism and semiotics, Marxist concepts of ideology, and psychoanalytic theory. The result was a twofold shift in the focus of analysis. Both structuralist/semiotic approaches and the renewed interest in the importance of ideology within culture led to a focus on the film (or other media product) as *text* – that is, as a complex structure of linguistic and visual codes organised to produce specific meanings – rather than as a collection of images or stereotypes. Semiotics (the application of Ferdinand de Saussure's structural linguistics to a more general study of how signs operate in society) had begun to investigate the codes, or textual systems, through which the film text is constructed. Although it might seem to be simply reflecting reality, it was argued, film is in fact like the written text in being both composed of textual segments (in the case of film, linked series of shots which form units of meaning), and structured by codes (socio-cultural codes like codes of dress and facial expression, and specifically cinematic codes like editing techniques). It is out of the combination of these codes, or textual systems, that meaning is produced.

The impression of realism we get from film, then, derives not so much from its ability to reflect the real, external world as from the extent to which it organises its meanings in accord with our 'common-sense' understandings of that world.

Its heroes embody the values of our society, and its villains represent those forces which seem to threaten it. These 'maps of meaning', through which a particular society makes sense of the world and according to which it organises its social institutions, are what constitute its *ideological* formation (Althusser 1984). They are always the product of specific power relations, functioning to defend the status quo and actively promote the values and interests of the dominant groups in society. It is film's conformity to these ideological 'maps of meaning' which, in this view, constitutes its apparent mirroring of reality. Moreover, film is a particularly effective carrier of ideology because its textual systems are based on the moving photographic image. Ideology works by effacing the signs of its own operation so that its interpretations of the world seem 'natural' or self-evident to us. Since film uses 'signs which do not look like signs' (Barthes 1977: 116), it is particularly effective in this process of 'naturalising' ideology. Textual analysis in the late 1960s therefore turned its attention not only to film's *textual* systems but also to its *ideological* structures, and to the extent to which the 'dominant ideology' of capitalism could be seen to be supported or critiqued in specific films.

Claire Johnston's work during the 1970s provides an example of the feminist appropriation of this approach to film analysis. Johnston adopts Althusser's definition of ideology as a system of *representations* of reality which is the product of a specific social structure but which presents itself as 'universal' or 'natural' to us, its subjects. She employs it, however, in an analysis not of capitalist but of *patriarchal* ideology. 'Within a sexist ideology and a male-dominated cinema', she writes, 'woman is presented as what she represents for man'. Thus women's bodies may be constantly on show as *spectacle* within film, but woman *as woman* is largely absent (1973: 26). The image of woman operates in film as a sign, she argues, but a sign which draws its meaning not from the reality of women's lives, but from the desires and fantasies of men. As an example of what Johnston means, we might cite the character of Vivian, played by Julia Roberts, in *Pretty Woman* (1990). Vivian derives her meaning not from reference to the lives of real prostitutes in America but from male fantasies of an ideal feminine sexual passivity. Referring to Roland Barthes's concept of 'myth' as the affixing of ideological values to signs, Johnston argues that 'myth transmits and transforms the ideology of sexism and renders it invisible' (1973: 25). Patriarchal myth, or ideology, empties the sign 'woman' of its meaning in relation to real women and replaces it with male fantasy. It is thus pointless to compare media stereotypes of women with the reality of women's lives. Instead, what must be examined is *how* the sign 'woman' operates within the specific film text – *what* meanings it is made to bear:

> woman is essentially a message which is being communicated in patriarchal culture, and it is in her inscription through stereotyping and myth as a sign which is being exchanged that she operates, finally, in the dominant cultural forms. In art, therefore, and hence in the film

text, the representation of woman is not primarily a sociological theme or problem, as is often thought, but a sign which is being communicated.

(Johnston 1975: 124)

But this process does not go uncontested – ideological operations are always liable to be resisted by those they seek to subordinate – and the figure of woman remains a source of anxiety within the patriarchal film text, threatening to escape its ideological straightjacket and disrupt the film's narrative and ideological coherence. The task of the feminist critic, therefore, is not only to uncover the ways in which patriarchal ideology constructs film 'women' as figures of male fantasy but also to identify a film's internal contradictions and disjunctures – those points at which it is 'splitting open under an internal tension' (Comolli and Narboni 1976: 27) in its efforts to impose patriarchal meanings on its female figures.

Visual Pleasures

In this emphasis on making visible the invisible, on uncovering hidden fantasies, desires and anxieties, Johnston's analysis draws on the terminology and methods of psychoanalytic theory as well as on semiotic and ideological analysis. Ideological operations in films are seen as in some sense unconscious, or repressed (Kuhn 1982: 86), to be uncovered by the feminist critic. Laura Mulvey's 1975 article, 'Visual Pleasure and Narrative Cinema', radically extended this use of psychoanalysis within feminist film theory, and also produced a second shift in analytic focus, towards a concern with the structures of identification and visual pleasure to be found in cinema: in other words, towards the *spectator–screen relationship*.

To Johnston's concern with woman as a sign in a patriarchal discourse, then, Mulvey added an analysis of how cinema as an 'apparatus'[1] creates a position for the film spectator, drawing on psychoanalysis to explain this positioning. Like Johnston's, her account highlights the ideological importance of cultural texts, but it also seeks to explain just what we as individuals have got invested in those texts. They are, it is argued, the scene of our search for identity and meaning; through them, we attempt to construct our sense of a gendered self. The images and representations which are the bearers of ideology are also those through which, by processes of identification, we construct our own identities as human subjects.[2]

Mulvey's essay sets out, then, to demonstrate 'the way the unconscious of patriarchal society has structured film form' (Mulvey 1989: 14). Like Johnston, she argues that the sign 'woman' in film is one constructed by and for a patriarchal culture, enabling man to 'live out his fantasies and obsessions ... by imposing them on the silent image of woman still tied to her place as bearer, not maker, of meaning' (1989: 15). Cinema's pleasures include erotic pleasure in looking, the fulfilment of desire through fantasy, and a return to the pleasures of infancy's 'mirror phase'[3] in which the child could imagine itself to be a whole and powerful individual by identifying with its own more perfect mirror image (provided in film by the figure of the hero). But these are pleasures provided only for the *male* spectator: 'In this world ordered by sexual imbalance, pleasure in looking has been split between active/male and passive/female' (1989: 19). Women are objects, not subjects, of the gaze, their bodies eroticised and often fragmented for the spectator's pleasure. Visual pleasure, however, has two aspects. The first is voyeuristic, the active (and often aggressive) gaze at the eroticised image of woman. The second is narcissistic, the pleasure of iden- tification with one's own 'ideal ego', that more perfect, more complete, more powerful figure first glimpsed by the infant in its idealised mirror image and now rediscovered in the person of the male movie star. The division between active/ male and passive/female, argues Mulvey, also structures film narrative. It is the film's hero who advances the story, controlling events, the woman, and the erotic gaze. 'Woman', in contrast, functions as erotic spectacle, interrupting rather than advancing the forward movement of the narrative as the camera slowly sweeps over her body.

Cinematic codes, then, construct meaning not only through visual images but also through film's ability to control the dimensions of time and space, through choice of shots, framing, editing and narrative pace. Film can 'create a gaze, a world and an object, thereby producing an illusion cut to the measure of [male] desire' (Mulvey 1989: 25). Its power and its pleasures come from the alignment of what Mulvey calls the 'three different looks' of cinema. What *we* see, as spectators, is determined by the gaze of the camera, and that in turn is aligned, through point-of-view shots, with the gaze of the film's characters at each other. In the latter, of course, it is the look of the central male character which is privi- leged, so that we see events largely through his eyes and identify with his gaze. Thus 'the power of the male protagonist as he controls events coincides with the active power of the erotic look', the combination providing for the male spectator 'a satisfying sense of omnipotence' (1989: 20).

The Female Spectator

If the early work of Johnston and Mulvey set the terms for a far more complex view of media representations, however, it also produced problems. B. Ruby Rich, in a 1978 discussion, summarises the difficulties in Mulvey's approach:

> According to Mulvey, the woman is not visible in the audience which is perceived as male; according to Johnston, the woman is not visible on the screen. She is merely a ... signifier for something else, etc. ... the cinematic codes have structured our absence to such an extent that the only choice allowed to us is to identify either with Marilyn Monroe or with

the man behind me hitting the back of my seat with his knees. What is there in a film with which a *woman viewer* identifies? [my emphasis]

(Citron et al. 1978: 87)

Psychoanalysis, she adds, may be a useful tool for analysing the patriarchal status quo, but it has nothing (or nothing useful) to say about *women*. If Mulvey's 'Visual Pleasure and Narrative Cinema' can be seen, then, as an inaugural moment in the study of the female viewer (Brunsdon 1991: 370), it is so, paradoxically, through the question it *doesn't* ask but which, as Rich's exasperated protest indicates, it most powerfully provokes. The search for answers to this question – Rich's 'What is there in a film with which a *woman viewer* identifies? – also produced a shift in analytic focus, away from mainstream male-centred narratives, and towards those genres specifically addressed to women.

Mary Ann Doane's analysis of the Hollywood 'woman's film' of the 1940s exemplifies this shift. What interests Doane is the position which these films construct for the female spectators whom they assume to be their audience. After all, if Mulvey is correct about cinema's structuring around a 'male' gaze, then these films, in seeking to address a *female* spectator, set themselves an impossible task. What she concludes is that they do indeed reveal internal contradictions and instabilities. On the one hand, they assume an *overidentification* of the female spectator with the screen image (as their familiar title 'weepies' suggests). Unlike its male counterpart, the female gaze is assumed to involve passivity and over-involvement rather than the distance necessary for voyeurism, so that the female spectator is invited to experience not *desire for* but *suffering with* the screen characters. On the other hand, however, since their narratives are centred on a female protagonist, these films *must* be driven by a female point of view, female desire and female activity. The woman *cannot* function merely as passive spectacle or no narrative would be possible. The result, argues Doane, is unstable and often incoherent narratives in which the woman may act and desire, only to be punished for such transgressions; she may exercise an 'active investigating gaze', only to end after all as victim (1984: 72). Loss, suffering and persecution characterise these films which centre on wives, mothers and daughters. What they – and the television soap operas which share many of their characteristics – offer to their female spectators is a *masochistic* fantasy, centred on suffering rather than on desire or the fantasy of omnipotence (Doane 1987: 19).

Doane's is a very depressing conclusion. Moreover, because she, like Mulvey, depends on psychoanalytic theory for her analysis, her account of the female spectator seems to offer no way out of the masochistic scenario she describes. To explain the power and pleasures of film, both she and Mulvey argue that it draws on the fundamental mechanisms by which our (sexed) identities are produced. But if this explains the ideological *power* of media representations, it seems to leave us little scope for *changing* the situation. After all, if film works by appealing to mechanisms which are both central to the construction of our (sexed) identities and *unconscious*, how can we hope to produce *different* media representations? Criticising this use of what she terms 'cine-psychoanalysis', Christine Gledhill sums up the impasse it produces: 'While these arguments have attracted feminists for their power to explain the alternate misogyny and idealization of cinema's female representations, they offer largely negative accounts of female spectatorship, suggesting colonized, alienated or masochistic positions of identification' (1988: 66).

Gledhill's own reading of melodrama and the 'woman's film' takes us in a rather different direction; one which seeks to retain a complex understanding of the way in which texts construct meaning, whilst at the same time returning to the questions asked within American mass communication research about the relationship of these texts to the real, historical *women* who comprise their audience(s). Melodrama and the 'woman's film', argues Gledhill, may indeed, as Johnston and Mulvey maintain, seek to reduce 'woman' to a symbol through which patriarchal fears and desires centring on the 'feminine' may be played out, but this is not the whole story. Because such films target a female audience, they must draw for their material on the romance novels and magazine stories which have traditionally comprised a subordinate 'woman's culture' – the 'woman's world' familiar to us from the shelves of newsagents and bookshops. Popular novels by Fannie Hurst and Olive Higgins Prouty, for example, were the source of 1930s and 1940s 'woman's films' such as *Imitation of Life* (1934), *Stella Dallas* (1937) and *Now, Voyager* (1942). This 'circuit of women's discourse', as Gledhill calls it (1987: 35), is one in which women's voices – in however circumscribed a way – *have* traditionally been heard. Thus, when films draw on such material for their narratives, what they produce is a figure, 'woman', who is a *contested* symbol – not merely a 'sign in a patriarchal discourse'. What we find is a 'struggle between male and female voices' (Gledhill 1987: 37), both within the film itself *and* in the different readings which male and female spectators make of it.

For Christine Gledhill, then, the 'woman's film' is both a product and a source of what she calls 'cultural negotiation', the negotiation between *competing* frames of reference and different experiences. The argument which she makes – that 'mass' or 'popular' culture is *always* 'fraught with tension, struggles and negotiations' (1987: 37) – is a long way from Laura Mulvey's vision of 'the silent image of woman ... tied to her place as bearer, not maker, of meaning'. To make it, Gledhill has shifted the theoretical terrain – away from what she calls 'cine-psychoanalysis', and towards a 'cultural studies' perspective. Such a break offers, she argues, a way out of the apparent impasse which the powerful and influential work of Mulvey, Johnston and Doane seemed to produce.

Negotiating the Popular

British Cultural Studies locates its institutional 'founding moment' in 1964, with the establishing at Birmingham University of the Centre for Contemporary Cultural Studies (CCCS). Conceptualising culture as '*both* ... a way of life – encompassing ideas, attitudes, languages, practices, institutions, and structures of power – and a whole range of cultural practices: artistic forms, texts, canons, architecture, mass-produced commodities, and so forth' (Nelson *et al.* 1992: 5), the Centre inaugurated an interdisciplinary methodology which would combine textual analysis with a focus on historical and social context. Most important, in the words of Stuart Hall, the Centre's director from 1968–79:

> From its inception, ... Cultural Studies was an 'engaged' set of disciplines, addressing awkward but relevant issues about contemporary society and culture, often without benefit of that scholarly detachment or distance which the passage of time alone sometimes confers on other fields of studies. The 'contemporary' ... was, by definition, hot to handle. This tension (between what might loosely be called 'political' and intellectual concerns) has shaped Cultural Studies ever since.
>
> (Hall 1980a: 17)

Like feminist film theory, cultural studies embraced the 'structuralist' theories of ideology and human subjectivity emerging in the 1960s and 1970s, since they offered a way of accounting for the ideological *power* of cultural institutions, texts and practices. The critical focus of cultural studies, however, was considerably broader than that of film theory, embracing both the texts and the practices of everyday, or 'popular' culture. Since its objects of study included both the mass media and their audiences, therefore, it found itself engaging critically not only with contemporary developments in cultural and film theory but with the American mass communication tradition of media research. What was needed was a model of the text-reader relationship which would account for the *whole* of the communicative process, not just for texts, or for 'effects' on audiences. Such a model is set out in Hall's 1973 paper, 'Encoding and Decoding in the Television Discourse'. Hall sees the media's communicative process as operating through three linked but distinctive 'moments'. The first is the moment of production (or 'encoding'), the second is that of the text, and the third is the moment of reception (or 'decoding'). Each is envisaged as the site of a struggle over meaning: the meanings given to an event or narrative ('encoded') by the producers; the meanings embodied in the text (Gledhill's 'struggle between [competing] voices'); and the meanings taken away ('decoded') by the audience/spectator (Hall 1980b: 128).

In Hall's model, then, not only are *texts* the site of a struggle over meaning; audiences, too, will be engaged in this struggle. As part of the same social formation as the text's producers, the reader/spectator will have access to broadly the same 'maps of meaning'. Because the reader/spectator's *position* in this social formation may be different, however – as working-class, as black, as a woman – the meanings 'preferred' by the text may be negotiated or even opposed by the reader/spectator. As women, for instance, we may privilege the subordinate rather than the dominant 'voice' in the 1930s 'woman's film'. Thus, although the text may limit the range of readings we can produce from it (it would be very difficult, for example, to read *Fatal Attraction* [1988] as a feminist text), it cannot *determine* them.

The 1978 collection by CCCS Women's Studies Group, *Women Take Issue*, makes it clear that the relationship between feminism and cultural studies was not always an easy one. Nevertheless, as Christine Gledhill's work demonstrates, in the concept of *negotiation* feminists could find an account of the text-reader relationship which might challenge the pessimism of 'cine-psychoanalysis'. The troubling gap within feminist film theory between the 'female spectator', that shadowy figure who, as Mary Ann Doane points out (1989: 143), is simply the spectator which the text imagines for itself, and *real* audiences of women might be closed. And with it might be closed the equally troubling gap between the feminist theorist, or critic, and the real, historical women on whose behalf she presumably speaks, but whose readings she never actually consults .Thus the 1980s saw a growing feminist interest in research which would move beyond the analysis of the textual positions constructed for the (imagined) female spectator to explore the actual readings which women made of such texts.

From Spectators to Audiences

There is … a great deal at stake when mass culture criticism takes as its subject those forms generally thought to be the most degraded, the most mindless of all, the female 'weepies', the soap opera and the romance. … If it can be demonstrated through the appropriate kind of 'reading' that the patriarchal surface of these texts conceals a womanly subtext and that, as a consequence, female audiences are capable of interpreting these forms against the grain, as it were, that is, as stories that explore the actual limitations of women's lives, we might better be able to understand just how often and how extensively women have managed to resist dominant practices of patriarchal signification. … In other words, there might be some hope of transforming the holding action of oppositional interpretation into the active resistance of alternative speech.

(Radway 1986: 98)

Janice Radway is discussing here the significance of her own research on popular romance fiction and its readers. Her account makes clear the *political* impetus behind such research into what Charlotte Brunsdon (1991: 365) calls 'mass cultural fictions of femininity' (soap opera, the 'woman's film', romantic fiction, girls' and women's magazines) and their readers/audiences. The most 'degraded' forms of mass culture, Radway suggests, are those identified with the feminine.

A feminist re-evaluation of them seeks to subvert a common critical judgement in which femininity is equated with the mindless consumption of the 'lowest' forms of mass culture, whilst masculinity is identified with the discriminating reader of 'high' culture. The women in Radway's study are demonstrated by her research to be active, resistant readers, not passive ideological dupes. Further, *in giving voice* to their readings, Radway's study challenges the cultural hierarchy in which women find themselves 'spoken' by patriarchal representations of 'woman' but are themselves denied a voice.

But Radway's account also raises a number of difficult questions. First, what precisely is the relationship between the *representations* of women to be found in these texts and the readings or uses made of them by their readers? Radway seems uncertain whether resistance to patriarchal structures is to be found within the texts themselves (a 'patriarchal surface' concealing a 'womanly subtext') or in the action of reading (the act of 'oppositional interpretation'). Second, and underlying this last uncertainty, what is the relationship of *Radway*'s reading of the texts ('the appropriate kind of "reading"'), and the readings of the (ordinary) women which she both offers and interprets? She clearly does not speak *as one of* them since she hopes to 'transform' their interpretations, but does she speak *for* them? Does she, rather, simply speak *about* them, constructing them as objects of her own (feminist) discourse? Perhaps it is not quite so easy to bridge that troubling gap between the feminist theorist and the real, historical women on whose behalf she seeks to speak.

Radway's study of female romance readers was published in 1984. Two years earlier, Dorothy Hobson's study of soap opera viewers, *'Crossroads': The Drama of a Soap Opera*, appeared. Like Radway, Hobson used an 'ethnographic'[4] research methodology. In order to study the viewing processes of *Crossroads'* female audience, she watched with the viewer, following such observation with a (transcribed) unstructured interview. Thus, she argues, 'I became part of the shared experience of viewing in that situation' (1982: 112–13). During the process, her view of the text-viewer relationship underwent a considerable shift. Finding that her subjects' readings not only differed according to their own experiences and understandings as women but were made through constant reference to those experiences, she moves away from the model with which she began, Hall's 'Encoding/Decoding' model. Instead of seeing meaning as produced by linked but determinate 'moments', Hobson now emphasises the moment of *reading* as that in which the text's meaning is produced. 'To try to say what Crossroads means to its audience is impossible,' she writes, 'for there is no single Crossroads, there are as many different Crossroads as there are viewers. Tonight twelve million, tomorrow thirteen million; with thirteen million possible understandings of the programme' (1982: 136).

Hobson's position here is very different from Janice Radway's project of 'transforming' the interpretations of her readers into a more 'active' resistance to patriarchy, yet both employ ethnographic research methods within a cultural studies framework. The difference between them centres on two key issues. The first is the question of where the power to determine meaning *primarily* lies: with the text or with the audience. Are female audiences limited by the text in the extent to which they can produce 'resistant' or 'oppositional' readings, as Radway suggests, or are they, as Hobson claims, able to 'remake' media texts according to their own needs and desires?

The second, related, issue concerns the relationship of the feminist theorist/researcher to the 'ordinary women' who provide the material for her research. Radway's approach has been termed 'recruitist' by Ien Ang (1988: 184–5), since its goal is to make 'them' (ordinary women) more like 'us' (feminists). Hobson's, on the other hand, like that of Ang herself in another 'ethnographic' study of soap opera viewers, *Watching Dallas* (1985), can be seen as what Charlotte Brunsdon (1989: 121) calls a 'redemptive reading' – one which sets out to find 'progressive' or even 'oppositional' potential in popular media texts. As Brunsdon points out, what drives such readings is the political need to align feminist theory more firmly with the experience of 'ordinary women' – who, after all, *enjoy Crossroads* or *Dallas* or Mills and Boon novels. But, she argues, in all such 'ethnographic' studies, what the analyst is in fact offering is a 'reading' of her audience no less theoretical or abstract than the 'readings' made by the textual critic. And in switching attention so thoroughly to the *audience* (as, for example, Hobson does when she claims that 'there are as many different Crossroads as there are viewers'), such approaches risk losing sight of both the complexities and the ideological power of the media *text*.

In an important (1984) essay, Annette Kuhn discusses the differences between approaches to the text-spectator relationship derived from feminist film theory and those emerging from ethnographic audience research. The differences can be represented in tabular form (Brunsdon 1991: 371):

Film Theory	**Audience Research**
(textual) spectator	social audience
femininity as a subject position	femaleness as a social gender
textual analysis	contextual enquiry
cinematic (or televisual) institution as context	historical context of production and reception
sexual difference constructed through look and spectacle	sexual difference constructed through flow, address and rhythm

The central question, once again, concerns the power of the media text in the construction of femininity (or masculinity). Do we produce 'feminine' readings of texts because that is the reading position which the text offers us (as Doane would argue), or because we are already positioned as 'feminine' when we come to the text (as Hobson would claim)? Kuhn's answer is to distinguish analytically between the *spectator* who is constructed by the film or TV text and the social *audience* which watches the film or television programme. 'Social audiences,' she writes, 'become spectators in the moment they engage in the processes and pleasures of meaning-making attendant on watching a film or TV programme'. On the other hand, when a group of spectators takes part in the *social act* of watching films or TV, they become a social audience (1987: 343). Thus, she argues, 'women's genres' *both* address themselves to an already gendered spectator *and* help to construct a feminine subject position.

Kuhn's framework seeks to bring together a historically specific analysis (what real audiences are/have been like) with psychoanalytically grounded theories of identity and subjectivity. What she argues is that our identities are formed, and constantly renegotiated, in the interaction between unconscious processes (our 'inner' world) and the 'outer' world of society. Representations – whether media representations or the representations of the world we make for ourselves in our 'lived experience' or memory – are the arena in which such negotiations take place. The cultural studies concept of 'negotiation' is thus extended here to include the 'inner' negotiations of our selves (our identities as women or men) as well as the negotiations we make with the meanings offered to us by media texts.

Beyond Gender

The cultural studies concept of 'negotiation' has proved influential and productive, with several recent accounts of media theory adopting it as an organising principle (Treichler and Wartella 1986; van Zoonen 1994; Macdonald 1995; Walters 1995). Nevertheless, it has recently been challenged from a number of directions. One of these has seen a questioning of the usefulness of generalisations about 'women'. What, it has been asked, do we *mean* when we talk about 'the female spectator' or 'the woman viewer'? Surely women are all positioned *differently* – by class, ethnicity, generation, sexual orientation, regionality. It is not merely an over-generalisation but an act of cultural imperialism for white, middle-class feminists to presume to analyse *a* 'female spectator'. Audiences are never 'just' gendered (Brunsdon 1993: 315). A second challenge comes from a move away from a focus on how we read specific texts – news, or soap opera or the 'woman's film' – to a broader concern with media 'use'. And such use is diverse, indeed often contradictory. I may, for example, read *Trouble & Strife* but I also enjoy *Coronation Street*; indeed, I may consume both at the same time. Even if I simply 'watch television', the range of programmes I might watch, the range of ways in which I might watch them, the range of ways in which they will appeal to me: all will vary enormously. As Annette Kuhn writes, 'Television asks us to be many things, not only at different times but also simultaneously: female is only one of them' (1989: 215). Such heterogeneity suggests that as human subjects, we are not merely 'split' between conscious and unconscious, as psychoanalysis would have it, but 'multiple' – composed of many different and contradictory fragments and able to be positioned in many different ways. How we might begin to analyse such diversity, and what role gender plays in it, are questions which become difficult to answer.

Underlying both of these challenges is a more far-reaching 'gender scepticism' (Ang and Hermes 1991: 323), which arises from feminism's engagement with postmodernism. If, as postmodern theory would suggest, we are all 'multiple' subjects, then it can be argued that such multiplicity should be *celebrated* as a way of evading stifling gender categorisations. Perhaps, indeed, we can all make and unmake, disassemble and reassemble our identities through playing with a range of media images and identities. Such an idea underlies, for example, much recent academic feminist writing about Madonna. In a 1990 article, Susan McClary writes that 'Madonna's art ... repeatedly deconstructs the traditional notion of the unified subject with finite ego boundaries. Her pieces explore ... various ways of constituting identities that refuse stability, that remain fluid, that resist definition' (1990: 2). Madonna's 'play' with identity in her videos, then, becomes a model for the kind of 'trying on' of identities in which we, as spectators, might engage.

New Directions?

To return to the questions with which this chapter began, we can see that four central issues have preoccupied feminist film and media theory since the 1960s (Kuhn 1989: 216). The first concerns the power of the media. How do the media form us? In what ways are our identities as women constructed through the media representations which surround us? The second concerns our own capacity for agency. How do *we* use the media? How far do we reshape their representations ('read against the grain') to serve our own pleasures and needs? In the balance between these two sets of questions lies much of the debate within feminist media theory, and it also determines the various responses to the third issue, that of the means we choose in order to answer these questions? Do we study texts, or media institutions, or audiences? Do we use psychoanalytic theory or theories of ideology or ethnographic study? Finally, there is the issue of the kind of knowledge we wish to produce, and the ways in which we wish to use it. In the sentences above I have assumed an identity between the feminist researcher and the women about whom she speaks – an all-inclusive 'we'. But the question of whether the feminist researcher is producing knowledge which *belongs to*, or knowledge *on behalf of*, or knowledge *about* female spectators or audiences, is not an easy one to answer. And with it comes the question of whether we are seeking to celebrate the experience of ordinary women as media consumers or in some way to *change* that experience – perhaps, as Radway suggests, by politicising it.

The most recent response to these questions, as we have seen, has been the emphasis of 'postmodern feminism' on the instability of gender identity and the need to celebrate the multiple and varied pleasures and meanings which the media can offer. Such an approach insists also upon the political importance of localised ethnographic studies as evidence of women's power to make meaning and evade narrow gender categories (Ang and Hermes 1991: 324). But it can also be argued that this celebration of multiplicity, diversity and the spectator's capacity for identificatory 'play' risks losing sight of the issue of media *power* which has been central to feminist concerns since the 1960s. The 'fluidity' of identity which we see represented in Madonna's videos conceals, as Susan Bordo points out, the way in which her body has been obsessively disciplined and regulated in order to produce these representations (1996: 54). And audience 'activity' and 'play' is not necessarily the same as *resistance* to oppressive ideologies – it may even distract from it. Thus a second response, exemplified, for example, in Jackie Stacey's combining of film theory with ethnographic research in *Star Gazing* (1994), has been to extend the concept of 'negotiation' which has been central to cultural studies approaches to the media. Arguing the need for 'an interactive model of text/audience/context to account for the complexity of the viewing process' (Stacey 1994: 47), this response continues to insist that our identities *are* formed (and re-formed) within representations, at the meeting point between the psychic and the social which is media consumption.

Notes

1. The 'cinematic apparatus', in Annette Kuhn's definition, is the 'entire context, structure and system of meaning production in cinema' (Kuhn 1982: 56).
2. The term 'subject' has a complex meaning here, combining three different uses of the word. The first is the *thinking* subject or self, as the term is usually used in philosophy. The second is the grammatical use – the subject of a sentence – which can be extended to refer to the subject of a *text*, or story (the character whom the story is about). The third use comes from political theory. We are all subjects *of* the state and hence subject *to* its laws, and its ideology. Combining the three meanings, then, suggests that as 'human subjects', our identities are both *individual* (as 'thinking subjects') and *determined* (by the culture and ideology into which we have been born).
3. This concept comes from Jacques Lacan's reworking of Freudian theory. In Madan Sarup's description, the mirror phase
   > is supposed to occur (usually between the age of six months and eighteen months) when the child has not fully mastered its own body. The mirror phase is a period at which, despite its imperfect control over its own activities, the child is first able to imagine itself as a coherent and self-governing entity. What happens is this: the child finds itself in front of a mirror. It stops, laughs at its reflection, and turns around towards whoever is holding it. It looks at its mother or its father, and then looks again at itself. For this necessary stage to occur, the child must have been separated from its mother's body (weaned) and must be able to turn around and see someone else *as* someone else. That is, it must be able to sense its discrete separation from an

Other, and must begin to assume the burden of an identity which is separate, discrete. (1992: 64)

It is this imaginary wholeness which the child internalises as an 'ideal ego'.

4. The term 'ethnography' is used loosely here to refer to a form of audience analysis which uses sources such as interviews, letters and observation to analyse audience viewing processes. The term is 'borrowed' from its source in anthropological research where it refers much more precisely to participant observation conducted over a substantial period of time.

References

Althusser, Louis (1984) *Essays on Ideology*, London and New York: Verso.

Ang, Ien (1985) *Watching Dallas: Soap Opera and the Melodramatic Imagination*, London: Methuen.

Ang, Ien (1988) 'Feminist Desire and Female Pleasure: On Janice Radway's *Reading the Romance*', in *Camera Obscura* 16:178–91.

Ang, Ien and Joke Hermes (1991) 'Gender and/In Media Consumption', in J. Curran and M. Gurevitch (eds) *Mass Media and Society*, London: Edward Arnold: 307–28.

Barthes, Roland (1973) *Mythologies*, London: Granada Publishing.

Barthes, Roland (1977) 'Introduction to the Structural Analysis of Narratives', in *Image-Music-Text*, London: Fontana.

Betterton, Rosemary (ed.) (1987) *Looking On: Images of Femininity in the Visual Arts and Media*, London and New York: Pandora.

Bordo, Susan (1996) '"Material Girl": the Effacements of Postmodern Culture', in H. Baehr and A. Gray (eds) *Turning it On*, London: Arnold: 44–57.

Brunsdon, Charlotte (1989) 'Text and Audience', in E. Seiter, H. Borchers, G. Kreutzner and E.-M. Warth (eds) *Remote Control: Television, Audiences and Cultural Power*, London and New York: Routledge: 116–29.

Brunsdon, Charlotte (1991) 'Pedagogies of the Feminine: Feminist Teaching and Women's Genres', *Screen* 32: 4: 364–81.

Brunsdon, Charlotte (1993) 'Identity in Feminist Television Criticism', *Media, Culture & Society* 15: 2: 309–20.

Busby, Linda J. (1975) 'Sex-Role Research on the Mass Media', *Journal of Communication*, Autumn: 107–31.

Citron, Michelle, Julia Le Sage, Judith Mayne, B. Ruby Rich, Anna Marie Taylor and the editors of *New German Critique* (1978) 'Women and Film: A Discussion of Feminist Aesthetics', *New German Critique* 13: 83–107.

Comolli, Jean-Louis and Jean Narboni (1976) 'Cinema/Ideology/Criticism', in B. Nichols (ed.) *Movies and Methods*, Berkeley and Los Angeles: University of California Press: 22–30.

Doane, Mary Ann (1984) 'The "woman's film": Possession and Address', in M. A. Doane, P. Mellencamp and L. Williams (eds) *Re-Vision: Essays in Film Criticism*, Los Angeles: American Film Institute: 67–82.

Doane, Mary Ann (1987) *The Desire to Desire: The Woman's Film of the 1940s*, Basingstoke and London: Macmillan.

Doane, Mary Ann (1989) Untitled entry, *Camera Obscura* 20/21: 142–7.

Friedan, Betty [1963] (1965) *The Feminine Mystique*, London: Penguin.

Gledhill, Christine (1987) 'The Melodramatic Field: An Investigation', in Gledhill (ed.) *Home is Where the Heart is: Studies in Melodrama and the Woman's Film*, London: BFI: 5–39.

Gledhill, Christine (1988) 'Pleasurable Negotiations', in E. D. Pribram (ed.) *Female Spectators: Looking at Film and Television*, London and New York: Verso: 64–89.

Hall, Stuart (1980a) 'Cultural Studies and the Centre: some problematics and problems', in S. Hall, D. Hobson, A. Lowe and P. Willis (eds) *Culture, Media, Language*, London: Hutchinson: 15–47.

Hall, Stuart (1980b) 'Encoding/decoding', in S. Hall, D. Hobson, A. Lowe and P. Willis (eds) *Culture, Media, Language*, London: Hutchinson, 1980: 128–38.

Hobson, Dorothy (1982) *'Crossroads': The Drama of a Soap Opera*, London: Methuen.

Johnston, Claire (1973) 'Women's Cinema as Counter-Cinema', in C. Johnston (ed.) *Notes on Women's Cinema*, Society for Education in Film and Television: 24–31.

Johnston, Claire (1975) 'Feminist Politics and Film History', *Screen* 16, 3: 115–25.

Johnston, Claire [1974] (1988) 'Dorothy Arzner: Critical Strategies', in C. Penley (ed.) *Feminism and Film Theory*, London: Routledge: 36–45.

Kaplan, E. Ann [1987] (1992) 'Feminist Criticism and Television', in Robert C. Allen (ed.) *Channels of Discourse*, London: Methuen; and *Channels of Discourse, Reassembled*, London: Routledge.

Kuhn, Annette (1982) *Women's Pictures: Feminism and Cinema*, London: Routledge & Kegan Paul.

Kuhn, Annette (1985) *The Power of the Image: Essays on Representation and Sexuality*, London: Routledge & Kegan Paul.

Kuhn, Annette (1987) 'Women's Genres: Melodrama, Soap Opera and Theory', in C. Gledhill (ed.), *Home is Where the Heart is: Studies in Melodrama and the Woman's Film*, London: BFI: 339–49.

Kuhn, Annette (1989) Untitled entry, *Camera Obscura* 20/21: 213–16.

Lopate, Carol (1978) 'Jackie!', in G. Tuchman (ed.) *Hearth and Home*, New York: Oxford University Press: 130–40.

Macdonald, Myra (1995) *Representing Women*, London: Edward Arnold.

McClary, Susan (1990) 'Living to Tell: Madonna's Resurrection of the Fleshy', *Genders* no. 7.

Mulvey, Laura [1975] (1989) 'Visual Pleasure and Narrative Cinema', in *Visual and Other Pleasures*, Basingstoke and London: Macmillan: 14–26.

Nelson, Cary, Paula A. Treichler and Lawrence Grossberg (1992) 'Cultural Studies: An Introduction', in L. Grossberg, C. Nelson and P. Treichler (eds) *Cultural Studies*, New York and London: Routledge, 1992: 1–16.

Pollock, Griselda (1977) 'What's Wrong with Images of Women?', *Screen Education* no. 24: 25–33.

Radway, Janice (1986) 'Identifying Ideological Seams: Mass Culture, Analytical Method, and Political Practice', *Communication* vol. 9: 93–123.

Radway, Janice [1984] (1987) *Reading the Romance*, London: Verso.

Sarup, Madan (1992) *Jacques Lacan*, Hemel Hempstead: Harvester Wheatsheaf.

Sprafkin, Joyce N. and Robert M. Liebert (1978) 'Sex-typing and Children's Television

Preferences', in G. Tuchman (ed.) *Hearth and Home*, New York: Oxford University Press: 228–39.

Stacey, Jackie (1994) *Staz Gazing: Hollywood Cinema and Female Spectatorship*, London and New York: Routledge.

Steeves, H. Leslie (1987) 'Feminist Theories and Media Studies', *Critical Studies in Mass Communication* 4: 2: 95–135.

Treichler, Paula A. and Ellen Wartella (1986) 'Interventions: Feminist Theory and Communication Studies', *Communication* vol. 9: 1–18.

Tuchman, Gaye (ed.) (1978) *Hearth and Home*, New York: Oxford University Press.

van Zoonen, Liesbet (1991) 'Feminist Perspectives on the Media', in J. Curran and M. Gurevitch (eds) *Mass Media and Society*, London: Edward Arnold: 33–54.

van Zoonen, Liesbet (1994) *Feminist Media Studies*, London: Sage.

Walters, Suzanna Danuta (1995) *Material Girls: Making Sense of Feminist Cultural Theory*, Berkeley, Los Angeles, London: University of California Press.

Williamson, Judith (1978) *Decoding Advertisements*, London: Marion Boyars.

Women and Film (1972) 'Editorial', *Women and Film* no. 1: 1–6.

Women's Studies Group, Birmingham CCCS (1978) *Women Take Issue*, London: Hutchinson.

Further Reading

Ang, Ien (1985) *Watching 'Dallas': Soap Opera and the Melodramatic Imagination*, London: Methuen.

Baehr, Helen (1980) *Women and Media*, Oxford: Pergamon Press.

Baehr, Helen and Gillian Dyer (eds) (1987) *Boxed In: Women and Television*, London: Pandora.

Baehr, Helen and Ann Gray (1996) *Turning it On: A Reader in Women and Media*, London: Arnold.

Betterton, Rosemary (ed.) (1987) *Looking On: Images of Femininity in the Visual Arts and Media*, London: Pandora.

Bobo, Jacqueline (1995) *Black Women as Cultural Readers*, New York: Columbia University Press.

Brown, Mary Ellen (ed.) (1990) *Television and Women's Culture*, London: Sage.

Brown, Mary Ellen (1994) *Soap Opera and Women's Talk*, London: Sage.

Brunsdon, Charlotte (1993) 'Identity in Feminist Television Criticism', in *Media, Culture and Society*, 15, 2: 309–20.

Coward, Rosalind (1984) *Female Desire*, London: Paladin.

Creedon, Pamela (ed.) (1989) *Women in Mass Communication: Challenging Gender Values*, London: Sage.

Davies, Kath, Julienne Dickey and Teresa Stratford (eds) (1987) *Out of Focus: Writing on Women and the Media*, London: The Women's Press.

Dyer, Richard, Christine Geraghty, Marion Jordan, Terry Lovell, Richard Paterson and John Stewart (1981) *Coronation Street* (BFI TV Monograph no. 13), London: BFI.

Gamman, Lorraine and Margaret Marshment (eds) (1988) *The Female Gaze: Women as Viewers of Popular Culture*, London: The Women's Press.

Geraghty, Christine (1991) *Women and Soap Opera: A Study of Prime Time Soaps*, Cambridge: Polity.

Gray, Ann (1992) *Video Playtime: The Gendering of a Leisure Technology*, London: Comedia/Routledge.

Kaplan, E. Ann (ed.) (1983) *Regarding Television*, Los Angeles: American Film Institute.

Kaplan, E. Ann (1992) Feminist Criticism and Television, in R. C. Allen (ed.) *Channels of Discourse, Reassembled*, London: Routledge.

Kuhn, Annette (1982) *Women's Pictures*, London: Routledge & Kegan Paul.

Kuhn, Annette (1985) *The Power of the Image: Essays on Representation and Sexuality*, London: Routledge & Kegan Paul.

Macdonald, Myra (1995) *Representing Women*, London: Edward Arnold.

McRobbie, Angela (1994) *Postmodernism and Popular Culture*, London: Routledge.

Mellencamp, Patricia (ed.) (1990) *Logics of Television*, Bloomington and London: Indiana University Press and BFI.

Modleski, Tania (1984) *Loving with a Vengeance: Mass Produced Fantasies for Women*, London: Methuen.

Modleski, Tania (ed.) (1986) *Studies in Entertainment: Critical Approaches to Mass Culture*, Bloomington: Indiana University Press.

Pribram, E. Deidre (1988) *Female Spectators: Looking at Film and Television*, London: Verso.

Radway, Janice (1987) *Reading the Romance*, London: Verso.

Seiter, Ellen, Hans Borchers, Gabriele Kreutzner and Eva-Maria Warth (eds) (1989) *Remote Control: Television, Audiences and Cultural Power*, London: Routledge.

Stacey, Jackie (1994) *Star Gazing: Hollywood Cinema and Female Spectatorship*, London and New York: Routledge.

Steeves, H. Leslie (1987) 'Feminist Theories and Media Studies', in *Critical Studies in Mass Communication*, 4, 2: 95–135.

Tuchman, Gaye et al. (eds) (1978) *Hearth and Home: Images of Women in the Media*, New York: Oxford University Press.

van Zoonen, Liesbet (1991) 'Feminist Perspectives on the Media', in J. Curran and M. Gurevitch (eds) *Mass Media and Society*, London: Edward Arnold.

van Zoonen, Liesbet (1994) *Feminist Media Studies*, London: Sage.

Walters, Suzanna Danuta (1995) *Material Girls: Making Sense of Feminist Cultural Theory*, Berkeley, Los Angeles, London: University of California Press.

Williamson, Judith (1978) *Decoding Advertisements*, London: Marion Boyars.

Winship, Janice (1987) *Inside Women's Magazines*, London: Pandora Press.

Women's Studies Group (eds) (1978) *Women Take Issue*, Centre for Contemporary Cultural Studies, London: Hutchinson.

Chapter 16

Theorising the Personal:
Using Autobiography in Academic Writing

Vicki Bertram

The writings that form the subject of this chapter do not constitute a coherent theory, so much as a methodology, or practice. They are particularly interesting because this methodology has evolved out of the earliest strategies of the Western Women's Liberation Movement of the 1970s. That famous slogan 'the personal is political' still serves as a useful summary of the impetus behind the more recent feminist work that forms the subject of this chapter, though definitions of precisely what constitutes 'personal' and 'political', or 'private' and 'public' are currently undergoing crucial changes. It is through their participation in these changes that the women I shall discuss are perhaps most significant.

The centrality of personal experience within the feminist movement of the 1970s is not hard to establish. Women began to speak out in consciousness-raising (CR) groups, sharing experiences of previously taboo subjects like abortion and domestic violence, as well as the less life-endangering experiences of frustration and confinement. Identifying common characteristics in their accounts, they started to construct their own explanations for female oppression. Feminists argued that existing theories which held the status of official knowledge, common sense or 'truth', were not true for everyone, but were founded on male experience dressed up as universal. A simple example would be early Marxist theory, in which 'work' actually meant paid labour outside the home, and effectively concealed the unpaid domestic labour of women.

Thus feminist theory was, from its outset, shaped out of women's personal experiences. Twenty years on, understanding of 'the personal' has undergone tremendous refinement. While, for the purposes of this book the emphasis is necessarily on feminist academic work, I believe there is a close relationship between this and feminist 'activist' politics. Personal experience is most significant as testimony: speaking out about what has happened to one, or what one has witnessed, is a matter of immediate practical and political importance. Without such accounts, for example, those of us outside the former Yugoslavia would not know the horrific extent of rape against women from all sides.

But while the debates I go on to discuss might seem far removed from such contexts, these writers are preoccupied with the processes whereby an indi-

232

vidual's testimony comes to be accepted (or not) as authoritative. In other words, their interest lies in the different value accorded different individuals' subjectivities. Their work emphasises the relativity of knowledge: how an individual's perception of 'facts' and 'common sense' depends on their social positioning. This is part of a far wider challenge (often linked to postmodernism) to what are now often referred to as universalising theories, or Grand Narratives.

Academics from many disciplines participate in this rather awkwardly designated activity, 'theorising the personal'; as a literary critic, I am most familiar with contributions from that angle, but will also address the work of sociologists and legal and cultural critics. I shall outline the main characteristics of this methodology briefly here, and illustrate them in more detail later by using examples from the writers themselves.

These writers share a profound suspicion of the concept of objectivity, and of the detached, impersonal style traditionally favoured by the academy (I use this term to refer to universities and related institutions such as funding panels and academic publishing houses in the West). They are committed to democratic methods of research and its dissemination; they aim to write in an accessible way, to engage the reader in dialogue and even to 'empower' her. They question why some information is accepted as 'knowledge' or 'fact', while some is dismissed or downgraded as 'anecdotal' or 'mere personal experience'; in this way they undertake a critique of epistemology (theories of knowledge production) in order to uncover its biases and exclusions. They are attentive to the power – and accompanying alienating effects – of publication, and the superior status of written over oral language. They recognise that a text is never innocent but always enmeshed in power structures, and they try to address the (often unintentional) effects that may be produced as a result. They are also often interested in the notion of the individual and its quasi-sacred position in western thought. They adopt a deliberate eclecticism, mixing anecdote, psychology, cultural analysis, literary theory, legal discourse and linguistics. Such a heady combination moves their writing outside the traditional orthodox boundaries of academic disciplines to which they ostensibly belong, and provokes controversy about the validity of their methods.

For clarity, it is useful to distinguish two different strands in this work. The first focuses predominantly on the style of academic writing, though the reasons for innovation here are more far-reaching than that might seem to suggest. Rejecting the detached impersonality of academic discourse, through explicitness about their own position or perspective, these writers aim to circumscribe the 'authority effect' (Tompkins 1989: 129) of their writing: to situate their knowledge rather than benefit from the apparently objective magisterial authority of conventional scholarship. The second strand uses autobiographical material as *part of* the data being analysed by the writer: in this way, the traditional distinction between researcher and object of research is disturbed. I shall discuss each below.

In practice both strands may be employed by one writer; in any case, they share similar aims: to bring about a radical shake-up of conventional epistemology. They seek to do this by flouting the rules governing what is considered legitimate as a topic for academic study, and by experimenting with new styles of academic writing. Their work reveals the invisible power relations that structure apparently neutral research methods. It demonstrates the need to work outside traditional academic discourse in order to produce new, more equitable, informed, and nuanced configurations of knowledge.

'The Authority Effect'

Some feminists (particularly critics of art and literature) have rejected the detached, measured tones of evaluation in favour of openly personalised response. Motivation may differ: this approach may feel more honest, or it may provide the opportunity for an implicit critique of the usual practice of critics. It may also reflect the writer's desired empathy with the individual or topic being researched. In her study of three Bloomsbury women, Mary Ann Caws writes from this position and calls her approach 'personal criticism'; she characterises it as demanding 'a certain intensity in the lending of oneself' to the subject of one's research (1990: 2), and as being 'the deliberate opposite of a cool science' (1990: 3).

Dissatisfaction with the unspoken but powerful convention of impersonality in academic writing was the force behind Jane Tompkins's now famous 1987 essay, 'Me and My Shadow', in which she wrote openly about her sense of an inner conflict between her 'academic' and her 'personal' side:

> There are two voices inside me … One is the voice of a critic … The other is the voice of a person who wants to write about her feelings (I have wanted to do this for a long time but have felt too embarrassed).
>
> (1989: 122)

She describes the academic style as feeling like a 'straitjacket' (138) and she explores her uneasiness with the impersonal, disembodied style of academic writing and the ways in which such a posture conceals the human frailty of the writer. In this brave piece, she tries to include more of herself, the three-dimensional person behind the pen. She describes the view from her window, and tells us when she needs to go to the toilet.

In her effort to discover why 'the person' has to be excised from 'the academic', Tompkins borrows ideas about the origins and development of academic thought from a colleague, Alison Jagger (1983):

> Western epistemology … is shaped by the belief that emotion should be excluded from the process of attaining knowledge. Because women in our culture are not simply encouraged but *required* to be the bearers of emotion, which men are culturally conditioned to repress,

an epistemology which excludes emotions from the process of attaining knowledge radically undercuts women's epistemic authority.

(Tompkins 1989: 123)

Thus she explores the place – or absence – of the subjective within epistemology, and the resulting invisible gender bias within it. In similar deliberations, Walter Ong suggests that the language of medieval study – Learned Latin, a second language taught only in schools, and thus only to boys – consequently 'had no direct connection with anyone's unconscious of the sort that mother tongues, learned in infancy, always have' (Ong 1972: 113). He speculates that this may have enhanced the 'exquisitely abstract world of medieval scholasticism'['s] rigorous exclusion of the emotions. The implications of this concealed gendering of knowledge are developed at greater length in the innovative work of Jane Gallop (1988). She explores the possibility and effects of introducing an embodied, female intellectual presence into the academy.

Caveats

Experiments in this kind of more personalised writing tend to be much easier to read than conventional academic prose. They preserve an immediacy; the reader feels directly addressed, and the effect is more like listening to a talk than reading a paper. This may be a deliberate attempt to avoid the aggrandising effects of publication. For example, in her 1991 collection of essays, *Getting Personal*, Nancy Miller prefaces each piece with an account of the circumstances and context of its original creation.

But there are drawbacks. There is obviously a fine line between situating one-self – giving details of one's political perspective, age, sexual orientation, etc. – and egotistical self-absorption. Furthermore, your or my detailed description of the room in which we are writing, and how we are feeling today, might not be received with the same degree of interest or tolerance as that offered to the similarly personal meditations of the 'big names' of feminist academia.

More dangerously, these voices are still predominantly those of educated, middle-class, white professional women from the West. Part of the impetus behind more personalised writing lay in an awareness of the risks of seeming to speak for 'all women', and it often signalled an attempt to be clearer about the limited perspective from which the individual wrote. Nevertheless, theories about the sources and solutions of female oppression are shaped from such experiential writing. Over-reliance on one's own subjective experience as a basis for generalisation about that of others is a temptation. Joan Smith suggests this accounts for the weakness in Naomi Wolf's work: in both *The Beauty Myth* (1990) and *Fire with Fire* (1993), she concentrates on a personal dilemma and turns it into a universal theory: all women are victims of the beauty myth; all women feel afraid of success and power (Smith 1995: 19)

There is a further problem in substituting the authority of personal experience for that of objectivity. The practice implies that the writer has authority because of her sex, race, or some other characteristic. Such essentialism has been the target of repeated attacks during the last decade. Furthermore, if the authority of experience is taken as the qualification for research, the effect is to draw sharp lines around the areas which an individual feminist is qualified to research. Jane Roland Martin discusses how this tendency becomes a 'prescription for the stunting of a field of intellectual inquiry' (Martin 1994: 631).

The risks of solipsism carry further political implications concerning the depoliticising effect of a focus on particularised facets of individual experience. In the 80s the emergence of increasingly individualised interest groups produced fragmentation that threatened the commonality vital to the feminist movement. As early as 1984 Bonnie Zimmerman tackled this issue in relation to the lesbian community. Laying claim to a 'lesbian' identity had, she acknowledged, been of tremendous importance for many women, but the accompanying emphasis on personal experience appeared to be undermining any feasible unity between women: 'The power of diversity has as its mirror image and companion the powerlessness of fragmentation' (Zimmerman 1984: 680). She called for a move away from the emphasis on personal experience:

> Perhaps we need to refocus our attention on the connecting exchange of language, rather than on the isolating structure of identity, allowing our political language to derive richness and variety from its many dialects.
>
> (682)

Autobiography as Data

The implications of this second strand can, I think, be regarded as more radical than the first. Incorporating their own subjectivity within their research not only disrupts the traditional distance between researcher and researched, it also alters the *kind* of knowledge produced. Such techniques cannot simply be dismissed as autobiographical asides because they affect the research methodology itself, challenging orthodox approaches and transgressing the boundaries of academic disciplines to borrow insights and methods from other spheres.

Feminist sociologists have produced the most interesting work in this area. An initial impetus was their unease with the conventional relationship between researcher and the object(s) of her research, which was ethically problematic for feminists. They were also unhappy with the extent to which women seemed to remain passive (and often victimised, or suffering) objects of sociological research, rather than agents.

The work of Frigga Haug (1987) has been particularly influential. Investigating the processes of female socialisation, Haug and her colleagues were concerned to do justice to the complexity of their own experience, and to restore female agency to accounts of the process. They created a methodology of 'memory work' : collective theorising, in which they were both the subjects and the objects of their research. They worked by recalling significant events from their pasts – not those usually regarded as significant, like losing one's virginity, but events that emerged spontaneously for them, and thus seemed to hold particular importance to their unconscious. These events were remembered in as much detail as possible; nothing was deemed irrelevant. The narrative progression of conventional autobiography was also rejected, because it so clearly borrows its versions of importance and notion of causality (with hindsight) from dominant ideological formations. In these ways they aimed to avoid simply reproducing the framework of research which had already mapped the terrain of female socialisation. Their pioneering work produced a more nuanced understanding of the perpetual interplay between society's 'norms' and an individual's desires. In the course of their research they also came to question the overvaluation of individuality, emphasising the degree to which individual identity is actually dependent upon collective social experience.

In the UK Liz Stanley and Sue Wise called for a similarly thorough interrogation of conventional sociological research methods in *Breaking Out* (1983). They argued that existing 'feminist' work failed to uncover the sexism embedded within the research methods it employed. According to this positivist model, the hallmarks of legitimate, authoritative research are objectivity, rationality and the use of experiments. Subjectivity, emotionality and experience are viewed as suspect (1983: 181). Suggesting that this dichotomy is itself part of the problem facing feminist sociologists, they outlined a more radical approach in which 'experience, theory and practice should exist in a mutual and immediate relationship with each other' (89).

More recent literary theorists have moved in comparable directions. Rereading Tompkins's essay in 1991, Nancy Miller argues that its weakness lies in the rejection of theory *per se*, rather than focusing on the way theorists rely on its authority effect to conceal the personal foundation of their own authority. (See also Williams 1993: 9–11.) Miller sets out to dismantle the traditional dichotomy between theory and subjectivity. Nothing prevents us bringing autobiographical material into our use of theory. She cites Jane Gallop as an example of a highly sophisticated theorist who freely acknowledges the place of personal experience within the process of theorising: 'at times I think through autobiography: that is to say, the chain of associations that I am pursuing in my reading passes through things that happened to me' (Gallop 1988: 4). Miller argues that to bring theory and the personal together is to create a profound challenge; it blows the cover of the impersonal as a masquerade of self-effacement ... and points to the narcissistic fantasy that inheres in the poses of self-sufficiency we identify with Theory: notably those of abstraction.

(Miller 1991: 24).

Miller's approach draws on poststructuralist critiques in order to avoid the problems of essentialism latent in earlier use of personal material to assure authenticity. Acknowledging that such material is not 'true' in any ultimate sense, she refers to 'the self-fiction of the personal voice', and describes it in terms of a self-conscious piece of theatre: 'by turning its authorial voice into spectacle, personal writing theorizes the stakes of its own performance: a personal materialism' (24).

Nicole Ward Jouve advances a similarly poststructuralist version of personal writing. Well aware of the slipperiness of identity in language, she maintains that the creation of a self can only ever be achieved 'through process and relationship' (Ward Jouve 1991: 10). She urges us to try out different subject positions: to learn to say 'as', conscious that we are not describing an identity but a position, 'an image and a relation. None the less true for that. Relations never amount to identity, never are fixed' (11).

Whether via sociological methods or the insights of poststructuralism, feminists have developed responses to criticisms of essentialism. However, the writers I have discussed so far have all been white. It is in the work of a number of black theorists that some of the most insightful contributions are to be found.

Patricia Williams, a black lawyer and Professor of Law at Columbia University, uses her own personal experience in her work – though it forms only one component of a critique of legal theory in which insights from 'psychology, sociology, history, criticism and philosophy' are harnessed (Williams 1993: 7). Examining the invisible biases in operation behind the law's espousal of neutrality, she shows how 'objective' decisions are in fact shaped by the racism and sexism of dominant ideology. She uses her experience of being refused entry to a branch of Benetton by a young white sales assistant as an example. (In New York, 'buzzer systems' allow shopworkers to control admission to the store, with the aim of reducing the threat of violence and theft.) When the account is published in a law review, reference to her race is removed because descriptions of physiognomy are 'against editorial policy'. She challenges this decision, pointing out that, without this information, the reader will either imagine she must be paranoid, or will have to deduce her colour, drawing on – and thus implicitly affirming – stereotypical presumptions that African Americans are more likely to be violent criminals than whites (1993: 47–8). She demonstrates how the legal acceptance of racism as a crime has inadvertently produced a situation in which all reference to race is avoided, while beliefs about racial differences continue to structure people's thoughts.

In essence, Williams focuses on differences in the authority accorded to different people's personal experience. She describes how blacks who live within a white-dominated culture are urged to internalise the dominant white perspective, to see themselves as others see them. As a result it is extremely difficult to develop a sense of one's own subjectivity and to feel secure in one's own sense of reality. The tyranny of this has profound effects:

> What links child abuse, the mistreatment of women, and racism is the massive external intrusion into psyche that dominating powers impose to keep the self from ever fully seeing itself. Since the self's power resides in another, little faith is placed in the true self, in one's own experiential knowledge. It is thus that children's, women's, and black's power is actually reduced to the 'intuitive' rather than to the real.
>
> (63)

The effect of this is to circumscribe minorities' access to objective discourse. Williams examines the concept of individual selfhood, showing that actual power differences between individual 'I's are concealed by the consensus that, in a democracy, we are all equal 'I's, possessing equal rights to freedom and choice. She identifies an extreme individualism at the heart of western society which exacerbates these differences: 'Very little in our language or culture encourages looking at others as parts of ourselves' (62).

Williams reveals the hierarchy of discourses that persists even within feminism. Despite their efforts to assert a theoretical methodology that resists abstraction, Black feminists' work is still often viewed as 'experiential' by whites. Back in 1981, Cherríe Moraga argued for a combination of political and personal insight:

> The danger lies in attempting to deal with oppression purely from a theoretical base. Without an emotional, heartfelt grappling with the source of our own oppression, without naming the enemy within ourselves and outside of us, no authentic, non-hierarchical connection among oppressed groups can take place.
>
> (Moraga and Anzaldúa 1981: 27)

Barbara Christian – defending herself against accusations of being 'anti-theory' – outlined a similar version of theorising:

> people of color have always theorized – but in forms quite different from the Western form of abstract logic ... our theorizing (and I intentionally use the verb rather than the noun) is often in narrative forms, in the stories we create, in riddles and proverbs, in the play with language, since dynamic rather than fixed ideas seem more to our liking ... My folk ... have always been a race of theory – though more in the form of the hieroglyph, a written figure which is both sensual and abstract, both beautiful and communicative.
>
> (Christian 1989: 226)

These interventions by black women illustrate the endurance of a troubling hierarchy arising from the process described by Williams, whereby some 'I's are more powerful than others, more easily accepted as legitimate knowledge producers. This situation has still not been adequately addressed. In 1992 Felly Nkweto Simmonds noted the way in which what she called 'High Feminist Theory' continued to marginalise issues around race and racism' (1992: 53). She quotes bell hooks describing the way white feminists responded to the challenge of their non-white sisters – not by relinquishing their central position, to let other women speak – but by exploring racism from their own perspective:

> White feminists could now centralize themselves by engaging in a discourse on race, 'the Other', in a manner which further marginalized women of color, whose works were often relegated to the realm of the experiential.
>
> (hooks 1991: 21)

Two Illustrations of Theorisations of Personal Material

The effects of these various methodologies are profound. In disregarding the conventional borders of academic disciplines, and admitting material previously excluded as inadmissible, they challenge the validity of those exclusions and of the knowledge produced by such a fiercely policed epistemological paradigm. I shall try to illustrate with a couple of examples.

Carolyn Steedman's *Landscape for a Good Woman: a story of two lives* is an autobiography with a difference: it questions and tests its own authenticity, and at the same time uses autobiographical material to interrogate accepted theories of class, psychology, psychoanalysis, cultural studies and feminism. Steedman argues that such theories are invariably shaped by individuals who are 'in a central relationship to the dominant culture' and thus ill-equipped to catch the very different nuances of 'lives lived out on the borderlands' (1986: 5) through, for example, poverty, class or ethnicity. Her book interweaves memories through these theoretical paradigms, and by applying the theories to her life and that of her parents, she shows the gaps in both.

Steedman argues, for example, that her early awareness of her father's powerlessness in the world meant that she didn't perform the classic psychoanalytic internalisation of patriarchal authority. Turning the spotlight onto theory in this way highlights the partial nature of its underlying perspective. For theories are usually shaped, in their original formation, out of the experiences of the theorist. Freud and his patients, as members of the middle classes, had no experience of the marginality and exclusion familiar to Steedman. Looking back on her mother's life, she suggests that within late capitalism women's reproductive capacity is something they own and can therefore exchange to further their aspirations; she reads her mother's refusal to 'mother' as resulting from her disappointment that the barter failed to bring her the consumer possessions and status for which she yearned. In this way she subverts research paradigms that never bother to consider what meaning motherhood might have, simply assuming that a biological impulse governs women's choice (where they have one) to become mothers. Like Haug and co., Steedman eschews linearity because she is concerned with the effects of the present on the past – not 'what really happened' (1986: 8), but how people use whatever stories or theories are available in order to tell the story of their lives. Furthermore, because of the personal nature of her subject, reading the book is deeply moving. It provokes emotional reactions not normally admissable within academic writing, but at the same time it is analytically sophisticated. Because it moves across genres, it is extremely difficult to categorise and summarise: it thus resists the taming effects of epistemology.

Liz Stanley's recent work is premised on the claim that autobiographical material can 'provide analytically sharp albeit experientially derived theory' (1993: 214). She analyses the diary she kept during her mother's decline after a stroke, not in order to explore her own psychology, but to reveal more about the impulses and function of narrative. She recalls the urgent need she felt to write it and, with hindsight, notes how odd were the kinds of things she recorded. This makes her consider what role the diary served: it offered reassurance during a bewildering time, when normal reference points (like the distinction between 'living' and 'dead', for her mother was severely brain-damaged) had been disrupted. She suggests that people use narrative as a way of papering over the cracks in their own awareness of the inconsistencies in their sense of identity: 'Narrative is highly complex and its referential claims frequently exist to repair what is actually an awareness of ontological complexity and fragmentation' (206).

Both Stanley and Steedman rework conventions of the life story, moving beyond the traditional arena of their academic discipline. Steedman is also challenging the intimidating authority of Freud and Marx, highlighting the ways in which their theories work to maintain the exclusion and illegitimacy of the experiences of those for whom it was/is different.

Caveats

All the writers I have discussed express a desire for dialogue with their readers, and the hope that their writing will somehow empower others. However, they cannot do anything to alter the controls that exist over access to publication, so the nature of such empowerment is perhaps dubious, certainly unmeasurable. Furthermore, their democratising impulse is slightly at odds with the complexity of their work. Stanley's wish for 'a rebellion of the active reader, a common reader who disputes academic insistence upon how texts "ought" to be read and interpreted' (1992: 91) downplays the degree of intellectual knowledge and sophistication that lies behind her clear prose. As Ward Jouve notes, '[I]t is no easier to say "I" than to make theory' (1991: 10).

The issue of empowerment is again problematic when feminist lecturers try to use aspects of this methodology in the classroom. Looking back on her attempts to legitimise her students' personal experience, McNeil records her misgivings. She points out that not only can the technique be as much of a deft, fictionalised performance as the traditional teacher's persona, but also that it really does nothing to alter power relations, since it is the teacher who decides when to authorise students' personal experiences (McNeil 1992: 22). (See also Williams (1993), whose unorthodox practice as a lecturer gets her into trouble with both students and academic authorities.)

In essence, what these approaches share is their recognition of the need to preserve a careful combination of subjective and objective knowledge-claims. Zimmerman's call for an approach that avoids both 'impersonal intellectualism and ... solipsism' (Zimmerman 1984: 682) is a succinct (and early) description. She wrote of the need to 'inscribe personal experience onto a body politic' (682). The metaphor retains – in its reference to a 'body politic' – a sense of the public, political sphere, but personalises that by also evoking the intimate resonances of 'body' . It conveys the way in which these inscriptions can actually change that sphere, marking and transforming it by *engraving* upon it. In the same way, the writers I have discussed hope to change theory through bringing it into collision with personal material.

What is needed in addition is an awareness of the point at which one ceases to be an individual, and finds oneself implicated in a larger system, within which one acquires status or characteristics that are not necessarily one's own. This is the distinction between the personal and the positional, and it is a crucial one. Miller suspects that it is the shifting boundary between these two that male academics have failed to understand, and Williams makes a similar point in relation to whites' lack of self-consciousness over the impact they have on others (Williams 1993: 72). Blacks and women, whose claims to legitimated objectivity are so much more tenuous, are more likely to find themselves viewed as representatives of a racial or gendered grouping, rather than as 'individuals'. Thus Sara Thornton, sentenced and then released for murdering her abusive partner, is treated by the media first as heroic survivor and then – once salacious information about her personal life becomes available – as an unpleasant, sexually voracious manipulator. Her 'fall from grace' has huge implications over the fate of future victims of domestic violence who try to appeal against murder charges because Thornton becomes, in public perception, a representative example of all of them. Her case illustrates women's precarious status before the law, and shows that 'we do have a very long way to go in terms of general acceptance that all women deserve justice – not just the ones who are flawless' (Bindel 1996).

Conclusions

What, then, are the implications of all these writers' methods? Below, I describe those I see as most exciting, and the work which I believe future feminists will develop.

The eclectic approaches employed by these writers play a significant part in the blurring of distinctions between academic disciplines. Importing methods from outside enables the writer to reveal how her own discipline's underlying methodological framework claims a neutrality that actually conceals its biases. In this way such frameworks function to maintain the status quo, effectively policing what are accepted as legitimate areas for research and excluding material that presents alternative perspectives. Challenging them results in surprising reconfigurations – as in the work of Haug and co., which not only shows women actively engaging with the social norms they encounter, but also produces a more complex understanding of the dynamic relation between individuals, society and ideology.

In Williams's irreverent multidisciplinary analysis of the law, supposedly neutral, objective truths are approached with scepticism; once these 'truths' are examined it becomes apparent that they are imbued with the gender- and race-blind assumptions of dominant ideology. Treating such truths as 'rhetorical gestures' allows us to move closer to a fuller and fairer system of justice, to 'fill in the gaps of traditional legal scholarship ... to write in a way that reveals the intersubjectivity of legal constructions' (Williams 1993: 7). The method allows 'room for the possibility of creatively mated taxonomies and their wildly unpredictable offspring' (1993: 10–11).

Responding to the fluid boundaries between personal and positional experience, the writers I have discussed embrace what Rosi Braidotti has called 'strategic essentialism'. Instead of putting all their faith in experiential claims to authority, they recognise the political potential in a more flexible concept of identity. One of the first to recognise this was the poet Denise Riley: 'I'd argue that it is compatible to suggest that "women" don't exist – while maintaining a politics of "as if they existed" – since the world behaves as if they unambiguously did' (Riley 1988: 112). This is to hold two apparently contradictory positions at the same time: to insist on positional reality *and* particularised differences which theoretically dissolve the viability of the category 'women'.

The approach I have been discussing has had a considerable impact on the way we approach education. Ward Jouve calls for greater personal involvement in intellectual work. In so doing, she undermines the conventional opposition at the heart of conventional epistemology: between intellect and feelings, private and professional. She argues that the critic must 'think with the whole of oneself, of one's life, rather than with one's (hermaphroditic, snail-like) brain' (105).

As can be seen from the pioneering work of Gallop in this area, the implications are far-reaching. Ward Jouve also advocates a suspicious attitude towards the academy, and urges women to resist the seductive temptations of integration, by continuing to disobey the rules 'in irreverent little ways' (114): by, for example, including quirky or taboo aspects of their experience in their academic work.

But perhaps the most profound outcome of this approach lies in its vision of theorising as an imaginative, intuitive activity. This is evident in the work of Christian, Moraga and Ward Jouve, among others. The creative potential of such a dynamic conception of theoretical endeavour can lead to the dissolution of genre distinctions, like that between theory and fiction. It guards against the tendency to reify theory. Even digests like this one, inevitably divorcing theoretical work from the contexts of its original creation, can inadvertently depoliticise the material. Theory that remains in intricate dialogue with practice, and with the subjectivity of the theorist, is far less likely to become abstracted in this way.

These developments span many different disciplines; I have only been able to draw examples from a few. But however various their research matter, these writers are connected through their preoccupation with subjectivity. Miller believes it is the struggle over subjectivity that lies at the heart of feminism's most profound challenge 'to recast the subject's relation to itself and to authority, the authority *in* theory. Where, then, will authority come from? The person(al)?' (21)

Her question, as yet, remains unanswered.

References

Bindel, Julie (1996) 'View from the pedestal', *The Guardian*, 11 June.

Caws, Mary Ann (1990) *Women of Bloomsbury: Virginia, Vanessa and Carrington*, London and New York: Routledge.

Christian, Barbara (1989) 'The Race for Theory', in L. Kaufmann (ed.) *Gender and Theory: Dialogues on Feminist Criticism*, Blackwell: Oxford.

Gallop, Jane (1988) *Thinking Through the Body*, New York: Columbia University Press.

Haug, Frigga (1987) *Female Sexualisation: A Collective Work of Memory*, Verso: London.

hooks, bell (1991) *Yearning: Race, Gender and Cultural Politics*, London: Turnaround.

Jagger, Alison (1983) *Feminist Politics and Human Nature*, Totowa, NJ: Rowman and Allenheld.

Martin, Jane Roland (1994) 'Methodological Essentialism, False Difference, and Other Dangerous Traps', *Signs* vol. 19(3): 630–57.

McNeil, Maureen (1992) 'Pedagogical Praxis and Problems: Reflections on Teaching about Gender Relations', in Hilary Hinds, Ann Phoenix and Jackie Stacey (eds) *Working Out: New Directions for Women's Studies*, London: The Falmer Press.

Miller, Nancy (1991) *Getting Personal*, London and New York: Routledge.

Moraga, Cherríe and Gloria Anzaldúa (eds) [1981] (1983) *This Bridge Called My Back: Writings by Radical Women of Color*, New York: Kitchen Table: Women of Color Press.

Ong, Walter (1972) *Orality and Literacy: The Technologizing of the Word*, London and New York: Methuen.

Riley, Denise (1988) *'Am I That Name?' Feminism and the Category of 'Women' in History*, London: Macmillan.

Simmonds, Felly Nkweto (1992) 'Difference, Power and Knowledge: Black Women in Academia', in Hilary Hinds, Ann Phoenix and Jackie Stacey (eds), *Working Out: New Directions for Women's Studies*, London: The Falmer Press.

Smith, Joan (1995) 'The seer and the sisters', *Independent on Sunday*, 15 October: 19.

Stanley, Liz (1993) 'The Knowing Because Experiencing Subject: Narratives, Lives and Autobiography', in *Women's Studies International Forum*, vol. 16(3): 205–15.

Stanley, Liz and Sue Wise [1983] (revised and reprinted 1993) *Breaking Out: Feminist Ontology and Epistemology*, London and New York: Routledge.

Steedman, Carolyn (1986) *Landscape for a Good Woman: A Story of Two Lives*, London: Virago.

Tompkins, Jane (1989) 'Me and My Shadow', in L. Kaufmann (ed.) *Gender and Theory: Dialogues on Feminist Criticism*, Oxford: Blackwell.

Ward Jouve, Nicole (1991) *White Woman Speaks with Forked Tongue: Criticism as Autobiography*, London and New York: Routledge.

Williams, Patricia (1993) *The Alchemy of Race and Rights*, London: Virago.

Wolf, Naomi (1990) *The Beauty Myth*, London: Chatto and Windus.

Wolf, Naomi (1993) *Fire with Fire: The New Female Power and How it Will Change the 21st Century*, London: Chatto and Windus.

Zimmerman, Bonnie (1984) 'The Politics of Transliteration: Lesbian Personal Narratives', *Signs* 9(4): 663–82.

Further Reading

Anderson, Linda (1986) 'At the threshold of the self: women and autobiography', in M. Monteith (ed.) *Women's Writing: A Challenge To Theory*, Brighton: Harvester Press.

Anderson, Linda (1996) *Women and Autobiography in the Twentieth Century*, Hemel Hempstead: Harvester Wheatsheaf.

Brodzi, Bella and Celeste Marguerite Schenck (eds) (1988) *Life/Lines: Theorising Women's Autobiography*, Ithaca: Cornell University Press.

Freedman, Diane et al. (1993) *The Intimate Critique: Autobiographical Literary Criticism*, Durham, NC: Duke University Press.

Gender and History (1989), vol. 2(i), special issue on autobiography, edited by Lucy Bland and Angela John.

MacLean, Gerald M. (1989) 'Citing the Subject', in L. Kaufmann (ed.) *Gender and Theory: Dialogues on Feminist Criticism*, Oxford: Blackwell.

Marcus, Laura (1994a) 'Personal Criticism and the Autobiographical Turn', in Sally Ledger et al. (eds) *Political Gender: Texts and Contexts*, Hemel Hempstead: Harvester Wheatsheaf.

Marcus, Laura (1994b) *Autobiographical Discourses: Theory, Criticism, Practice*, Manchester and New York: Manchester University Press.

Smith, Dorothy E. (1974) 'Women's perspective as a radical critique of sociology', *Sociological Quarterly* 44: 7–13.

Smith, Dorothy E. (1989) 'Sociological Theory: Methods of Writing Patriarchy', in R. A. Wallace (ed.) *Feminism and Sociological Theory*, London: Sage Publications.

Smith, Sidonie (1993) *Subjectivity, Identity, and the Body. Women's Autobiographical Practices in the Twentieth Century*, Indiana: Indiana University Press.

Stanley, Liz (1992) *The Auto/biographical I: The Theory and Practice of Feminist Auto/biography*, Manchester: Manchester University Press.

Swindells, Julia (1995) *The Uses of Autobiography*, Basingstoke: Taylor & Francis.

Women's Studies International Forum (1987) vol. 10(i), special issue on 'Personal Chronicles: Women's Autobiographical Writings', edited by Dale Spender.

Chapter 17

Women's Studies

Mary Maynard

Women's studies first appeared in the United States in the second half of the 1960s, with courses and degree programmes emerging in other Western countries during the 1970s. Subsequently, expansion has been so great that women's studies is now something of a global educational phenomenon. Initially, Western women's studies were set up as part of a thorough-going feminist critique of patriarchal institutions which was taking place within the Women's Liberation Movement. It was argued that neither the construction of knowledge, nor the practices involved in education, were exempt from oppressive and exploitative processes. As one facet of the educational wing of the Women's Movement, women's studies had two particular and interrelated aims. The first was to provide information and analyses about the lives of women, with a view to bringing about social changes which would end gender inequalities and women's subordination. The second was to develop a critique of existing knowledge forms which would demonstrate how, and why, women's lives, views and perspectives remained largely hidden in the existing academic disciplines. It was suggested that academic scholarship had either ignored women, assumed their experiences were the same as men's (thereby overlooking the importance of gender as a dimension of analysis) or treated them as deviant (Spender 1981: 2).

In this chapter I will be looking at how different kinds and forms of feminist theory have informed the nature, shape and content of women's studies, particularly in the US and in Britain. However, such an endeavour is not without difficulties. The issue of the relevance or otherwise of feminist theory has led to heated debate on many women's studies courses (Stacey 1993: 49). Some, who emphasise the link between feminist theory and practice, argue that it is important to engage with and challenge existing forms of theoretical knowledge (Evans 1982; Fildes 1983). Others regard theorising as an arid, abstract and masculine form of activity, bearing little relationship to women's everyday lives and experiences (Kelly and Pearson 1983; Currie and Karl 1987). Still more occupy the middle ground somewhere between the two opposing positions. On the one hand, some forms of feminist theory are undoubtedly very reified, elitist and difficult to comprehend. On the other, if we take feminist theory to mean a body of knowledge which offers critical explanations of and challenges to women's subordination then it is clear that some use of analytical categories is required. These enable us to move beyond description, anecdote or individual cases to more general levels of understanding (Stacey 1993: 50).

The focus in this chapter is on three particular kinds of feminist theory and this is reflected in its structure. The first section is concerned with epistemology and the feminist theoretical critique of male knowledge as the grounds for setting up autonomous women's studies. The second focuses on the theoretical ideas which have influenced both the content and practice of women's studies and how these have changed over time. The third section concentrates on the changing shape of those kinds of feminist theory which have been concerned with analysing the social situation of women. The chapter concludes by looking at three crucial aspects of theorising which women's studies should confront in future years.

The Feminist Critique of Male Knowledge

A feminist critique of existing knowledge forms began to develop as academic feminists started to discover the difficulties inherent in using existing discipline-based frameworks to explore the ideas which were emerging from the grassroots Women's Movement. Initially, certainly in Britain, the impetus for this critique came from the social sciences, although it was soon being debated, to a greater or lesser extent, within other disciplinary contexts (Spender 1981). A very early version, for instance, is to be found in the existential feminism of Simone de Beauvoir, who wrote, in *The Second Sex*, about how men both made the world and went on to represent it from their own point of view, which they then confused with the absolute truth (1972). The American feminist, Catharine MacKinnon, has since dubbed this position 'the male epistemological stance'. Writing about the sexist, biased and exclusionary nature of much of what, prior to feminism, counted as knowledge, MacKinnon observes that: 'men create the world from their own point of view, which then *becomes* the truth to be described ... *Power to create the world from one's point of view is power in the male form*' (1982: 23–4).

MacKinnon's arguments draw attention not just to what might have been overlooked or left out from a woman's point of view in various knowledge-creating processes. It also points to the fact that the issues which have been given attention, together with the ways this has been achieved, have derived from male interests and ways of seeing. This was previously the case, it has been suggested, even when women have been involved in producing knowledge. Because the content, concepts, theories and methods of academic subjects have largely derived from a male perspective of the universe, this has had a profound influence on which aspects of the world have been regarded as significant for study and how they have been perceived as structured and ordered (Smith 1974). For instance, prior to the 1970s, much sociology in the US and Britain focused on public issues such as work, production, class and belief systems which were of relevance to men. Where there was interest in more private matters, such as the family, this ignored those aspects of particular concern to women, such as housework, motherhood, the role of emotions and sexuality. It is only since women's studies has come to be regarded as a legitimate area of scholarship that aspects of women's experiences such as these have been properly researched.

Another point which MacKinnon makes is that the social world, as it is constructed from a male perspective, affords men a privileged position. Dorothy Smith endorses this, and refers to the existence of two worlds, the male and the female, in sociology, where the domestic sphere has been constructed as the domain of women and portrayed as dependent on, as well as subordinate to, the world of men (1974). Smith claims that the implications of this are that women have been forced to conceptualise their world in terms derived from those of men. This means that, prior to women's studies at least, women have been alienated from their experiences because they have not been able to represent and understand them on their own terms. A similar point has also been made by feminist historians and literary critics, who have criticised the ways in which their subjects have been determined on the basis of men's interests and criteria (Spender 1981).

A further aspect to which MacKinnon draws attention – the concern about objectivity – was also a significant characteristic of early feminist debates about knowledge and, indeed, still features prominently in them today. Feminists have been critical about claims as to the possibility of producing value-neutral accounts about the nature of the social world. Firstly, the supposed objectivity of masculinist knowledge has been exposed as a sham, due to its partial nature and gender-blindness. Feminists, along with other critics, have also been sceptical about the possibilities of ever being able to produce completely objective understandings or 'truth'. This is because, they argue, it is impossible for researchers to stand outside of a social situation, since their taken-for-granted biographical and cultural assumptions will always be implicated in the questions that are asked, how these are studied and the interpretations that are made. For this reason, more reliable knowledge will be produced if we are reflexively aware of the hidden agendas that will be brought to the practice of research and knowledge-creation more generally (Acker, Barry and Esseveld 1983).

It is against criticisms of conventional forms of knowledge such as these that women's studies has emerged. Women's studies seeks to address the fact that individual disciplines themselves are gender-blind, presenting male values and experiences as general human ones and as representative of all. Autonomous women's studies are required, it is argued, because of the necessity for all women to alter their frames of reference to ones in which women's different and differing ideas, knowledge, experiences, needs and interests are accepted as legitimate in their own right and form the basis of research, and knowledge-creation (Bowles and Duelli Klein 1983). Different perspectives exist on how this might be achieved. Some argue for a *multi-disciplinary* approach, whereby the most useful parts of different disciplines are critiqued and brought to bear on a topic in differing ways. Others argue for an *interdisciplinary* perspective in which this is done in more holistic and integrative ways. A further possibility, albeit more difficult to achieve, is to develop a *trans-disciplinary* framework in which existing disciplines are transcended (Klein 1991). Each kind of women's studies, however, involves theorising the gendered power relations inherent in current knowledge-creation processes. In placing women themselves at the centre of research and analysis, they question how previous meanings have been constructed and evaluated (Robinson 1993).

The Content and Practice of Women's Studies

In terms of the content of its courses and scholarship, women's studies has moved through three broad and interconnected phases, each influenced by the current stage reached in theorising about feminist knowledge (de Groot and Maynard 1993). The first, recuperative, phase aimed to challenge the silencing, stereotyping, marginalisation and misrepresentation of women in historical, social science, literary and cultural studies. It questioned assumptions, discovered and disseminated empirical evidence, and grappled with the conceptual and explanatory implications of restoring the female half of humanity as a proper and necessary part of research and analysis. Women's lives, experiences and perspectives were brought into the picture by designing practical research projects and explanatory frameworks which might redress the situation. Such endeavours were influenced and informed by the activist agendas of those who, during the 1970s, were involved in various kinds of feminist politics both inside and outside of educational institutions. This interaction between academic and activist approaches to women's position and problems became a significant feature of feminism and women's studies.

During the second, reconstructive, phase the terms and topics which structured the practices of existing disciplines have been re-evaluated and redesigned. Whereas the recuperative phase largely involved 'adding' women into existing knowledge, the reconstructive focused on new areas of concern and the generation of new concepts and theories. Substantive issues such as those of sexuality, violence towards women and 'the body' came to the fore. Particularly important was the way in which knowledge was transformed by a continuing insistence on the relevance of 'private' phenomena and not just the masculinist emphasis on the public sphere. Further, there were also serious conceptual and theoretical disagreements over questions such as the nature of patriarchy or male power, the relationship between gender power and inequality and other forms of domination and exploitation, and the extent to which women shared their subordination or whether this was influenced by other factors, such as those of social class.

It is, however, the third phase, the reflexive, which has raised issues which have been, and continue to be, particularly difficult and painful. This has involved feminists in being both self-critical and self-aware about their women's studies work. Recently, questions have been raised about the white, Western, privileged, heterosexist and other biases (both political and intellectual) in women's studies (Ramazanoglu 1989). In the early days, cosy assumptions were made, both explicitly and implicitly, that all women could be defined in terms of a universal 'sisterhood', meaning that they could be described in terms of the things they experienced and shared in common. Challenges to these ideas have come from a variety of sources, but many originated from Black women in the US and Britain (Bhavnani 1993; Collins 1990; hooks 1984). They argue that the focus in women's studies work on white women's experiences, to the virtual exclusion of Black and Third World women's lives, constitutes a form of racism, in which the concerns of a small group of white women are prioritised and treated as the norm. Further, women's studies has suppressed the ideas of Black women, to the extent that few manage to find their way into mainstream debate. Similar criticisms have been made by women from other groups. Disabled women, for example, have been critical of the ways in which their experiences are treated as isolated and individualised, resulting in their virtual exclusion from women's studies research (Morris 1995). Frustrations around heterosexism have led some lesbians to set up their own lesbian studies courses (Staddon 1995).

These are crucial matters for women's studies to confront. One way in which this has been attempted is via the introduction of the concept 'difference'. This is intended to signal a move away from assumptions about homogeneity, emphasising, instead, the diverse nature and variety of women's lives. Much more work needs to be done, however, in order to attain the inclusiveness to which women's studies should aspire. As June Jordan has remarked, 'most of the women of the world persist far from the heart of the usual women' studies syllabus' (1995: 27).

If women's studies have involved challenging the gendered nature of courses and scholarship, they have also been concerned with adopting a critical stance towards teaching and learning. In part, this is associated with theorising the relationship between education, hierarchy and power. Initially, many feminists were influenced by the writings of Paulo Freire (1972), who was critical of what he referred to as the 'banking' model of education, whereby students are assumed to know nothing and it is the role of the teacher to deposit knowledge in them. Freire's argument was that, through this process, the teacher wielded power over students, thereby reinforcing relations of domination and subordination. Instead, he advocated the 'problem-posing' model of education in which oppression and its causes are the topics of study, with students and teachers collaborating to gain a greater understanding both of themselves and of the world.

It is not difficult to see why such a form of pedagogy, which closely resonates with feminist politics, should prove attractive in women's studies. For a start, its emphasis on cooperation, dialogue and the use of experience in the classroom challenges the idea of a hierarchy of learning and the teacher as expert. It promotes the idea of education as an empowering activity, where the possibilities of personal and social changes are facilitated through listening to and respecting others, and through pooling resources. Such a form of pedagogy allows the tensions between the emotional, subjective and experiential understandings of women and the intellectualised (so-called) objective, expertise of mainstream knowledge to be highlighted. In emphasising such factors as supportive and egalitarian classroom relationships, the value of each individual, experience as a learning resource, together with joint projects, small group work and other non-traditional forms of discussion and assessment, it is possible to problematise the contradictory positions held by women's studies students and teachers, in relation to each other, to the academic world and to the practice of feminism (hooks 1989; Lubelska 1991; Robinson 1993; Welch 1994).

More recently, however, concern has been expressed as to just how far these objectives are being, or ever could be, met. Some commentators, for example, have argued that the institutionalisation of women's studies, particularly within higher education, has led to its de-radicalisation (Brimstone 1991; Currie 1993; Currie and Kazi 1987). The need to accommodate the structures and procedures of universities and colleges places severe limitations on the challenges that women's studies can adopt. Not only is the academic side of women's studies dominated by white, heterosexual and educated women, but the decline of a high-profile grass-roots women's movement means that, today, most feminist theory is produced in universities, rather than in activist groups (Welch 1994). There is a danger that women's studies have begun to grow into a knowledge industry of their own (Rowbotham 1989). As bell hooks says:

> Given the way universities work to reinforce and perpetuate the status quo, the way knowledge is offered as a commodity, Women's Studies can easily become a place where revolutionary feminist thought and feminist activism are submerged or made secondary to the goals of academic careerism.
>
> (1989: 51)

Such a position is reinforced, particularly in countries such as Britain, by contemporary socio-political factors, such as high unemployment, the rhetoric of consumerism, market-led higher education, citizenship charters and heightened student expectations. Beverley Skeggs points out how women's studies has expanded through the rapid growth of places, without adequate resourcing and at a time of rationalisation and constraint (1995), which means that demands from students are far greater than what can be provided. The difficulties are com-pounded by expectations that, in addition to more teaching, academics will undertake increased administration and research. For Skeggs, this means that 'in our present conditions the attention required by increased numbers of students at all levels and the ideals of feminist pedagogy are very difficult to meet' (1995: 482). Thus, the current institutional position works against the interests of both feminist students and staff, making it very difficult to deliver many aspects of what had been theorised as good feminist educational practice.

The Changing Nature of Feminist Theory in Women's Studies

For many commentators the term 'feminist theory' is associated, in particular, with the analysis and explanation of women's subordinate social situation. Until recently, it was customary to categorise different ways of doing this in terms of three major perspectives, each with their own historical tradition and legacy. The first of these, liberal feminism, is depicted as focusing on individual rights and on the concepts of equality, justice and equal opportunities; women are presented as being prevented from achieving equality with men by certain social barriers. It is argued, therefore, that specific legal and social policy changes are the necessary tools for rectifying women's inferior position. The second position – marxist feminism – is identified by a concern with women's oppression as it is tied to forms of capitalist exploitation of labour, where women's paid and unpaid work are each analysed in relation to their function within the capitalist economy. Thirdly, racial feminism is 'radical' because, unlike the previous two, it eschews existing theoretical frameworks and attempts to formulate new ways of theoris-ing women's relationship to men. In particular, men's social control of women through various mechanisms of patriarchy is emphasised – especially violence, heterosexuality and reproduction, where men as a group are seen as responsible for maintaining women's oppression.

The problem of portraying feminist theory in terms of the 'Big Three', how-ever, is that this formulation could never totally encompass and encapsulate every strand of feminism (Maynard 1995). Not only were a number of prominent thinkers excluded by such categorisation, but there was not always agreement as to which writers should be given which label. Further difficulties in attempting to classify theories in this way lay in the fact that this was largely a white, Western feminist endeavour. As a consequence, the ideas of Black women became even more marginalised and invisible. Additionally, during the 1980s, as the external intellectual and political influences on feminist theories began to increase, so the number of categories to describe them also proliferated. The introduction of labels such as dual systems, materialist, psychoanalytic, postmodern, Black, lesbian, together with other forms of feminist thinking, suggests that, currently, it is more appropriate to view feminist theorising as a complex, dynamic and evolving process, rather than in terms of narrow and static stereotypes. It is no longer useful to portray feminist theory in terms of discrete positions which can be 'mugged up', learnt parrot-fashion and applied in unproblematic ways. Not only is theory more pluralistic than was previously conceived, it now encompasses a number of organisational axes which cannot be regarded as absolute.

There have been two specific theoretical trends which have influenced the development of feminist theory in the late 1980s and 1990s, as they have other disciplinary areas. These are the psychoanalytic thinking of Jacques Lacan (1968, 1979) and the post-structuralist ideas of Michel Foucault (1979, 1981). Some feminists have used their concepts and theories to explore such areas as sexuality, desire and the body, although such work is not uncontentious (Ramazanoglu 1995). However, it is not these more substantive issues which are of concern here. Rather, the focus is on the more general influence that Lacan and Foucault have had on the nature of feminist theory and the parameters which it can be said to encompass. Their ideas about knowledge have affected what such theory can be expected to acheive and how its various elements should be structured.

For example, the importance assigned by Lacan and Foucault to language and discourse has meant something of a re-focusing of women's studies interests away from the material aspects of women's lives (and a concern with such matters as economics, the labour market, the sexual division of labour) to an emphasis on symbolisation, representation and textual analysis. In other words, changes in theoretical emphasis have increasingly led women's studies to focus less on social and more on cultural phenomena. As a consequence, explorations of the meanings of 'difference' for women have begun to involve less of a concern with diversity of experience and more of an emphasis on the deconstruction of subjectivity. The self is no longer presented as rationalistic, monolithic and unified, and gender itself becomes a problematic term. Instead, each is portrayed as fragmented, pluralistic and continually changing. What constitutes 'woman', it is argued, can no longer be taken for granted and accepted at face value. Through the processes of deconstruction, the multiple subjectivities, identities and complexities of womanhood are displayed.

Another way in which writers such as Lacan and Foucault have had an impact on feminist theory is in terms of their criticisms of attempts to produce grand theories or meta-narratives. Many feminists have accepted the arguments that the latter provide falsely homogenising accounts, which are obsessed with monocausal and universalistic explanations. Instead, they are currently more likely to theorise in ways which acknowledge the specifics of cultural and historical location, and which shy away from overly expansive and totalising claims. This may be seen, for instance, in two particular developments. The first is the move away from foundationalism, the assumption that theories need to be based upon some fundamental core to which all other elements of which they are comprised can be reduced. This involves rejecting any claim that there can be *a* specific *cause* of women's subordination (be this male violence, capitalism's need for a docile work force or discriminatory laws) which is primary to all others. Relatedly, the second involves the move away, in feminist theory, from positioning women as a group within some overarching oppressive structure or system, whether patriarchy, capitalism or a male-defined liberal democracy. This is because the connotations of passivity and determinism in such a formulation deny women agency and the ability to struggle and resist. Thus, concepts such as patriarchy have given way to more pluralistic notions, such as patriarchal relations, taken to signify that relationships between men and women are not uniform and can, indeed, be contradictory. This, further, facilitates an understanding of the unevenness of power. Not all of women's experiences are negative, neither are they necessarily and inherently those of being oppressed. Additionally, some women may be in positions from which they can exercise power over other women. As may be seen, developments such as these signify considerable changes in the nature and content of what constitutes feminist theory, when compared to the earlier 'perspectives' approach.

Looking Forward

Many of the changes brought about by the influence of Lacanian and Foucauldian ideas have been tremendously significant in opening up debate and questioning some of the silences which previously existed in feminists' thinking. Some commentators, however, have argued that feminists' acceptance of postmodern ideas has gone too far (Walby 1992). This has resulted in an over-emphasis on fragmentation and on culture, to the detriment of being able to understand how women are variously socially positioned. It is, therefore, important that women's studies confront three particular issues in future years.

First, there is the need to redress the current theoretical hype about culture, discourse and representation, which suggests that these are the only possible and legitimate areas for study (Barrett 1992). This has huge implications for women's studies, for it ignores the ways in which material processes influence the cultural practices which are available to individuals. Our lived experience is mediated not just through discourse or text but also through material structures and relationships. These may range from family and friends, to access to knowledge and learning, to the amount of money, food and other resources which are available. Such things need to be taken into account because of the ways in which they influence how men and women may be restricted or empowered in their everyday lives.

Second, attempts to theorise the diversity of women's experiences should be put at the heart of the women's studies agenda. Currently, 'difference' is treated either in terms of the postmodern concern with multiple subjectivities or at the level of rhetoric. To state an awareness of 'difference' (whether race, sexual orientation, disability, etc.) is the trendy, 'politically correct' and 'done' thing to do. Less often do such issues permeate throughout a project and even then there is a tendency to treat the 'other' as if they deviate from some kind of accepted norm. Even more infrequent are attempts to problematise the 'norm' itself and expose differences held by the powerful (whiteness, heterosexuality, able-bodiedness) to analytical scrutiny.

Finally, it is necessary for white Western women's studies to adopt a more all-encompassing and global framework. Ethnocentrism has encouraged a focus on indigenous culture. Not only has women's studies tended to ignore the circumstances of non-white women who live in their midst, it has also disregarded those who live in different parts of the world. Yet, despite the postmodern emphasis on fragmentation and the inward turning gaze which this promotes, the world order is characterised by increasing political and economic globalisation. Moreover, overall, women do two-thirds of the world's work, earn one-tenth of its income and own less than one-third of its property. In disregarding such matters, women's studies is guilty of both racism and cultural imperialism. As the next millenium approaches, 'the global hegemony of western feminism' must be challenged (Mohanty 1991: 52).

References

Acker, J., J. Barry and J. Esseveld (1983) 'Objectivity and truth: problems in doing feminist research', *Women's Studies International Forum*, 6, 4: 423–35.

Barrett, M. (1992) 'Words and things', in M. Barrett and A. Phillips (eds) *Destabilizing Theory*, Cambridge: Polity.

Bhavnani, K.-K. (1993) 'Talking racism and the editing of women's studies', in D. Richardson and V. Robinson (eds) *Introducing Women's Studies*, London: Macmillan.

Bowles, G. and R. Duelli Klein (1983) (eds) *Theories of Women's Studies*, London: Routledge.

Brimstone, L. (1991) 'Out of the margins and into the soup: some thoughts on incorporation', in J. Aaron and S. Walby (eds) *Out of the Margins*, London: Taylor & Francis.

Collins, P. H. (1990) *Black Feminist Thought*, London: HarperCollins.

Currie, D. (1993) 'Unhiding the hidden: race, class and gender in the construction of knowledge', *Humanity and Society*, 17, 1: 3–27.

Currie, D. and H. Kazi (1987) 'Academic feminism and the process of de-radicalization: re-examining the issues', *Feminist Review*, 25: 77–98.

de Beauvoir, S. (1972) *The Second Sex*, Harmondsworth: Penguin.

de Groot, J. and M. Maynard (1993) 'Doing things differently? A context for women's studies for the next decade', in J. de Groot and M. Maynard (eds) *Women's Studies in the 1990s*, London: Macmillan.

Evans, M. (1982) 'In praise of theory: the case for women's studies', *Feminist Review*, 10: 61–74.

Fildes, S. (1983) 'The inevitability of theory', *Feminist Review*, 14: 62–70.

Foucault, M. (1979) *Discipline and Punish*, Harmondsworth: Penguin.

Foucault, M. (1981) *The History of Sexuality, Volume One*, Harmondsworth: Pelican.

Freire, P. (1972) *Pedagogy of the Oppressed*, Harmondsworth: Penguin.

hooks, b. (1984) *Feminist Theory: From Margin to Center*, Boston MA: South End Books.

hooks, b. (1989) *Talking Back: Thinking Feminist, Thinking Black*, London: Sheba.

Jordan, J. (1995) 'Report from the Bahamas', in M. L. Anderson and P. H. Collins (eds) *Race, Class and Gender. An Anthology*, Belmont CA: Wadsworth.

Kelly, L. and R. Pearson (1983) 'Women's studies: women studying or studying women?', *Feminist Review*, 15: 76–80.

Klein, R. D. (1991) 'Passion and politics in women's studies in the 1990s', in J. Aaron and S. Walby (eds) *Out of the Margins*, London: Taylor & Francis.

Lacan, J. (1968) *The Language of Self: The Function of Language in Psychoanalysis*, Baltimore: Johns Hopkins University Press.

Lacan, J. (1979) *Four Fundamental Concepts of Psychoanalysis*, Harmondsworth: Penguin.

Lubelska, C. (1991) 'Teaching methods in women's studies: challenging the mainstream', in J. Aaron and S. Walby (eds) *Out of the Margins*, London: Taylor and Francis.

MacKinnon, C. (1982) 'Feminism, marxism, method and the state: an agenda for theory', in N. O. Keohane, M. Rosaldo and B. Gelpi (eds) *Feminist Theory*, Brighton, Sussex: Harvester Press.

Maynard, M. (1995) 'Beyond the "big three": the development of feminist theory into the 1990s', *Women's History Review*, 4, 3: 259–81.

Mohanty, C. T. (1991) 'Under western eyes', in C. T. Mohanty, A. Russo and L. Torres (eds) *Third World Women and the Politics of Feminism*, Bloomington and Indianapolis: Indiana University Press.

Morris, J. (1995) 'Personal and political: a feminist perspective on researching physical disability', in J. Holland and M. Blair (eds) *Debates and Issues in Feminist Research and Pedagogy*, Buckingham: Open University Press.

Ramazanoglu, C. (1989) *Feminism and the Contradictions of Oppression*, London: Routledge.

Ramazanoglu, C. (ed.) (1995) *Up Against Foucault*, London: Routledge.

Robinson, V. (1993) 'Introducing women's studies', in D. Richardson and V. Robinson (eds) *Introducing Women's Studies*, London: Macmillan.

Rowbotham, S. (1989) *The Past is Before Us*, Harmondsworth, Penguin.

Skeggs, B. (1995) 'Women's studies in Britain in the 1990s. Entitlement cultures and institutional constraints', *Women's Studies International Forum*, 18, 4: 475–85.

Smith, D. (1974) 'Women's perspective as a radical critique of sociology', *Sociological Inquiry*, 44, 1: 7–13.

Spender, D. (ed.) (1981) *Men's Studies Modified*, Oxford: Pergamon.

Stacey, J. (1993) 'Untangling feminist theory', in D. Richardson and V. Robinson (eds) *Introducing Women's Studies*, London: Macmillan.

Staddon, P. (1995) 'Lesbian studies: an opportunity not to be missed', in M. Maynard and J. Purvis (eds) *(Hetero)sexual Politics*, London: Taylor & Francis.

Walby, S. (1992) 'Post-post-modernism? Theorizing social complexity', in M. Barrett and A. Phillips (eds) *Destabilizing Theory*, Cambridge: Polity.

Welch, P. (1994) 'Is a feminist pedagogy possible?', in S. Davies, C. Lubelska and J. Quinn (eds) *Changing the Subject: Women in Higher Education*, London: Taylor & Francis.

Further Reading

Anderson, M. L. and P. H. Collins (eds) (1995) *Race, Class and Gender: An Anthology*, Belmont CA: Wadsworth.

Butler, J. and J. W. Scott (eds) (1992) *Feminists Theorize the Political*, London: Routledge.

Collins, P. H. (1990) *Black Feminist Thought*, London: HarperCollins.

Crowley, H. and S. Himmelweit (eds) (1992) *Knowing Women: Feminism and Knowledge*, Cambridge: Polity and Open University Press.

Gunew, S. (ed.) (1991) *A Reader in Feminist Knowledge*, London: Routledge.

Maynard, M. (1995) 'Beyond the "Big Three": the development of feminist theory into the 1990s', *Women's History Review*, 4, 3: 259–81.

Maynard, M. and J. Purvis (eds) (1996) *New Frontiers in Women's Studies: Knowledge, Identity and Nationalism*, London: Taylor & Francis.

Mohanty, C. T. (1991) 'Under Western eyes: feminist scholarship and colonial discourses, in C. T. Mohanty, A. Russo and L. Torres (eds) *Third World Women and the Politics of Feminism*, Bloomington and Indianapolis: Indiana University Press.

Morris, J. (1995) 'Personal and political: a feminist perspective on researching disability', in J. Holland and M. Blair (eds) *Debates and Issues in Feminist Research and Pedagogy*, Buckingham: Open University Press.

Richardson, D. and V. Robinson (eds) (1997) *Introducing Women's Studies*, 2nd edn, London: Macmillan.

Stanley, L. and S. Wise (1993) *Breaking Out Again*, London: Routledge.

Whelehan, I. (1995) *Modern Feminist Thought*, Edinburgh: Edinburgh University Press.

Notes on Contributors

Lisa Adkins is Research Fellow in the Research School of Social Sciences at the Australian National University. Her research interests are focused on the sociology of gender, especially in relation to economic life and sexuality. Recent publications include *Gendered Work: Sexuality, Family and the Labour Market* (1995) and *Sexualizing the Social: Power and the Organization of Sexuality* (co-edited with V. Merchant, 1996).

Vicki Bertram is Senior Lecturer in English Studies at Oxford Brookes University. She is editor of *Kicking Daffodils: Twentieth-Century Women Poets* (Edinburgh University Press, 1997) and is working on *Gendered Poetics*.

Deborah Cameron is Professor of English Language at the University of Strathclyde. She is the author of *Feminism and Linguistic Theory* (Macmillan, 1992) and *Verbal Hygiene* (Routledge, 1995), editor of *The Feminist Critique of Language* (Routledge, 1990) and co-editor with Jennifer Coates of *Women in their Speech Communities* (Longman, 1988).

Elizabeth Frazer is Fellow and Tutor in Politics at New College, Oxford. She is co-author with Nicola Lacey of *The Politics of Community: A Feminist Critique of the Liberal-Communitarian Debate* (Harvester Wheatsheaf, 1993). Currently she is continuing work on the theme of community, and also on normative conceptions of public life.

Caroline Gonda is Fellow and Director of Studies in English at St Catharine's College, Cambridge. She is the author of *Reading Daughters' Fictions, 1709–1834: Novels and Society from Manley to Edgeworth* (Cambridge University Press, 1996) and editor of *Tea and Leg-Irons: New Feminist Readings from Scotland* (Open Letters, 1992).

Penelope Harvey is Senior Lecturer in Social Anthropology at the University of Manchester and author of *Hybrids of Modernity: Anthropology, the Nation State and the Universal Exhibition* (Routledge, 1996). She edited *Sex and Violence: Issues of*

259

Representation and Experience together with Peter Gow (Routledge, 1994) and has published widely on the ethnic and gender politics of communicative practice in the Peruvian Andes.

Maggie Humm is Professor of Women's Studies at the University of East London. She is author of ten books, notably *Border Traffic* (Manchester University Press, 1991) which looks at strategies of contemporary women writers; *Feminisms: A Reader* (1992); *The Dictionary of Feminist Theory* (2nd edition, 1995) and *Practising Feminist Criticism* (1995) all published by Harvester Wheatsheaf. Her latest book is *Feminism and Film* (Edinburgh University Press, 1997). Currently she is researching the photography and visual aesthetics of Virginia Woolf and other modernists for her book *Borderline*.

Stevi Jackson is Professor of Women's Studies and Director of the Centre for Women's Studies at the University of York. She is the author of *Christine Delphy* (Sage, 1996) and co-editor of *Women's Studies: A Reader* (Harvester Wheatsheaf, 1993), *The Politics of Domestic Consumption* (Prentice Hall/Harvester Wheatsheaf, 1995), and *Feminism and Sexuality: A Reader* (Edinburgh University Press, 1996). She has also written on romance, sexuality and family relationships and is currently working with Sue Scott, Kathryn Milburn and Jennifer Harden researching the impact of risk and adult risk anxiety on the everyday world of children. Forthcoming books include *Concerning Heterosexuality* (Sage), and *Childhood and Sexuality Revisited* (Macmillan).

Jackie Jones is Editorial Director at Edinburgh University Press. She manages the academic and trade imprints and commissions books in Feminist Theory, Literary Studies, Media and Cultural Studies, and Linguistics. She has written on feminist publishing and is developing a book project on narrative and nostalgia in the inter-war period.

Kadiatu Kanneh is Lecturer in English at the University of Birmingham. She has published in postcolonial theory, Black feminisms and Black writing. Her recent publications are included in, for example, *New Feminist Discourses* (Routledge, 1992); *Political Gender: Texts and Contexts* (Harvester Wheatsheaf, 1994); *Writing: A Woman's Business* (Manchester University Press, 1997). Her book, *African Identities*, is in press (Routledge, 1998).

Mary Maynard is Professor in the Department of Social Policy at the University of York. Her interests and publications relate to issues in feminist theory and methodology, the interface between gender, 'race' and other social divisions, and violence towards women. She is currently developing a project on age, ageing and widowhood and completing a book, *Feminists and Social Research: Pragmatics, Politics and Power*, for UCL Press.

Sara Mills is Research Professor in Cultural Studies at Sheffield Hallam University. She has written on feminism and colonial/post-colonial discourse in *Discourses of Difference* (Routledge, 1991); on feminist theory in *Gendering the Reader* (Harvester Wheatsheaf, 1994) and with Lynne Pearce, in *Feminist Readings/ Feminists Reading* (Prentice Hall/Harvester Wheatsheaf, 1996); on feminist linguistics in *Feminist Stylistics* (Routledge, 1995) and (ed.) *Language and Gender* (Longman, 1995). She is currently writing a book on *Gender and Colonial Space*.

Jane Scoular lectures in Law and Women's Studies at the University of Strathclyde. Her research interests are in the area of gender, sexuality and the Law. She is currently writing on the subject of feminist perspectives on mediation and is working on a book, with colleague Denise Mina, on False Memory Syndrome.

Sue Thornham is Principal Lecturer in Media and Cultural Studies at the University of Sunderland. She is co-editor of *Media Studies: A Reader* (Edinburgh University Press, 1996), author of *Passionate Detachments: An Introduction to Feminist Film Theory* (Edward Arnold, 1997), and editor of *Feminist Film Theory: A Reader* (Edinburgh University Press, forthcoming).

Sue Vice is Lecturer in English Literature at the University of Sheffield. She is editor of *Psychoanalytic Criticism: A Reader* (Polity Press, 1996) and author of *Introducing Bakhtin* (Manchester University Press, 1997). She is working on a book entitled *Holocaust Fiction* to be published by Routledge in 1999.

Patricia Waugh is Professor of English Literature at the University of Durham. Her publications include *Metafiction: The Theory and Practice of Self-Conscious Fiction* (Methuen, 1984), *Feminine Fictions: Revisiting the Postmodern* (Routledge, 1989), *Practising Postmodernism/Reading Modernism* (Edward Arnold, 1992), *Harvest of the Sixties* (Oxford University Press, 1995), and *Revolutions of the Word: Intellectual Contexts for the Study of Modern Literature* (Edward Arnold, 1997). She is currently writing a book on science and the concept of utopia.

Subject Index

academic disciplines, male bias, 248–9
academic writing
  and autobiography, 232–44
  style, 233, 234–6
academy, the
  and feminist theory, 2, 4–6
  and lesbian theory, 113, 124–6
affidamento (entrustment), 109
African-American women and Jewish women, 92
African culture
  and American feminism, 90–1
  and European culture, 93–4
agency
  development, 39, 43
  importance, 35
alterity, 178, 184, 187
American feminism and African culture, 90–1
Andean marriages, wife-beating as a
    characteristic, 74–5
animal/human communication, 201–2
anthropology and feminism, 73–81, 82; *see also*
    biological sex and gender
Arena 3, 113–14
audiences
  and the media, 226
  reactions to film, 219–20, 222–5
Australian aborigines and women's knowledge,
    80–1
autobiography
  in academic writing, 232–44
  as data, 236–41

Barnard College conference (1982), 119
biological sex and gender, 133, 134; *see also*
    anthropology and feminism; gender;
    sexuality
'Black' and 'Blackness', meaning, 86–7, 92–4
Black feminisms, 86–94
  and African culture, 90–1
  and autobiography, 238–40

  in Britain, 92–3
  and culture, 86, 90–4, 98
  and postmodernism, 94–5
  and 'Third World', 88, 92, 93
  in the United States, 87–92, 93
  see also feminism; White feminism
Black feminist literary criticism, 199–200
blacks, experiences under legal system, 69
body, the, 142
  and embodiment, 78–9
  see also reflexive production
border criticism, 208
Britain
  and Black feminisms, 92–3
  understanding of 'Black', 86–7, 92–3
British women in India, 104–5, 106

capitalism
  and the labour market, 14, 16–18
  and male dominance, 13–14, 15, 16–19
  representations, 26–7
  women's subordination, 22
Cartesianism, 185
Centre for Contemporary Cultural Studies
    (CCCS) (Birmingham), 221
cine-psychoanalysis, 220, 222
cinema
  and femininity, 173
  see also film
cinematic apparatus, 217, 227n
Civil Rights Act 1964, 63
civil society, 41
class
  and language, 157
  and lesbianism, 122, 123
class relations, 18, 19, 27
colonialism, 103, 110n
  characterisation of women, 101–5
  and domesticity, 102–3
  effects, 99–100

Name Index